THE INTERNATIONAL PSYCHO-ANALYTICAL LIBRARY
No. 5

ESSAYS IN APPLIED PSYCHO-ANALYSIS

BY

ERNEST JONES, M. D.

PRESIDENT OF THE INTERNATIONAL PSYCHO-ANALYTICAL ASSOCIATION
AND OF THE BRITISH PSYCHO-ANALYTICAL SOCIETY

THE INTERNATIONAL PSYCHO-ANALYTICAL PRESS
LONDON   MCMXXIII   VIENNA

CONTENTS

PREFACE

One fifth only of this book has previously been published in English. It has all been revised and the greater part largely re-written.

The light which psycho-analysis is capable of throwing on the deeper problems of human thought and conduct is only beginning to be appreciated. The field over which it can be applied is almost indefinitely large. The parts touched on in the present volume constitute of course only a selection, yet they are sufficiently diverse· political psychology, artistic and literary creation, national and individual characterology, and the study of superstition, history, religion, and folk-lore.   E. J.

December 1922.

ESSAYS IN
APPLIED PSYCHO-ANALYSIS

CHAPTER I

A PSYCHO-ANALYTIC STUDY OF HAMLET[1]

1

PSYCHOLOGISTS have as yet devoted relatively little attention to individual analytic study of genius and of artistic creativeness, and have mainly confined themselves to observations of a general order. They seem to share the shyness or even aversion displayed by the world at large against too searching an analysis of a thing of beauty, the feeling expressed in Keats' lines on the prismatic study of the rainbow. The fear that beauty may vanish under too scrutinizing a gaze, and with it our pleasure, is, however, only in part justified; much depends on the nature of the pleasure and on the attitude of the analyst. Experience has shewn that intellectual appreciation in particular is only heightened by understanding, and to further this is one of the recognised social functions of the critic. Since, moreover, intellectual appreciation comprises an important part of the higher forms of aesthetic

---

[1] This chapter is founded on an essay which appeared in the *American Journal of Psychology*, January 1910, an enlarged version of which was published in German as Heft 10 of the Schriften zur angewandten Seelenkunde under the name 'Das Problem des Hamlet und der Oedipus-Komplex', 1911.

appreciation, a deepened understanding can but increase this also.

It has been found that with poetic creations this critical procedure cannot halt at the work of art itself; to isolate this from its creator is to impose artificial limits to our understanding of it. As Masson,[1] in defending his biographical analysis of Shakespeare, justly says: 'not till every poem has been, as it were, chased up to the moment of its organic origin, and resolved into the mood or intention, or constitutional reverie, out of which it sprang, will its import be adequately felt or understood.' A work of art is too often regarded as a finished thing-in-itself, something almost independent of the creator's personality, so that little would be learned about the one or the other by connecting the two studies. Informed criticism, however, shews that a correlated study of the two sheds light in both directions, on the inner nature of the composition and on the mentality of its author. The two can be separated only at the expense of diminished appreciation, whereas to increase our knowledge of either automatically deepens our understanding of the other. Masson[2] well says: 'What a man shall or can imagine, equally with what he shall or can desire, depends ultimately on his own nature, and so even on his acquisitions and experiences . . . Imagination is not, after all, creation out of nothing, but only re-combination, at the bidding of moods and of conscious purposes, out of the materials furnished by memory, reading and experience; which materials vary with the individual cases.' In asserting this deterministic point of view, one characteristic also of modern clinical psychology, Masson gives us a hint of one of the sources of the prevailing aversion from psycho-

[1] Masson: Shakespeare Personally, 1914, p. 13.
[2] idem: op. cit., pp. 129, 130.

logical analysis—namely, the preference for the belief that poetic ideas arise in their finished form, perhaps from some quasi-divine source, rather than as elaborations of simple and familiar elements devoid in themselves of glamour or aesthetic beauty. This attitude becomes still more comprehensible when one realises that the deeper, unconscious mind, which is doubtless the actual source of such ideas, as of all abstract ideas, is comprised of mental material discarded or rejected by the conscious mind as being incompatible with its standards, material which has to be extensively transformed and purified before it can be presented to consciousness. The attitude, in short, is one more illustration of the constant resistance that man displays against any danger he may be in of apprehending his inner nature.

The artist himself has always avoided a closely analytic attitude towards his work, evidently for the same reason as the common man. He usually dissociates the impelling motive force from his conscious will, and sometimes ascribes it to an actual external agency, divine or demonic. D'Annunzio, for example, in his 'Flame of Life' makes his artist-hero think of 'the extraordinary moments in which his hand had written an immortal verse that had seemed to him not born of his brain, but dictated by an impetuous deity to which his unconscious organ had obeyed like a blind instrument'. Nowhere is the irresistible impetuosity of artistic creation more perfectly portrayed than in the memorable passage in 'Ecce Homo' where Nietzsche describes the birth of 'Also sprach Zarathustra', and its involuntary character has been plainly indicated by most great writers, from Socrates to Goethe. I wish to lay special stress on this feature, on the artist's unawareness of the ultimate source of his creation, for it is cognate to the argument of the present essay.

1*

Within the past few years the analytic investigation of the workings of genius has been infused with fresh interest by the luminous studies of Freud, who has revealed some of the fundamental mechanisms by which artistic and poetic creativeness proceeds.[1] He has shewn that the main characteristics of these mechanisms have much in common with those underlying many apparently dissimilar mental processes, such as dreams, wit, and neurotic symptoms,[2] further, that all these processes bear an intimate relation to fantasy, to the realisation of non-conscious wishes, to psychological 'repression', to the revival of childhood memories, and to the psycho-sexual life of the individual. It was to be expected that the knowledge so laboriously gained by the psycho-analytic method devised by Freud would prove of great value in the attempt to solve the psychological problems concerned with the obscurer motives of human action and desire. In fact it is hard to think of any other scientific mode of approach to such problems than through the patient dissecting of the deeper and more hidden elements of the mind which is the aim of this procedure. The results already obtained by Abraham,[3] Ferenczi,[4] Hitschmann,[5]

[1] Freud: Der Wahn und die Träume in W. Jensen's Gradiva, 1907; 'Der Dichter und das Phantasieren,' *Neue Revue*, 1908, Nr. 10, S. 716; 'Das Motiv der Kästchenwahl,' *Imago*, 1913, S. 257; Eine Kindheitserinnerung des Leonardo da Vinci, 1910.

[2] idem: Die Traumdeutung, 1900, Der Witz und seine Beziehung zum Unbewußten, 1905; Drei Abhandlungen zur Sexualtheorie, 1905; Sammlung kleiner Schriften, 1906-18.

[3] Abraham: Traum und Mythus. Eine Studie zur Völkerpsychologie, 1909; 'Amenhotep IV. Psychoanalytische Beiträge zum Verständnis seiner Persönlichkeit und des monotheistischen Aton-Kultes', *Imago*, 1912, S. 334.

[4] Ferenczi: Contributions to Psycho-Analysis (Engl. Transl.), 1916.

[5] Hitschmann: Gottfried Keller, 1919.

Rank,[1] Sadger,[2] myself,[3] and others are only a foretoken of the applications that will be possible when this method has been employed over a larger field than has hitherto been the case.

II

The particular problem of Hamlet, with which this essay is concerned, is intimately related to some of the most frequently recurring problems that are presented in the course of psycho-analytic work, and it has thus seemed possible to secure a fresh point of view from which an answer might be proffered to questions that have baffled attempts made along less technical lines. Some of the most competent literary authorities have freely acknowledged the inadequacy of all the solutions of the problem that have hitherto been suggested, and when judged by psychological standards their inadequacy is still more evident. The aim of the present essay is to expound and bring into relation with other work an hypothesis suggested some twenty years ago by Freud in a footnote to his 'Traumdeutung'.[4] Before attempting this it will be necessary to make a few general remarks about the nature of the problem and the previous solutions that have been offered.

The problem presented by the tragedy of 'Hamlet' is one of peculiar interest in at least two respects. In the

[1] Rank: Der Künstler. Ansätze zu einer Sexual-psychologie, 1907; Der Mythus von der Geburt des Helden, 1909; Die Lohengrinsage, 1911, Das Inzest-Motiv in Dichtung und Sage, 1912, Psychoanalytische Beiträge zur Mythenforschung, 1919.

[2] Sadger: Konrad Ferdinand Meyer. Eine pathographisch-psychologische Studie, 1908; Aus dem Liebesleben Nicolaus Lenaus, 1909; Friedrich Hebbel, 1920.

[3] Ernest Jones: Papers on Psycho-Analysis, 1918; Essays in Applied Psycho-Analysis, 1922.

[4] Freud: Die Traumdeutung, 1900, S. 183.

first place, the play is almost universally considered to be the chief masterpiece of one of the greatest minds the world has known. It probably expresses the core of Shakespeare's philosophy and outlook on life as no other work of his does. Bradley[1] writes, for instance: 'Hamlet is the most fascinating character, and the most inexhaustible, in all imaginative literature. What else should he be, if the world's greatest poet, who was able to give almost the reality of nature to creations totally unlike himself, put his own soul straight into this creation, and when he wrote Hamlet's speeches wrote down his own heart?' Figgis[2] calls Hamlet 'Shakespeare's completest declaration of himself'. Taine's[3] opinion also was that 'Hamlet is Shakespeare, and at the close of a gallery of portraits, which have all some features of his own, Shakespeare has painted himself in the most striking of them all.' It may be expected, therefore, that anything which will give us the key to the inner meaning of the play will necessarily provide a clue to much of the deeper workings of Shakespeare's mind.

In the second place, the intrinsic interest of the play itself is exceedingly great. The central mystery in it— namely, the cause of Hamlet's hesitancy in seeking to obtain revenge for his father's murder[4]—has well been called the Sphinx of modern Literature.[5] It has given rise to a regiment of hypotheses and to a large library of critical

[1] Bradley: Oxford Lectures on Poetry, 1909, p 357.
[2] Darrell Figgis: Shakespeare: A Study, 1911, p. 320.
[3] Taine: Histoire de la Litterature Anglaise, 1866, t. II, p. 254.
[4] The desperate effort has been made, e g. by J. M. Robertson (The Problem of 'Hamlet', 1919, pp. 16, 17) to deny the existence of this delay, only, however, for it to be found necessary on the very next page to admit it and propound a reason for it.
[5] It is but fitting that Freud should have solved the riddle of this Sphinx, as he has that of the Theban one.

and controversial literature. No detailed account of them will here be attempted, for this is obtainable in the writings of Loening,[1] Döring,[2] and others, but the main points of view that have been put forward must be briefly mentioned.

Of the solutions that have been offered many will probably be remembered on account of their very extravagance.[3] Allied if not belonging to this group are the hypotheses that see in Hamlet only allegorical tendencies of various kinds. Thus Gerth[4] sees in the play an elaborate defence of Protestantism, Rio[5] and Spanier[6] on the contrary a defence of Roman Catholicism. Stedefeld[7] regards it as a protest against the scepticism of Montaigne, Feis[8] as one against his mysticism and bigotry. A writer under the name of Mercade[9] maintains that the play is an allegorical philosophy of history: Hamlet is the spirit of truth-seeking which realises itself historically as progress, Claudius is the type of evil and error, Ophelia is the Church, Polonius its

[1] Loening· Die Hamlet-Tragödie Shakespeares, 1893. This book is especially to be recommended, for it is certainly the most critical work on the subject.

[2] Döring. 'Ein Jahrhundert deutscher Hamlet-Kritik', *Die Kritik*, 1897, Nr. 131.

[3] Such as, for instance, the view developed by Vining (The Mystery of Hamlet, 1881) that Hamlet's weakness is to be explained by the fact that he was a woman wrongly brought up as a man. A writer in the *New Age* (February 22, 1912) suggested that Hamlet's delay was simply due to the necessity of making the play a presentable length!

[4] Gerth: Der Hamlet von Shakespeare, 1861.

[5] Rio: Shakespeare, 1864.

[6] Spanier: Der 'Papist' Shakespeare im Hamlet, 1890.

[7] Stedefeld: Hamlet, ein Tendenzdrama Shakespeare's gegen die skeptische und kosmopolitische Weltanschauung des M. de Montaigne, 1871.

[8] Feis: Shakspere and Montaigne, 1884. The importance of Montaigne's influence on Shakespeare, as shewn in Hamlet, was first remarked by Sterling (*London and Westminster Review,* 1838, p. 321), and has been clearly pointed out by J. M. Robertson, in his book 'Montaigne' and Shakespeare, 1897.

[9] Mercade· Hamlet; or Shakespeare's Philosophy of History, 1875.

Absolutism and Tradition, the Ghost is the ideal voice of Christianity, Fortinbras is Liberty, and so on. Many writers, including Plumptre[1] and Silberschlag,[2] have read the play as a satire on Mary, Queen of Scots, and her marriage with Bothwell after the murder of Darnley, and Winstanley[3] has recently made out a case for the view that the figure of Hamlet was largely taken from that of James VI of Scotland, the heir to the English throne, while Elze,[4] Isaac,[5] and others have found in it a relation to the Earl of Essex's domestic experiences. Such hypotheses overlook a characteristic of all Shakespeare's works, and indeed those of any great artist—namely, the subordination of either current or tendencious interests to the inspiration of the work as an artistic whole.

The most important hypotheses that have been put forward are sub-varieties of three main points of view. The first of these sees the difficulty about the performance of the task in Hamlet's temperament, which is not fitted for effective action of any kind; the second sees it in the nature of the task, which is such as to be almost impossible of performance by any one; and the third in some special feature of the task that renders it peculiarly difficult or repugnant to Hamlet.

The *first* of these views, sometimes called the 'subjective' one, which would trace the inhibition to some general defect in Hamlet's constitution, was independently elaborated more than a century ago by Mackenzie,[6] Goethe,[7] Coleridge,[8]

---

[1] Plumptre: Observations on Hamlet, 1796.
[2] Silberschlag· 'Shakespeare's Hamlet', *Morgenblatt,* 1860, Nr. 46, 47.
[3] Lilian Winstanley: Hamlet and the Scottish Succession, 1920
[4] Elze: *Shakespeare's Jahrbuch,* Bd. III.
[5] Isaac: *Shakespeare's Jahrbuch,* Bd. XVI.
[6] Henry Mackenzie: *The Mirror,* April 18, 1780.
[7] Goethe: Wilhelm Meister's Lehrjahre, 1795, Bd. IV, Kap. XIII
[8] Coleridge: Lectures on Shakespeare, 1808.

and Schlegel.[1] Partly because of its association with Goethe, who promulgated the view as a young man when under the influence of Herder[2] (who, by the way, later abandoned it[3]), it has been the most widely held view of Hamlet, and he is still almost always represented on the stage in this light. Hardly any literary authorities, however, have held it in the past half century, though in 1850 Gervinus[4] could still write: 'Since this riddle has been solved by Goethe in his Wilhelm Meister, we can scarcely conceive that it was one'. Türck[5] suggestively remarks that Goethe's view of Hamlet was a projected account of his own Werther. The oft-quoted passage describing Hamlet runs as follows. 'To me it is clear that Shakespeare meant to present a great deed imposed as a duty upon a soul that is too feeble for its accomplishment. Here is an oak-tree planted in a costly vase that should have nurtured only the most delicate flowers: the roots expand; the vase is shattered. A pure, noble, highly moral disposition, but without that energy of soul which constitutes the hero, sinks under a load, which it can neither support nor resolve to abandon.'

Thus the view is essentially that Hamlet, for temperamental reasons, was inherently incapable of decisive action of any kind. These temperamental reasons are variously stated by different writers: by Mackenzie as 'an extreme sensibility of mind, apt to be too strongly impressed by its situation, and overpowered by the feelings which that situation excites', by Goethe as 'over-sensitiveness', by

---

[1] Schlegel: Vorlesungen über dramatische Kunst und Litteratur, III, 1809.

[2] Herder: Von deutscher Art und Kunst, 1773.

[3] idem: Aufsatz über Shakespeare im dritten Stück der Adrastea, 1801.

[4] Gervinus. Shakespeare, Dritte Auflage, Bd. II, S. 98. English Transl. p. 550.

[5] Hermann Türck: Das psychologische Problem in der Hamlet-Tragödie, 1890, S. 8.

Coleridge as 'overbalance in the contemplative faculty', by Schlegel as 'reflective deliberation—often a pretext to cover cowardice and lack of decision', by Vischer[1] as 'melancholic disposition', and so on; Trench[2] recently described Hamlet as 'a man of contemplation reacting only mentally, being from the first incapable of the required action'. It will be noticed that while some of these writers lay stress on the over-sensitiveness of feeling, others think rather of an unduly developed mental activity. A view fairly representative of the pure Coleridge school,[3] for instance, would run somewhat as follows: Owing to his highly developed intellectual powers, Hamlet could never take a simple or single view of any question, but always saw a number of different aspects and possible explanations with every problem. A given course of action never seemed to him unequivocal and obvious, so that in practical life his scepticism and reflective powers paralysed his conduct. He thus stands for what may roughly be called the type of an intellect over-developed at the expense of the will, and in the Germany of the past he was frequently held up as a warning example to university professors who shewed signs of losing themselves in abstract trains of thought at the risk of diminished contact with external reality.[4]

[1] Vischer: Kritische Gänge. Neue Folge. 1861, Heft 2.

[2] W. F. Trench: Shakespeare's Hamlet· A New Commentary, 1913, pp. 74-9, 119, 137.

[3] An expanded account of Coleridge's view is given by Edward Strachey: Shakespeare's Hamlet: An Attempt to find the Key to a Great Moral Problem by Methodical Analysis of the Play, 1848.

[4] See for instance Köstlin: Shakespeare und Hamlet, *Morgenblatt*, 1864, Nr. 25, 26. Already in 1816 Börne in his Dramaturgischen Blättern had amusingly developed this idea. He closes one article with the words 'If it had been a German who had written Hamlet I should not have been at all surprised. A German would need only a fine legible hand for it. He describes himself and there you have Hamlet'. Frank Harris (The Man Shakespeare and his Tragic Life-Story, 1909, p. 267) writes

There are at least three grave objections to this view of Hamlet's hesitancy, one based on general psychological considerations and the others on objective evidence furnished by the text of the play. It is true that at first sight increasing scepticism and reflection might appear to weaken motive, inasmuch as they tear aside common illusions as to the value of certain lines of conduct; this is well seen, for example, in such a matter as social reform, where a man's energy in carrying out minor philanthropic undertakings wanes in proportion to the amount of clear thought he gives to the subject. But closer consideration will shew that this debilitation is a qualitative rather than a quantitative one. Scepticism merely leads to a simplification of motive in general, and to a reduction in the number of those motives that are efficacious; it brings about a lack of adherence to certain conventional ones rather than a general failure in the springs of action. Every student of individual psychology knows that any such general weakening in energy is invariably due to other causes than intellectual scepticism—namely, to the results of buried intra-psychical conflicts. This train of thought need not be further developed here, for it is really irrelevant to discuss the cause of Hamlet's general aboulia if, as will presently be maintained, this did not exist; the argument, then, must remain unconvincing except to those who already apprehend its validity.

Unequivocal evidence of the inadequacy of the hypothesis under discussion may be obtained from perusal of the play. In the first place, as was first emphatically pointed out by Hartley Coleridge,[1] there is every reason

---

that Hamlet 'became a type for ever of the philosopher or man of letters who, by thinking, has lost the capacity for action'.

[1] Hartley Coleridge. 'On the Character of Hamlet', *Blackwood's Magazine*, 1828.

to believe that, apart from the task in question, Hamlet
is a man capable of very decisive action. This could be
not only impulsive, as in the killing of Polonius, but
deliberate, as in the arranging for the death of Guildenstern
and Rosencrantz. His biting scorn and mockery towards
his enemies, and even towards Ophelia, his cutting
denunciation of his mother, his lack of remorse after the
death of Polonius, these are not signs of a gentle, yielding
or weak nature. His mind was as rapidly made up about
the organisation of the drama to be acted before his
uncle, as it was resolutely made up when the unpleasant
task had to be performed of breaking with the no longer
congenial Ophelia. He shews no trace of hesitation when
he stabs the listener behind the curtain,[1] when he makes
his violent onslaught on the pirates, leaps into the grave
with Laertes or accepts his challenge to what he must
know was a duel, or when he follows his Father's spirit on
to the battlements;[2] nor is there any lack of determination in his resolution to meet the ghost:

> I'll speak to it, though hell itself should gape
> And bid me hold my peace,

or in his cry when Horatio clings to him.

> Unhand me, gentlemen;
> By heaven! I'll make a ghost of him that lets me;
> I say, away!

On none of these occasions do we find any sign of that
paralysis of doubt which has so frequently been imputed

---

[1] I find Loening's detailed argument quite conclusive that Hamlet
did not have the King in his mind when he struck this blow (op. cit.,
S. 242-4, 362-3).

[2] Meadows (Hamlet, 1871) considers that Hamlet's behaviour on
this occasion is the strongest proof of his mental health and vigour.

to him. On the contrary, not once is there any sort of failure in moral or physical courage except only in the matter of the revenge. Bradley, who calls Hamlet 'a heroic, terrible figure',[1] writes of the Coleridge view:[2] 'The theory describes, therefore, a man in certain respects like Coleridge himself, on one side a man of genius, on the other side, the side of will, deplorably weak, always procrastinating and avoiding unpleasant duties, and often reproaching himself in vain; a man, observe, who at *any* time and in *any* circumstances would be unequal to the task assigned to Hamlet. And thus, I must maintain, it degrades Hamlet and travesties the play. For Hamlet, according to all the indications in the text, was not naturally or normally such a man, but rather, I venture to affirm, a man who at any *other* time and in any *other* circumstances than those presented would have been perfectly equal to his task; and it is, in fact, the very cruelty of his fate that the crisis of his life comes on him at the one moment when he cannot meet it, and when his highest gifts, instead of helping him, conspire to paralyse him.'

In the second place, as will later be expounded, Hamlet's attitude is never that of a man who feels himself not equal to the task, but rather that of a man who for some reason cannot bring himself to perform his plain duty. The whole picture is not, as Goethe depicted, one of a gentle soul crushed beneath a colossal task, but one of a strong man tortured by some mysterious inhibition.

Already in 1827 a protest was raised by Hermes[3] against Goethe's interpretation, and since then a number

[1] Bradley: Shakespearean Tragedy, 2nd. Ed. 1905, p. 102.
[2] idem: op. cit., p. 107.
[3] Hermes: Ueber Shakespeare's Hamlet und seine Beurteiler, 1827.

of hypotheses have been put forward in which Hamlet's temperamental deficiencies are made to play a very subordinate part. The *second* of the group of views here discussed goes in fact to the opposite extreme, and finds in the difficulty of the task itself the sole reason for the non-performance of it; it has therefore been termed the 'objective', in contrast to the former 'subjective' hypothesis. This view was first hinted by Fletcher,[1] perhaps deriving from Hartley Coleridge, and was independently developed by Klein[2] and Werder.[3] It maintains that the extrinsic difficulties inherent in the task were so stupendous as to have deterred anyone, however determined. To do this it is necessary to conceive the task in a different light from the usual one. As a development largely of the Hegelian teachings on the subject of abstract justice, Klein, and to a lesser extent Werder, contended that the essence of Hamlet's revenge consisted not merely in slaying the murderer, but of convicting him of his crime in the eyes of the nation. The argument, then, runs as follows: The nature of Claudius' crime was so frightful and so unnatural as to render it incredible unless supported by a very considerable body of evidence. If Hamlet had simply slain his uncle, and then proclaimed, without a shred of supporting evidence, that he had done it to avenge a fratricide, the nation would infallibly have cried out upon him, not only for murdering his uncle to seize the throne himself, but also for selfishly seeking to cast an infamous slur on the memory of a man who could no longer defend his

---

[1] Fletcher: *Westminster Review*, September 1845.

[2] Klein: 'Emil Devrient's Hamlet', *Berliner Modenspiegel, eine Zeitschrift fur die elegante Welt*, 1846, Nr. 23, 24.

[3] Werder: 'Vorlesungen über Shakespeare's Hamlet', *Preußische Jahrbucher* 1873-4; reprinted in book form, 1875. Translated by E. Wilder, 1907, under the title of 'The Heart of Hamlet's Mystery'.

honour. This would have resulted in the sanctification of the uncle, and so the frustration of the revenge. In other words it was the difficulty not so much of the act itself that deterred Hamlet as of the situation that would necessarily result from the act.

Thanks mainly to Werder's forcible presentation of this view, several prominent critics, including Furness,[1] Halliwell-Phillips,[2] Widgery,[3] Hudson,[4] Corson,[5] and Rolfe,[6] have given it their adherence: Werder himself confidently wrote of his thesis: 'That this point for a century long should never have been seen is the most incomprehensible thing that has ever happened in aesthetic criticism from the very beginning of its existence'. It has not, however, found much favour in the Hamlet literature proper, and has been crushingly refuted by a number of able critics, more particularly by Hebler,[7] Baumgart,[8] Bulthaupt,[9] Ribbeck,[10] Loening,[11] Bradley,[12] Tolman,[13] and Robertson.[14]

I need, therefore, do no more than mention one or two of the objections that can be raised to it. It will be

[1] Furness: A New Variorum Edition of Shakespeare, Vols. III and IV, 1877.

[2] Halliwell-Phillips: Memoranda on the Tragedy of Hamlet, 1879.

[3] W. H. Widgery: Harness Prize Essays on the First Quarto of Hamlet, 1880.

[4] Hudson: Shakespeare's Life, Art, and Characters, 2nd. Ed, 1882.

[5] Corson: Cited by Rolfe, op. cit.

[6] Rolfe: Introduction to the English Translation of Werder, op. cit., 1907.

[7] Hebler: Aufsatze über Shakespeare, 2. Ausg., 1874, S. 258-78.

[8] Baumgart: Die Hamlet-Tragödie und ihre Kritik, 1877, S. 7-29.

[9] Bulthaupt: Dramaturgie des Schauspiels, 4. Aufl. 1891, II. S. 237.

[10] Ribbeck: Hamlet und seine Ausleger, 1891, S. 567.

[11] Loening: op. cit., S. 110-13 and 220-4.

[12] Bradley: op. cit, Art. 'Hamlet'.

[13] Tolman: Views about Hamlet and other Essays, 1904.

[14] J. M. Robertson: The Problem of 'Hamlet', 1919, pp. 21-3.

seen that to support this hypothesis the task has in two respects to be made to appear more difficult than it really is: first it is assumed to be not a simple revenge in the ordinary sense of the word, but a complicated bringing to judgement in a more or less legal way; and secondly the importance of the external obstacles has to be greatly exaggerated. This distortion of the meaning of the revenge is purely gratuitous and has no warrant in any passage of the play, nor elsewhere where the word is used in Shakespeare. [1] Hamlet never doubted that he was the legitimately appointed instrument of punishment, and when at the end of the play he secures his revenge the dramatic situation is correctly resolved, although the nation is not even informed, let alone convinced, • of the murder that is being avenged. To secure evidence that would convict the uncle in a court of law was from the nature of the case impossible, and no tragical situation can arise from an attempt to achieve what is evidently impossible, nor could the interest of the spectator be aroused for an obviously one-sided struggle.

The external situation is similarly distorted for the needs of this hypothesis. On which side the people would have been in any conflict is clearly enough perceived by Claudius, who dare not even punish Hamlet for killing Polonius (Act IV, Sc. 3)

> Yet must not we put the strong law on him;
> He's loved of the distracted multitude,
> Who like not in their judgment, but their eyes;

[1] Loening (op. cit., Cap. VI) has made a detailed study of the significance of revenge in Shakespeare's period and as illustrated throughout his works; his conclusion on the point admits of no questioning

and again in Act IV, Sc. 7,

> The other motive,
> Why to a public count I might not go,
> Is the great love the general gender bear him;
> Who, dipping all his faults in their affection,
> Would, like the spring that turneth wood to stone,
> Convert his gyves to graces; so that my arrows,
> Too lightly timber'd for so loud a wind,
> Would have reverted to my bow again,
> And not where I had aim'd them.

The ease with which the people could be roused against Claudius is well demonstrated after Polonius' death, when Laertes carried them with him in an irresistible demand for vengeance, which would promptly have been consummated had not the king immediately succeeded in convincing the avenger that he was innocent. Here the people, the false Danish dogs whose loyalty to Claudius was so feather-light that they gladly hailed as king even Laertes, a man who had no sort of claim on the throne, were ready enough to believe in the murderous guilt of their monarch without any shred of supporting evidence, when the accusation was not even true, and where no motive for murder could be discerned at all approaching in weight the two powerful ones that had actually led him to kill his brother. Where Laertes succeeded, it is not likely that Hamlet, the darling of the people, would have failed. Can we not imagine the march of events during the play before the court, had Hamlet there shewn the same mettle as Laertes did: the straining observation of the fore-warned nobles, the starting up of the guilty monarch who can bear the spectacle no longer, the open murmuring of the audience, the resistless impeachment by the avenger, and the instant execution effected by him and his devoted friends? Indeed, the whole

2

Laertes episode seems almost deliberately to have been woven into the drama so as to shew the world how a pious son should really deal with his father's murderer, how possible was the vengeance in just these particular circumstances, and by contrast to illuminate the ignoble vacillation of Hamlet whose honour had been doubly wounded by the same treacherous villain.

The deeper meaning of the difference in the behaviour of the two men in a similar situation has been aptly pointed out by Storfer:[1] 'When we compare the earlier versions of the Hamlet theme with Shakespeare's tragedy, Shakespeare's great psychological intuition becomes evident. The earlier versions turned on a political action relating to the state: the heir to the throne wreaks vengeance on the usurper for the murder of the king. In Shakespeare the family tragedy is placed in the foreground. The origin of all revolutions is the revolution in the family. Shakespeare's Hamlet is too philosophical a man, too much given to introspection, not to feel the personal and family motive behind the general political undertaking. Laertes, on the other hand, is blind and deaf to this etymology of feeling, to the unconscious mind; his response to his father Polonius' murder is a political revolt. The behaviour of the two men whose fathers had been murdered well characterises the conscious and the unconscious mind in the psychology of the revolutionary and of the political criminal.'

Most convincing proof of all that the tragedy cannot be interpreted as residing in difficulties produced by the external situation is Hamlet's own attitude towards his task. He never behaves as a man confronted with a straightforward task, in which there are merely external difficulties to overcome. If this had been so surely he

---

[1] Storfer. Zur Sonderstellung des Vatermordes, 1911, S. 14.

would from the first have confided in Horatio and his other friends who so implicitly believed in him, as he did in the pre-Shakespearean versions of the play when there really were external difficulties of a more serious nature than in Shakespeare's, and would deliberately have set to work with them to formulate plans by means of which these obstacles might be overcome. Instead of this he never makes any serious attempt to deal with the external situation, and indeed throughout the play makes no concrete reference to it as such, even in the significant prayer scene when he had every opportunity to disclose to us the reason for his non-action. There is therefore no escape from the conclusion that so far as the external situation is concerned the task was a possible one, and was regarded as such by Hamlet.

If Hamlet is a man capable of action, and the task one capable of achievement, what then can be the reason that he does not execute it? Critics who have realised the inadequacy of the hypotheses mentioned above—and this is true of nearly all modern critics—have been hard pressed to answer this question. Some, struck by Klein's suggestion that the task is not really what it appears to be, have offered novel interpretations of it. Thus Mauerhof [1] maintains that the Ghost's command to Hamlet was not, as is generally supposed, to avenge his father by killing the king, but merely to put an end to the life of depravity his mother was still leading, and that Hamlet's problem was how to accomplish this without tarnishing her name by disclosing the truth. Dietrich [2] put forward the singular view that Hamlet's task was to restore to Fortinbras the lands that had been unjustly filched from the latter's father.

---

[1] Mauerhof: Ueber Hamlet, 1882.

[2] Dietrich: Hamlet, der Konstabel der Vorsehung; eine Shakespeare-Studie, 1883.

When straits such as these are reached it is little wonder that many competent critics have taken refuge in the conclusion that the tragedy is in its essence inexplicable, incoherent and incongruous. This view, first critically sustained by Rapp in 1846,[1] has been developed by a number of writers, including von Friefen,[2] Rümelin,[3] Benedix,[4] Robertson,[5] and many others. The causes of the dramatic imperfection of the play have been variously given: by Dowden[6] as a conscious interpolation by Shakespeare of some secret, by Reichel[7] as the defacement by an uneducated actor called Shakspere of a play by an unknown poet called Shakespeare, and so on.

The argument, however, has usually taken the form of direct criticism of the poet's capacity, and therefore is found chiefly among writers of the eighteenth century, such as Hanmer[8] and Mackenzie,[9] i. e. a time before bardolatry had developed, or else at the time when this reached its acme, during the tercentenary of 1864, by authors who headed the revulsion against it, including Von Friefen, Rümelin, and Benedix; the last-named of these ascribes Hamlet's delay solely to the number of wholly superfluous episodes which occupy time in the play. It has lately been revived in a weightier form by J. M. Robertson, basing himself on the recent discoveries concerning the sources of the play. Robertson's thesis is that Shakespeare, finding in

---

[1] Rapp: Shakespeare's Schauspiele übersetzt und erläutert, Bd. VIII, 1846.

[2] Von Friefen: Briefe über Shakespeare's Hamlet, 1864.

[3] Rümelin: Shakespeare-Studien, 1886.

[4] Benedix: Die Shakespereomanie, 1873.

[5] Robertson: op. cit.

[6] Dowden: Shakespeare; his development in his works, 1875.

[7] Reichel: Shakespeare-Litteratur, 1887.

[8] Hanmer: Some Remarks on the Tragedy of Hamlet, 1736.

[9] Mackenzie: op. cit.

the old play 'an action that to his time-discounting sense was one of unexplained delay, elaborated that aspect of the hero as he did every other',[1] 'finally missing artistic consistency simply because consistency was absolutely excluded by the material';[2] he concludes that 'Hamlet' is 'not finally an intelligible drama as it stands',[3] that 'the play cannot be explained from within'[4] and that 'no jugglery can do away with the fact that the construction is incoherent, and the hero perforce an enigma, the snare of idolatrous criticism'.[5] In a still more recent work, by Shore, the view is taken that the character is badly drawn, and that 'Shakespeare had no clear idea himself of what he meant Hamlet to be'.[6] This seems to be the position on the whole prevailing at the present day; to deny the possibility of a solution, or even the real existence of the problem, has always been the last resort when faced with an apparently insoluble enigma.

Many upholders of this negative conclusion have consoled themselves with the thought that in this very obscurity, so characteristic of life in general, lie the power and attractiveness of the play. Even Grillparzer[7] saw in its impenetrability the reason for its colossal effectiveness; he adds 'it becomes thereby a true picture of universal happenings and produces the same sense of immensity as these do'. Now vagueness and obfuscation may or may not be characteristic of life in general, but they are certainly not the attributes of a successful drama. No disconnected and intrinsically meaningless drama could have produced the effect on its audiences that 'Hamlet' has continuously done for the past three

---

[1] Robertson: op. cit., p. 18.
[2] idem: op. cit., p. 85.
[3] idem: op. cit., p. 27.
[4] idem: op. cit., p 29.
[5] idem: op. cit., p. 67.
[6] W. T. Shore: Shakespeare's Self, 1920, p. 146.
[7] Grillparzer: Studien zur Litterärgeschichte, 3. Ausgabe, 1880.

centuries. The underlying meaning of its main theme may be obscure, but that there is one, and one which touches matters of vital interest to the human heart, is empirically demonstrated by the uniform success with which the drama appeals to the most diverse audiences. To hold the contrary is to deny all the accepted canons of dramatic art: 'Hamlet' as a masterpiece stands or falls by these canons.

III

We are compelled then to take the position that there is some cause for Hamlet's vacillation which has not yet been fathomed. If this lies neither in his incapacity for action in general, nor in the inordinate difficulty of the particular task in question, then it must of necessity lie in the third possibility—namely in some special feature of the task that renders it repugnant to him. This conclusion, that Hamlet at heart does not want to carry out the task, seems so obvious that it is hard to see how any open-minded reader of the play could avoid making it.[1] Some of the direct evidence for it furnished in the play will presently be brought forward when we discuss the problem of the cause of the repugnance, but it will first be necessary to mention some of the views that have been expressed on the subject.

The first writer clearly to recognise that Hamlet was a man not baffled in his endeavours but struggling in an internal conflict was Ulrici,[2] in 1839. The details of Ulrici's hypothesis, which like Klein's originated in the Hegelian views of morality, are not easy to follow, but the essence

---

[1] Anyone who doubts this conclusion is recommended to read Loening's convincing chapter (XII), 'Hamlet's Verhalten gegen seine Aufgabe'.

[2] Ulrici: Shakespeare's dramatische Kunst; Geschichte und Charakteristik des Shakespeare'schen Dramas, 1839.

of it is the contention that Hamlet gravely doubted the
moral legitimacy of revenge. He was thus plunged into a
struggle between his natural tendency to avenge his father
and his highly developed ethical and Christian views, which
forbade the indulging of this instinctive desire. This hypothesis has been further developed on moral, ethical and
religious planes by Liebau,[1] Mézières,[2] Gerth,[3] Baumgart,[4]
Robertson,[5] and Ford.[6] Kohler[7] ingeniously transferred the
conflict to the sphere of jurisprudence, maintaining that
Hamlet represented a type in advance of his time in
recognising the superiority of legal punishment over private
revenge or family vendetta and was thus a fighter in the
van of progress; he writes:[8] 'Hamlet is a corner-stone in
the evolution of law and morality'. A similar view has
been developed more recently by Rubinstein.[9] This special
pleading has been effectually refuted by Loening[10] and
Fuld;[11] it is contradicted by all historical considerations.
Finally, Schipper[12] and, more recently, Gelber[13] have suggested

[1] Liebau Studien über William Shakespeares Trauerspiel Hamlet.
Date not stated.

[2] Mézières· Shakespeare, ses oeuvres et ses critiques, 1860.

[3] Gerth· op. cit.

[4] Baumgart: op. cit.

[5] J. M. Robertson: Montaigne and Shakspere, 1897, p. 129.

[6] Ford: Shakespeare's Hamlet A New Theory, 1900.

[7] Kohler· Shakespeare vor dem Forum der Jurisprudenz, 1883; and
Zur Lehre von der Blutrache, 1885. See also *Zeitschrift für vergleichende
Rechtswissenschaft*, Bd. V, S. 330.

[8] Kohler: Shakespeare etc.; op. cit., S. 189.

[9] Rubinstein: Hamlet als Neurastheniker, 1896.

[10] Loening: *Zeitschrift für die gesamte Strafrechtswissenschaft*,
Bd. V, S. 191.

[11] Fuld: 'Shakespeare und die Blutrache', *Dramaturgische Blätter
und Bühnen-Rundschau*, 1888, Nr. 44.

[12] Schipper: Shakespeare's Hamlet, ästhetische Erläuterung des
Hamlet, 1862.

[13] Gelber: Shakespeare'sche Probleme, Plan und Einheit im
Hamlet, 1891.

that the conflict was a purely intellectual one, Hamlet being
unable to satisfy himself of the adequacy or reliability of
the Ghost's evidence. In his recent interesting work Figgis
combines these views by insisting that the play is a tragedy
of honour, Hamlet's main instinct: 'In striking at the King
without a full assurance of his guilt, was to him not only
to strike at the legal monarch of the realm, but also to
seem as though he was seizing a pretext to strike for the
throne, he being the next in succession':[1] 'What seems
like indecision in the early portion of the play is really the
honourable desire not to let his mere hatred of the King
prick him into a capital action against an innocent man, to
prove that the apparition of his father was no heated
fantasy, and, above all, not to take action till he was
assured that his action would not involve his mother'.[2]

The obvious question that one puts to the upholders
of any of the hypotheses just mentioned is: why did Hamlet
in his monologues give us no indication of the nature of
the conflict in his mind? As we shall presently note, he
gave several pretended excuses for his hesitancy, but never
once did he hint at any doubt about what his duty was
in the matter. He was always clear enough about what he
ought to do; the conflict in his mind ranged about the
question why he couldn't bring himself to do it. If Hamlet
had at any time been asked whether it was right for him
to kill his uncle, or whether he really intended to do so,
no one can seriously doubt what his instant answer would
have been. Throughout the play we see his mind irrevocably
made up as to the necessity of a given course of action,
which he fully accepts as being his bounden duty; indeed,
he would have resented the mere insinuation of doubt on
this point as an untrue slur on his filial piety. Ulrici,

[1] Figgis: op. cit., p. 213.
[2] idem: op. cit., p. 232.

Baumgart and Kohler try to meet this difficulty by assuming that the ethical objection to personal revenge was never clearly present to Hamlet's mind; it was a deep and undeveloped feeling which had not fully dawned. I would agree that only in some such way as this can the difficulty be logically met, and further that in recognising Hamlet's non-consciousness of the cause of his repugnance to his task we are nearing the core of the mystery. But an invincible obstacle in the way of accepting any of the causes of repugnance suggested above is that the nature of them is such that a keen and introspective thinker, as Hamlet was, would infallibly have recognised some indication of their presence, and would have openly debated them instead of deceiving himself with a number of false pretexts in the way we shall presently recall. Loening[1] well states this in the sentence: 'If it had been a question of a conflict between the duty of revenge imposed from without and an inner *moral* or *juristic* counter-impulse, this discord and its cause *must* have been brought into the region of reflection in a man so capable of thought, and so accustomed to it, as Hamlet was'.

In spite of this difficulty the hint of an approaching solution encourages us to pursue more closely the argument at that point. The hypothesis just stated may be correct up to a certain stage and then have failed for lack of special knowledge to guide it further. Thus Hamlet's hesitancy may have been due to an internal conflict between the impulse to fulfil his task on the one hand and some special cause of repugnance to it on the other; further, the explanation of his not disclosing this cause of repugnance may be that he was not conscious of its nature; and yet the cause may be one that doesn't happen to

---

[1] Loening: Die Hamlet-Tragödie Shakespeares, 1893, S. 78.

have been considered by any of the upholders of this
hypothesis. In other words, the first two stages in the
argument may be correct, but not the third. This is the
view that will now be developed, but before dealing with
the third stage of the argument it is first necessary to
establish the probability of the first two—namely, that
Hamlet's hesitancy was due to some special cause of
repugnance for his task and that he was unaware of the
nature of this repugnance.

A preliminary obstruction to this line of thought,
based on some common prejudices on the subject of
mental dynamics, may first be considered. If Hamlet was
not aware of the nature of his inhibition, doubt may be
felt as to the possibility of our penetrating to it. This
pessimistic thought was expressed by Baumgart[1] as follows: 'What hinders Hamlet in his revenge is for him
himself a problem and therefore it must remain a problem
for us all.' Fortunately for our investigation, however,
psycho-analytic studies have demonstrated beyond doubt
that mental trends hidden from the subject himself may
come to external expression in ways that reveal their
nature to a trained observer, so that the possibility of
success is not to be thus excluded. Loening[2] has further
objected to this hypothesis that the poet himself has not
disclosed this hidden mental trend, or even given any indication
of it. The first part of his objection is certainly true—
otherwise there would be no problem to discuss, but we
shall presently see that the second is by no means true.
It may be asked: why has the poet not put in a clearer
light the mental trend we are trying to discover? Strange
as it may appear, the answer is probably the same as
with Hamlet himself—namely, he could not because he

[1] Baumgart: op. cit., S. 48.
[2] Loening: op. cit., S. 78, 79.

was unaware of its nature. We shall later deal with this question in connection with the relation of the poet to the play.

As Trench well says:[1] 'We find it hard, with Shakespeare's help, to understand Hamlet: even Shakespeare, perhaps, found it hard to understand him: Hamlet himself finds it impossible to understand himself. Better able than other men to read the hearts and motives of others, he is yet quite unable to read his own.' But, if the motive of the play is so obscure, to what can we attribute its powerful effect on the audience, for, as Kohler[2] asks, 'Who has ever seen Hamlet and not felt the fearful conflict that moves the soul of the hero?' This can only be because the hero's conflict finds its echo in a similar inner conflict in the mind of the hearer, and the more intense is this already present conflict the greater is the effect of the drama.[3] Again, it is certain that the hearer himself does not know the inner cause of the conflict in his own mind, but experiences only the outer manifestations of it. So we reach the apparent paradox that the hero, the poet, and the audience are all profoundly moved by feelings due to a conflict of the source of which they are unaware.

The fact, however, that such a conclusion should appear paradoxical is in itself a censure on popular ignorance of the actual workings of the human mind and before undertaking to sustain the assertions made in the preceding paragraph it will first be necessary to make a few observations on the prevailing views of motive and conduct in general. The new science of clinical psychology

---

[1] Trench: op. cit., p. 115.

[2] Kohler: Shakespeare vor dem Forum der Jurisprudenz, 1883, S. 195.

[3] It need hardly be said that the play, like most others, appeals to its audience in a number of different respects. We are here considering only the main appeal, the central conflict in the tragedy.

stands nowhere in sharper contrast to the older attitudes toward mental functioning than on this very matter. Whereas the generally accepted view of man's mind, usually implicit and frequently explicit in psychological writings, regards it as an interplay of various processes that are for the most part known to the subject, or are at all events accessible to careful introspection on his part, the analytic methods of clinical psychology have on the contrary decisively proved that a far greater number of these processes than is commonly surmised arises from origins that he never even suspects. Man's belief that he is a self-conscious animal, alive to the desires that impel or inhibit his actions, is the last stronghold of that anthropomorphic and anthropocentric outlook on life which has so long dominated his philosophy, his theology, and, above all, his psychology. In other words, the tendency to take man at his own valuation is rarely resisted, and we assume that the surest way of finding out why a person commits a given act is simply to ask him, relying on the knowledge that he, as we ourselves would in a like circumstance, will feel certain of the answer and will almost infallibly provide a plausible reason for his conduct. Special objective methods of penetrating into the more obscure mental processes, however, disclose the most formidable obstacles in the way of this direct introspective route, and reveal powers of self-deception in the human mind to which a limit has yet to be found. If I may quote from a former paper:[1] 'We are beginning to see man not as the smooth, self-acting agent he pretends to be, but as he really is, a creature only dimly conscious of the various influences that mould his thought and action, and blindly resisting with all the means at his command

[1] 'Rationalisation in Every Day Life,' *Journal of Abnormal Psychology*, 1908, p. 168.

the forces that are making for a higher and fuller consciousness.'

That Hamlet is suffering from an internal conflict the essential nature of which is inaccessible to his introspection is evidenced by the following considerations. Throughout the play we have the clearest picture of a man who sees his duty plain before him, but who shirks it at every opportunity and suffers in consequence the most intense remorse. To paraphrase Sir James Paget's well-known description of hysterical paralysis: Hamlet's advocates say he cannot do his duty, his detractors say he will not, whereas the truth is that he cannot will. Further than this, the deficient will-power is localised to the one question of killing his uncle; it is what may be termed a *specific aboulia*. Now instances of such specific aboulias in real life invariably prove, when analysed, to be due to an unconscious repulsion against the act that cannot be performed (or else against something closely associated with the act, so that the idea of the act becomes also involved in the repulsion). In other words, whenever a person cannot bring himself to do something that every conscious consideration tells him he should do—and which he may have the strongest conscious desire to do—it is always because there is some hidden reason why he doesn't want to do. it; this reason he will not own to himself and is only dimly if at all aware of. That is exactly the case with Hamlet. Time and again he works himself up, points out to himself his obvious duty, with the cruellest self-reproaches lashes himself to agonies of remorse—and once more falls away into inaction. He eagerly seizes at every excuse for occupying himself with any other matter than the performance of his duty, just as on a lesser plane a person faced with a distasteful task, e. g. writing a difficult letter, will whittle away his time in arranging, tidying, and fidgetting.

with any little occupation that may serve as a pretext for procrastination. Bradley[1] even goes so far as to make out a case for the view that Hamlet's self-accusation of 'bestial oblivion' is to be taken in a literal sense, his unconscious detestation of his task being so intense as to enable him actually to forget it for periods.

Highly significant is the fact that the grounds Hamlet gives for his hesitancy are grounds none of which will stand a moment's serious consideration, and which continually change from one time to another. One moment he pretends he is too cowardly to perform the deed, at another he questions the truthfulness of the ghost, at another—when the opportunity presents itself in its naked form—he thinks the time is unsuited, it would be better to wait till the King was at some evil act and then to kill him, and so on. When a man gives at different times a different reason for his conduct it is safe to infer that, whether consciously or not, he is concealing the true reason. Wetz,[2] discussing a similar problem in reference to Iago, truly observes: 'nothing proves so well how false are the motives with which Iago tries to persuade himself as *the constant change in these motives*'. We can therefore safely dismiss all the alleged motives that Hamlet propounds, as being more or less successful attempts on his part to blind himself with self-deception. Loening's[3] summing-up of them is not too emphatic when he says: 'they are all mutually contradictory; *they are one and all false pretexts*'. The alleged motives excellently illustrate the psychological mechanisms of evasion and rationalisation

[1] Bradley: op. cit., pp. 125, 126, 410, 411.
[2] Wetz: Shakespeare vom Standpunkt der vergleichenden Litteraturgeschichte, 1890, Bd. I, S. 186.
[3] Loening: op. cit , S. 245.

I have elsewhere described.[1] It is not necessary, however, to discuss them here individually, for Loening has with the greatest perspicacity done this in full detail and has effectually demonstrated how utterly untenable they all are.[2]

Still, in his moments of self-reproach Hamlet sees clearly enough the recalcitrancy of his conduct and renews his efforts to achieve action. It is interesting to notice how his outbursts of remorse are evoked by external happenings which bring back to his mind that which he would so gladly forget, and which, according to Bradley, he does at times forget: particularly effective in this respect are incidents that contrast with his own conduct, as when the player is so moved over the fate of Hecuba (Act II, Sc. 2), or when Fortinbras takes the field and 'finds quarrel in a straw when honour's at the stake' (Act IV, Sc. 4). On the former occasion, stung by the monstrous way in which the player pours out his feeling at the thought of Hecuba, he arraigns himself in words which surely should effectually dispose of the view that he has any doubt where his duty lies.

What's Hecuba to him or he to Hecuba
That he should weep for her? What would he do
Had he the motive and the cue for passion
That I have? He would drown the stage with tears,
And cleave the general ear with horrid speech,
Make mad the guilty and appal the free,
Confound the ignorant, and amaze indeed
The very faculties of eyes and ears.
Yet I

---

[1] op. cit., p. 161.
[2] See especially his analysis of Hamlet's pretext for non-action in the prayer scene. op. cit., S. 240-2.

A dull and muddy-mettled rascal, peak,
Like John-a-dreams, unpregnant of my cause, [1]
And can say nothing; no, not for a king,
Upon whose property and most dear life
A damn'd defeat was made. Am I a coward?
Who calls me villain? breaks my pate across?
Plucks off my beard, and blows it in my face?
Tweaks me by the nose? gives me the lie i' the throat,
As deep as to the lungs? Who does me this?
Ha!
'Swounds, I should take it; for it cannot be
But I am pigeon-liver'd, and lack gall
To make oppression bitter; or ere this
I should have fatted all the region kites
With this slave's offal. Bloody, bawdy villain!
Remorseless, treacherous, lecherous, kindless villain!
O, vengeance!
Why, what an ass am I! This is most brave,
That I, the son of a dear father murder'd,
Prompted to my revenge by heaven and hell,
Must, like a whore, unpack my heart with words,
And fall a-cursing, like a very drab,
A scullion!

The readiness with which his guilty conscience is stirred into activity is again evidenced on the second appearance of the Ghost, when Hamlet cries,

Do you not come your tardy son to chide,
That, lapsed in time and passion, lets go by
The important acting of your dread command?
Oh, say!

[1] How the essence of the situation is conveyed in these four words.

The Ghost at once confirms this misgiving by answering,

Do not forget: this visitation
Is but to whet thy almost blunted purpose.

In short, the whole picture presented by Hamlet, his deep depression, the hopeless note in his attitude towards the world and towards the value of life, his dread of death,[1] his repeated reference to bad dreams, his self-accusations, his desperate efforts to get away from the thoughts of his duty, and his vain attempts to find an excuse for his procrastination; all this unequivocally points to a tortured conscience, to some hidden ground for shirking his task, a ground which he dare not or cannot avow to himself. We have, therefore, to take up the argument again at this point, and to seek for some evidence that may serve to bring to light the hidden counter-motive.

The extensive experience of the psycho-analytic researches carried out by Freud and his school during the past quarter of a century has amply demonstrated that certain kinds of mental processes shew a greater tendency to be inaccessible to consciousness (put technically, to be 'repressed') than others. In other words, it is harder for a person to realise the existence in his mind of some mental trends than it is of others. In order therefore to

---

[1] Tieck (Dramaturgische Blätter, II, 1826) saw in Hamlet's cowardly fear of death a chief reason for his hesitancy in executing his vengeance. How well Shakespeare understood what this fear was like may be inferred from Claudio's words in 'Measure for Measure':
> The weariest and most loathed worldly life
> That age, ache, penury and imprisonment
> Can lay on nature is a paradise
> To what we fear of death.

gain a proper perspective it is necessary briefly to inquire into the relative frequency with which various sets of mental processes are 'repressed'. Experience shews that this can be correlated with the relation between these various sets and their degree of compatibility with the ideals and standards accepted by the conscious ego; the less compatible they are with these the more likely are they to be 'repressed'. As the standards acceptable to consciousness are in a great measure derived from the immediate environment, one may formulate the following generalisation: those processes are most likely to be 'repressed' by the individual which are most disapproved of by the particular circle of society to whose influence he has chiefly been subjected during the period when his character was being formed. Biologically stated, this law would run: 'That which is unacceptable to the herd becomes unacceptable to the individual member', it being understood that the term herd is intended here in the sense of the particular circle defined above, which is by no means necessarily the community at large. It is for this reason that moral, social, ethical or religious tendencies are hardly ever 'repressed', for, since the individual originally received them from his herd, they can hardly ever come into conflict with the dicta of the latter. This merely says that a man cannot be ashamed of that which he respects; the apparent exceptions to this rule need not be here explained.

The language used in the previous paragraph will have indicated that by the term 'repression' we denote an active dynamic process. Thoughts that are 'repressed' are actively kept from consciousness by a definite force and with the expenditure of more or less mental effort, though the person concerned is rarely aware of this. Further, what is thus kept from consciousness typically possesses an energy of its own; hence our frequent use of such expressions as 'trend', 'tendency', etc. A little consideration of the genetic aspects of the matter will make it comprehensible that the trends most likely to be 'repressed' are those belonging to what are called the natural instincts, as contrasted with secondarily acquired ones. Loening [1] seems very discerningly to have grasped this, for, in commenting on a remark of Kohler's to the effect that 'where a feeling impels us to action or to omission, it is replete with a hundred reasons—with reasons that are as light as soap-bubbles, but which through self-deception appear to us as highly respectable and compelling motives, because they are hugely magnified in the (concave) mirror of our own feeling', he writes: 'but this does not hold good, as Kohler and others believe, when we are impelled by *moral* feelings of which reason *approves* (for these we admit to ourselves, they need no excuse), only for feelings that arise from our *natural man*, those the gratification of which is *opposed by our reason*'. It only remains to add the obvious corollary that, as the herd unquestionably selects from the 'natural' instincts the sexual one on which to lay its heaviest ban, so it is the various psycho-sexual trends that are most often 'repressed' by the individual. We have here the explanation of the clinical experience that the more intense and the more obscure is a given case of deep mental conflict the more certainly will it be found on adequate analysis to centre about a sexual problem. On the surface, of course, this does not appear so, for, by means of various psychological defensive mechanisms, the depression, doubt, despair and other manifestations of the conflict are transferred on to more tolerable and permissible topics, such as anxiety about worldly success or failure,

---

[1] Loening: op. cit., S. 245, 246.

3*

about immortality and the salvation of the soul, philosophical considerations about the value of life, the future of the world, and so on.

Bearing these considerations in mind, let us return to Hamlet. It should now be evident that the conflict hypotheses discussed above, which see Hamlet's conscious impulse towards revenge inhibited by an unconscious misgiving of a highly ethical kind, are based on ignorance of what actually happens in real life, for misgivings of this order belong in fact to the more conscious layers of the mind rather than to the deeper, unconscious ones. Hamlet's intense self-study would speedily have made him aware of any such misgivings and, although he might subsequently have ignored them, it would almost certainly have been by the aid of some process of rationalisation which would have enabled him to deceive himself into believing that they were ill-founded; he would in any case have remained conscious of the nature of them. We have therefore to invert these hypotheses and realise that the positive striving for vengeance, the pious task laid on him by his father, was to him the moral and social one, the one approved of by his consciousness, and that the 'repressed' inhibiting striving against the act of vengeance arose in some hidden source connected with his more personal, natural instincts. The former striving has already been considered, and indeed is manifest in every speech in which Hamlet debates the matter: the second is, from its nature, more obscure and has next to be investigated.

This is perhaps most easily done by inquiring more intently into Hamlet's precise attitude towards the object of his vengeance, Claudius, and towards the crimes that have to be avenged. These are two: Claudius' incest with the Queen, and his murder of his brother. Now it is of great importance to note the profound difference in Hamlet's attitude towards these two crimes. Intellectually of course he abhors both, but there can be no question as to which arouses in him the deeper loathing. Whereas the murder of his father evokes in him indignation and a plain recognition of his obvious duty to avenge it, his mother's guilty conduct awakes in him the intensest horror. Furnivall [1] well remarks, in speaking of the Queen, 'Her disgraceful adultery and incest, and treason to his noble father's memory, Hamlet has felt in his inmost soul. Compared to their ingrain die, Claudius' murder of his father—notwithstanding all his protestations—is only a skin-deep stain'.

Now, in trying to define Hamlet's attitude towards his uncle we have to guard against assuming off-hand that this is a simple one of mere execration, for there is a possibility of complexity arising in the following way: The uncle has not merely committed *each* crime, he has committed *both* crimes, a distinction of considerable importance, for the *combination* of crimes allows the admittance of a new factor, produced by the possible inter-relation of the two, which prevents the result from being simply one of summation. In addition it has to be borne in mind that the perpetrator of the crimes is a relative, and an exceedingly near relative. The possible inter-relationship of the crimes, and the fact that the author of them is an actual member of the family, gives scope for a confusion in their influence on Hamlet's mind which may be the cause of the very obscurity we are seeking to clarify.

Let us first pursue further the effect on Hamlet of his mother's misconduct. Before he even knows that his father has been murdered he is in the deepest depression, and evidently on account of this misconduct. The connection

---

[1] Furnivall: Introduction to the 'Leopold' Shakespeare, p. 72.

between the two is unmistakable in the monologue in Act I,
Sc. 2, in reference to which Furnivall[1] writes: 'One must
insist on this, that before any revelation of his father's
murder is made to Hamlet, before any burden of revenging
that murder is laid upon him, he thinks of suicide as a
welcome means of escape from this fair world of God's,
made abominable to his diseased and weak imagination by
his mother's lust, and the dishonour done by her to his
father's memory'.

> O! that this too too solid[2] flesh would melt,
> Thaw and resolve itself into a dew;
> Or that the Everlasting had not fix'd
> His canon 'gainst self-slaughter! O God! O God!
> How weary, stale, flat, and unprofitable
> Seem to me all the uses of this world!
> Fie on 't! O fie! 'tis an unweeded garden
> That grows to seed; things rank and gross in nature
> Possess it merely. That it should come to this!
> But two months dead! nay, not so much, not two;
> So excellent a king; that was, to this,
> Hyperion to a satyr; so loving to my mother
> That he might not beteem the winds of heaven
> Visit her face too roughly. Heaven and earth!
> Must I remember? why, she would hang on him,
> As if increase of appetite had grown
> By what it fed on; and yet, within a month—
> Let me not think on 't—Frailty, thy name is woman!
> A little month! or ere those shoes were old
> With which she follow'd my poor father's body,
> Like Niobe, all tears; why she, even she—

[1] Furnivall: op. cit., p. 70

[2] Dover Wilson (*Times Literary Supplement*, May 16, 1918) brings
forward good reasons for thinking that this word is a misprint for
'sullied'.

O God! a beast, that wants discourse of reason,
Would have mourn'd longer,—married with my uncle,
My father's brother, but no more like my father
Than I to Hercules. Within a month?
Ere yet the salt of most unrighteous tears
Had left the flushing in her galled eyes,
She married. O, most wicked speed, to post
With such dexterity to incestuous sheets!
It is not nor it cannot come to good;
But break, my heart, for I must hold my tongue!

According to Bradley,[1] Hamlet's melancholic disgust at life was the cause of his aversion from 'any kind of decided action'. His explanation of the whole problem of Hamlet is 'the moral shock of the sudden ghastly disclosure of his mother's true nature',[2] and he regards the effect of this shock, as depicted in the play, as fully comprehensible. He says:[3] 'Is it possible to conceive an experience more desolating to a man such as we have seen Hamlet to be; and is its result anything but perfectly natural? It brings bewildered horror, then loathing, then despair of human nature. His whole mind is poisoned . . . A nature morally blunter would have felt even so dreadful a revelation less keenly. A slower and more limited and positive mind might not have extended so widely through the world the disgust and disbelief that have entered it.'

But we can rest satisfied with this seemingly adequate explanation of Hamlet's weariness of life only if we accept unquestioningly the conventional standards of the causes of deep emotion. Many years ago Connolly,[4] the well-known

---

[1] Bradley: op. cit., p. 122.
[2] Idem: op. cit., p. 117.
[3] Idem: op. cit, p. 119.
[4] Connolly: A Study of Hamlet, 1863, pp. 22, 23.

psychiatrist, pointed out the disproportion here existing between cause and effect and gave as his opinion that Hamlet's reaction to his mother's marriage indicated in itself a mental instability, 'a predisposition to actual unsoundness'; he writes: 'The circumstances are not such as would at once turn a healthy mind to the contemplation of suicide, the last resource of those whose reason has been overwhelmed by calamity and despair.' We have unveiled only the exciting cause, not the predisposing cause. The very fact that Hamlet is content with the explanation arouses our grave suspicions, for, as will presently be expounded, from the very nature of the emotion he cannot be aware of the true cause of it. If we ask, not what ought to produce such soul-paralysing grief and distaste for life, but what in actual fact does produce it, we are compelled to go beyond this explanation and seek for some deeper cause. In real life speedy second marriages occur commonly enough without leading to any such result as is here depicted, and when we see them followed by this result we invariably find, if the opportunity for an analysis of the subject's mind presents itself, that there is some other and more hidden reason why the event is followed by this inordinately great effect. The reason always is that the event has awakened to increased activity mental processes that have been 'repressed' from the subject's consciousness. His mind has been specially prepared for the catastrophe by previous mental processes with which those directly resulting from the event have entered into association. This is perhaps what Furnivall means when he speaks of the world being made abominable to Hamlet's 'diseased imagination'. In short, the special nature of the reaction presupposes some special feature in the mental predisposition. Bradley himself has to qualify his hypothesis by inserting the words 'to a man such as we have seen Hamlet to be'.

Those who have devoted much time to the study of such conditions will recognise the self-description given in this monologue as a wonderfully accurate picture of a particular mental state which is often loosely and incorrectly classified under the name of 'neurasthenia'. [1] Analysis of such states always reveals the operative activity of some forgotten group of mental processes, which on account of their unacceptable nature have been 'repressed' from the subject's consciousness. Therefore if Hamlet has been plunged into this abnormal state by the news of his mother's second marriage it must be because the news has awakened into activity some slumbering memory of an associated kind, which is so painful that it may not become conscious.

[1] Hamlet's state of mind more accurately corresponds, as Freud has pointed out, with that characteristic of a certain form of hysteria.

In the past this little problem in clinical diagnosis seems to have greatly exercised psychiatrists. Rosner (Shakespeare's Hamlet im Lichte der Neuropathologie, 1895) described Hamlet as hystero-neurasthenic, a view sharply criticised by Rubinstein (op. cit.) and Landmann (Zeitschr. fur Psychologie, 1896, Bd. XI).

Kellog (Shakespeare's Delineations of Insanity, 1866), de Boismon (Annales médico-psychologiques, 1868, 4e. sér., 12e. fasc.), Hense (Jahrbuch der deutschen Shakespeare-Gesellschaft, 1876, Jahrg. XIII), Nicholson (Trans. New Shakespeare Society, 1880-85, Part II) and Laehr (Die Darstellung krankhafter Geisteszustände in Shakespeare's Dramen, 1898) hold that Hamlet was suffering from melancholia, a conclusion rejected by Ominus (Rev. des deux Mondes, 1876, 3e. sér., 14e. fasc.). Laehr (op. cit., S. 179 and elsewhere) has a particularly ingenious hypothesis which maintains that Shakespeare, having taken over the Ghost episode from the old saga, was obliged to depict Hamlet as a melancholic, because this was theatrically the most presentable form of insanity in which hallucinations occur!

Thierisch (Nord und Süd, 1878, Bd. VI) and Sigismund (Jahrbuch der deutschen Shakespeare-Gesellschaft, 1879, Jahrg. XVI) also hold that Hamlet was insane, without particularising the form of insanity.

For some deep-seated reason, which is to him unacceptable, Hamlet is plunged into anguish at the thought of his father being replaced in his mother's affections by someone else. It is as though his devotion to his mother had made him so jealous for her affection that he had found it hard enough to share this even with his father and could not endure to share it with still another man. Against this thought, however, suggestive as it is, may be urged three objections. First, if it were in itself a full statement of the matter, Hamlet would have been aware of the jealousy, whereas we have concluded that the mental process we are seeking is hidden from him. Secondly, we see in it no evidence of the arousing of an old and forgotten memory. And, thirdly, Hamlet is being deprived by Claudius of no greater share in the Queen's affection than he had been by his own father, for the two brothers made exactly similar claims in this respect—namely, those of a loved husband. The last-named objection, however, leads us to the heart of the situation. How if, in fact, Hamlet had in years gone by, as a child, bitterly resented having had to share his mother's affection even with his own father, had regarded him as a rival, and had secretly wished him out of the way so that he might enjoy undisputed and undisturbed the monopoly of that affection? If such thoughts had been present in his mind in childhood days they evidently would have been 'repressed', and all traces of them obliterated, by filial piety and other educative influences. The actual realisation of his early wish in the death of his father at the hands of a jealous rival would then have stimulated into activity these 'repressed' memories, which would have produced, in the form of depression and other suffering, an obscure aftermath of his childhood's conflict. This is at all events the mechanism that is actually found in the real Hamlets who are investigated psychologically.

IV

I am aware that those Shakespearean critics who have enjoyed no special opportunities for penetrating into the obscurer aspects of mental activities, and who base their views of human motive on the surface valuation given by the agents themselves—to whom all conduct whether good or bad at all events springs from purely conscious sources—are likely to regard the suggestion put forward above as merely constituting one more of the extravagant and fanciful hypotheses of which the Hamlet literature in particular is so replete. For the sake, however, of those who may be interested to apprehend the point of view from which this strange hypothesis seems probable I feel constrained to interpolate a few considerations on two matters that are not at all commonly appreciated at their true importance—namely, a child's feelings of jealousy and his ideas on the subject of death.

The whole subject of jealousy in children is so clouded over with prejudice that even well-known facts are either ignored or are not estimated at their true significance. Stanley Hall, for instance, in his encyclopaedic treatise, makes a number of very just remarks on the importance of the subject in adolescence, but implies that before the age of puberty this passion is of relatively little consequence. It was reserved for the genetic studies of psycho-analytic research to demonstrate the lasting and profound influence that infantile jealousies may have upon later character reactions and upon the whole course of a person's life.[1]

---

[1] A recent example of this is afforded by J. C. Flügel's study: 'On the Character and Married Life of Henry VIII,' *Internat. Journ. of Psycho-Analysis,* 1920, Vol. I, p. 24. See also his valuable work on The Psycho-Analytic Study of the Family (No. 3 of the Internat. Psycho-Analytical Library, 1921).

The close relation between adult jealousy and the desire for the removal of the rival by the most effective means, that of death, and also the common process of suppression of such feelings, is clearly illustrated in a remark of Stanley Hall's [1] to the effect that ｢'Many a noble and even great man has confessed that mingled with profound grief for the death and misfortune of their best friends, they were often appalled to find a vein of secret joy and satisfaction, as if their own sphere were larger or better.｣ He has doubtless in mind such passages as the following from La Rochefoucauld: 'Dans l'adversité de nos meilleurs amis, il y a quelque chose qui ne nous déplait pas.' A similar thought is more openly expressed by Bernard Shaw [2] when he makes Don Juan, in the Hell Scene, remark. 'You may remember that on earth—though of course we never confessed it—the death of any one we knew, even those we liked best, was always mingled with a certain satisfaction at being finally done with them.' Such cynicism in the adult is exceeded to an incomparable extent by that of the child, with its notorious, and to the parents often heartbreaking, egotism, with its undeveloped social instincts, and with its ignorance of the dread significance of death. A child very often unreasoningly interprets the various encroachments on its privileges, and the obstacles interposed to the immediate gratification of its desires, as meaningless cruelty, and the more imperative is the desire that has been thwarted the more pronounced is the hostility towards the agent of this supposed cruelty, most often of course a parent. The most important encroachment, and the most frequent, is that made on the child's desire for affection. The resulting hostility is very often seen on the occasion of the birth of a subsequent

[1] Stanley Hall: Adolescence, 1908, Vol. I, p. 358.
[2] Bernard Shaw: Man and Superman, 1903, p. 94.

child, and is usually regarded with amusement as an added contribution to the general gaiety called forth by the happy event. When a child, on being told that the doctor has brought him another playfellow, responds with the cry 'Tell him to take it away again', he intends this, however, not, as is commonly believed, as a joke for the entertainment of his elders, but as an earnest expression of his intuition that in future he will have to renounce his previously unquestioned pre-eminence in the family circle, a matter that to him is serious enough.

The second point, on which there is also much misunderstanding, is that of the child's attitude toward the subject of death, it being commonly assumed that this is necessarily the same as that of an adult. When a child first hears of anyone's death, the only part of its meaning that he realises is that the person is *no longer there,* a consummation which time and again he has fervently desired when being interfered with by the persons around him. It is only gradually that the grimmer implications of the phenomenon are borne in upon him. When, therefore, a child expresses the wish that a given person, even a near relative, would die, our feelings would not be so shocked as they sometimes are, were we to interpret the wish from the point of view of the child. The same remark applies to the dreams of adults in which the death of a near and dear relative takes place, dreams in which the underlying repressed wish is usually concealed by an emotion of grief. But on the other hand the significance of these death-wishes is not to be under-estimated, either, for the later conflicts they may give rise to can be of the utmost importance for the person's mental welfare, and this in spite of the fact that in the vast majority of cases they remain merely wishes. Not that they always remain wishes, even in children. Some years ago (in two editorial articles entitled 'Infant Murderers' in the *British Journal of Children's Diseases,* Nov. 1904, p. 510, and June 1905, p. 270) I collected a series of murders committed by jealous young children, and, referring to the constant occurrence of jealousy between children in the same family, pointed out the possible dangers arising from the imperfect realisation by children of the significance of death.

Of the infantile jealousies the most important, and the one with which we are here occupied, is that experienced by a boy towards his father. The precise form of early relationship between child and father is in general a matter of vast importance in both sexes and plays a predominating part in the future development of the child's character; the theme has been expounded in an interesting essay by Jung,[1] where he gives it its due importance, though to the one-sided exclusion of the mother's influence. The only aspect that at present concerns us is the resentment felt by a boy towards his father when the latter disturbs, as he necessarily must, his enjoyment of his mother's exclusive affection. This feeling is the deepest source of the world-old conflict between father and son, between the younger and the older generation, the favourite theme of so many poets and writers, the central *motif* of most mythologies and religions. The fundamental importance that this conflict, and the accompanying breaking away of the child from the authority of his parents, has both for the individual and for society is clearly stated in the following passage of Freud's:[2] 'The detachment of the growing individual from the authority of the parents is one of the most necessary, but also

[1] Jung: 'Die Bedeutung des Vaters für das Schicksal des Einzelnen', *Jahrb. f. psychoanalyt. u. psychopathol. Forschungen,* 1909, Bd. I.
[2] Personal communication quoted by Rank: Der Mythus von der Geburt des Helden, 1909, S. 64.

one of the most painful, achievements of development. It is absolutely necessary for it to be carried out, and we may assume that every normal human being has to a certain extent managed to achieve it. Indeed, the progress of society depends in general on this opposition of the two generations.'

It was Freud[1] who first demonstrated, when dealing with the subject of the earliest manifestations of the sexual instinct in children, that the conflict rests in the last resort on sexual grounds. He has shewn[2] that this instinct does not, as is generally supposed, differ from other biological functions by suddenly leaping into being at the age of puberty in all its full and developed activity, but that like other functions it undergoes a gradual evolution and only slowly attains the particular form in which we know it in the adult. A child has to learn how to love just as it has to learn how to walk, although the former function is so much more intricate and delicate in its adjustment than the latter that the development of it is a correspondingly slower and more involved process. The earliest sexual manifestations are so palpably unadapted to what is generally considered to be the ultimate aim of the function, and are so general and tentative in contrast with the relative precision of the later ones, that the sexual nature of them is commonly not recognised at all.

This important theme cannot be further pursued here, but it must be mentioned how frequently these earliest dim awakenings are evoked by the intimate physical relations existing between the child and the persons of his

[1] Freud: Die Traumdeutung, 1900, S. 176-80. He has strikingly illustrated the subject in a detailed study of a young boy: 'Analyse der Phobie eines fünfjährigen Knaben', *Jahrb. f. psychoanalyt. u. psycho-pathol. Forschungen*, 1909, Bd. I.

[2] Freud: Drei Abhandlungen zur Sexualtheorie, 4. Aufl. 1920.

immediate environment, above all, therefore, his mother.
There is a considerable variability in both the date and
the intensity of these early sexual impressions, this depending partly on the boy's constitution and partly on the
mother's. When the attraction exercised by the mother is
excessive it may exert a controlling influence over the
boy's later destiny; a mass of evidence in demonstration
of this, too extensive to refer to in detail, has been
published in the psycho-analytical literature. Of the various
results that may be caused by the complicated interaction
between this influence and others only one or two need
be mentioned. If the awakened passion undergoes an
insufficient 'repression'—an event most frequent when
the mother is a widow—then the boy may remain
throughout life abnormally attached to his mother and unable
to love any other woman, a not uncommon cause of
bachelorhood. He may be gradually weaned from the
attachment if it is less strong, though it often happens
that the weaning is incomplete so that he is able to fall
in love only with women who in some way resemble the
mother; the latter occurrence is a frequent cause of
marriage between relatives, as has been interestingly pointed out by Abraham.[1] The maternal influence may also
manifest itself by imparting a strikingly tender feminine
side to the later character.[2] When, on the other hand,

[1] Abraham: 'Verwandtenehe und Neurose', *Neurologisches Zentralblatt*, 1908, S. 1150.

[2] This trait in Hamlet's character has often been the subject of
comment. See especially Bodensted: 'Hamlet', *Westermanns Illustrierte
Monatshefte*, 1865; Vining's suggestion that Hamlet really was a woman
has been mentioned earlier in the present essay. That the same trait
was a prominent one of Shakespeare's himself is well known (see, for
instance, Bradley's works), a fact which the appellation of 'Gentle Will'
sufficiently recalls; Harris (op. cit., p. 273) even writes: 'Whenever we
get under the skin, it is Shakespeare's femininity which startles us.'

the aroused feeling is intensely 'repressed' and associated with shame, guilt, and similar reactions the submergence may be so complete as to render the person incapable of experiencing any feeling at all of attraction for the opposite sex; to him all women are as forbidden as his mother. This may declare itself in pronounced misogyny or even, when combined with other factors, in actual homosexuality, as Sadger[1] has shewn.

The attitude towards the successful rival, namely the father, also varies with—among other factors—the extent to which the aroused feelings have been 'repressed'. If this is only slight, then the natural resentment against the father may be more or less openly manifested later on, a rebellion which occurs commonly enough, though the true meaning of it is not recognised. To this source many social revolutionaries—perhaps all—owe the original impetus of their rebelliousness against authority, as can often be plainly traced—for instance, with Shelley and Mirabeau.[2] The unimpeded train of thought in the unconscious logically culminates in the idea, or rather the wish, that the father (or his substitute) may disappear from the scene, i. e. that he may die. Shakespeare himself provides a good example of this (King Henry IV, Part II) in the scene between the dying king and his son:

Prince Henry. I never thought to hear you speak again.
King Henry. Thy wish was father, Harry, to that thought.

If, on the other hand, the 'repression' is considerable, then the hostility towards the father will be correspondingly

---

[1] Sadger:· 'Fragment der Psychoanalyse eines Homosexuellen', *Jahrb. f. sex. Zwischenstufen,* 1908, Bd. IX; 'Ist die konträre Sexualempfindung heilbar?', *Zeitschr. f. Sexualwissenschaft,* Dez. 1908; 'Zur Aetiologie der konträren Sexualempfindung', *Mediz. Klinik,* 1909, Nr. 2.

[2] See Wittels: Tragische Motive, 1911, S. 153.

concealed from consciousness; this is usually accompanied by the development of the opposite sentiment, namely of an exaggerated regard and respect for him, and a morbid solicitude for his welfare, which completely cover the true underlying relationship.

The complete expression of the 'repressed' wish is not only that the father should die, but that the son should then espouse the mother. This was openly expressed by Diderot in speaking of boys: 'If we were left to ourselves and if our bodily strength only came up to that of our phantasy we would wring our fathers' necks and sleep with our mothers.' The attitude of son to parents is so transpicuously illustrated in the Oedipus legend,[1] as developed for instance in Sophocles' tragedy, that the group of mental processes in question is generally known under the name of the 'Oedipus-complex'.

We are now in a position to expand and complete the suggestions offered above in connection with the Hamlet problem.[2] The story thus interpreted would run somewhat as follows.

As a child Hamlet had experienced the warmest affection for his mother, and this, as is always so, had contained elements of a disguised erotic quality. The presence of

[1] See Freud: Die Traumdeutung, 1900, S. 181. Valuable expositions of the mythological aspects of the subject are given by Abraham, Traum und Mythus, 1909, and Rank, op. cit. Rank has also worked through in great detail the various ways in which the same theme is made use of in literature: Das Inzest-Motiv in Dichtung und Sage, 1912, especially Kap. VIII which contains an excellent analysis of the Oedipus legend.

[2] Here, as throughout this essay, I closely follow Freud's interpretation given in the footnote previously referred to. He there points out the inadequacy of the earlier explanations, deals with Hamlet's feelings toward his mother, father, and uncle, and mentions two other matters that will presently be discussed, the significance of Hamlet's reaction against Ophelia and of the probability that the play was written immediately after the death of Shakespeare's own father.

two traits in the Queen's character go to corroborate this assumption, namely her markedly sensual nature and her passionate fondness for her son. The former is indicated in too many places in the play to need specific reference, and is generally recognised. The latter is also manifest; Claudius says, for instance (Act IV, Sc. 7), 'The Queen his mother lives almost by his looks'. Nevertheless Hamlet seems to have with more or less success weaned himself from her and to have fallen in love with Ophelia. The precise nature of his original feeling for Ophelia is a little obscure. We may assume that at least in part it was composed of a normal love for a prospective bride, though the extravagance of the language used (the passionate need for absolute certainty, etc.) suggests a somewhat morbid frame of mind. There are indications that even here the influence of the old attraction for the mother is still exerting itself. Although some writers, following Goethe,[1] see in Ophelia many traits of resemblance to the Queen, surely more striking are the traits contrasting with those of the Queen. Whatever truth there may be in the many German conceptions of Ophelia as a sensual wanton[2]—misconceptions that have been confuted by Loening[3] and others—still the very fact that it needed what Goethe happily called the 'innocence of insanity' to reveal the presence of any such libidinous thoughts demonstrates in itself the modesty and chasteness of her habitual demeanour. Her naive piety, her obedient resignation and her unreflecting simplicity sharply contrast with the

---

[1] Goethe: Wilhelm Meister, IV, 14. 'Her whole being hovers in ripe, sweet voluptuousness'. 'Her fancy is moved, her quiet modesty breathes loving desire, and should the gentle Goddess Opportunity shake the tree the fruit would at once fall'.

[2] For instance, Storffrich. Psychologische Aufschlüsse über Shakespeares Hamlet, 1859, S. 131; Dietrich, op. cit., S. 129; Tieck, Dramaturgische Blätter, II, S. 85, etc.

[3] Loening · op. cit., Cap. XIII. 'Charakter' und Liebe Ophelias.

Queen's character, and seem to indicate that Hamlet by a characteristic reaction towards the opposite extreme had unknowingly been impelled to choose a woman who should least remind him of his mother. A case might even be made out for the view that part of his courtship originated not so much in direct attraction for Ophelia as in an unconscious desire to play her off against his mother, just as a disappointed and piqued lover so often has resort to the arms of a more willing rival. It would be hard otherwise to understand the readiness with which he later throws himself into this part. When, for instance, in the play scene he replies to his mother's request to sit by her with the words 'No, good mother, here's metal more attractive' and proceeds to lie at Ophelia's feet, we seem to have a direct indication of this attitude; and his coarse familiarity and bandying of ambiguous jests with the woman he has recently so ruthlessly jilted are hardly intelligible unless we bear in mind that they were carried out under the heedful gaze of the Queen. It is as though his unconscious were trying to convey to her the following thought: 'You give yourself to other men whom you prefer to me. Let me assure you that I can dispense with your favours and even prefer those of a woman whom I no longer love.' His extraordinary outburst of bawdiness on this occasion, so unexpected in a man of obviously fine feeling, points unequivocally to the sexual nature of the underlying turmoil.

Now comes the father's death and the mother's second marriage. The association of the idea of sexuality with his mother, buried since infancy, can no longer be concealed from his consciousness. As Bradley[1] well says: 'Her son was forced to see in her action not only an astounding shallowness of feeling, but an eruption of coarse sensuality,

[1] Bradley: op. cit., p. 118.

"rank and gross," speeding post-haste to its horrible delight'. Feelings which once, in the infancy of long ago, were pleasurable desires can now, because of his repressions, only fill him with repulsion. The long 'repressed' desire to take his father's place in his mother's affection is stimulated to unconscious activity by the sight of someone usurping this place exactly as he himself had once longed to do. More, this someone was a member of the same family, so that the actual usurpation further resembled the imaginary one in being incestuous. Without his being in the least aware of it these ancient desires are ringing in his mind, are once more struggling to find conscious expression, and need such an expenditure of energy again to 'repress' them that he is reduced to the deplorable mental state he himself so vividly depicts.

There follows the Ghost's announcement that the father's death was a willed one, was due to murder. Hamlet, having at the moment his mind filled with natural indignation at the news, answers normally enough with the cry (Act. I, Sc. 5):

> Haste me to know 't, that I, with wings as swift
> As meditation or the thoughts of love,
> May sweep to my revenge.

The momentous words follow revealing who was the guilty person, namely a relative who had committed the deed at the bidding of lust.[1] Hamlet's second guilty wish had thus also been realised by his uncle, namely to procure the fulfilment of the first—the possession of the mother—by a personal deed, in fact by murder of the father. The two recent events, the father's death and the

---

[1] It is not maintained that this was by any means Claudius' whole motive, but it was evidently a powerful one and the one that most impressed Hamlet.

mother's second marriage, seemed to the world to have no inner causal relation to each other, but they represented ideas which in Hamlet's unconscious fantasy had for many years been closely associated. These ideas now in a moment forced their way to conscious recognition in spite of all 'repressing forces', and found immediate expression in his almost reflex cry: 'O my prophetic soul! My uncle?'. The frightful truth his unconscious had already intuitively divined his consciousness had now to assimilate, as best it could. For the rest of the interview Hamlet is stunned by the effect of the internal conflict thus re-awakened, which from now on never ceases, and into the essential nature of which he never penetrates.

One of the first manifestations of the awakening of the old conflict in Hamlet's mind is his reaction against Ophelia. This is doubly conditioned, by the two opposing attitudes in his own mind. In the first place, there is a complex reaction in regard to his mother. As was explained above, the being forced to connect the thought of his mother with sensuality leads to an intense sexual revulsion, one that is only temporarily broken down by the coarse outburst discussed above. Combined with this is a fierce jealousy, unconscious because of its forbidden origin, at the sight of her giving herself to another man, a man whom he had no reason whatever either to love or to respect. Consciously this is allowed to express itself, for instance after the prayer scene, only in the form of extreme resentment and bitter reproaches against her. His resentment against women is still further inflamed by the hypocritical prudishness with which Ophelia follows her father and brother in seeing evil in his natural affection, an attitude which poisons his love in exactly the same way that the love of his childhood, like that of all children, must have been poisoned. He can forgive a woman neither her

rejection of his sexual advances nor, still less, her alliance
with another man. Most intolerable of all to him, as
Bradley well remarks, is the sight of sensuality in a quarter
from which he had trained himself ever since infancy
rigorously to exclude it. The total reaction culminates in the
bitter misogyny of his outburst against Ophelia, who is devast-
ated at having to bear a reaction so wholly out of proportion
to her own offence and has no idea that in reviling her Hamlet
is really expressing his bitter resentment against his mother.[1]
'I have heard of your paintings too, well enough;
God has given you one face, and you make yourselves
another; you jig, you amble, and you lisp, and nickname
God's creatures, and make your wantonness your ignorance.
Go to, I'll no more on't; it hath made me mad' (Act III,
Sc. 1). On only one occasion does he for a moment escape
from the sordid implication with which his love has been
impregnated and achieve a healthier attitude toward
Ophelia, namely at the open grave when in remorse he
breaks out at Laertes for presuming to pretend that his
feeling for her could ever equal that of her lover.

The intensity of Hamlet's repulsion against woman in
general, and Ophelia in particular, is a measure of the
powerful 'repression' to which his sexual feelings are being
subjected. The outlet for those feelings in the direction
of his mother has always been firmly dammed, and now
that the narrower channel in Ophelia's direction has also
been closed the increase in the original direction

---

[1] His similar tone and advice to the two women shew plainly
how closely they are identified in his mind. Cp. 'Get thee to a nun-
nery: why wouldst thou be a breeder of sinners' (Act III, Sc. 2) with
'Refrain to-night; And that shall lend a kind of easiness To the next
abstinence' (Act III, Sc. 4).

The identification is further demonstrated in the course of the
play by Hamlet's killing the men who stand between him and these
women (Claudius and Polonius).

consequent on the awakening of early memories tasks all
his energy to maintain the 'repression.' His pent up feelings
find a partial vent in other directions. The petulant irascib-
ility and explosive outbursts called forth by his vexation at
the hands of Guildenstern and Rosencrantz, and especially of
Polonius, are evidently to be interpreted in this way, as also
is in part the burning nature of his reproaches to his mother.
Indeed towards the end of his interview with his mother
the thought of her misconduct expresses itself in that
almost physical disgust which is so characteristic a manifestation of intensely 'repressed' sexual feeling.

> Let the bloat king tempt you again to bed;
> Pinch wanton on your cheek; call you his mouse;
> And let him, for a pair of reechy kisses,
> Or paddling in your neck with his damn'd fingers,
> Make you to ravel all this matter out, (Act III, Sc. 4)

Hamlet's attitude towards Polonius is highly instructive. Here the absence of family tie and of other similar
influences enables him to indulge to a relatively unrestrained
extent his hostility towards the prating and sententious
dotard. The analogy he effects between Polonius and
Jephthah[1] is in this connection especially pointed. It is
here that we see his fundamental attitude towards moralis-
ing elders who use their power to thwart the happiness
of the young, and not in the over-drawn and melodramatic
portrait in which he delineates his father: 'A combination
and a form indeed, where every god did seem to set his
seal to give the world assurance of a man.'

---

[1] What Shakespeare thought of Jephthah's behaviour towards his
daughter may be gathered from a reference in Henry VI, Part III,
Act V, Sc. 1. See also on this subject Wordsworth: On Shakespeare's
Knowledge and Use of the Bible, 1864, p. 67.

It will be seen from the foregoing that Hamlet's attitude towards his uncle-father is far more complex than is generally supposed. He of course detests him, but it is the jealous detestation of one evil-doer towards his successful fellow. Much as he hates him, he can never denounce him with the ardent indignation that boils straight from his blood when he reproaches his mother, for the more vigorously he denounces his uncle the more powerfully does he stimulate to activity his own unconscious and 'repressed' complexes. He is therefore in a dilemma between on the one hand allowing his natural detestation of his uncle to have free play, a consummation which would stir still further his own horrible wishes, and on the other hand ignoring the imperative call for the vengeance that his obvious duty demands. His own evil prevents him from completely denouncing his uncle's, and in continuing to 'repress' the former he must strive to ignore, to condone, and if possible even to forget the latter; *his moral fate is bound up with his uncle's for good or ill.* In reality his uncle incorporates the deepest and most buried part of his own personality, so that he cannot kill him without also killing himself. This solution, one closely akin to what Freud[1] has shewn to be the motive of suicide in melancholia, is actually the one that Hamlet finally adopts. The course of alternate action and inaction that he embarks on, and the provocations he gives to his suspicious uncle, can lead to no other end than to his own ruin and, incidentally, to that of his uncle. Only when he has made the final sacrifice and brought himself to the door of death is he free to fulfil his duty, to avenge his father, and to slay his other self—his uncle.

[1] Freud: 'Trauer und Melancholie', Vierte Sammlung kleiner Schriften, 1918, Kap. XX.

There is a second reason why the call of duty to kill his step-father cannot be obeyed, and that is because it links itself with the unconscious call of his nature to kill his mother's husband, whether this is the first or the second; the absolute 'repression' of the former impulse involves the inner prohibition of the latter also. It is no chance that Hamlet says of himself that he is prompted to his revenge 'by heaven and hell'.

In this discussion of the motives that move or restrain Hamlet we have purposely depreciated the subsidiary ones, which also play a part, so as to bring out in greater relief the deeper and effective ones that are of preponderating importance. These, as we have seen, spring from sources of which he is quite unaware, and we might summarise the internal conflict of which he is the victim as consisting in a struggle of the 'repressed' mental processes to become conscious. The call of duty, which automatically arouses to activity these unconscious processes, conflicts with the necessity of 'repressing' them still more strongly; for the more urgent is the need for external action the greater is the effort demanded of the 'repressing' forces. Action is paralysed at its very inception, and there is thus produced the picture of apparently causeless inhibition which is so inexplicable both to Hamlet [1] and to readers

[1] The situation is perfectly depicted by Hamlet in his cry (Act IV, Sc. 4) ·

> I do not know
> Why yet I live to say 'this thing's to do',
> Sith I have cause, and will, and strength, and means,
> To do 't.

With greater insight he could have replaced the word 'will' by 'pious wish', which as Loening (op. cit, S. 246) points out, it obviously means. Curiously enough, Rolfe (op. cit, p. 23) quotes this very passage in support of Werder's hypothesis that Hamlet was inhibited by the thought of the external difficulties of the situation, which shews the straits the supporters of this untenable hypothesis are driven to.

of the play. This paralysis arises, however, not from physical or moral cowardice, but from that intellectual cowardice, that reluctance to dare the exploration of his inner soul, which Hamlet shares with the rest of the human race. 'Thus conscience does make cowards of us all.'

V

We have finally to return to the subject with which we started, namely poetic creation, and in this connection to inquire into the relation of Hamlet's conflict to the inner workings of Shakespeare's mind. It is here maintained that this conflict is an echo of a similar one in Shakespeare himself, as to a greater or lesser extent with all men. As was remarked earlier in this essay, the view that Shakespeare depicted in Hamlet the most important part of his own inner self is a wide-spread and doubtless a correct one. [1] Bradley, [2] who says that in Hamlet Shakespeare wrote down his own heart, makes the interesting comment: 'We do not feel that the problems presented to most of the tragic heroes could have been fatal to Shakespeare himself. The immense breadth and clearness of his intellect would have saved him from the fate of Othello, Troilus, or Anthony. We do feel, I think, and he himself may have felt, that he could not have coped with Hamlet's problem.' It is, therefore, as much beside the point to inquire into Shakespeare's conscious intention, moral, political or otherwise, in the play as it is with most works of genius. The play is simply the form in which his deepest,

[1] See especially Döring Shakespeare's Hamlet seinem Grundgedanken und Inhalte nach erläutert, 1865; Taine: Histoire de la littérature anglaise, 1866, t. II, p. 254; Vischer: Altes und Neues, 1882, Heft 3; Hermann: Ergänzungen und Berichtigungen der hergebrachten Shakespeare-Biographie, 1884.

[2] Bradley: Oxford Lectures on Poetry, 1909, p. 357.

unconscious feelings find their spontaneous expression, without any inquiry being possible on his part as to the essential nature or source of those feelings.

It is, of course, probable that in writing the play Shakespeare was not only inspired from the personal and intimate sources we have indicated, but was also influenced by his actual conscious experiences. For instance, there is reason to suppose that in painting the character of Hamlet he had in mind some of his contemporaries, notably William Herbert, later Lord Pembroke,[1] and Robert Earl of Essex.[2] Some authors[3] have provided us with complete schemes indicating exactly which contemporary figures they surmise to be mirrored in each one in the play. The repeated allusion to the danger of Ophelia's conceiving illegitimately may be connected with both Herbert, who was imprisoned for being the father of an illegitimate child, and the poet himself, who hastily married to avoid the same stigma. Frank Harris,[4] following up Tyler's suggestions[5] concerning the poet's relations to Mary Fitton, has persuasively expounded the view that Shakespeare wrote 'Hamlet' as a reaction against his deep disappointment at being betrayed by his friend Herbert. Many of Harris' suggestions are easily to be reconciled with the theory here advanced. The following passage, for instance, may be quoted.[6] 'Why did Hamlet hate his mother's lechery? Most men would hardly have condemned it, certainly would not have suffered their thoughts to dwell on it

---

[1] Döring. Hamlet, 1898, S. 35.

[2] Isaac. 'Hamlet's Familie', *Shakespeare's Jahrbuch*, Bd. XVI, S. 274.

[3] For instance, French: Shakespeareana Genealogica, 1869, p. 301.

[4] Harris: op cit. See also his Shakespeare and His Love, 1910, and The Women of Shakespeare, 1911.

[5] Tyler: Shakespeare's Sonnets, 1890.

[6] Harris: The Man Shakespeare, 1909, p. 269.

beyond the moment;[1] but to Hamlet his mother's faithlessness was horrible, shameful, degrading, simply because
Hamlet-Shakespeare had identified her with Miss Fitton,
and it was Miss Fitton's faithlessness, it was her deception
he was condemning in the bitterest words he could find.
He thus gets into a somewhat unreal tragedy, a passionate
intensity which is otherwise wholly inexplicable.' Indeed,
Harris considers[2] that 'Shakespeare owes the greater part
of his renown to Mary Fitton'. As is well known, the
whole Mary Fitton story rests on a somewhat slender
basis, but it is certainly reasonable to suppose that if
Shakespeare had passed through such an experience it
would have affected him very deeply because of his peculiar
sensitiveness to it; one cannot forget that it was he who
wrote 'Othello'. If, therefore, there is any historical truth
in Harris' suggestions we should have an excellent example
of what Freud has termed 'over-determination', that is to
say, the action of two mental impulses in the same
direction. It was pointed out above that Hamlet's excessive
reaction to his mother's conduct needed some other
explanation than the mere fact of this conduct, but if
part of this excess arose from Shakespeare's feeling about
Miss Fitton,[3] part of it arose from a deeper source still.
Behind Queen Gertrude may stand Mary Fitton, but behind
Mary Fitton certainly stands Shakespeare's mother.

Much light is thrown on our subject by an historical
study of the circumstances under which the play arose,

---

[1] In their judgements on this point how much nearer Bradley is
than Harris to the fount of feeling.

[2] Harris: op. cit., p. 231.

[3] The fact is certainly noteworthy 'that throughout the great
tragic period of Shakespeare's work, one of the prevailing notes towards
the whole sex-question is of absolute nausea and abhorrence' (Figgis:
op. cit., p. 284).

though such a study also raises some further questions that have not yet been satisfactorily answered. The exact source of Shakespeare's plot and the date at which he wrote the play are two of the knottiest problems in the history of English literature, and we shall see that they both possess a considerable interest for our purpose. To know precisely what versions of the Hamlet story were accessible to Shakespeare before he wrote his play would tell us what were his own contributions to it, a piece of knowledge that would be invaluable for the study of his personality. Again, to know the exact date of his composition might enable us to connect the impulse to write the play with significant events in his own life.

As far as has been at present ascertained, the facts seem to be somewhat as follows. Shakespeare must certainly have taken not only the skeleton of the plot, but also a surprising amount of detail, from earlier writings. It is not absolutely known, however, which of these he had actually read, though it is probable that most of the following sources were available to him, all derived from the Hamlet legend as narrated early in the thirteenth century by Saxo Grammaticus. This was printed, in Latin, in 1514, translated into German by Hans Sachs in 1558, and into French by Belleforest in 1570.[1] It is very probable that a rough English translation of Belleforest's version—we say version rather than translation, for it contains numerous modifications of the story as told by Saxo—was extant throughout the last quarter of the sixteenth century, but the only surviving copy, entitled 'The Hystorie of Hamblet', actually dates from 1608,

---

[1] Belleforest· Histoires tragiques (1564), t. V. 1570. This may have been derived directly from Saxo, but more likely from another intermediary now unknown.

and Elze[1] has given reasons for thinking that whoever issued it had first read an English 'Hamlet', possibly Shakespeare's own. For at least a dozen years before Shakespeare wrote his 'Hamlet' there was a drama of the same name being played in England; references to it were made in 1589 by Nash[2] and in 1596 by Lodge.[3] The suggestion, first made by Malone[4] in 1821, that this play is from the hand of Thomas Kyd has been strongly confirmed by later research[5] and may now be regarded as almost certainly established. There is contemporary evidence[6] shewing that it was played at Newington Butts' about 1594 by the Lord Chamberlain's company, of which Shakespeare was at that time a member. Henslowe incidentally makes it plain that it was a very common practice for dramatists to avail themselves freely of the material, whether of plot, character, or even language, supplied by their predecessors or contemporaries, and, apart from the moral certainty that Shakespeare must have been familiar with this play and drawn on it for his own, there is good reason for thinking that he incorporated actual parts of it in his 'Hamlet'.[7]

Now unfortunately no copy of Kyd's play has survived. We can compare Shakespeare's 'Hamlet' with the Belleforest translation of Saxo's prose story and also with

[1] Elze: William Shakespeare, 1876.

[2] Nash: 'To the Gentlemen Students of both Universities', prefixed to Greene's Menaphon, or Arcadia, 1589.

[3] Lodge: Wits miserie, and the Worlds madnesse, 1596.

[4] Malone: Variorum, 1821, Vol. II.

[5] See Widgery: op. cit., pp 100 et seq; Fleay: Chronicle of the English Drama, 1891, Sarrazin: Thomas Kyd und sein Kreis, 1892; Corbin: The Elizabethan Hamlet, 1895.

[6] Henslowe's Diary, 1609, reprinted by the Shakespeare Society, 1845.

[7] See Sarrazin: op. cit.; and Robertson: The Problem of 'Hamlet', 1919, pp 34-41.

the English modification of this, the 'Hystorie of Hamblet', both of which he *probably* used; but not with the Elizabethan play, which he almost *certainly* used. We therefore cannot tell with surety which of his deviations from the original story originated with Shakespeare and which of them were merely taken over from Kyd. And it is just from deviations such as these that we can learn much of the personality of the writer; they are unmistakably his own contributions, whether they consist in positive additions or in negative omissions.

Still the case is not quite so desperate as it seems. In the first place we have a copy—late, it is true, being printed only in 1710—of a German play, 'Der bestrafte Brudermord oder Prinz Hamlet aus Dänemark,' which was played at least as early as 1626 in Dresden, and which intrinsic evidence proves to emanate, at all events in great part, from a very early and probably pre-Shakespearean version of 'Hamlet'.[1] The differences between it and Shakespeare's 'Hamlet' will be discussed later. In the second place a comparison can be instituted between 'Hamlet' and the surviving plays of Kyd, for instance 'The Spanish Tragedy' where there is also the theme of motiveless hesitation on the part of a hero who has to avenge his next-of-kin's murder. The characteristics of the two writers are so distinct that it is not very difficult for expert critics to tell with which a given passage or part of a plot is likely to have originated. The third consideration is a purely psychological one. It is in the last resort not of such absorbing interest whether Shakespeare took only part of a plot or the whole of it from other sources; the

---

[1] Bernhardy: 'Shakespeare's Hamlet. Ein literar-historisch kritischer Versuch,' *Hamburger literarisch-kritische Blätter*, 1857; Cohn: Shakespeare in Germany, 1865; Latham: Two Dissertations, 1872.

essential point is that he took, or made, a plot of such
a kind as to enable him to express his deepest personal
feelings and thoughts. The intrinsic evidence from the play
decisively shews that Shakespeare projected into it his
inmost soul; the plot, whether he made it or found it,
became his own, inasmuch as it obviously corresponded
with the deepest part of his own nature. One has only
for a moment to compare the treatment of the similar
themes in 'Hamlet' and in 'The Spanish Tragedy' to
realise how fundamentally different was Shakespeare's and
Kyd's reaction to them.

In addition to these definite sources ruder accounts
of the old Amleth story, of Irish and Norse origin, were
widely spread in England, and the name Hamlet itself, or
some modification of it, was common in the Stratford
district.[1] As is well known, Shakespeare in 1585 christened
his only son Hamnet, a frequent variant of the name;
the boy died in 1596. For all these reasons it is plain
that the plot of the tragedy must have been present in
Shakespeare's mind for many years before it actually took
form as a new composition. When this happened is a
matter of some uncertainty and considerable bearing. Many
arguments, which need not be repeated here, have been
given in favour of various dates between 1599 and 1602;
more authorities can be cited to the effect that it was
written in the winter of 1601-2 than at any other time.
On the basis of this Freud has made the highly interesting
suggestion that it followed as a reaction on the death of
Shakespeare's father; this event, which may well be supposed to have had the same awakening effect on old
'repressed' death-wishes as the death of Hamlet's father

---

[1] Elton: William Shakespeare. His Family and Friends, 1904,
p. 223.

had with Hamlet, took place in September 1601. It is certainly noteworthy that the only other play in which he depicted a son's intimate relation to his mother, 'Coriolanus', was written just after the death of Shakespeare's mother, in 1608 (though Frank Harris would doubtless retort that this was also the year in which Mary Fitton finally left London).

'Hamlet' was actually registered at Stationer's Hall on July 26, 1602, with the words added 'as it was lately acted.' In 1603 appeared the notorious pirated edition in quarto, the official version (Q. 2) following in 1604. In a recent remarkable textual study of the two quartos Dover Wilson[1] comes to the following conclusions. The first, pirated quarto and the second, definitely Shakespearean one were derived from the same source, an actor's copy used in the theatre from 1593 onward. He dates Kyd's play as being before 1588 and thinks that Shakespeare partly revised this about 1591-2; this revision was mainly confined to the ghost scenes. The Elizabethan 'Hamlet', therefore, used by the Lord Chamberlain Players in the sixteen-nineties would be a combination of Kyd's and Shakespeare's work, possibly recast by these and even by other dramatists from time to time. It is evident, however, that Shakespeare countered the 1602 piracy by issuing what was practically a re-written play, and the dates go to confirm Freud's suggestion that this was done while he was still under the influence of the thoughts stirred by his father's death, an event which is usually the turning-point in the mental life of a man.

If Dover Wilson's conclusions prove to be correct, as seems probable, then we may have an answer to the

---

[1] Dover Wilson: The Copy for 'Hamlet', 1603, and the 'Hamlet' Transcript, 1593; 1919.

riddle provided by Harvey's marginal comments in his copy of Speght's Chaucer, which were presumably written before February 1601, as fixed by the date of Essex' death; in these he refers to Shakespeare's 'Hamlet'. Renewed interest in the point has been aroused by Moore Smith's [1] discovery of the copy in question which had been missing for over a century. The passage in Harvey and also the inferred dates are by no means unequivocal, but even if the conclusion is accepted that it proves Shakespeare's 'Hamlet' to have been in existence a couple of years before the date usually allotted to its composition there is left the possibility that the reference is to the early acting version only, which may well by that time have become more associated with Shakespeare's name than with Kyd's, and not to the play that we know as 'Shakespeare's Hamlet'.

The play that Shakespeare wrote next after 'Hamlet' was probably 'Measure for Measure', the main theme of which Masson [2] considers to be 'mutual forgiveness and mercy'. Just about the some time, more likely before than after 'Hamlet', was written 'Julius Caesar', a play that calls for some special consideration here. Here we have a drama apparently devoid of any sexual problem or motive, and yet it has been shewn, in Otto Rank's excellent analysis, [3] that the inspiration of the main theme is derived from the same complex as we have studied in Hamlet. His thesis is that Caesar represents the father, and Brutus the son, of the typical Oedipus situation. Psycho-analytic work has shewn that a ruler, whether king, emperor, president or what not, is in the unconscious

---

[1] Moore Smith: Gabriel Harvey's Marginalia, 1913, pp. viii-xii and 232.

[2] Masson: op. cit., p. 133.

[3] Rank: op. cit, S. 204-9.

mind a typical father symbol, [1] and in actual life he tends
to draw on to himself the ambivalent attitude characteristic
of the son's feelings for the father. On the one hand a
ruler may be piously revered, respected and loved as the
wise and tender parent; on the other he may be hated
as the tyrannical authority against whom all rebellion is
justified. Very little experience of life is enough to shew
that the popular feelings about any ruler are always
disproportionate, whether they are positive or negative;
one has only to listen to the different opinions expressed
about any actual ruler, e.g. Wilson, Lloyd George, or
Clemenceau. The most complete nonentity may, if only
he finds himself in the special position of kingship, be
regarded either as a model of all the virtues, to whom
all deference is due, or as a heartless tyrant whom it
would be a good act to hurl from his throne. We have
pointed out earlier the psychological origin of revolutionary
tendencies in the primordial rebellion against the father,
and it is with these that we are here mainly concerned.
In Hamlet the two contrasting elements of the normal
ambivalent attitude towards the father were expressed
towards two sets of people; the pious respect and love
towards the memory of his father, and the hatred, contempt and rebellion towards the father-substitutes, Claudius
and Polonius. In other words, the original father has been
transformed into two fathers, one good, the other bad,
corresponding with the division in the son's feelings. With
Caesar, on the other hand, the situation is simpler. He is
still the original father, both loved and hated at once,
even by his murderer. That the tyrant aspect of Caesar,
the Caesar who has to be killed by a revolutionary, was
in Shakespeare's mind associated with Polonius, another

---

[1] See Ernest Jones: Papers on Psycho-Analysis, 1918, p. 143.

'bad' father who has to be killed, is indicated by a curious identification of the two in the 'Hamlet' play: Polonius when asked what part he had ever played answers (Act. III, Sc. 2) 'I did enact Julius Caesar: I was killed i' the Capitol; Brutus killed me.' Those who always underestimate the absolute strictness with which the whole of our mental life is determined will pass this by; to those, however, who are accustomed to trace out the determining factors in unsparing detail it serves as one more example of how fine are the threads connecting our thoughts. Polonius might have quoted any other part on the stage, but it is an unescapable fact that he chose just this one.

Appropriate estimates disclose the curious fact, first pointed out by Craik,[1] that Shakespeare made more frequent allusions to Caesar in his works than to any other man of all past time; of all men in the range of history Caesar seems to have been the one who most fascinated his imagination. There are so many passages mocking at Caesar's hook nose and tendency to brag that Masson[2] concludes these must have constituted special features in Shakespeare's recollection of him. These exhibitionistic symbols accord well with the fact that the boy's 'repressed' antipathy towards his father always centres about that part of his father whose functioning most excites his envy and jealousy.

That the two noble characters of Hamlet and Brutus have a great deal in common has often been remarked.[3] The resemblances and differences in which the 'son's' attitudes towards the 'father' come to expression in the two plays are of very great interest. In 'Julius Caesar' they are expressed by being incorporated in three different

[1] Craik: The English of Shakespeare, 3rd. Ed., 1864.
[2] Masson: op. cit., p. 177.
[3] See, for instance, Brandes: William Shakespeare, 1896, S. 456

'sons'. Thus, as Rank points out,[1] Brutus represents the son's rebelliousness, Cassius his remorsefulness, and Anthony his natural piety,[2] the 'father' remaining the same person. In 'Hamlet', on the other hand, the various aspects of the son's attitude are expressed[3] by the device of describing them in regard to three different 'fathers', the love and piety towards his actual father, the hatred and contempt towards the father-type Polonius, and the conflict of both towards his uncle-father, Claudius (conscious detestation and unconscious sympathy and identification, one paralysing the other). The parricidal wish in Shakespeare is allowed to come to expression in the two plays by being concealed in two different ways. In 'Hamlet' it is displaced from the actual father to the father-substitutes. In 'Julius Caesar' there is supposed to be no actual blood relation between the two men, the 'son' and 'father' types. But a highly significant confirmation of the interpretation here adopted is the circumstance that Shakespeare in composing his tragedy entirely suppressed the fact that Brutus was the actual, though illegitimate, son of Caesar; this fact is plainly mentioned in Plutarch, the source of Shakespeare's plot, one which he almost literally followed otherwise.[4] Even Caesar's famous death-cry 'Et tu, mi fili, Brute!' appears in Shakespeare only in the weakened form 'Et tu, Brute!'. Rank comments on the further difference between the two plays that the son's relation to the

---

[1] Rank: op. cit., S. 209

[2] Against our treating Brutus, Cassius, and Anthony as types in this way it may be objected that they were after all actual historical personages. But we are discussing them as they appear in Shakespeare, to whom they owe most of their life; what we know of them historically is colourless and lifeless by comparison.

[3] That is, in the main. As is indicated elsewhere in the text, certain 'son' aspects are also depicted by, for instance, Laertes.

[4] Delius: 'Casar und seine Quellen' *Shakespeare-Jahrbuch*, Bd. XVII.

mother, the other side of the whole Oedipus complex, is omitted in 'Julius Caesar', whereas, as we have seen, it is strongly marked in 'Hamlet'. Yet even of this there is a faint indication in the former play. In his great speech to the citizens Brutus says 'Not that I loved Caesar less, but that I loved Rome more' (Act. III, Sc. 2). Now it is not perhaps altogether without interest in this connection that cities, just like countries, are unconscious symbols of the mother, [1]—this being an important source of the conscious feeling of patriotism—so that the passage reads as if Brutus, in a moment of intense emotion, had revealed to his audience the unconscious motive from which his action sprang.

Besides Shakespeare's obvious interest in Caesar, noted above, there is another set of considerations, some of which were certainly known to Shakespeare, connecting Brutus and Hamlet, and it seems likely that they constituted an additional influence in determining him to write the one play so soon after the other. They are these. Belleforest [2] pointed out some striking resemblances between Saxo's story of Amleth and the Roman legend of the younger Brutus (Lucius Junius Brutus), and it is probable that Saxo derived much of his story from the Latin sources. [3] Both Plutarch and Belleforest were certainly accessible to Shakespeare. In both cases a son has to avenge a father who had been slain by a wicked uncle who usurped the throne—for the usurper Tarquinius Superbus had slain his brother-in-law, Brutus' father, as

[1] See, for instance, Rank: 'Um Stadte werben', *Internationale Zeitschrift fur Psychoanalyse*, Bd. II, S. 50.

[2] I quote from York Powell in Elton's translation of Saxo's Danish History, 1894, pp. 405 et seq.

[3] Saxo's two main sources were the Roman one and the Icelandic Hrólf Saga.

well as Brutus' brother[1]—and in both cases the young man feigned madness in order to avoid arousing the suspicions of the tyrant, whom in both cases he finally overthrew. Of further incidental interest, though of course not known to Shakespeare, is the fact that the name Hamlet[2] has the same signification as that of Brutus, both words meaning 'doltish', 'stupid'; the interest of this fact will be pointed out presently.

There are numerous other indications of the influence of his Oedipus complex throughout Shakespeare's works, especially in the earlier ones—there are actually son-father murders in Henry VI and Titus Andronicus—but as this subject has been dealt with so exhaustively by Rank in his work 'Das Inzest-Motiv in Dichtung und Sage' it is not necessary to repeat his discussion of it here.

VI

It is for two reasons desirable at this point to interpolate a short account of the mythological relations of the original Hamlet legend, first so as to observe the personal contribution to it made by Shakespeare, and secondly because knowledge of it serves to confirm and amplify the psychological interpretation given above.

Up to the present point in this essay an attempt has been made on the whole to drive the argument along a dry, logical path and to shew that prior to that given by Freud all the explanations of the mystery end in blind alleys. So far as I can see, there is no escape from the conclusion that the cause of Hamlet's hesitancy lies in some unconscious source of repugnance to his task; the next step of the argument, however, in which a motive for this repugnance

---

[1] Dionysius Halic: Antiquitates Romanae, 1885, Vol. IV, pp. 67, 77.
[2] See Detter: *Zeitschrift für deutsches Altertum*, 1892, Bd. VI, S. 1 et seq.

is supplied, is avowedly based on considerations not generally appreciated, though I have tried to minimise the difficulty by assimilating the argument to some commonly accepted facts. Now, there is another point of view from which this labour would have been superfluous, in that Freud's explanation would appear directly obvious. To anyone familiar with the modern interpretation, based on psycho-analytic researches, of myths and legends, that explanation of the Hamlet problem would immediately occur on the first reading through of the play. The reason why this strong statement can be made is that the story of Hamlet is merely an unusually elaborated form of a vast group of legends, the psychological significance of which is now, thanks to Freud and his co-workers, well understood. It would exceed our purpose to discuss in detail the historical relationship of the Hamlet legend to the other members of this group [1] and I shall content myself here with pointing out the psychological resemblences; Jiriczek [2] and Lessmann [3] have adduced much evidence to shew that the Norse and Irish variants of it are descended from the ancient Iranian legend of Kaikhosrav and there is no doubt of the antiquity of the whole group, some members of which can be traced back to the beginning of history.

The fundamental theme common to all the members of the group [4] is the success of a young hero in displacing

[1] See Zinzow: Die Hamlet-Sage an und mit verwandten Sagen erläutert. Ein Beitrag zum Verständnis nordisch-deutscher Sagendichtung, 1877.

[2] Jiriczek: 'Hamlet in Iran', *Zeitschrift des Vereins für Volkskunde,* 1900, Bd. X.

[3] Lessmann: Die Kyrossage in Europa. Wissenschaftliche Beilage zum Jahresbericht der städtischen Realschule zu Charlottenburg, 1906.

[4] In the exposition of this group of myths I am largely indebted to Otto Rank's excellent volume, 'Der Mythus von der Geburt des Helden', 1909, in which most of the original references may also be found.

a rival father. In its simplest form the hero is persecuted by a tyrannical father, who has usually been warned of his approaching eclipse, but after marvellously escaping from various dangers he avenges himself, often unwittingly, by slaying the father. The persecution mainly takes the form of attempts to destroy the hero's life just after his birth, by orders that he is to be drowned, exposed to cold and starvation, or otherwise done away with. A good example of this simple form, illustrating all the features just mentioned, is the Oedipus legend, from which of course is derived the technical term 'Oedipus complex' so familiar in modern psychopathology. The underlying motive is openly betrayed by the hero marrying his mother Jocasta after having slain his father. This incestuous marriage also takes place in the same circumstances in the many Christian versions of the legend, for example, in those pertaining to Judas Iscariot and St. Gregory.

The intimate relation of the hero to the mother may be indicated in other ways than marriage, for instance by their both being persecuted and exposed together to the same dangers, as in the legends of Feridun, Perseus, and Telephos. In some types of the story the hostility to the father is the predominating theme, in others the affection for the mother, but as a rule both of these are more or less plainly to be traced.

The elaboration of the more complex variants of the myth is brought about chiefly by three factors, namely: an increasing degree of distortion engendered by greater psychological 'repression', complication of the main theme by subsidiary allied ones, and expansion of the story by repetition due to the creator's decorative fancy. In giving a description of these three processes it is difficult sharply to separate them, but they are all illustrated in the following examples.

The *first,* and most important disturbing factor, that
of more pronounced 'repression,' manifests itself by the
same mechanisms as those described by Freud in connection
with normal dreams,[1] psychoneurotic symptoms, etc. The
most interesting of these mechanisms of myth formation
is that known as 'decomposition,' which is the opposite of
the 'condensation' so characteristic of dreams. Whereas in
the latter process attributes of several individuals are fused
together in the creation of one figure, much as in the
production of a composite photograph, in the former process
various attributes of a given individual are disunited and
several òther individuals are invented, each endowed with
one group of the original attributes. In this way one person
of complex character is dissolved and replaced by several,
each of whom possesses a different aspect of the character
which in a simpler form of the myth was combined in one
being; usually the different individuals closely resemble one
another in other respects, for instance in age. A great
part of Greek mythology must have arisen in this way. A
good example of the process in the group now under
consideration is seen by the figure of a tyrannical father
becoming split into two, a father and a tyrant. We then
have a story told about a young hero's relation to two
older men, one of whom is a tender father, the other a
hated tyrant. The resolution of the original figure is often
not complete, so that the two resulting figures stand in a
close relationship to each other, being indeed as a rule
members of the same family. The tyrant who seeks to
destroy the hero is then most commonly the grandfather,
as in the legends of the heroes Cyrus, Gilgam, Perseus,
Telephos, and others, or the grand-uncle, as in those of
Romulus and Remus and their Greek predecessors Amphion

[1] Cp Abraham: Traum und Mythus, 1908.

and Zethod. Less often is he the uncle, as in the Hamlet and Brutus legends, though there is an important Egyptian example in the religious myth of Horus and his uncle Set.[1]

When the decomposition is more complete the tyrant is not of the same family as the father and hero, though he may be socially related, as with Abraham whose father Therach was the tyrant Nimrod's commander-in-chief. The tyrant may, however, be a complete stranger, as in the examples of Moses and Pharoah, Feridun and Zohâk, Jesus and Herod, and others. It is clear that this scale of increasing decomposition corresponds with, and is doubtless due to, further stages of 'repression'; the more 'repressed' is the idea that the father is a hateful tyrant, the more completely is the imaginary figure of the persecuting tyrant dissociated from the recognised father. In the last two instances, and in many others, there is a still higher degree of 'repression,' for not only are the mother and son, but also the actual father himself, persecuted by the tyrant; it will be recalled how Jesus, Joseph and Mary all fled together to Egypt from Herod, and when we think that the occasion of the flight was the parents' desire to save their son from the tyrant it is impossible to conceive a more complete dissociation of the loving, solicitous father from the figure of the dreaded tyrant.

There is a more disguised variant yet, however, in which the loving father is not only persecuted by the tyrant, typically in company with the son and mother, but is actually slain by him. In this variant, well represented by the Feridun legend, the son adores his father and avenges his murder by killing their common enemy. It is of special interest to us here because it is the original form of the Hamlet legend as narrated by Saxo Grammaticus,

[1] Flinders Petrie: The Religion of Ancient Egypt, 1908, p. 38.

where Feng (Claudius) murders his brother Horwendil and marries the latter's wife Gerutha, being slain in his turn by Amleth. The dutiful Laertes springing to avenge his murdered father Polonius is also an example of the same stage in the development of the myth. The picture here presented of the son as avenger instead of slayer of the father illustrates the highest degree of psychological 'repression,' in which the true meaning of the story is concealed by the identical mechanism that in real life conceals 'repressed' hostility and jealousy in so many families, namely, the exactly opposite attitude of exaggerated solicitude, care and respect. Nothing is so well calculated to conceal a given feeling as to emphasise the presence of its precise opposite; one can imagine the bewilderment of an actual Feridun, Amleth, or Laertes if they were told that their devotion to their father and burning desire to avenge his murder constituted a reaction to their own buried death-wishes! There could be no more complete repudiation of the primordial hostility of the son.

Yet even in this form of the legend the 'repressed' death-wish does after all come to expression; the father is really murdered, although at the hands of a hated tyrant. Myths are like dreams in being only products of the imagination, and if a man who was being psychoanalysed were to dream that a third person murdered his father he would not long be able to blame the third person for the idea, which obviously arose in his *own* mind. The process constitutes psychologically what Freud has termed 'the return of the repressed'. In spite of the most absolute conscious repudiation of a death-wish the death does actually come about. From this point of view it must be said that the 'tyrant' who commits the murder is a substitute for the son who repudiates the idea: Zohâk, who kills Feridun's father Abtin, is a substitute for Feridun,

Feng for Amleth, and, in the Polonius section of Shake-speare's drama, Hamlet for Laertes. So that the figure of the 'tyrant' in this exceedingly complex variant of the myth is really a compromise-formation representing at one and the same time the hated father and the murderous son. On the one side he is identified with the primordial father, being hated by the young hero who ultimately triumphs over him; on the other with the young hero himself, in that he kills the hero's father.[1]

In Shakespeare's modification of the Hamlet legend there is an even more complicated distortion of the theme, the young hero now shrinking from playing the part of the avenging son. Psychologically it betokens not a further degree of 'repression', but rather a 'regression'. The son really refuses to repudiate the murder-wish; he cannot punish the man who carried it out. Claudius is identified with the son almost as much as with the primary father-figure of the myth. Shakespeare's marvellous intuition has, quite unconsciously, penetrated beneath the surface of the smooth Amleth version. He lifts for us at least one layer of the concealing 'repression' and reveals something of the tumult below.[2]

Not only may the two paternal attributes mentioned above, fatherliness and tyranny, be split off so as to give rise to the creation of separate figures, but others also.

---

[1] For this reason Claudius should always be cast as midway in age between the two Hamlets, linking both together psychologically; in a recent London production, by William Poel, this was done, Claudius appearing about ten years only older than Hamlet.

[2] One or two friends have made the reproach to me that my work on Hamlet diminished their aesthetic appreciation of the play. On the contrary I cannot but think that a fuller understanding of Shakespeare's work, its profound truth, its psychological correctness throughout, the depth of its inspiration, must enormously heighten our appreciation of its wonder.

For instance, the power and authority of the parent may be incorporated in the person of a king or other distinguished man, who may be contrasted with the actual father.[1] In the present legend, as has already been indicated, it is probable that the figure of Polonius may be thus regarded as resulting from 'decomposition' of the paternal archetype, representing a certain group of qualities which the young not infrequently find an irritating feature in their elders. The senile nonentity, concealed behind a show of fussy pomposity, who has developed a rare capacity to bore his audience with the repetition of sententious platitudes in which profound ignorance of life is but thinly disguised by a would-be worldly-wise air; the prying busybody whose meddling is, as usual, excused by his 'well-meaning' intentions, constitutes a figure that is sympathetic only to those who submissively accept the world's estimate of the superiority of the merely decrepit. Because of his greater distance from the original Oedipus situation, not being a member of the royal family, he draws on to himself the son-hero's undisguised dislike, untempered by any doubts or conflicts, and Hamlet finds it possible to kill him without remorse. That he is but a substitute for the step-father, i. e. a father *imago*, is shewn by the ease with which the two are identified in Hamlet's mind: after stabbing him he cries out 'Is it the king?'

The *second* disturbing factor in the primary Oedipus scheme is that due to the interweaving of the main theme of jealousy and incest between parent and son with others of a similar kind. We noted above that in the simplest form of decomposition of the paternal attributes the tyrannical rôle is most often relegated to the grandfather. It is no mere chance that this is so, and it is by no

---

[1] The best example of this is to be found in the Jesus myth.

means fully to be accounted for by incompleteness of the decomposition. There is a deeper reason why the grandfather is peculiarly suited to play the part of tyrant and this will be readily perceived when we recollect the large number of legends in which he has previously interposed all manner of obstacles to the marriage of his daughter, the future mother. He opposes the advances of the would-be suitor, sets in his way various conditions and tasks apparently impossible of fulfilment—usually these are miraculously carried out by the lover—and even as a last resort locks up his daughter in an inaccessible spot, as in the legends of Gilgam, Perseus, Romulus, Telephos and others. The underlying motive in all this is that he grudges giving up his daughter to another man, not wishing to part with her himself (father-daughter complex). We are here once more reminded of events that may be observed in daily life by those who open their eyes to the facts, and the selfish motive is often thinly enough disguised under the pretext of an altruistic solicitude for the daughter's welfare; Gretna Green is a repository of such complexes. In two articles giving an analysis of parental complexes[1] I have shewn that they are ultimately derived from infantile ones of the Oedipus type, the father's complex in regard to his daughter, called by Putnam[2] the 'Griselda complex',[3] being a later development and manifestation of his own original Oedipus complex for his mother.

When this grandfather's commands are disobeyed or circumvented his love for his daughter turns to bitterness

---

[1] 'The Significance of the Grandfather for the Fate of the Individual' and 'The Phantasy of the Reversal of Generations', Ch. XXXVIII and XXXIX of my Papers on Psycho-Analysis, 1918.

[2] Putnam: 'Bemerkungen über einen Krankheitsfall mit Griselda-Phantasien', *Internationale Zeitschrift für Psychoanalyse*, 1913, Bd. I, S. 205; reprinted in his Addresses on Psycho-Analysis, 1921.

[3] Rank: 'Der Sinn der Griseldafabel', *Imago*, 1912, Bd. I, S. 34.

and he pursues her and her offspring with insatiable hate. When the grandson in the myth, the young hero, avenges himself and his parents by slaying the tyrannical grandfather it is as though he realised the motive of the persecution, for in truth he slays the man who endeavoured to possess and retain the mother's affections, i. e. his own rival. Thus in this sense we again come back to the primordial father, for whom to him the grandfather is but an *imago,* and see that from the hero's point of view the distinction between father and grandfather is not so radical as it might at first sight appear. We perceive, therefore, that for two reasons this resolution of the original father into two persons, a kind father and a tyrannical grandfather, is not a very extensive one.

The foregoing considerations throw more light on the figure of Polonius in the present play. In his attitude towards the relationship between Hamlet and Ophelia are many of the traits that we have just mentioned as being characteristic of the father-daughter complex displayed by the grandfather of the myth, though by the mechanism of rationalisation they are here skilfully disguised under the guise of worldly-wise advice. Hamlet's resentment against him is thus doubly conditioned, in that first Polonius, through the mechanism of 'decomposition', personates a group of obnoxious elderly attributes, and secondly presents the equally objectionable attitude of the dog-in-the-manger father who grudges to others what he possesses but cannot himself enjoy. In this way, therefore, Polonius represents the antipathetic characteristics of both the father and the grandfather of mythology, so we are not surprised to find that, just as Perseus 'accidentally' slew his grandfather Acrisios, who had locked up his daughter Danae so as to preserve her virginity, so does Hamlet 'accidentally' slay Polonius, by a deed that resolves the situation as

6

correctly from the dramatic as from the mythological point of view. With truth has this act been called the turning-point of the play, for from then on the tragedy relentlessly proceeds with ever increasing pace to its culmination in the doom of the hero and his adversary.

The characteristics of the father-daughter complex are also found in a similar one, the brother-sister complex. As analytic work shews every day, this also, like the former one, is a derivative of the fundamental Oedipus complex. When the incest barrier develops early in the life of the young boy it begins first in regard to his relationship with the mother, and only later sets in with the sister as well; indeed, erotic experiences between brother and sister in early childhood are exceedingly common. The sister is usually the first replacement of the mother as an erotic object; through her the boy learns to find his way to other women. His relationship to his sister duplicates that of the two parents to each other, and in life he often plays a father-part in regard to her (care, protection, etc.). In the present play the attitude of Laertes towards his sister Ophelia is quite indistinguishable from that of their father Polonius.

Hamlet's relation to Laertes is, mythologically speaking, a double one, a fusion of two primary Oedipus schemes, one the reverse of the other. On the one hand Laertes, being identified with the old Polonius in his attitude towards Ophelia and Hamlet, represents the tyrant father, Hamlet being the young hero; Hamlet not only keenly resents Laertes' open expression of his devoted affection for Ophelia — in the grave scene — but at the end of the play kills him, as he had killed Polonius, in an accurate consummation of the mythological motive. On the other hand, however, as was remarked earlier, from another point of view we can regard Hamlet and Polonius as two figures resulting from 'decomposition' of Laertes' father, just as we did with the elder Hamlet and Claudius in relation to Hamlet. For in the relationship of the three men Hamlet kills the father Polonius, just as the tyrant father kills the good father in the typical Feridun form of the myth, and Laertes, who is from this point of view the young hero, avenges this murder by ultimately slaying Hamlet. An interesting confirmation of this view that the struggle between the two men is a representation of a father-son contest has been pointed out by Rank.[1] It is that the curious episode of the exchange of rapiers in the fatal duel is an evident replacement of a similar episode in the original saga, where it takes place in the final fight between Hamlet and his step-father, when Hamlet kills the latter and escapes unwounded. From this point of view we reach the interesting conclusion that Laertes and Claudius are psychological and mythological equivalents or duplicates. Each represents aspects of both generations, the father who is to be killed and the revolutionary, murderous son, thus differing from Polonius, the Ghost, and the elder Hamlet himself, who are all pure father-figures. The equivalence of the two men is well brought out dramatically. Not only does the King's sword of the saga become Laertes' rapier in the play, but in the duel scene it is evident that Laertes is only a tool in Claudius' hand, carrying out his intention with what was his own weapon. Throughout the play, therefore, we perceive the theme of the son-father conflict recurring again and again in the most complicated interweavings.

That the brother-sister complex was operative in the original Hamlet legend also is evidenced in several ways. From a religious point of view Claudius and the Queen stood to each other in exactly the same relationship as do

---

[1] Rank: Das Inzestmotiv in Dichtung und Sage, 1912, S. 226, 227.

brother and sister, which is the reason why the term
'incestuous' is always applied to it and stress laid on the
fact that their guilt exceeded that of simple adultery.[1] Of
still more interest is the fact that in the saga — plainly
stated in Saxo and indicated in Belleforest — Ophelia (or
rather her nameless precursor) was said to be a foster-
sister of Amleth; she bore here no relation to Polonius,
this being an addition made by the dramatist with an
obvious motivation. This being so, we would seem to trace
a still deeper reason for Hamlet's misogynous turning from
her and for his jealous resentment of Laertes. This theme
of the relation between siblings, however, is much less
prominent in the Hamlet legend than in some others of
the same group, e. g. those of Cyrus, Karna, etc., so that
it will not be dwelt on further here.

The *third* factor to be considered is the process
technically known to mythologists as 'doubling' of the
principal characters. The chief motive for its occurrence
seems to be the desire to exalt the importance of these,
and especially to glorify the hero, by decoratively filling
in the stage with lay figures of colourless copies whose
neutral movements contrast with the vivid activities of the
principals; it is perhaps more familiar in music than in
other products of the imagination. This factor is sometimes
hard to distinguish from the first one, for it is plain that
a given multiplying of figures may serve at the same time
the function of decomposition and that of doubling; in
general it may be said that the former function is more
often fulfilled by the creation of a new person who is
related to the principal character, the latter by the creation
of one who is not, but the rule has many exceptions. In

---

[1] It may be noted that Shakespeare accepted Belleforest's alteration
of the original saga in making the Queen commit incest during the life
of her first husband.

the present legend Claudius seems to subserve both functions. It is interesting to note that in many legends it is not the father's figure who is doubled by the creation of a brother, but the grandfather's. This is so in some versions of the Perseus legend and, as was referred to above, in those of Romulus and Amphion; in all three of these the creation of the king's brother, as in the Hamlet legend, subserves the functions of both decomposition and doubling. Good examples of the simple doubling process are seen with the maid of Pharaoh's daughter in the Moses legend and in many of the figures of the Cyrus one.[1] Perhaps the purest examples in the present play are the colourless copies of Hamlet presented by the figures of Horatio, Marcellus and Bernardo; the first of these was derived from a foster-brother of Hamlet's in the saga. Laertes and the younger Fortinbras, on the other hand, are examples of both doubling and decomposition of the main figure. Laertes is the more complex figure of the two, for in addition to representing, as Claudius also does, both the son and father aspects of Hamlet's mentality, in the way explained above, he evinces also the influence of the brother-sister complex and in a more positive form than does Hamlet. Hamlet's jealousy of Laertes' interference in connection with Ophelia is further to be compared with his resentment at the meddling of Guildenstern and Rosencrantz. They are therefore only copies of the Brother of mythology and, like him, are killed by the Hero. Common to Hamlet, Laertes, and Fortinbras is the theme of revenge for murder or injury done to a dead father. It is noteworthy that neither of the latter two shew any sign of inhibition in the performance of this task and that with neither is any reference made to his mother. In Hamlet, on the other

[1] This is very clearly pointed out by Rank: Der Mythus von der Geburt des Helden, 1909, S. 84, 85.

hand, in whom 'repressed' love for the mother is at least as strong as 'repressed' hostility against the father, inhibition appears.

The interesting subject of the actual mode of origin of myths and legends, and the relation of them to infantile phantasies, will not here be considered,[1] since our interest in the topic is secondary to the main one of the play of 'Hamlet' as given to us by Shakespeare. Enough perhaps has been said of the comparative mythology of the Hamlet legend to shew that in it are to be found ample indications of the working of all forms of incestuous fantasy. We may summarise the foregoing consideration of this aspect of the subject by saying that *the main theme of this story is a highly elaborated and disguised account of a boy's love for his mother and consequent jealousy of and hatred towards his father;* the allied one in which the brother and sister respectively play the same part as the father and mother in the main theme is also told, though with subordinate interest.

Last of all in this connection may be mentioned a matter which on account of its general psychological interest has provoked endless discussion, namely Hamlet's so-called 'simulation of madness'. I do not propose to review the extraordinarily extensive literature that has grown up over this matter,[2] for before the advent of the new science of psychopathology such discussions were bound to be little better than guesswork and now possess only an historical interest. There is of course no question of insanity in the proper sense of the word; Hamlet's

---

[1] Those who wish to pursue the subject from the psycho-analytical point of view are referred to the writings of Freud, Rank and Abraham.

[2] The earlier part of this will be found in Furness' Variorum Shakespeare, 'Hamlet', Vol. II, pp. 195-235; See further Delbrück: Über Hamlets Wahnsinn, 1893.

behaviour is that of a psychoneurotic and as such naturally
aroused the thought on the part of those surrounding him
that he was suffering from some inner affliction. The traits
in Hamlet's behaviour that are commonly called 'feigning
madness' are brought to expression by Shakespeare in
such a refined and subtle manner as to be not very
transpicuous unless one compares them with the corresponding part of the original saga. The fine irony exhibited
by Hamlet in the play, which enables him to express contempt and hostility in an indirect and disguised form—
beautifully illustrated, for instance, in his conversations
with Polonius—is a transmutation of the still more concealed mode of expression adopted in the saga, where
the hero's audience commonly fails to apprehend his meaning.
He here combines a veiled form of speech, full of obvious
equivocations and intent to deceive, with a curiously
punctilious insistence on verbal truthfulness. Saxo gives
many examples of this and adds:[1] 'He was loth to be
thought prone to lying about any matter, and wished to
be held a stranger to falsehood; and accordingly he mingled
craft and candour in such wise that, though his words did
not lack truth, yet there was nothing to betoken the
truth and betray how far his keenness went'. Even in the
saga, however, we read[2] that 'some people, therefore,
declared that his mind was quick enough, and fancied that
he only played the simpleton in order to hide his understanding, and veiled some deep purpose under a cunning
feint'. The king and his friends applied all sorts of tests
to him to determine this truth, tests which of course the
hero successfully withstands. It is made plain that Amleth
deliberately adopts this curious behaviour in order to

[1] Saxo Grammaticus: Danish History, translated by Elton, 1894,
p. 109.
[2] Saxo: op. cit., p. 108.

further his scheme of revenge, to which—thus differing from Hamlet—he had whole-heartedly devoted himself. The actual mode of operation of his simulation here is very instructive to observe, for it gives us the clue to a deeper psychological interpretation of the process. His conduct in this respect has three characteristics, first the obscure and disguised manner of speech just referred to, secondly a demeanour of indolent inertia and general purposelessness, and thirdly conduct of childish and at times quite imbecillic foolishness (*Dummstellen*); the third of these is well exemplified by the way in which he rides into the palace seated backwards on a donkey, imitates a cock crowing and flapping its wings, rolling on the floor, and similar asininities. His motive in so acting was, by playing the part of a harmless fool, to deceive the king and court as to his projects of revenge, and unobserved to get to know their plans and intentions; in this he admirably succeeded. Belleforest adds the interesting touch that Amleth, being a Latin scholar, had adopted this device in imitation of the younger Brutus: as was remarked earlier, both names signify 'doltish', 'stupid'; the derived Norwegian word 'amlod' is still a colloquialism for 'fool'.[1] Belleforest evidently did not know how usual it was for famous young heroes to exhibit this trait; similar stories of 'simulated foolishness' are narrated of David, Moses, Cyros, Kaikhosrav, William Tell, Parsifal, and many others besides Hamlet and Brutus.[2]

The behaviour assumed by Amleth in the saga is not that of any form of insanity. It is a form of syndrome well-known to occur in hysteria to which various names have been given: 'simulated foolishness' (Jones), 'Dummstellen', 'Moria' (Jastrowitz), 'ecmnésie' (Pitres), 'retour

[1] Assen: Norsk Ordbog, 1877.
[2] See Rank: Das Inzest-Motiv, S. 264, 265.

à l'enfance' (Gandy), 'Witzelsucht' (Oppenheim), 'puér-
ilisme mental' (Dupré), and so on. I have published
elsewhere[1] a clinical study of the condition, with a description of a typical case; Rank[2] has reached similar conclusions from his extensive mythological studies. The
complete syndrome comprises the following features:
foolish, witless behaviour, an inane, inept kind of funniness
and silliness, and childishness. Now, in reading the numerous
examples of Amleth's 'foolish' behaviour as narrated by
Saxo one cannot help being impressed by the *childish*
characteristics manifested throughout in them. His peculiar
riddling sayings, obviously aping the innocence of childhood,
his predilection for dirt and for smearing himself with
filth, his general shiftlessness, and above all the highly
characteristic combination of fondness for deception as a
thing in itself (apart from the cases where there is a
definite motive) with a punctilious regard for verbal truth,
are unmistakably childish traits. The whole syndrome is an
exaggeration of a certain type of demeanour displayed at
one time or another by most children, and psycho-analysis
of it has demonstrated beyond any doubt that their motive
in behaving so is to simulate innocence and often extreme
childishness, even 'foolishness', in order to delude their
elders into regarding them as being 'too young to
understand' or even into altogether disregarding their
presence. The purpose of the artifice is that by these
means children can view and overhear various private
things which they are not supposed to. It need hardly be

[1] 'Simulated Foolishness in Hysteria', *American Journal of
Insanity*, 1910, reprinted as Ch. XXIV of my Papers on Psycho-
Analysis, 1918.

[2] Rank: Die Lohengrin-Sage, 1911; 'Die Nacktheit in Sage und
Dichtung', *Imago*, 1913; numerous passages in his other works
previously quoted, especially: Das Inzestmotiv, Der Mythus von der
Geburt des Helden, etc.

said that the curiosity thus indulged in is in most cases concerned with matters of a directly sexual nature; even marital embraces are in this way investigated by quite young children far oftener than is generally suspected or thought possible. The core of Amleth's attitude is secrecy and spying: secrecy as to his own thoughts, knowledge, and plans; spying as regards those of his enemy, his step-father. These two character traits are certainly derived from forbidden curiosity about secret, i. e. sexual matters in early childhood. So is the love of deception for its own sake, a trait which sometimes amounts to what is called pathological lying; it is a defiant reaction to the lies almost always told to the child, and always detected by him. In so behaving the child is really caricaturing the adult's behaviour to himself, as also in the punctiliousness about verbal truth that is sometimes combined with the tendency to deceive; he is pretending to tell the truth as the parent pretended to tell it to him, deceiving going on all the while in both cases. That the theme of the Amleth *motif* is derived from an infantile and sexual source can easily be shewn from the material provided in the saga itself. The main test applied to him by Feng in order to discover whether he was really stupid or only pretending to be so was to get a young girl (the prototype of Ophelia) to seduce him away to a lonely part of the woods and then send retainers to spy on them and find out whether he knew how to perform the sexual act or not. Then follows a long story of how Amleth is warned of the plot and manages to outwit the spies and also to attain his sexual goal. This passage, so obviously inappropriate if taken literally as applying to a man of Amleth's age and previous intelligence, can only be understood by correlating it with the unconscious source of the theme, and this always emanates from the impulses of childhood.

'Knowledge' is often felt to be synonymous with 'sexual knowledge', the two terms being in many contexts interchangeable: for instance, the legal expression 'to have knowledge of a girl', the Biblical one 'and Adam knew Eve his wife' (after eating of the tree of knowledge), and so on. If a child has mastered the great secret he feels that he knows what matters in life; if he hasn't he is in the dark. And, as in the Amleth saga, to prove that someone is ignorant of this fundamental matter is the supreme test of his stupidity and 'innocence'.

Spying and overhearing play such a constant part in the Amleth saga as to exclude the possibility of their being unconnected with the central theme of the story. After the plot just mentioned had failed Feng's counsellor, the prototype of Polonius, devises another in which Amleth is to be spied on when talking to his mother in her bedroom. During the voyage to England the king's retainers enter Amleth's bedroom to listen to his conversation. Before this Amleth had spied on his companions and replaced their letter by one of his own. In the later part of the saga, not utilised by Shakespeare, two other instances of spying occur. In 'Hamlet' Shakespeare has retained these scenes and added one other. The first time is when the interview between Hamlet and Ophelia, doubtless taken from the test described above, is overlooked by the king and Polonius ; the second when Hamlet's interview with his mother is spied on by Polonius, who thereby loses his life; and the third when the same interview is watched by the Ghost. It is appropriate to the underlying theme of sexual curiosity that two out of these should take place in the mother's bedchamber, the original scene of such curiosity; on both occasions the father-substitute comes *between* Hamlet and his mother, as though to separate them, the reversal of a theme common in primitive cosmogonies. The most striking example in 'Hamlet' of a spying scene is the famous 'play within a play', for in a very neat analysis Rank[1] has shewn that this play scene is a disguised representation of the infantile curiosity theme discussed above.

From this point of view we can specify more nearly the precise aspect of the father that is represented by the 'decomposed' figure Polonius. It is clearly the spying, watching, 'all-knowing' father, who is appropriately outwitted by the cunning youth. Now it is interesting that, apart from Falstaff and the subordinate names of Reynaldo and Gonzago,[2] Polonius is the only person whose name Shakespeare changed in any of his plays, and one naturally wonders why he did so. In the Kyd play and also in the first Quarto the name was Corambis. The plausible suggestion has been made[3] that the name Polonius was taken from Polonian, the name for a Pole in Elizabethan English, for the reason that even at that date Poland was the land pre-eminent in policy and intrigue.

Amleth's feigned stupidity in the saga is very crudely depicted and its meaning is quite evident. The use Shakespeare made of this unpromising material, and the way in which he made it serve his aim of completely transforming the old story, is one of the master-strokes of the drama. Amleth's gross acting, for a quite deliberate purpose, is converted into a delicately drawn character trait. Merciless satire, caustic irony, ruthless penetration together with the old habit of speaking in riddles: all these betray not simply the caution of a man who has to keep his secret

---

[1] Rank: 'Das "Schauspiel" in Hamlet', *Imago*, Bd. IV, S. 41.

[2] The story of the Gonzago play is taken from a murder by a man of that name of a duke which was committed in 1538 by means of pouring poison into his ear.

[3] By Furness: op. cit., p. 242.

from those around him, as with Amleth, but the poignant sufferings of a man who is being torn and tortured within his own mind, who is struggling to escape from knowing the horrors of his own heart. With Amleth the feigned stupidity was the weapon used by a single-hearted man in his fight against external difficulties and deliberate foes; with Hamlet it — or rather what corresponds to it, his peculiar behaviour — was the agent by which the secret of a man torn by suffering was betrayed to a previously unsuspecting foe[1] and increasing difficulties were created in his path where none before existed. In the issue Amleth triumphed; Hamlet was destroyed. The different use made of this feature in the story symbolises more finely than anything else the transformation effected by Shakespeare. An inertia pretended for reasons of expediency becomes an inertia unavoidably forced on the hero from the depths of his nature. In this he shews that the tragedy of man is within himself, that, as the ancient saying goes: Character is Fate. It is the essential difference between pre-historic and civilised man; the difficulties with which the former had to contend came from without, those with which the latter have to contend really come from within. This inner conflict modern psychologists know as neurosis, and it is only by study of neurosis that one can learn the fundamental motives and instincts that move men. Here, as in so many other respects, Shakespeare was the first modern.

VII

It is highly instructive now to review the respects in which the plot of 'Hamlet' deviates from that of the original saga. We are here, of course, not concerned with the poetic and literary representation, which not merely

[1] On the way in which Hamlet's conduct inevitably led him into ever increasing danger see Loening, op. cit., S. 385, et seq.

revivified an old story, but created an entirely new work of genius. The changes effected were mainly two and it can be said that Shakespeare was only very slightly indebted to others for them. The first is as follows: In the saga Feng (Claudius) had murdered his brother in public, so that the deed was generaly known, and further had with lies and false witnesses sought to justify the deed by pretending it was done to save the Queen from the cruel threats of her husband.[1] This view of the matter he successfully imposed on the nation, so that, as Belleforest has it, 'son péché trouva excuse à l'endroit du peuple et fut reputé comme justice envers la noblesse—et qu'au reste, en lieu de le poursuyvre comme parricide[2] et incestueux, chacun des courtisans luy applaudissoit et le flattoit en sa fortune prospere'. Now was the change from this to a secret murder effected by Shakespeare or by Kyd? It is of course to be correlated with the introduction of the Ghost, of whom there is no trace in either Saxo or Belleforest. This must have been done early in the history of the Elizabethan 'Hamlet', for it is referred to by Lodge[3] in 1596 and is also found in 'Der bestrafte

---

[1] Those acquainted with psycho-analytic work will have no difficulty in discerning the infantile sadistic origin of this pretext (See Freud. Sammlung kleiner Schriften, Zweite Folge, 1909, S. 169). Young children commonly interpret an overheard coitus as an act of violence imposed on the mother and they are in any case apt to come to this conclusion whichever way they are enlightened on the facts of sex. The view in question is certainly an aggravating cause of the unconscious hostility against the father.

This point again confirms our conclusion that Claudius partly incorporates Hamlet's 'repressed' wishes, for we see in the saga that he not only kills the father-king but also gives as an excuse for it just the reason that the typical son feels.

[2] Saxo also has 'parricidium', which was of course occasionally used to denote the murder of other near relatives than the parents.

[3] Lodge : loc. cit.

Brudermord', though neither of these reasons is decisive for excluding Shakespeare's hand. But purely literary considerations make it likely enough, as Robertson [1] has pointed out, that the change was introduced by Kyd, who seems to have had a partiality for Ghost scenes. In the saga there was delayed action due to the external difficulties of penetrating through the king's watchful guard. Kyd seems to have retained these external difficulties as an explanation for the delay, though his introduction of the Ghost episode for reasons of his own—probably first in the form of a prologue—somewhat weakened them as a justification, since to have the Ghost episode the murder had to be a secret one—otherwise there would be nothing for the Ghost to reveal and no reason for his appearance. But his Hamlet, as in the saga, had a quite single-hearted attitude towards the matter of revenge; he at once confided in Horatio, secured his help, and devoted himself entirely to his aim. There was no self-reproaching, no doubt, and no psychological problem. Shakespeare, however, saw the obvious advantages of the change in the plot—if he did not introduce it himself—for his intention of transforming the play from an external struggle into an internal tragedy. The change minimises the external difficulties of Hamlet's task, for plainly it is harder to rouse a nation to condemn a crime and assist the avenger when it has been openly explained and universally forgiven than when it has been guiltily concealed. If the original plot had been retained there would be more excuse for the Klein-Werder hypothesis, though it is to be observed that even in the saga Hamlet successfully executed his task, herculean as it was. The present rendering makes still more conspicuous Hamlet's recalcitrancy, for it disposes of the

[1] Robertson: op. cit, pp. 44, 55, 56.

only justifiable plea for delay. That Shakespeare saw the value of the change thus unwittingly and ununderstandingly introduced by Kyd is proved by the fact that later on he took steps to remove the last traces of even a relative publicity concerning the murder. In the first Quarto Hamlet secures his mother's promise to help him in his plans of revenge, and later Horatio in an interview with the Queen speaks with knowledge of Hamlet's plans of revenge and learns from the Queen that she sympathises with them. Both these passages were omitted in the second Quarto. The omission unmistakably indicates Shakespeare's intention to depict Hamlet not as a man dismayed by external difficulties and naturally securing the cooperation of those he could trust, but as a man who could not bring himself to speak to his best friend about his quite legitimate desire for revenge, simply because his own mind was in dire conflict on the matter.

The second and all-important respect in which Shakespeare, and he alone, changed the story and thus revolutionised the tragedy is the vacillation and hesitancy he introduced into Hamlet's attitude towards his task, with the consequent paralysis of his action. In all the previous versions Hamlet was throughout a man of rapid decision and action wherever possible, not—as with Shakespeare's version—in everything except in the one task of vengeance. He had, as Shakespeare's Hamlet felt he should have, swept to his revenge unimpeded by any doubts or scruples and had never flinched from the straightforward path of duty. With him duty and natural inclination went hand in hand; from his heart he wanted to do that which he believed he ought to do, and thus was harmoniously impelled by both the summons of his conscience and the cry of his blood. There was none of the deep-reaching conflict that was so disastrous to Shakespeare's Hamlet.

It is as though Shakespeare, on reading the story, had realised that had *he* been placed in a similar situation he would not have found the path of action so obvious as was supposed, but would on the contrary have been torn in a conflict which was all the more intense for the fact that he could not explain its nature. Bradley, in the passage quoted earlier, might well say that this was the only tragic situation to which Shakespeare himself would not have been equal, and we now know the reason must have been that his penetration had unconsciously revealed to his feeling, though not to his conscious intelligence, the fundamental meaning of the story. His own Oedipus complex was too strong for him to be able to repudiate it as readily as Amleth and Laertes had done and he could only create a hero who was unable to escape from its toils.

In this transformation Shakespeare exactly reversed the plot of the tragedy. Whereas in the saga this consisted in the overcoming of external difficulties and dangers by a single-hearted hero, in the play these are removed and the plot lies in the fateful unrolling of the consequences that result from an internal conflict in the hero's soul. From the struggles of the hero issue dangers which at first did not exist, but which, as the effect of his untoward essays, loom increasingly portentous until at the end they close and involve him in final destruction. More than this, every action he so reluctantly engages in for the fulfilment of his obvious task seems half-wittingly to be disposed in such a way as to provoke destiny, in that, by arousing the suspicion and hostility of his enemy, it defeats its own purpose and helps to encompass his own ruin. The conflict in his soul is to him insoluble and the only steps he can make are those which inexorably draw him nearer and nearer to his doom. In him, as in every victim of a powerful unconscious conflict, the Will to Death is fundamentally stronger than the Will to Life, and his struggle is at heart one long despairing fight against suicide, the least intolerable solution of the problem. Being unable to free himself from the ascendency of his past he is necessarily impelled by Fate along the only path he can travel—to Death. In thus vividly exhibiting the desperate but unavailing struggle of a strong man against Fate Shakespeare achieved the very essence of the Greek conception of tragedy, but he went beyond this and shewed that the real nature of man's Fate is inherent in his own soul.

There is thus reason to believe that the new life which Shakespeare poured into the old story was the outcome of inspirations that took their origin in the deepest and darkest regions of his mind. He responded to the peculiar appeal of the story by projecting into it his profoundest thoughts and emotions in a way that has ever since wrung wonder from all who have heard or read the tragedy. It is only fitting that the greatest work of the world-poet should have had to do with the deepest problem and the intensest conflict that have occupied the mind of man since the beginning of time—the revolt of youth and of the impulse to love against the restraint imposed by the jealous eld.

CHAPTER II

ON 'DYING TOGETHER'

WITH SPECIAL REFERENCE TO HEINRICH VON KLEIST'S SUICIDE [1]

In a recent interesting monograph on Heinrich von Kleist Sadger[2] has called attention to a number of considerations bearing on the psychology of the impulse to die together with a loved one, to share death in common. As it is possible in a special journal to pursue an analysis more freely than in writings intended for a lay audience, I wish to comment here on two points in this connection which Sadger—I assume, with intention—left untouched.

Of the general psycho-sexual significance of the idea of death nothing need be added here. Freud, Stekel, and others have fully described the masochistic phantasies in which the idea may become involved, and this is also clearly illustrated in Sadger's monograph. The common mythological and folk-loristic conception of death as a spirit that violently attacks one mainly originates in this source.

The question of 'dying together' is, however, more complicated, the tendency being determined by several motives. The most obvious of these is that underlying a

[1] Published in the *Zentralblatt für Psychoanalyse,* September 1911, Jahrgang I, S. 563.
[2] Sadger: Heinrich von Kleist. Eine pathographisch-psychologische Studie, 1910.

7*

belief in a world beyond, a region where all hopes that
are denied in this life will come true. The wish-fulfilment
comprised in this belief subserves, of course, a similar
function to that operative in the neuroses and psychoses;
the consolation it yields, as is well-recognised by theologians, is naturally greater at times when life is filled with
disappointment and sorrow. The same is true of the desire
to die together with one's beloved, as is well illustrated
by the accessory factors that helped to drive von Kleist
to suicide.[1] With him, however, as Sadger clearly shews,[2]
there was a specific and irresistible attraction toward the
act, one which is not at all accounted for by the attendant
circumstances. Most psycho-analysts will probably agree
with Sadger's conclusions[3] that 'the wish to die together
is the same as the wish to sleep and lie together (originally,
of course, with the mother)', and that 'the grave so longed
for by Kleist is simply an equivalent of the mother's bed'.
Von Kleist's own words plainly confirm this: he writes,
'I must confess to you that her grave is dearer to me
than the beds of all the empresses[4] of the world.' The idea
that death consists in a return to the heaven whence we
were born, i. e. to the mother's womb, is familiar to us
in religious and other spheres of thought.

Deeper motives connect the subject with that of
necrophilia. First of these may be mentioned the sadistic
impulse, which can be inflamed at the thought of communion with a dead person—partly through the helpless
resistlessness of the latter, and partly through the idea
that a dead mistress can never be wearied by excessive

---

[1] idem: op. cit., S. 60, 61.

[2] idem: op. cit., S. 56-8.

[3] idem: op. cit., S. 60.

[4] Empress, like Queen, is a well-known unconscious symbol of the
mother.

caresses, can endure without limit, is forever loyal. The latter thought of the insatiability of the dead often recurs in the literature on vampyrism; it is indicated in the verses where Heine, in his dedication to 'Der Doktor Faust', makes the returned Helena say:

> Du hast mich beschworen aus dem Grab
> Durch deinen Zauberwillen,
> Belebtest mich mit Wollustglut --
> Jetzt kannst du die Glut nicht stillen.

> · Preß deinen Mund an meinen Mund;
> Der Menschen Odem ist göttlich!
> Ich trinke deine Seele aus,
> Die Toten sind unersättlich.

> (Thou hast called me from my grave
> By thy bewitching will;
> Made me alive, feel passionate love,
> A passion thou canst never still.

> Press thy mouth close to my cold mouth;
> Man's breath is god-like created.
> I drink thy essence, I drink thy soul,
> The dead can never be sated.)

In my psycho-analytical experience of neurotics, necrophilic tendencies have further[1] invariably been associated with both coprophilic and birth phantasies. Freud[2] first pointed out the connection between the two phantasies just named, and this has since been amply confirmed by most observers. On the one hand, faecal material is dead

---

[1] The connection here implied between sadism and coprophilia is discussed at length in a later paper republished as Chapter XXXI of the author's 'Papers on Psycho-Analysis', Second Edition.

[2] Freud: Sammlung kleiner Schriften, Zweite Folge, S. 168.

matter that was once part of a living body, but is now decomposing, facts that make it easy for an association to be formed between it and a corpse: and on the other hand it is, according to a common 'infantile theory', the material out of which children are made, and, in the form of manure, is a general fertilising principle. Love for, or undue horror at, a dead body may thus betoken a reversion to the infantile interest and fondness for faecal excrement. This explains the frequency with which the twin motives of (1) a dead woman giving birth to a child, and (2) a living woman being impregnated by a dead husband, occur in folklore, literature, mythology and popular belief.[1] Interesting indications of both, which need not be detailed here, are to be found in von Kleist's short story 'Die Marquise von O.' The same combination of coprophilic and birth phantasy probably underlay his remarkable proposal to Wilhelmine von Zenge that they should leave everything else and adopt a peasant's life; as is well known, when she refused to fulfil this 'love condition' he heartlessly broke off their engagement. Sadger quotes the following passage of his in this connection: 'With the Persian magi there was a religious law to the effect that a man could do nothing more pleasing to the gods than *to till a field, to plant a tree, and to beget a child.*[2] I call that wisdom, and no truth has yet penetrated so deeply into my soul as this has. That is what I *ought* to do, I am *absolutely* sure. Oh, Wilhelmine, what unspeakable joy there must be in the knowledge that one is fulfilling one's destiny *entirely* in accord with the will

[1] Numerous examples of this are quoted by Hanusch: *Zeitschrift für deutsche Mythologie,* Jahrgang IV, S. 200; Hock: Die Vampyrsagen und ihre Verwertung in der deutschen Literatur, 1900, S. 24, 37, 43; Horst: Zauber-Bibliothek, 1821, Erster Teil, S. 277; Krauss: Slavische Volksforschungen, 1908, S. 130; Sepp: Occident und Orient, 1903, S. 268.

[2] The italics are mine (in this instance only)

of Nature.' I thus fully agree with Sadger[1] when he
maintains that this has 'eine versteckte sexuelle Bedeutung'
('a hidden sexual meaning'). I have further observed, though
I do not know if it is a general rule, that patients having this
complex often display an attitude of wonderful tenderness
towards the object of their love, just like that of a fond
mother for her babe; this was very pronounced in von Kleist's
final outburst of 'dithyrambic rapture' towards Henriette,
with its 'exchange of pet names that bordered on lunacy'.[2]

Sadger further comments on the 'travelling' significance
of dying together. The connection between the ideas of
death and travel is primaeval; one thinks at once of the
Grecian and Teutonic myths of the procession of dead souls,
and of Hamlet's 'undiscovered country, from whose bourn
no traveller returns'. The fact, now becoming generally
recognised since Freud first called attention to its importance (Die Traumdeutung, 1900), that children essentially
conceive of death as a 'going away', as a journey, evidently renders this association a natural and stable one.
With von Kleist it can be brought into line with his
curious mania for travelling, which seemed so objectless
and inexplicable to his friends. Two motives in this connection lie fairly near the surface. In the first place, death
is conceived of as a voyage of discovery, as a journey to
a land where hidden things will be revealed; I have had
several religious patients whose curiosity, sexual and otherwise, had been largely transferred on to this idea.[3] Sadger
points out how passionate was von Kleist's desire to reach
absolute, certain truth,[4] and quotes his statement: *'Education*

---

[1] Sadger: op. cit., S. 62.

[2] idem: op. cit., S. 59.

[3] One of my patients eagerly looked forward to discovering in the
next world the authorship of the Letters of Junius!

[4] Sadger: op. cit., S. 62.

seemed to me the only goal worthy of endeavour, *truth*[1]
the only wealth worthy of possession.' When he studied
Kant's destructive criticism of the concept of the Absolute,
and of a life hereafter, he was shaken to the depths of
his being. He wrote: 'And my only thought, which my
soul in this utmost tumult laboured on with burning dread,
was always this: thy *sole* aim, thy loftiest goal, has declined.'
In the second place, a journey can be undertaken in company,
and it is significant that in von Kleist's fugue-like escapes
this was practically always so. Sadger traces this tendency
ultimately to the infantile desire to defy the father and
escape with the mother to some distant place where he
cannot disturb their mutual relations; therefore dying together
can signify in the unconscious to fly with the mother and
thus gratify secret desires.[2] The travelling mania is one of
many tendencies that may come to expression in flying
dreams,[3] and in this connection I should like to throw
out a few suggestions. Freud traces the ultimate source
of these dreams to the pleasurably exciting chasing of
childhood,[4] and has also laid special stress on the relation
between bodily movements in general and sexuality.[5] In
several psycho-analyses I have found associated with this
various anal-erotic motives, which may therefore furnish
something towards the later desires. The fact itself that
the common expression for defaecation is 'movement', and
for faeces 'motion', points to an inner connection between

---

[1] On the intimate association between the ideas of truth and nudity
see Furtmüller: *Zeitschrift für Psychoanalyse,* 1913, Bd. I, S. 273.

[2] Sadger: op. cit., S 60.

[3] It is perhaps not without interest that the name of the woman
with whom von Kleist departed on his endless journey was Vogel (i.e. 'Bird').

[4] Freud: Die Traumdeutung, 2e Aufl, S. 195.

[5] Idem: Drei Abhandlungen, 2e Aufl., S. 53, 54. See also Sadger:
'Haut-, Schleimhaut- und Muskelerotik', *Jahrbuch der Psychoanalyse,*
Bd. III, S. 525.

two subjects that at first sight appear to be quite unrelated.[1]
I need not here go into the different grounds for the
association, but will only remark that when the act of
defaecation is especially· pleasurable it is apt to acquire
the significance of a sexual 'projecting',[2] just as of urine
and semen. I have collected much evidence, from both
actual psycho-analyses and from folk-lore, which I hope
to detail elsewhere,[3] indicating that (a) this connotation of
sexual projecting, and of movement in general, is especially
closely associated in the unconscious with the act of
passing flatus,[4] and (b) that this latter act, on account of
the idea of penetration to a distance, is sometimes conceived
of by children as constituting the essential part of coitus,
which thus consists of expelling flatus into the female cloaca.
The latter phantasy would, through its association with
movement (and therefore flying through a gaseous medium
—the air), be particularly well adapted to find expression,
together with the other coprophilic, sadistic, and incestuous
tendencies referred to above, in the love-condition of dying
together, and I would suggest that it might be worth
while to investigate future cases of the kind from this
point of view.

---

[1] This association plays a prominent part in the common symptom
known as *Reisefieber,* and in the allied 'packing' dreams

[2] It is noteworthy that the common vulgarism for the act is etymo-
logically cognate with the word 'to shoot'.

[3] Since the present paper was written this has been done in two
monographs published in the *Jahrbuch der Psychoanalyse.*

[4] It is noteworthy that the common vulgarism for this both in
English and in German singularly resembles the German for travel,
'Fahrt'.

CHAPTER III

AN UNUSUAL CASE OF 'DYING TOGETHER'[1]

THE following dramatic event, which took place here[2] this week, seems to lend itself to some considerations of psycho-analytical interest.

A man and wife, aged 32 and 28 respectively, went from Toronto to spend a week-end at Niagara Falls. In company with several other people they ventured on to the great bridge of ice that forms every winter just at the foot of the Falls, and which then joins the American and Canadian shores of the river. The ice-bridge began to crack and drift from its moorings, and a river-man, who knew the locality well and who was on the ice at the time, shouted to the others to make for the Canadian side where there was more chance of getting ashore. The couple in question ignored this advice and rushed towards the American shore, but were soon stopped by open water. They then ran in the other direction (about 150 yards), but when about 50 yards from safety the woman fell down exhausted, crying 'I can't go on! let us die here!'. The husband, aided by another man, dragged her onward until they reached the edge. This was three yards from the shore, and the intervening water was covered with

---

[1] Published in the *Zentralblatt für Psychoanalyse*, May 1912, Jahrgang II, S. 455.
[2] i. e. Toronto.

soft ice. The river-man begged them to cross this, pointing out that the ice would prevent their sinking, and guaranteed to bring them to safety; he demonstrated the possibility of the feat by crossing himself, and later by returning to save another man. The woman, however, declined to take the risk, and her husband refused to go without her. The mass of ice now began to drift down the river, breaking into smaller pieces as it went, and slowly but surely approaching the terrible Rapids that lead to the Niagara Whirlpool. In an hour's time they had drifted to where a railway bridge crosses the ravine, over 60 yards above their heads, and were on the point of being caught up by the swift rapids. A rope, with an iron harpoon at the end, had been lowered from the bridge and this was obviously their last hope of safety. As the ice-floe, now moving rapidly, swept under the bridge, the man successfully seized the rope, but apparently the woman refused to trust to it unless it was fastened around her. At all events the man was seen to be vainly fumbling, with fingers numbed by cold, to tie the rope around his wife's waist. Failing in this in the short time at his disposal before the floe passed onwards, he flung the rope aside, knelt down beside the woman and clasped her in his arms; they went thus to their death, which was now only a matter of seconds.

These are the main facts as published in all the newspapers. The only additional ones I could discover, from a friend of mine who happened to know the couple well, were: that they were devotedly fond of each other, that they had been married for seven years, and that they, the woman in particular, were sad at never having had any children.

The husband's conduct does not call for any special comment, being dictated by sufficiently obvious motives.

To these I will only add that he was in the presence of a large audience, the banks of the ravine being lined by thousands of people who had accumulated during the fateful hour, and that it would be difficult or impossible for a man to hold up his head again if he deserted any woman in such a situation, let alone his own wife.

There is, however, more to be said about the woman's conduct, or rather lack of conduct. It is evident that she was throughout overcome by panic and fright, or else convinced of the inevitableness of the fate awaiting her. Her efforts at escape were either paralysed or else *actively hindering*, and she did not respond even to the powerful motive of saving her husband. Now it is known to psychoanalysts, as Freud first pointed out in reference to certain dreams,[1] that emotional paralysis is not so much a traumatic effect of fright as a manifestation of inhibition resulting from a conflict between a conscious and unconscious impulse. A familiar example is that of a woman who cannot protect herself with her whole strength against being raped, part of her energy being inhibited by the opposing unconscious impulse which is on the side of the assailant. The question thus arises whether any such process can be detected in the present case. If so then the woman's conduct would have to be viewed as expressing an unconscious desire for death, an automatic suicide. The available evidence, as just narrated, is so meagre that any hypothesis of this kind must necessarily be very tentative, but when correlated with psycho-analytical experience in general the probability of its being true is, in my opinion, very considerable.

There is no reason to believe that any desire for death that might have existed could have been other than symbolic; indeed the description I obtained of the woman's state of mind on the day before the calamity makes the

[1] Freud: Die Traumdeutung, 1900, S. 228.

idea of any direct suicidal intent highly improbable. We have therefore to ask what other ideas could have been symbolised by that suicide. It is known through analysis not on y that the ideas of sex, birth, and death are extensively associated with one another, but also that the idea of dying in the arms of the loved one—*'gemeinsames Sterben'*—symbolises certain quite specific desires of the unconscious. Of these, which have been pointed out especially by Sadger[1] and myself,[2] one in particular may be recalled—namely, the desire to beget a child with the loved one. The unconscious associative connections between this desire and the notion of common suicide are too rich and manifold to discuss here; besides which they are now well enough known to justify one in assuming an understanding of them in expert circles. I will therefore content myself with indicating some of the respects in which the present situation was adapted for supporting this associative connection.

The association between Niagara and death, especially suicide, is one that has been enforced by countlessly repeated experiences. It is not so generally known, however, that the association between it and birth is also very intimate. Niagara is a favourite honeymoon resort—possibly more so for Toronto people than for those of other places in the neighbourhood, on account of the romantic journey thither across the Lake of Ontario. So much is this so that Niagara town is commonly known—in Toronto at all events—as 'the Baby City', from the high percentage of conceptions that date from a visit there. The couple in question were very fond of spending their holidays there, the unconscious attraction being possibly the same as that which drew women of old to the Temple of Aesculapius and

[1] Sadger: Heinrich von Kleist, 1910, S. 59-62.
[2] Chapter II of these Essays.

which still draws women to various healing waters. They
had never been there before in winter time, a rather
strange circumstance, for it is almost as popular with
Toronto people in the winter as in the summer because
of the beautiful ice effects to be seen at that time. It is
conceivable that they were this time drawn by the idea
of winter (death, cold, etc.) which was beginning to correspond with their attitude of hopelessness about ever
getting a child.

Coming next to the calamity itself we see how similar
was the conscious affect investing the two ideas which we
suppose became associated; the hope of giving birth to a child
was almost as small as that of escaping from the threatened
doom. That this doom was one of drowning—in the
horrible form of being swept under in an ice-cold whirlpool—is a circumstance of considerable significance in
the light of all we know about the symbolic meaning of
water in general and of drowning in particular (cp. Freud,
Rank, Abraham, Stekel, etc.). If the whole story were told
to one as constituting a dream one would have no hesitation in interpreting it as a childbirth fantasy of a sterile
woman, the floating *on a block of ice* in a dangerous
current of water, in company with the lover, in sight of
all the world and yet isolated from it, the threatening
catastrophe of drowning, and the rapid movement of being
passively swept to and fro (in the article referred to above
I have insisted on the significance of movement in this
connection)—all this forms a perfect picture.

Though the actual situation was not a dream but a
grim reality, nevertheless the circumstances detailed above
are just such as would, especially in a moment of acute
emotion, strongly appeal to the latent complex in question
and stimulate it to activity. It should be remembered that
in times of despair (defeat, severe illness, danger,

enfeeblement, approaching death, and so on) there is a universal tendency to fly from reality by having recourse to the primitive system of thought (Freud's primary *Lustprinzip,* Jung's *phantastisches Denken*), mostly in the form of infantile wishes relating to the mother; indeed I have elsewhere[1] expressed the opinion that the idea of personal death does not exist for the unconscious, being always replaced by that of sexual communion or of birth. We may thus imagine the woman in question as reacting to her frightful situation by rapidly transforming it in the unconscious and replacing reality by the fantasy of the gratification of her deepest desire. The external outcome of this act of transformation illustrates very well the contrast between the practical value of the pleasure principle and that of the reality principle.[2]

One might speculate whether the outcome would have been different if the woman's thoughts concerning childbirth had been more accustomed to assume the common form of the fantasy of saving, or of being saved.[3] It is even possible that this fantasy was operative, and that her objection to being saved by the river-man and by the men who were holding the rope from the bridge was due fundamentally to her excessive marital fidelity, to her determination that no one should save her except her husband. But at this point our speculations become so filmy as to float away into the region of the completely unknown.

---

[1] *Journal of Abnormal Psychology,* April, 1912.

[2] See Freud: 'Die zwei Prinzipien des psychischen Geschehens', *Jahrbuch der Psychoanalyse,* Bd. III, S. 1.

[3] See Chapter X of my Papers on Psycho-Analysis, 1918.

CHAPTER IV

THE SYMBOLIC SIGNIFICANCE OF SALT
IN FOLKLORE AND SUPERSTITION[1]

I

IN THE course of some highly suggestive remarks on the
subject of superstition Freud[2] writes: 'I take it that this
conscious ignorance and unconscious knowledge of the
motivation of psychical accidents is one of the psychical
roots of superstition.' He maintains in general that the
undue significance attached by the superstitious to casual
external happenings arises from associative connections that
exist between these and important thoughts and wishes of
which the subject is quite unaware, and that it constitutes
a projection of the significance really belonging to these
unconscious thoughts· the feeling of significance, therefore,
is fully justified, though it has been displaced into a false
connection. The object of the present communication is to
examine in the light of this thesis one of the most familiar
and wide-spread of superstitions—namely, the belief that it
is unlucky to spill salt at table. In doing so the endeavour
will be made to use the inductive method only, that is to
say, to construct hypotheses only when they appear to be
legitimate inferences from definitely ascertained facts and

[1] Published in *Imago*, 1912, Bd. I, S. 361 and 454.
[2] Freud: Zur Psychopathologie des Alltagslebens, 1904, S. 82.

then to test them in their capacity to resume the whole range of accessible evidence.

Two primary considerations may be mentioned at the outset. First that in all ages salt has been invested with a significance far exceeding that inherent in its natural properties, interesting and important as these are. Homer calls it a divine substance, Plato describes it as especially dear to the Gods,[1] and we shall presently note the importance attached to it in religious ceremonies, covenants, and magical charms. That this should have been so in all parts of the world and in all times shews that we are dealing with a general human tendency and not with any local custom, circumstance or notion. Secondly, the idea of salt has in different languages lent itself to a remarkable profusion of metaphorical connotations, so that a study of these suggests itself as being likely to indicate what the idea has essentially stood for in the human mind, and hence perhaps the source of its exaggerated significance.

We may begin by considering the chief characteristic properties of salt that have impressed themselves on popular thought and have in this way become associated with more general ideas of an allied nature. Perhaps the most prominent of these is the *durability* of salt and its *immunity against decay*. On account of this property salt was regarded as emblematic of durability and permanence,[2] and hence of eternity and immortality;[3] in the middle ages it was thought that the devil for this reason detested salt.[4] In connection with eternity is also mentioned the idea of wisdom, which

[1] Plutarch : Morals (Goodwin's English Edition), 1870, Vol. II, p. 338.

[2] Lawrence : The Magic of the Horse-Shoe : with other Folk-Lore Notes, 1899, Ch. III, 'The Folk-Lore of Common Salt,' p. 157.

[3] Seligmann : Der böse Blick und Verwandtes, 1910, Bd. II, S. 33.

[4] Bodin : De la Démonomanie des Sorciers, 1593, p. 278.

salt is likewise supposed to symbolise,[1] though Pitré[2] says that this comes merely from a play on the words *sedes sapientiae* and *sale e sapienza*. Brand,[3] however, quotes an introductory address delivered at a German university in the seventeenth century that seems to shew an intrinsic connection between the two ideas· 'The sentiments and opinions both of divines and philosophers concur in making salt the *emblem of wisdom or learning*; and that not only on account of what it is composed of, but also with respect to the several uses to which it is applied. As to its component parts, as it consists of the purest matter, so ought wisdom to be pure, sound, immaculate, and incorruptible: and similar to the effects which salt produces upon bodies ought to be those of wisdom and learning upon the mind.' This explanation of the association between the ideas of salt and wisdom sounds a little too strained to be altogether convincing and suggests that perhaps there may be other determining factors besides those just mentioned. Wisdom was frequently personified holding a salt-cellar, and the bestowal of *Sal Sapientiae*, the Salt of Wisdom, is still a formality in the Latin Church. The heavenly Sophia appears in mystical science as sodium, and her colour is yellow, the colour of burning salt.[4]

The idea of durability in regard to salt is evidently an important cause of the old association between it and the topic of *friendship* and *loyalty*.[5] Owing to its lasting

[1] Collin de Plancy: Dictionnaire Infernal, 1818, t. II, p. 278; Lawrence: ibid

[2] Pitré: Usi e costumi, credenze e pregiudizi del popolo Siciliano, 1889, Vol. III, p. 426

[3] Brand: Observations on the Popular Antiquities of Great Britain, 1849, Vol. I, p. 433.

[4] Bayley: The Lost Language of Symbolism, 1912, Vol. I, p. 228.

[5] See Victor Hehn: Das Salz. Eine kulturhistorische Studie, 2e Aufl., 1901, S. 10-12.

and incorruptible quality it was regarded as the emblem of perpetual friendship,[1] and from this several secondary meanings are derived. One corollary, for instance, is that the spilling of salt is supposed to involve a quarrel or breaking of friendship.[2] Salt has played an important part in matters of *hospitality*. Stuckius[3] tells us that the Muscovites thought a prince could not shew a stranger a greater mark of affection than by sending to him salt from his own table. In Eastern countries it is a time-honoured custom to place salt before strangers as a token and pledge of friendship and good-will,[4] and in Europe it was usually presented to guests before other food, to signify the abiding strength of friendship.[5] When an Abyssinian desires to pay an especially delicate attention to a friend or guest he produces a piece of rock-salt and graciously permits the latter to lick it with his tongue.[6] In the most diverse countries and at all ages, from Ancient Greece to modern Hungary, salt has been used to *confirm oaths and compacts*,[7] according to Lawrence, 'in the East, at the present day, compacts between tribes are still confirmed by salt, and the most solemn pledges are ratified by this substance.' Such compacts are inviolable, and in the same way 'to eat a man's salt,' a phrase still in current use, carries with it the obligation of *loyalty;* during the Indian mutiny of 1857 a chief motive of restraint among the Sepoys was said to

---

[1] Brand. op. cit, Vol. III, p. 162; Lawrence: op cit., pp. 169, 171.

[2] Wuttke: Der deutsche Volksaberglaube der Gegenwart, Dritte Bearbeitung, 1900, S 211; Brand: loc. cit.

[3] Stuckius: Antiquitatum Convivialium, 1690, S. 17.

[4] Lawrence: op cit., p 156

[5] Lawrence: op. cit., p. 169.

[6] Lawrence: op. cit, p. 188.

[7] Schleiden: Das Salz. Seine Geschichte, seine Symbolik und seine Bedeutung im Menschenleben, 1875, S. 71-3; Lawrence: op. cit., pp. 164-6.

have been the fact that they had sworn by their salt to be loyal to the Queen.[1] Byron, in 'The Corsair', refers to this group of beliefs as follows:

> Why dost thou shun the salt? that sacred pledge,
> Which, once partaken, blunts the sabre's edge,
> Makes even contending tribes in peace unite,
> And hated hosts seem brethren to the sight!

Closely allied to the preceding feature of incorruptibility is the capacity salt possesses of *preserving other bodies from decay*. It is generally supposed that this is the reason for the power salt has of warding off the devil and other malignant demons, who have a horror of it.[2] The same property has also greatly aided in establishing the association between salt and immortality; the connection is plainly seen in the Egyptian custom of using salt for embalming. It is one reason for the custom, obtaining until recently in every part of Great Britain, of placing salt on a corpse;[3] usually earth was added, 'the earth being an emblem of the corruptible body, the salt an emblem of the immortal spirit.' In later years this was said to be done so as to prevent decomposition,[4] an idea probably akin to the original one. A Welsh elaboration of the custom was to place a plate of bread and salt over the coffin (the combination of bread and salt will be discussed later); the professional 'sin-eater' of the district then arrived, murmured an incantation and ate the salt, thereby taking upon himself all the sins of the deceased.[5]

[1] Manley: Salt and other Condiments, p. 90.

[2] Conway: Demonology and Devil-Lore, 1879, Vol. I, p. 288; Moresin: Papatus, etc., 1594, p. 154, Bodin: loc. cit.

[3] Dalyell: The Darker Superstitions of Scotland, 1835, p. 102; Sikes: British Goblins, 1880, p. 328; Brand: op. cit., Vol. II, pp. 234, 235.

[4] Brand and Sikes: loc. cit.

[5] Sikes: op. cit., pp. 324, 326.

An important conception of salt is that of its constituting the *essence* of things, particularly of life itself. This seems to include two sub-ideas, those of necessary presence and of value respectively. The idea of ultimate essence no doubt underlies the Biblical phrase (Matthew v. 13) 'Ye are the salt of the earth', and in many other expressions it is used in the sense of aristocratic, quintessential, and the like.[1] In alchemy salt was considered to be one of the three ultimate elements out of which the seven noble metals were generated. Mercury symbolised the spirit, sulphur the soul, and salt the body; mercury represented the act of illumination, sulphur that of union, and salt that of purification. Herrick, in his Hesperides (p. 394), ranks salt even more highly:

> The body's salt the soule is, which when gone,
> The flesh soone sucks in putrefaction.

In Ancient Egypt salt and a burning candle represented life, and were placed over a dead body to express the ardent desire of prolonging the life of the deceased.[2] The following argument was employed by Latin writers, e. g. Plutarch: 'After death all parts of the body fall apart. In life the soul maintains the parts intact and in connection with one another. In the same way salt maintains the dead body in its form and connection, thus representing—so to speak—the soul.'[3] The culmination of eulogies, in which the idea of value is also prominent, is to be found in a treatise on salt, published in 1770, where the writer launches forth in impassioned style the most extravagant encomiums upon this substance, which he avers to be

[1] Oxford English Dictionary, Vol. VIII, p. 59.
[2] Moresin: op. cit., p. 89.
[3] ibid.

the quintessence of the earth. Salt is here characterised as a Treasure of Nature, an Essence of Perfection, and the Paragon of Preservatives. Moreover, whoever possesses salt thereby secures a prime factor of human happiness among material things.[1]

Salt is closely associated with the idea of *money* or *wealth*, and indeed this is one of the connotations of the word. Nowadays the implication is even of excessive or unfairly high value, as in the colloquial phrase 'a salt or salty price'; similarly in French 'il me l'a bien salé' means 'he has charged me an excessive price'. In commercial circles the expression 'to salt a mine or property' means to add a small quantity of some valuable substance to it so as artificially to raise its selling price. In Ancient Rome soldiers and officials were paid in salt instead of money, whence (from salarium) the modern words 'salair' and 'salary' and the phrase 'to be worth one's salt' (= to be capable, to earn one's salary). A salt currency was in vogue in Africa in the sixth century, and in the middle ages this was so also in England,[2] as well as in China, Tibet, and other parts of Asia.[3] The name of the Austrian coin 'Heller' is derived from an old German word for salt, 'Halle'.[4] The Montem ceremony at Eton,[5] which consisted in collecting money in exchange for salt, was continued until 1847. Salt-Silver was the term used to denote the money paid by tenants to their lord as a commutation for the service of bringing him salt from market.[6] In parts of Germany the game is played of placing some sand, some salt, and

[1] Elias Artista Hermetica. Das Geheimnis vom Salz, 1770
[2] Brand: op. cit., Vol. I, p. 436.
[3] Schleiden : op. cit, S. 68-70, 82
[4] Hehn : op. cit., S. 90.
[5] Brand: op. cit, pp. 433-40
[6] Brand: op. cit., p 403

a green leaf on the table and making a blind-folded person grope for them ; if he seizes the salt it denotes wealth.[1]

These and other considerations have invested the idea of salt in the popular mind with a sense of *general importance*. Waldron[2] states that in the Isle of Man 'no person will go out on any material affair without taking some salt in their pockets, much less remove from one house to another, marry, put out a child, or take one to nurse, without salt being mutually exchanged; nay, though a poor person be almost famished in the streets, he will not accept any food you will give him, unless you join salt to the rest of your benevolence'. To carry salt with one on moving to a new dwelling is a very wide-spread custom;[3] it is related that when the poet Burns, in 1789, was about to occupy a new house at Ellisland, he was escorted there by a procession of relatives in whose midst was carried a bowl of salt.[4] The Arabs of Upper Egypt, before setting out on a journey, burn salt to prevent ill-luck.[5] The laying of salt at the table was in the middle ages a tremendous ceremony. The other implements were disposed with minute care in their relation to the salt, which throughout was treated with special deference.[6] With the Romans it was a matter of religious principle that no other dish was placed upon the table until the salt was in position. Rank and precedence among the guests were precisely indicated by their seat above or below the salt and their exact distance from it. Schleiden[7] remarks: 'How great was the importance attached to

[1] Wuttke : op. cit., S. 233.
[2] Waldron. Description of the Isle of Man, 1725, p. 187.
   Wuttke: op. cit., S. 396.
[4] Rogers: Scotland, Social and Domestic, 1869, Vol. III, p. 288.
[5] Burckhardt : Travels in Nubia, 1822, p. 169
[6] Lawrence : op. cit., pp. 197-205.
[7] Schleiden : op. cit., S. 70.

salt is also seen from the fact that hardly a place existed in which salt was produced where this was not expressed in the name of the place, from the Indian Lavanápura ("Salt-town") and the Austrian Salzburg ("Salt-town") to the Prussian Salzkotten and the Scottish Salt-coats.'

The high importance attaching to salt led to various *magical powers* being ascribed to it, and it has been very extensively employed in magical procedures. It could be used for these and other purposes by placing it on the tongue or by rubbing the body with it, but the favourite method was to dissolve it in water and bathe the person with this. The principal function of salt in this connection, like that of most other charms, was to ward off harm, chiefly by averting the influence of malignant spirits. Salt is almost universally thought to be abhorrent to evil demons,[1] the only exception I know of being in Hungarian folk-lore, where on the contrary evil beings are fond of salt.[2] Salt was always missing from the devil's and witches' banquets.[3] Salt has therefore been one of the staple charms against the power of the devil,[4] of magicians,[5] of witches,[6] of the evil eye,[7] and of evil influences in general:[8] such beliefs are found in countries so far apart as Arabia[9]

---

[1] Bodin: loc. cit.; Collin de Plancy: op. cit, pp. 277, 278; Schleiden: op. cit., S. 78.

[2] Lawrence: op. cit., p 159.

[3] Wright: Sorcery and Magic, 1851, p. 310

[4] Bodin and Collin de Plancy: loc. cit

[5] Grimm: Deutsche Mythologie, Vierte Ausgabe, 1876, S. 876.

[6] Krauss: Slavische Volksforschungen, 1908, S. 39; Mannhardt: Germanische Mythen, 1858, S. 7; Seligmann: op. cit., Band II, S. 33; Wuttke: op. cit., S. 95, 258, 283. Grimm: op cit, Nachtrag, S. 454.

[7] Seligmann: op cit., Band I, S. 312, 313, 320, 331, 344, 346, 365, 377, 389; Band II, S. 73, 144, 220, 376.

[8] Lawrence: op. cit, p 177.

[9] Burckhardt: loc cit.

and Japan.[1] Cattle are also protected against witchcraft in
the same way.[2] In India and Persia one can even determine by means of salt whether a given person has been
bewitched or not.[3] Salt will also protect the fields from
evil influences.[4] It was further used to prevent the souls
of the dead from returning to earth and to secure them
peace in Purgatory.[5]

These practices were performed with especial frequency with *children*. The custom of rubbing new-born
infants with salt is referred to in the Bible (Ezekiel
xvi, 4). The use of salt to guard the new-born against
evil demons and evil influences, either by placing a little
on the tongue or by immersing the infant in salt and
water, was in vogue throughout Europe from early times,
and certainly antedated Christian baptism;[6] in France the
custom lasted until 1408 of putting salt on children until
they were baptised, when it was considered no longer
necessary.[7] At the present day it is still placed in the cradle
of the new-born child in Holland.[8] In Scotland it was
customary to put salt into a child's mouth on entering a
stranger's house for the first time.[9] Salt was also placed in
the mouth of a new-born calf for similar purposes as with
children.[10]

[1] Bousquet: Le Japon de nos jours, 1877, t. I, p. 94; Griffis: The
Mikado's Empire.

[2] Seligmann: op. cit., Band II, S. 104, 241, 329; Wuttke: op. cit.,
S. 40, 435, 438; Krauss: loc. cit.

[3] Seligmann. op. cit., Band I, S. 262, 264.

[4] Seligmann: op cit., Band II, S. 374.

[5] Wuttke: op. cit, S 465, 472.

[6] Conway: op. cit, Vol II, p. 217, Lawrence: op. cit., pp. 174,
175; Seligmann: op. cit., S 34, Wuttke: op. cit., S. 382, 387.

[7] Schleiden: op. cit., S 79.

[8] *New York Times*, November 10, 1889.

[9] Dalyell: op. cit., p. 96.

[10] Seligmann: op. cit., S. 58; Wuttke: op. cit. S. 436, 443.

Salt has been extensively used for *medicinal purposes*. It was believed to have the function of both preventing[1] and curing[2] diseases, as was already commented on by Pliny, particularly those caused by occult influences. It is possible that the Latin word 'salus' (= health), the earliest connotation of which was 'well-preserved', was originally related to the word 'sal'.

Another important function of salt was its use in furthering *fecundity*. As this obviously cannot have been derived from any natural property of the substance, it must represent some symbolic significance in harmony with the general importance attached to it. Schleiden[3] makes the following interesting remarks in this connection: 'The sea was unquestionably the fructifying, creative element. Leaving aside the few marine mammals, the offspring of sea creatures are to be counted by thousands and hundreds of thousands. This was all the more easily ascribed to the salt of the sea, since other observations believed to have been made were connected with it. It was recalled that in dog-breeding the frequent use of salt increased the number of the progeny, and that on ships carrying salt the number of mice multiplied to such an extent as to give rise to the idea of parthenogenesis, i. e. to the view that mice could beget young without the coöperation of a male. The conviction was thus formed that salt must stand in a close relation to physical love, so that salt became the *symbol of procreation.*' It was used in this connection in two ways, to promote fecundity and to avert barrenness or impotence. The latter is illustrated by Elisha's action of throwing salt into the fountain of Jericho (2 Kings ii. 21): 'Thus saith the Lord, I have healed these waters;

---

[1] Wuttke: op. cit., S. 374.

[2] Dalyell: op. cit., pp. 98, 99, 102; Lawrence: op. cit., p. 180, Seligmann: op. cit., Band I, S. 278; Wuttke: op. cit, S. 336.

[3] Schleiden: op. cit., S. 92, 93

and for the future they shall not be the occasion either of death or barrenness.' Gaume[1] states that salt has the specific function of promoting fecundity, and its symbolic significance in this direction is seen in the following Indian practice:[2] A woman who wishes for a child, particularly for a son, fasts on the fourth lunar day of every dark fortnight and breaks her fast only after seeing the moon. A dish of twenty-one balls of rice, one of which contains salt, is then placed before her, and if she first lays her hand on the ball containing the salt she will be blessed with a son. In this case no more is eaten; otherwise she goes on until she takes the salted ball. The ceremony may be observed only a limited number of times; if in these she fails altogether to pick out the salted ball first she is doomed to barrenness. In Belgium salt is mixed with the food of a pregnant mare or cow so as to make the birth easy,[3] in Normandy it is given to cows so as to ensure plenty of butter.[4] In East Friesland[5] and Scotland[6] salt is put into the first milk after calving with the object of securing a plentiful supply of good milk. In Bohemia a special cake containing salt is given to a pregnant cow so that she may bear a choice calf and yield plenty of milk.[7] In Ireland when the seed is being sown the mistress of the house first puts salt into the field,[8] and a similar custom exists in East Prussia.[9]

[1] Gaume: L'Eau Bénite au Dix-neuvième Siècle. 1866. Cited by Conway

[2] Indian Notes and Queries, Vol. IV, p. 106.

[3] Von Reinsberg-Düringsfeld: 'Volksgebräuche in Kempen', Ausland, 1874, S. 471.

[4] Kuhn: Märkische Sagen und Marchen, 1843, S. 388.

[5] Wuttke: op. cit., S. 446.

[6] Dalyell: op. cit., p. 101.

[7] Wuttke: op. cit., S. 442.

[8] Gough's Edition of Camden's Britannia: 1789, Vol. III, p 659 and Vol. IV, p. 470.

[9] Seligmann: op. cit., Band II, S. 34; Wuttke: op. cit., S. 419.

In Bavaria to obtain a rich harvest the first load is sprinkled with salt and water.[1]

It is only natural that the general importance attached to salt should have been reflected in the sphere of *religion,* and we find that this was so in a remarkable degree. Salt was an essential constituent of sacrificial offerings in Ancient Egypt,[2] as well as in Greece and Rome;[3] Brand says of the latter: 'Both Greeks and Romans mixed salt with their sacrificial cakes; in their lustrations also they made use of salt and water, which gave rise in after times to the superstition of holy water.' In Judaism we find descriptions of three different usages taught by the Bible. As in other countries, salt formed a necessary part of sacrificial offerings: 'Every oblation of thy meat offering shalt thou season with salt; neither shalt thou suffer the salt of the covenant of thy God to be lacking from thy meat offering: With all thine offerings thou shalt offer salt' (Leviticus ii. 13).[4] A covenant, especially a religious covenant, was ratified by means of salt: 'It is a covenant of salt for ever, before the Lord' (Numbers xviii. 19); 'The Lord God of Israel gave the kingdom over Israel to David for ever, even to him, and to his sons, by a covenant of salt' (2 Chronicles xiii. 5). The idea of a bond of loyalty through eating salt also occurs: the passage 'we have maintenance from the king's palace' (Ezra iv. 14) means literally 'we are salted with the salt of the palace.'[5] The salt sources in Germany, which later became associated with the doings of witches, had a considerable religious significance; Ennemoser[6]

---

[1] Wuttke. op. cit, S. 423.

[2] Arrian: De Expeditione Alexandri, lib. iii, cap. i.

[3] Brand: op. cit, Vol. III, p. 161.

[4] In Job i. 22, the literal rendering of the passage 'In all this Job sinned not, nor charged God foolishly' is 'In all this Job sinned not, nor gave God unsalted'. (Conway: op. cit., Vol. II, p. 150.)

[5] Lawrence: op. cit., p. 156.

[6] Ennemoser: Geschichte der Magie, Zweite Aufl., 1844, S. 839.

writes of them: 'their yield was regarded as a direct gift of the near Divinity, and the winning and distributing of the salt as a holy occupation—probably sacrifices and folk festivities were connected with the drying of the salt.

In the Roman Catholic Church salt was introduced for baptismal purposes in the fourth century[1] and has played a prominent part there ever since.[2] According to Schleiden,[3] this was derived from the Jewish use of salt at the circumcision rite. The celebration of baptism in Scotland by a layman was afterwards confirmed by a priest administering a particle of salt.[4] Gratian, in his Decretalia, explains that the use of consecrated salt in the mouth of one about to be baptised is to render the rite more efficacious.[5] In the baptismal ceremonies of the Church of England in mediaeval times salt was placed in the child's mouth, and its ears and nostrils were touched with saliva—practices which became obsolete at the time of the Reformation.[6] As a rule, however, salt is applied in the dissolved state, the well-known 'Salzstein',[7] composed of salt and water that has been separately blessed beforehand. The holy water thus constituted was extensively used in both Catholic and Protestant countries, and for the identical purposes for which simple salt and water had previously been used by the common people, the only difference being that the latter was not quite so efficacious as the consecrated mixture. Thus it was officially employed by the Roman Catholic Church for profiting the health of

---

[1] Pfannenschmid: Das Weihwasser im heidnischen und christlichen Cultus, 1870.

[2] See Lawrence: op. cit., p. 182.

[3] Schleiden: op. cit., S. 76.

[4] Dalyell: op. cit., p. 97.

[5] Cited by Dalyell: loc. cit.

[6] Lawrence: op. cit., p. 176.

[7] Seligmann: op. cit., Band I, S. 322; Wuttke: op. cit, S. 142.

the body and for the banishing of demons,[1] by the English Church to prevent the devil from entering churches and dwellings,[2] and by the Scottish Church for expelling demons, for sanctifying religious rites, and to prevent new-born babies from becoming changelings.[3] Holy water was also used, and to some extent is still used, to avert the evil eye,[4] to prepare for a journey,[5] to cure demoniac possession,[6] to make the cattle thrive,[7] to prevent witches from turning the butter sour,[8] and to ensure the fortunate delivery of a pregnant cow.[9] In the same connection may be mentioned certain African taboos concerning salt. A demon who inhabited a lake in Madagascar was so averse from salt that whenever any was being carried past the lake it had to be called by another name, or it would all have been dissolved and lost.[10] A West African story relates how a man was told that he would die if ever the word 'salt' was pronounced in his hearing; one day the fatal word was pronounced, amd he promptly died.[11]

We may now consider another attribute of salt which has given rise to many symbolic connotations—namely, its peculiar *taste*. Seligman[12] says. 'Salt is on account of its piquant power a life-furthering material', and he associates with this the beliefs in the influence exerted by

---

[1] Gaume : loc cit., Moresin : op. cit, pp. 153, 154.

[2] Ady : A Perfect Discovery of Witches, 1661.

[3] Napier Folk Lore, or Superstitious Beliefs in the West of Scotland within this Century, 1879.

[4] Seligmann: op cit., Band I, S. 325 ; Band II, S 315, 396

[5] Wuttke: loc. cit.

[6] Reginald Scot: The Discoverie of Witchcraft, 1584, p. 178.

[7] Wuttke : op. cit., S. 439.

[8] Wuttke : op. cit., S 448.

[9] Wuttke: op. cit., S 142.

[10] Sibree: The Great African Island, 1880, p. 307.

[11] Nassau : Fetichism in West Africa, 1904, p. 381.

[12] Seligmann : op. cit., Band I, S. 278.

salt when it penetrates into other substances, e. g. bread, and also the belief in its capacity to cure disease. This property of salt has been especially connected with speech in various metaphorical ways. Lawrence[1] writes· 'Owing to the importance of salt as a relish, its Latin name sal came to be used metaphorically as signifying a savoury mental morsel, and, in a general sense, wit or sarcasm . . . The characterization of Greece as the "salt of nations" is attributed to Livy, and this is probably the origin of the phrase "Attic salt", meaning delicate, refined wit.' A pungent or pithy remark or jest is termed salt,[2] as in such expressions as 'there is no salt in his witticisms', though the use of the word in this sense is becoming obsolescent in English, in French a similar one obtains, in expressions such as 'une epigramme salé', 'il a répandu le sel à pleines mains dans ses écrits', etc. In the Biblical passage (Epistle to the Corinthians iv. 6) 'Let your speech be always with grace, seasoned with salt' this connotation is probably present, as well as that previously mentioned of wisdom or sense. The same metaphor is also applied in a general way, apart from speech, as in denoting an insipid man as 'having no sense or salt', lacking in piquancy or liveliness, just as in Latin the word insalsus (= unsalted) meant stupid. This metaphorical attribute of salt is evidently closely akin to the one previously mentioned of 'essentialness'.

A property of salt that has been extensively exploited by the popular imagination is the ease with which it *dissolves in water*. That a substance otherwise so durable should disappear when put into water and, though leaving no visible trace of its presence, should endow the water with its peculiar properties (capacity to preserve from

[1] Lawrence: op. cit., p. 161. See also Schleiden . op. cit., S. 91.
[2] See Oxford English Dictionary, loc. cit.

decay, pungent taste, etc.) has always impressed the people
as being a remarkable characteristic, and is perhaps partly
responsible for the mysterious significance attaching to holy
water. One obvious practical application, of which frequent
use has been made, is to estimate the amount of moisture
in the atmosphere by the varying avidity of salt for it.
It has thus been quite rationally used to *foretell the weather*.[1]
From this have been derived the following symbolical uses
of it for the same purpose.[2] An onion is cut into twelve
pieces, which are strewn with salt and named after the
twelve months; the piece that becomes specially moist
denotes a wet month in the coming year. The same may
be done with twelve nutshells, which have to be examined
at midnight. Or a piece of salt is placed on each corner
of the table to denote the four seasons of the year; the
one that has collected most moisture by the morning
indicates the wettest season. The last-mentioned practice
is also used to find out if the coming harvest will be
valuable or not.[3] This foretelling capacity of salt has
naturally been generalised far beyond its original sphere.
Thus, according as a particular heap of salt remains dry
or not it is concluded that a corresponding person will or
will not survive the coming year, that a given undertaking
will be successful or the reverse, and so on.[4]

Water is not the only substance into which salt can
be absorbed with the production of peculiar changes.
Indeed, the capacity of salt to *enter into combination with
a second substance* may be regarded as one of its most
salient characteristics. The substance with which it is by
far the most often associated in this way is *bread*. The

[1] Willsford · Nature's Secrets, p. 139.
[2] Wuttke: op. cit., S. 231.
[3] Wuttke: op. cit., S. 230.
[4] Wuttke: op. cit., S. 231.

combination of the two has been used for practically all the purposes enumerated above in connection with salt, and in folk beliefs the two are almost synonymous. Thus bread and salt are both absent from the devil's feasts;[1] the combination of them is potent against witches,[2] and against the evil eye,[3] it guards cattle against disease,[4] ensures a plentiful supply of milk,[5] and removes obstacles to the churning of butter.[6] It is equally efficacious with adults and infants. It is carried into a new dwelling to avert evil influences and to bring good luck;[7] in Hamburg nowadays this custom is replaced by that of carrying at processional times a cake covered with chocolate, in the form of a bread roll, and a salt-cellar of marzipan filled with sugar. The combination of salt and bread has also been extensively used to confirm oaths,[8] and is still so used in Arabia at the present day.[9]

The mixture of *wheat and salt* was used for the same purpose as that of bread and salt. It was an important part of the Roman propitiatory sacrifices,[10] and also of the Jewish oblations.[11] In Russia it was offered as congratulatory to strangers,[12] as we have seen salt alone was in other

[1] Grimm: op, cit, S. 877.

[2] Seligmann· op. cit, Band II, S. 37, 52, 93, 94; Grimm op. cit., Nachtrag, S. 454, Wuttke: op cit, S. 129, 282.

[3] Wuttke: op. cit, S 282; Seligmann· op cit, Band I, S. 398, Band II, S. 37, 38, 93, 94, 100, 250, 334.

[4] Dalyell: op cit, p. 100.

[5] Seligmann: op cit., Band II, S. 38; Dalyell loc. cit.

[6] Seligmann· loc. cit

[7] Seligmann: op cit, S. 37.

[8] Dekker's Honest Whore, 1635, Sc. 13; Blackwood's *Edinburgh Magazine*, Vol I, p. 236, Lawrence· op. cit, p. 164.

[9] Lawrence. op. cit., p. 185.

[10] Brand· op. cit., Vol. III, p. 163; Dalyell· op. cit, pp. 99, 100.

[11] Dalyell: op. cit., p. 99.

[12] Dalyell: loc. cit.

countries. In Ireland women in the streets, and girls from the windows, sprinkled salt and wheat on public functionaries when they assumed office.[1]

Lastly may be mentioned the attribute of salt as a *means of purification*. That salt water possesses this quality in a high degree was observed at an early stage of civilisation, and by Roman ladies it was actually regarded as a means of attaining beauty.[2] Especially in regard to the sea this feature has led to numerous poetical applications and also to the development of many superstitions. It is intelligible that this purifying attribute should have played an important part in the use of salt in religious cults, and this we find was so, notably in Egypt and Greece.[3] We shall return to the subject later on when discussing the relation of purification to baptism.

II

We may now survey the facts just related. While it has only been possible in the allotted space to give a relatively few examples of the numerous ways in which ideas concerning salt have played a part in folk belief and custom—it would need a special treatise to record them all—it is probable that the most prominent and typical of them have been mentioned; at all events no special selection whatever has been made, beyond relegating sexual ones to the background. It is hardly necessary to say that the grouping here adopted is unduly schematic, being one of convenience in presentation only; a given custom would mostly be dictated by interest in other properties of salt as well as the one under which it is here mentioned.

[1] Brand: op. cit., p. 165, Dalyell: loc. cit.
[2] Schleiden: op. cit., S. 84.
[3] Schleiden: op. cit., S. 84, 85.

In regard now to the matter that formed our starting-point—namely, the superstitious fear of spilling salt—it is plain that here a significance is attached to an act which does not inherently belong to it, and it is equally plain that the same is true of most of the customs and beliefs related above. There are two possible explanations that may be offered for this state of affairs. The *first* would run somewhat as follows. The present-day superstition has no meaning beyond an historical one; it is simply an instance of the tendency of mankind to retain traditional attitudes for no intelligible reason, and is an echo of the time when the idea of salt was properly invested with a greater psychical value than it now is. In former times the significance attached to the idea of salt that we now regard as excessive was not so, being justified in fact and to be accounted for quite naturally by the real importance of the substance. There is undeniably a certain amount of truth in this view. Salt, being a substance necessary to life and in some countries obtainable only with considerable difficulty,[1] was inevitably regarded as both important and valuable, though this consideration must lose much of its weight in regard to most parts of the world where the supply is plentiful. Again, the curious properties of salt, its preserving capacity, its power of penetrating other substances, etc., would naturally impress the primitive mind, and the view just described would doubtless try to account for the belief in its magical powers by pointing out that such minds work on a simpler plane of thought than do ours. To this argument, however, comparative psychology could object that, although this type of thought—just as that of children—certainly often differs from what we term rational thinking, careful investigation always shews that it

---

[1] Lawrence: op. cit , p. 187.

is very far from being so bizarre and unintelligible as it may at first sight appear; the formation of illogical connections is not meaningless, but has a perfectly definite and comprehensible reason for it. The general criticism, therefore, that must be passed on this explanation is that while it adduces unquestionably important considerations these are only partly capable of accounting for the facts, and are inadequate as a complete explanation of them. Other factors must have been operative in addition to those just mentioned.

The *second* explanation would supplement the first by regarding the excessive significance attaching to the idea of salt as an example of what Wernicke called an *Über-wertige Idee*, that is to say, an idea overcharged with psychical significance. Only some of this inherently belongs to the idea itself, the rest being of adventitious origin. Such processes are, of course, very familiar in daily life: a banknote, for instance, is valued not for the intrinsic worth of the paper but for the worth that extrinsic circumstances give it. Psycho-analytic investigation has shewn on the one hand that such transference of affect from one idea to another allied one is much commoner even than was previously realised, and on the other hand that very often the subject is quite unaware of the occurrence. Thus a person may experience an intense affect —fear, horror, etc.—in regard to a given idea or object purely through the idea having formed strong associative connections with another idea which is justifiably invested with this affect; the intrinsic attributes of the idea do not account for the strong affect attached to it, this being in the main derived from a different source. The most striking manifestations of this process are seen in the psychoneuroses; the patient has a terror of a certain object which is not customarily regarded with terror, the reason being that the idea of the object is unconsciously connected in his mind with that of another object in regard to which the terror is quite comprehensible. In such cases the secondary idea may be said to represent or symbolise the primary one.[1] The more bizarre and apparently unintelligible is the phobia or other symptom, the more strained is as a rule the connection between it and the original idea, and the stronger is the emotion investing the latter. Apart from the neuroses instances of exceedingly strained connections are less common. What happens as a rule is that the affect belonging to the two ideas, the symbolised and the symbolising one, is very similar, so that the affect transferred from the one to the other accounts for only part of the affect accompanying the secondary idea. In this case the intrinsic qualities of the idea account for some of the affect, but not for all, the affect is appropriate in quality, but disproportionate in quantity. Unless the cause of this exaggeration is appreciated there is an unavoidable tendency to overlook the fact itself on rationalistic grounds; then the intrinsic qualities of the secondary idea are erroneously regarded as constituting an adequate explanation of the affect in question.

The main difference, therefore, between the two explanations is this: the first assumes that the affect, or psychical significance, attaching to the idea of salt was once not disproportionate to its real value, whereas the second, regarding the affect as disproportionate, maintains that some of it must be derived from an extraneous source.

In seeking for this source we have two distinct clues to guide us. In the first place, the universality of the beliefs and customs under discussion, and the remarkably

---

[1] On the precise distinction between symbolism and other forms of indirect mental representation see Ch.VII of my Papers on Psycho-Analysis, 1918, 'The Theory of Symbolism'.

high and even mystical significance that has been attached
to the idea of salt, indicate that any further idea from
which this may have been derived must be both a general
one, common to all mankind, and one of fundamental
psychical importance. In the second place, the association
between the idea of salt and any further one must have
been formed through the resemblances, real or fancied, of
the corresponding qualities of the two ideas. It becomes
necessary, therefore, to consider with closer attention the
popular conception of these qualities that was described
above.

This conception may be summarised as follows. Salt
is a pure, white, immaculate and incorruptible substance,
apparently irreducible into any further constituent elements,
and indispensable to living beings. It has correspondingly
been regarded as the essence of things in general, the
quintessence of life, and the very soul of the body. It has
been invested with the highest general significance —far more
than that of any other article of diet -was the equivalent
of money and other forms of wealth, and its presence was
indispensable for the undertaking of any enterprise, particularly any new one. In religion it was one of the most
sacred objects, and to it were ascribed all manner of
magical powers. The pungent, stimulating flavour of salt,
which has found much metaphorical application in reference
to pointed, telling wit or discourse, doubtless contributed
to the conception of it as an essential element; to be without
salt is to be insipid, to have something essential lacking.
The durability of salt, and its immunity against decay, made
it an emblem of immortality. It was believed to have an
important influence in favouring fertility and fecundity, and
in preventing barrenness, this idea is connected with other
attributes than the one just mentioned, probably indeed
with them all. The permanence of salt helped to create

the idea that for one person to partake of the salt of
another formed a bond of lasting friendship and loyalty
between the two, and the substance played an important
part in the rites of hospitality. A similar application of it
was for confirming oaths, ratifying compacts, and sealing
solemn covenants. This conception of a bond was also
related to the capacity salt has for combining intimately
with a second substance and imparting to this its peculiar
properties, including the power to preserve against decay;
for one important substance—namely, water—it had in
fact a natural and curious affinity.

If we now try to discover what other idea these ideas
could arise in reference to, besides that of salt, the task
is surely not difficult. If the word salt had not been mentioned in the preceding description anyone accustomed to
hidden symbolism, and many without this experience, would
regard it as a circumlocutory and rather grandiloquent
account of a still more familiar idea—that of human semen.
In any case a substance possessing the attributes just
mentioned would lend itself with singular facility to such
an association. Indeed, the mere fact that salt has been
regarded as the emblem of immortality and wisdom is in
itself suggestive to anyone who is alive to such possibilities,
for the other well-known emblem of these two concepts is
the snake, which is in mythology and elsewhere the phallic
symbol *par excellence*. The surmise that the idea of salt
has derived much of its significance from its being unconsciously associated with that of semen fulfils at least one
postulate of all symbolic thinking—namely, that the idea
from which the excessive significance is derived is more
important psychically than the idea to which this is transferred; the radiation of the affect, like that of electricity,
is always from the site of more intense concentration to
that of less.

At the present stage of our investigation it is plain that the inference just drawn cannot be regarded as being much more than a surmise, or at the most a working hypothesis, one which will appear more or less plausible according to the experience of unconscious symbolism by which it is viewed. It must next be tested by the ordinary rules of science —namely, by its capacity to predict and by its power of satisfactorily reducing to simple terms a series of disparate phenomena.

If the hypothesis is correct then one could foretell that customs and beliefs would be found shewing a direct relation between the idea of salt on the one hand and such ideas as those of marriage, sexual intercourse, and potency on the other, as well as a larger number shewing a plainly symbolical relation between the two sets of ideas, further, that the ideas concerning salt and water mirror similar, more primitive ones concerning semen and urine, and that the partaking of salt would be connected with ideas relating to sexual intercourse and impregnation. It will presently be seen that anthropological and folk-loristic material provides ample confirmation of these expectations.

The supposed action of salt in favouring fecundity and in preventing barrenness has been mentioned above. It was a classical belief that mice became impregnated through eating salt;[1] any objection to our hypothesis, therefore, that the connection between the ideas of salt and semen is too remote for them ever to have been brought together, except artificially, at once falls to the ground, for here we have a direct identification of the two substances. In the Pyrenees the wedding couple before setting out for church put salt into their left pocket to guard against the man's being impotent. In Limousin,

[1] Pliny. Nat. Hist. x. 85.

Poitou, and Haut-Vienne the bridegroom alone does this, in Altmark the bride alone. In Pamproux salt is put into the clothes of the wedding couple with the same motive.[1] In Germany salt is strewn in the bride's shoe.[2] In Scotland on the night before the wedding salt is strewn on the floor of the new home with the object of protecting the young couple against the evil eye;[3] I have elsewhere[4] shewn that the idea of maleficium, with which that of the evil eye is practically identical, mainly arises from the pervading dread of impotence, and Seligmann[5] actually mentions the use of salt to counteract the 'ligature', i. e. the spell cast over the sexual functions by evil influences.

Salt has often, especially in former times, been considered to have an exciting influence on the nervous system, and it was thus thought to possess the attribute of arousing passion and desire.[6] Schleiden[7] writes. 'The Romans termed a man in love "salax", and this view still survives with us when we jokingly say that the cook who has put too much salt into the soup must be in love.' In Belgium the custom of visiting one's sweetheart in the nights after festivals is called 'turning one's love into salt'.[8] Shakespeare evidently uses it in the same sense in the passage 'Though we are justices . . . we have some salt of our youth in us'.[9] In some stories collected among African

---

[1] The preceding examples are all taken from Seligmann: op. cit., Band II, S. 35, 36, or from Schleiden: op. cit., S. 71, 79.

[2] Schell. 'Das Salz im Volksglauben', *Zeitschrift des Vereines für Volkskunde*, Jahrg. XV, S. 137.

[3] Seligmann· op. cit, S 35

[4] Ernest Jones: Der Alptraum in seiner Beziehung zu gewissen Formen des mittelalterlichen Aberglaubens, 1912, S 107, 108.

[5] Seligmann: op. cit., Band I, S. 291.

[6] Schleiden: op. cit., S. 92.

[7] Schleiden: op. cit, S. 93.

[8] Von Reinsberg-Düringsfeld: op. cit, S 472.

[9] The Merry Wives of Windsor: Act II, Sc. 3.

natives by Frobenius[1] salt is referred to as a direct equivalent of semen. Paracelsus, in his 'De Origine Morborum Invisibilium',[2] teaches that Incubi and Succubi emanate from the sperma found in the imagination of those who commit the unnatural sin of Onan, but that this is no true sperma, only corrupted salt.

The following are two metaphorical applications of the same idea. Salt is used to keep the fire always burning,[3] and there are examples, which need not be quoted, of the combination of salt and fire being used for every purpose in regard to which salt alone has superstitiously been used. At the Osiris festivals in Egypt all those taking part had to light lamps the oil of which had had salt mixed with it.[4] The idea of fire, however, in poetry as well as in mythology,[5] is constantly used to represent the ideas of the fire of life and the fire of love. Again, lameness is often brought into symbolic association with impotence (incapacity, inability), and in Sicily salt is used specifically to prevent lameness.[6]

The initiatory ceremonies universally performed by ruder peoples at the age of puberty commonly include a sacrificial or propitiatory act; circumcision is a replacement of such ceremonies, having been put back to the age of infancy just as baptism has been by most Christian Churches. In Egypt salt is strewn when circumcision is performed.[7] In various initiations, both earnest and jocular, at universities and schools salt played a central part, and the phrase

---

[1] Frobenius: Schwarze Seelen (Privately printed), 1913, S. 433. Dr. Otto Rank kindly informs me of this.

[2] Hartmann's Life of Paracelsus: 1667, p. 90.

[3] Mühlhauser: Urreligion des deutschen Volkes, 1860, S. 133.

[4] Schleiden: op. cit., S. 76.

[5] Cp. Abraham: Traum und Mythus, 1909, S. 31, etc.

[6] Pitré: loc. cit.

[7] Seligmann: op. cit, Band II, S. 37.

'to salt a freshman' is still in vogue.[1] Of late years it has been replaced in this respect by the more convenient alcohol, another unconscious symbol for semen,[2] but the feeling-attitude remains the same—namely, that the young man needs the administration of an essential substance before he can be regarded as having attained full virility.

It is known that there exists an intimate connection between extreme *abstinence* attitudes of all kinds and excessive sexual 'repression'; over-great prudishness is apt to be accompanied by a desire to abolish all alcohol from the universe, as we see at the present day in America. In the same way salt has been brought into manifold relation with the idea of sexual abstinence. The workers in the salt-pans near Siphoum, in Laos, must abstain from all sexual relations at the place where they are at work, the motive being a purely superstitious one.[3] The celibate Egyptian priests had at certain times to abstain wholly from the use of salt, on the ground of its being a material that excited sensual desires too much.[4] Abstinence both from sexual relations and from the partaking of salt is enjoined for several days on men of the Dyak tribes after returning from an expedition in which they have taken human heads,[5] and for three weeks on a Pima Indian who has killed an Apache;[6] in the latter case the man's wife

---

[1] Cp. Brand: op. cit., Vol. I, pp. 433-9

[2] Abraham. 'Die psychologischen Beziehungen zwischen Sexualität und Alkoholismus', *Zeitschrift für Sexualwissenschaft,* 1908, S. 449.

[3] Aymonier· Notes sur le Laos, 1885, p. 141

[4] Schleiden· op. cit., S. 93.

[5] Tromp: 'Uit de Salasial van Koetei', *Bijdragen tot de Taal-Land- en Volkenkunde van Nederlandsch-Indië,* 1888, Vol. XXXVII, p. 74.

[6] Bancroft: Native Races of the Pacific States, 1875, Vol. I, p. 553; Grossman, in Ninth Annual Report of the Bureau of Ethnology, 1892, p. 475.

also has to abstain from salt during the same period.[1] The
full account of these customs clearly shews that they
constitute rites of purification and expiation. Abstinence
both from sexual relations and from salt is also frequently
prescribed during important undertakings or on weighty
occasions: thus on Lake Victoria Nyanza while fishing,[2]
and in the island of Nias while traps are being laid for
wild animals.[3] In Uganda any man who has either committed
adultery or eaten salt is not allowed to partake of the
sacred fish-offering.[4] In Mexico the Huichol Indians undergo
the same double abstinence while the sacred cactus-plant,
the gourd of the God of Fire, is being gathered.[5] Similar
double observances obtain in other countries in connection
with the promotion of fertility; in fact the last-named custom
is related to this, for the main benefits that the sacred
cactus is supposed to bestow are plentiful rain-supply, good
crops, and the like. The Indians of Peru abstain for as
long as six months both from sexual intercourse and from
eating salt on the occasion of the birth of twins; one of
the twins was believed to be the son of the lightning, the
lord and creator of rain.[6] Other examples of the same double
abstinence are: in Peru preceding the Acatay mita festival,
the object of which is to ripen the fruit, and which is
followed by a sexual orgy;[7] in Nicaragua from the time

---

[1] Russell: 'The Pima Indians', Twenty-Sixth Annual Report of the
Bureau of American Ethnology, 1908, p. 204.

[2] Frazer: The Golden Bough, Third Edition, Part II, Taboo,
1911, p. 194.

[3] Thomas 'De jacht op het eiland Nias', Tijdschrift voor Indische
Taal- Land- en Volkenkunde, 1880, Vol. XXVI.

[4] Roscoe: 'Further Notes on the Manners and Customs of the
Baganda', Journal of the Royal Anthropological Institute, 1902, Vol.
XXXII, p 56.

[5] Lumholtz: Unknown Mexico, 1903, Vol II, p. 126.

[6] Frazer: op. cit, Part I, The Magic Art, 1911, Vol I, p. 266

[7] Frazer. op. cit., Vol. II, p 98.

that the maize is sown until it is reaped.[1] In Behar in
India the Nagin women, sacred prostitutes known as 'wives
of the Snake-God', periodically go about begging and during
this time they may not touch salt; half of their proceeds
go to the priests and half to buying salt and sweetmeats
for the villagers.[2]

Attention may be called to two features of the preceding
collection of customs. First that they occur in all parts of
the globe, instances having been cited from Europe, Africa,
Asia, and America, North, South, and Central. Secondly,
that to a great extent they duplicate the customs previously
described in connection with salt alone, thus in relation to
religion, to the weather, to important undertakings, and to
the production of fertility. Where in one country the presence
of salt is indispensable, in another one abstinence from
salt - and at the same time from sexual intercourse - is
equally essential. Both cases agree in regarding salt as an
important agent in these respects; whether this is for good
or for evil is of secondary interest, the main point being
its significance. If, as is here suggested, the idea of salt is
generally connected in the unconscious mind with that of
semen, it is throughout intelligible that abstinence from
sexual relations should tend to be accompanied by abstinence
from salt as well (radiation of the affect); it is in perfect
accord with all we know of primitive, symbolic thinking.
The unconscious logic of the argument seems to be that
abstinence from sexuality is incomplete unless all forms of
semen, even symbolic forms, are abstained from.

This bipolar attitude of regarding salt as either exceedingly beneficial or exceedingly harmful reminds one of
two current controversies—namely, whether alcohol and sexual

[1] Frazer: op cit., p. 105.
[2] Crooke: Popular Religion and Folk-Lore of Northern India,
1896, Vol. II, p 138.

intercourse respectively are beneficial or harmful to health. Indeed, as with these, there have been at various times propagandist movements started in which salt has been denounced as the cause of numerous bodily evils.[1] About 1830 there was published a volume by a Dr. Arthur Howard entitled: 'Salt, the forbidden fruit or food; and the chief cause of diseases of the body and mind of man and of animals, as taught by the ancient Egyptian priests and wise men and by Scripture, in accordance with the author's experience of many years'. It was described by the *Lancet* as 'worthy of immortality'. As may be imagined from the title, the author treats of salt as a most obnoxious substance, abstinence from which is essential to the maintenance of health. It is possible even that unconscious associations of the kind under consideration may not have been altogether without influence in relation to more recent medical views. It had long been noticed that urine contained solid constituents which were either evident as such or could be recovered from their soluble state by means of evaporation; these were regarded on the one hand as comprising the essence of the fluid, being thus identified with semen, and on the other as salts, which indeed they mostly are.[2] The sufferings due to the excessive accumulation of these salts, in the form of calculi, attracted a great deal of attention and play a very important part in early surgical writings. When the chemical constituents of urine came to be carefully studied by exact methods there arose a tendency, which reached its acme in the late eighties, to attribute a considerable number of disorders to the presence in the system of an excessive amount of these constituents. Thus,

---

[1] Lawrence. op. cit., pp. 189-92.

[2] The unconscious association between semen and urine on the one hand and salt and water on the other will be dealt with at length later in this essay.

to mention only a few examples, gout was thought to be simply a question of poisoning by uric acid, uraemia to be poisoning with urea, diabetic oma (exhaustion following on the continued loss of a ital substance) poisoning by acetone (an occasional urinary constituent), rheumatism poisoning by lactic acid (milk, a sexual secretion, is almost constantly identified with semen in the unconscious), and so on. is interesting that the two diseases in regard to which this idea was most firmly fixed—namely, gout and rheumatism —are joint diseases, and hence lend themselves to the series of unconscious associations 'lameness incapacity— impotence'. Of late years the tendency has taken at the same time simpler and more complex directions. On the one hand there is a return to salt itself, and a 'salt-free diet' is vaunted as the sovereign agent for the prevention of arterial disease and old age (impotency), for the cure of epilepsy, and so on. It will also be remembered how, when Brown-Séquard's attempt to recapture youthful vigour by means of the injection of canine semen shocked the medical profession in London, efforts were made to substitute the more respectable, because unconscious, symbo of this—common salt. On the other hand there is a restless search for more complex organic poisons, usually in the intestinal contents, which are now being as extensively exploited as the urine was forty years ago. The belief in the prime importance of organic poisons is even generally extended to psychosexual maladies, such as hysteria, 'neurasthenia', and dementia praecox. It may be questioned whether the important advance in knowledge represented by the toxic theory of disease would not have met with more resistance than it did had it not appealed to a fundamental complex in the human mind, in which, among others, the ideas of poison and semen are closely associated.

A few derivative symbolisms concerning salt may next be considered, which receive an added significance in the light of the hypothesis put forward above. The power of salt is enhanced when it is placed on an object resembling the male organ. Cattle are thus protected by making them step over a bar of iron, or a hatchet, which has been sprinkled with salt;[1] the Esthonians cut a cross[2] under the door through which the cattle have to pass, and fill the furrows of it with salt to prevent evil spirits from harming them.[3]

In Bohemia when a girl goes out for a walk her mother sprinkles salt on the ground so that she may not 'lose her way',[4] this over-solicitous precaution becomes more intelligible when we read Wuttke's[5] explanation that the object of it is to prevent the girl from falling in love. A belief at first sight quite foolish and meaningless is that a boy can be cured of home-sickness by placing salt in the hem of his trousers (!) and making him look up the chimney.[6] We now know, however, that excessive home-sickness is due to over-attachment, rooted in unconscious incestuous wishes, to some member of the family, usually the mother, which has the effect of 'fixing' his powers of love and rendering it incapable of being transferred in the normal way to a stranger. To look up the chimney symbolises the daring to face another dark, inaccessible and dangerous passage (the very word 'chimney' is derived from the Greek κάμινος = oven, a common unconscious

---

[1] Wuttke: op. cit., S. 440.

[2] The phallic significance of the cross symbolism has been pointed out by many investigators. See, for instance, Inman: Ancient Pagan and Modern Christian Symbolism, 1874.

[3] Frazer: op. cit., p. 331

[4] Lawrence: op. cit., p. 182.

[5] Wuttke: op. cit., S. 367.

[6] Lawrence: op. cit., p. 181.

equivalent for the mother's lap or womb). The belief, therefore, which means that if someone can succeed in 'making a man of him' he will be freed from his homesickness, is not so unintelligible as it appears, and is merely the clothing in symbolic language of a fundamental fact in human nature. One may learn from it how invaluable a knowledge of unconscious symbolism is for the understanding of superstition, and how impossible it is to comprehend it without this knowledge.

The *Salt-cellar*, the receptacle of the salt, has been held in as much superstitious reverence as its contents.[1] The symbolism of it is usually a feminine one,[2] as indeed is indicated by the Spanish compliment of calling a sweetheart 'salt-cellar of my love'.[3] Salt-cellars, often of great magnificence, were, and still are, favourite wedding-presents. In Rome they constituted a special heirloom, the paternum salinum, which was handed down from generation to generation with especial care. In general it is just as evident that an excessive amount of affect, of extraneous origin, has been invested in the idea of a salt-cellar as it is in salt itself. In classical times the salt-cellar partook of the nature of a holy vessel, associated with the temple in general, and more particularly with the altar.[4] To those who are familiar with the female symbolism of the altar[5] this will be quite comprehensible. The etymology of the word 'salt-cellar' is of considerable interest in the present connection. The second part 'cellar' is derived from the French '*salière*' (salt-cellar), so that the whole

[1] Schleiden: op. cit., S. 74; Lawrence: op. cit., pp. 196-205.

[2] Though the late Dr. Putnam related to me the case of a man in whose dreams a salt-cellar appeared as a symbol of the scrotum.

[3] Andrée: *Globus*, 1867, Band XI, S. 140.

[4] Schleiden: op. cit., S. 74.

[5] G. W. Cox: The Mythology of the Aryan Nations, 1870, Vol. II, pp. 113-21; Inman: op. cit., p. 74.

is a redundancy, meaning salt-salt-receptacle. We see here an instructive example of linguistic assimilation, for a 'cellar' (a dark chamber under the house) has the same feminine symbolic meaning as *salière* itself. The sound resemblance of the words *salière* and cellar naturally made the assimilation easier, but the instinctive intuition of the people was probably the underlying factor in bringing it about.

The offering of salt as a special mark of favour, and as a sign of hospitality, has been mentioned above; we have now to note the reverse of this. In England[1] and France[2] it was considered unlucky to be helped to salt at table; this superstition still obtains in Anglican circles and finds popular expression in the saying 'Help me to salt, help me to sorrow'. In Russia the quarrel that would otherwise follow can be averted if one smiles amicably when proffering the salt.[3] A clue to the original meaning of the superstition is found in the attitude formerly obtaining in Italy,[4] where a courtesy of this kind was thought to be a mark of undue familiarity, when salt was offered by one man to the wife of another it was a sufficient cause for jealousy and even quarrel. This is perfectly intelligible in the light of the hypothesis advanced above, but is hardly otherwise to be explained.

In the North of England to give salt to someone is considered dangerous, for it puts the giver into the power of the recipient;[5] the same belief also used to be held in

---

[1] Brand: op. cit., Vol III, p. 162.

[2] Brand: ibid., p. 163.

[3] *Revue des Traditions populaires*, 1886, t. I, Sikes: op. cit., p. 329.

[4] Boyle: A Theological and Philosophical Treatise of the Nature and Goodness of Salt, 1612.

[5] Henderson: Notes on the Folk-Lore of the Northern Counties of England, 1879, p 217.

Russia.[1] In other places the act gives one possession or power over the recipient, and with salt one can acquire either men or knowledge;[2] this idea is probably allied to those of loyalty and of the magical properties of salt (see above). Light is thus thrown on the quaint saying: 'to catch a bird you must put salt on his tail'. This is commonly accounted for with the obvious remark that to catch a bird one must get near enough to it to be able to touch it, but this does not explain why it should be just salt that has to be applied, nor why it should be just to the tail. Realisation of the belief in the magical power of salt makes the saying rather more intelligible, but the explanation thus afforded is still only a general one; constructions of the phantasy, including superstitious beliefs and sayings, are determined not only generally, but precisely and in their finest details. Additional help is furnished by an old legend narrated by Lawrence,[3] in which a young man playfully threw some salt on to the back of a woman who was sitting next to him at table; she happened to be a witch, and was so weighted down by the salt that she was unable to move until it was brushed away. We have here, therefore, again the idea of salt brought into relation with that of weight which prevents movement. Now witches were conceived to be incorporeal beings, and in fact one of the chief ways of finding out whether a given woman was a witch was by weighing her;[4] the difference in weight made by a pinch of salt was therefore quite considerable, or could metaphorically be imagined to be so. This attribute of witches was closely related to their power of flying by night, and therefore with bird

[1] Schleiden: op cit., S 71
[2] Oxford Dictionary: loc cit
[3] Lawrence: op. cit., p. 179.
[4] Bekker: Die Bezauberte Welt, 1692, Theil I, S. 209.

10*

mythology altogether. The bird has always been a common phallic symbol[1]—sometimes quite consciously so, as with the winged phallus charms of the Roman ladies—and the tail is a still more familiar one in common speech; further the act of flying from the ground is frequently associated in the unconscious with the phenomenon of erection.[2] The significance of salt (= semen) in this connection is obvious; favouring and hindering are treated as synonymous terms here as elsewhere in superstition, just as in the unconscious mind, the main point being the significance.

Finally may be mentioned the belief that to see salt in a dream indicates illness.[3] When one recalls the frequency with which the ideas of nocturnal emission and of illness or loss of strength are associated, it is not difficult to divine the source of this particular belief.

III

In the preceding section of this essay we dealt chiefly with the *adult* roots of salt symbolism and superstitions, and we have now to turn our attention to the deeper *infantile* roots. The reason why the word 'deeper' is used here will presently become evident; it has to do with the ontogenetic, as well as phylogenetic, antiquity of symbolism in general.

Before passing to the next stage of the investigation, therefore, it will be necessary briefly to refer to some aspects of infantile mental life that without being realised play an important part in adult life—namely, certain views developed by young children concerning the begetting of

---

[1] Abraham: Traum und Mythus, 1909, S. 30, 63, etc.

[2] Federn: Cited by Freud, Die Traumdeutung, Dritte Aufl., 1911, S. 204.

[3] Schleiden: op. cit., S. 80.

children.[1] These are forgotten long before puberty, so
that the adult is quite unaware of their existence and is
extremely surprised to hear of their great frequency in
childhood life. They survive nevertheless in the unconscious mind, and exert a considerable influence on later
interests and views.

Early realising, in spite of the untruths told him by
the parents, that a baby is born of the mother and grows
inside her, the child sets to work to solve the problem as
best he can, the full answer being concealed from him.
Knowing nothing of other organs he conceives of the
'inside', particularly the abdomen, as simply a receptacle
for food, a view amply confirmed by his experience of
indigestion and other sensations. The baby, therefore, must
have been formed out of food, an inference that is largely
correct. Further, there being no other mode of exit
possible—at least so far as he is aware—the baby must
have then reached the exterior in the same way as digested
food (cloaca theory), as it actually does in all animals
except mammalia. There is thus established in the child's
mind a close connection between the ideas of food, faeces,
and babies, one that explains among many other things
many an hysterical symptom in later life.

The child next comes to the notion that, since food
alone does not in his personal experience have this result,
a mixing of two substances must be necessary. On the
basis of his excremental interests he observes that there
are three possible materials available, for it is only excep-
tionally that he thinks the fertilising material is of non-
human origin. The phantasy may combine these three
materials—solid, liquid, and gaseous—in different ways, the
commonest of which, in my experience and in that of

[1] See Freud: Sammlung kleiner Schriften zur Neurosenlehre, Zweite
Folge, 1911, S. 159-64, 'Über infantile Sexualtheorien'.

other observers, are in order: liquid—solid, liquid—liquid, solid—solid, and gaseous—solid. A knowledge of these facts is indispensable for the full understanding of salt symbolism. As the objection may be raised that they are artefacts of the psycho-analytic method of investigation, it will be well to refer to a little of the mass of purely anthropological evidence that proves the universal occurrence of similar beliefs in what corresponds with the childhood of the race.[1]

The belief that fertilisation, and even delivery, can take place through some other orifice than the vagina has been held in the most diverse countries of the world and is still quite prevalent. Any orifice or indentation may be implicated, the nostril, eye, ear, navel, and so on. An interesting historical example was the mediaeval belief that the Virgin Mary conceived through the ear, one widely held in the Roman Catholic Church.[2] The mouth, however, was the orifice most frequently thought of in this connection, as is apparent from the very numerous legends and beliefs in which eating or drinking bring about pregnancy. The peasantry in England still believe that peahens are impregnated in this way[3] and similar views are entertained in other countries in respect of different animals; we noted above that according to which female mice are impregnated by eating salt.

The belief that women can conceive as the result of eating various articles of diet has existed in most parts

---

[1] Since this essay was written a highly interesting paper of Otto Rank's has appeared ('Völkerpsychologische Parallelen zu den infantilen Sexualtheorien', *Zentralblatt für Psychoanalyse,* Jahrg. II, Heft 8) in which a large quantity of additional data is given that both confirms and amplifies the conclusions here enunciated.

[2] See Ch. VIII of these Essays, which is devoted to an examination of this belief.

[3] Hartland: Primitive Paternity, 1909, Vol. I, p. 151.

of the world;[1] usually the particular food is one to which some sexual symbolism is attached, such as rice, fish, cocoanuts, and so on. In the more civilised countries this has been reduced to the belief that partaking of such substances will cure barrenness in women or promote their fecundity; Hartland[2] relates a huge number of practices of this kind carried out, mostly at the present day, for the purpose of securing conception.

A digression must here be made on a matter of some importance to the present theme—namely, the association between food as taken into the body and food as it is given out, two ideas which are by no means so remote from each other in the primitive mind, including that of the child, as they usually are in that of the civilised adult. In the first place many savage tribes have the custom of devouring ordure of all kinds, including their own, and indeed seem to partake of it with special relish;[3] a contemptuous reference to it may be found in 2 Kings xviii. 27. In more civilised countries this has long been replaced by sausages[4] (a word, by the way, of the same etymological derivation as salt), and other products of abdominal organs.[5] The ordure of sacred men has in many countries a high religious significance, being used to

---

[1] Hartland: op. cit, pp. 4-16. Numerous examples.

[2] Hartland· op. cit, pp. 32-41, 47, 48, 54-72.

[3] Bourke: Scatalogic Rites of All Nations, 1891, pp. 33-7.

[4] In England in the present generation the belief was acted on that a stolen sausage had the power of curing barrenness (Hartland: op. cit., p. 56).

[5] The wife of the Elector of Hanover, in a letter to her niece, the sister-in-law of Louis XIV, writes as follows:

Hanovre, 31 Octobre, 1694.
Si la viande fait la merde, il est vrai de dire que la merde fait la viande. Est-ce que dans les tables les plus délicates, la merde n'y est pas servie en ragoûts? Les boudins, les andouilles, les saucisses, ne sont-ce pas de ragoûts dans des sacs à merde?

anoint kings, to guard against evil demons, and so on.[1]
That it is not very rare for insane patients to eat their
own excrement is of course well-known;[2] in such cases
the long-buried infantile association may come to open
expression in the patient's remark, pointing to the excrement, that he has just produced a baby. Cases of sterco-
phagy are occasionally met with apart from any psychosis,
as I know from personal experience of several instances.
An association is often formed between the ideas of excrement and corpses, probably through the common notion
of decomposition of something that was once a living
human body, or part of one. Both ideas are connected
with that of fecundity. Hartland[3] refers to 'numerous
stories wherein portions of dead bodies, given to maidens
and other women, render them pregnant'. One of the
most widely-spread practices in India and elsewhere for
remedying sterility is to perform various symbolic acts in
relation to dead bodies: thus, to creep under the coffin,
to wash in the blood of decapitated criminals, to bathe
over a dead body or underneath a person who has been
hanged, and so on.[4] The Hungarians hold that a dead
man's bone shaved into drink and given to a woman will
promote conception, or if given to a man will enhance his
potency.[5] It is clear that other factors also enter into
these last-mentioned beliefs, notably forms of ancestor-
worship, but we are concerned here only with the one
element of the association between putrefaction and fecundity, one which has of course an extensive real justification

---

[1] Bourke: op. cit., pp. 42-53.
[2] According to Obersteiner (*Psychiatrisches Centralblatt*, 1871,
Band III, S. 95) this is true of one per cent of such patients, more
often with men.
[3] Hartland: op. cit., p. 77
[4] Hartland: op. cit., pp. 74-6.
[5] Von Wlislocki. Aus dem Volksleben der Magyaren, 1893, S. 77.

in agriculture (manure and fertility). The bone, being a rigid hollow tube containing a vital marrow,[1] is a very frequent phallic symbol in anthropological data and in the unconscious mind generally: the following Egyptian myth also illustrates its power of impregnation.[2] A bone thrown on a dung-heap (!) grew up into so fine a tree (another familiar symbol) that no one had ever seen its like. The daughter of the man who had thrown the bone was desirous of seeing this wonderful tree; when she witnessed its beauty she was so entranced that she embraced it and kissing it took a leaf into her mouth. As she chewed it she found the taste sweet and agreeable and swallowed the leaf; at the same instant she conceived by the will of God.

Mainly derived from the same source are the beliefs and customs relating to the endless magical properties attaching to dead bodies, and notably to their most putrefactive elements (saliva, excretions, etc.).[3] It would be out of place to follow this subject further here, but mention may be made of a West German belief to the effect that unless the person who has clothed the dead body rubs his hands *with salt* his limbs will go to sleep.[4] This is evidently akin to sympathetic magic, the meaning being that close contact with the corpse may transfer his state of deadness to the person; the deeper meaning is that salt (= semen) will protect the member(s) from the risk of death, i. e. impotency.

A more constant unconscious association is that between the ideas of *gold* and *faeces*,[5] one of far-reaching

---

[1] Cp. the curse: 'May his bones lose their sap'.

[2] Oestrup: Contes de Damas, 1897, p. 26.

[3] Hartland: The Legend of Perseus, 1895, Vol. II, pp. 162-74, 313-32, etc.

Wuttke: op. cit., S. 463.

[5] Freud: op. cit., S. 136, 137; Ferenczi: Contributions to Psycho-Analysis, 1916, Ch. XIII, 'The Ontogenesis of the Interest in Money'; Ernst Jones: Papers on Psycho-Analysis, 1918, pp. 676-8.

significance in mythology as well as in the reactions of every-day life. Gold as fertilising principle usually in conjunction with a second sexual symbol is a favourite theme in mythology; perhaps the best known instance is that of Danae being impregnated by a shower of golden rain. Apples, fish, and other objects, made of or resembling gold, are also familiar instances of the same type of story. This association explains the extensive connection noted earlier between salt and money or wealth (both being symbols of fertilising excrement), of which a few other examples may be given. In Pomerania at the close of a wedding breakfast a servant carries round a plate containing salt, upon which the guests put money;[1] the combination of the two substances plainly symbolises fertility. Seligmann[2] refers to a German custom of carrying salt and money together in the pocket as a protection against impotence, so that here we have our surmise directly confirmed as to the meaning of the combination. A more complex variant is found in the Chemnitz saying· 'if one washes one's money in clear water and puts it with salt and bread, the dragon and evil people cannot get it'.[3]

Pregnancy has been brought about just as frequently by drinking as it has by eating: all manner of fluids have been efficacious in this respect, the sacred soma-juice milk, the sap of grass, leaves and plants, the juice of roots, fruit and flowers, and so on.[4] The idea of a *liquid* stimulus to conception thus stands in contrast with that of a solid one. The practice of drinking various fluids for the purpose of aiding conception is even more widely spread, and exists throughout Europe at the present day. In every country

---

[1] Schleiden: op. cit., S. 71.
[2] Seligmann: op. cit., S. 38.
[3] Grimm: op. cit., Nachtrag, S. 434,
[4] Hartland: Primitive Paternity, 1909, Vol. 1 Numerous instances.

women wishing to have children drink water from various holy springs or wells, the most potent of which is perhaps that at Lourdes.[1] Apart from this numerous allied practices exist, of which the following selection may be given.[2] In Thuringia and Transylvania women who wished to be healed of unfruitfulness drank consecrated (salt) water from the baptismal font; in Rügen such water was efficacious if poured before the door of a childless couple. In Hungary a barren woman drinks from a spring that she has never before seen. A Malagasy woman who has not been blessed with issue is made to go on swallowing water until her stomach is so full that it will not hold another drop. Masur women in West Prussia make use of the water that drips from a stallion's mouth after he has drunk.

As might be expected, more personal fluids are extensively used for the same purpose, this being the primary sense of the proceeding. In Bombay a woman cuts off the end of the robe of another woman who has borne children, steeps it, and drinks the infusion. Other women in India drink the water squeezed from the loin-cloth of a sanyási, or devotee. Saliva has been very extensively employed in this connection, it being almost universally treated as a seminal equivalent (hence the expression 'he is the very spit of his father'). Saliva in fact forms throughout in folk-lore and superstition a regular duplicate of salt, bearing the same relation to hospitality, friendship, compacts, baptism, magical powers and charms, religious significance, and the rest;[3] the theme cannot be further pursued here and obviously needs separate exposition. Other fluids that may be mentioned are the milk of another woman, blood from the navel of a new-born child, water in which the

[1] Hartland: op. cit., pp. 64-7.
[2] Hartland: op. cit., pp. 67-71.
[3] Hartland: Perseus, op. cit., pp. 258-75.

navel has been soaked, the lochial discharge of a woman at her first child-bed, water in which the placenta has been soaked, water from the first bath of a woman after delivery. The original sense of all these beliefs and customs is revealed by consideration of the numerous myths and legends, which recur in every part of the world without exception, describing how pregnancy followed the imbibing of semen, deliberate or accidental.

A great part of our mental life, however, is the echo of childhood thoughts, and the child knows nothing about semen. To him the corresponding potent fluid is *urine,* a topic which must next concern us. The prediction was ventured above that the various ideas noted in regard to salt and water would be found to mirror earlier corresponding ones relating to semen and urine. Confining ourselves for the present to the subject of salt water and urine, we find that the resemblances between the ideas relating to them are very striking. They may be considered by following the order in which the properties of salt were enumerated at the outset.

The significance of salt for friendship, loyalty, hospitality, and the ratifying of pacts, was dwelt on above: the same customs and ideas can be duplicated in respect of urine. Until about three centuries ago it was the vogue in Europe to pledge a friend's health in urine,[1] exactly as we now do in wine, and in the same circumstances; by this, perpetual friendship and loyalty, or even love attachment, might be ensured. The same custom still obtains in Siberia, where it also signifies a pact of peace.[2] At a Moorish wedding the bride's urine is thrown in the face of any unmarried man or stranger on whom it is wished to bestow

[1] Bourke op. cit., p. 129. Numerous references. ('Cobblers' punch' means urine with a cinder in it.)

[2] Melville: In the Lena Delta, 1885, p. 318.

a distinguished favour,[1] just as in other countries salt is presented with the same intention. In parts of Russia it was customary for the bride to wash her feet and then use the water for sprinkling the bridal bed and the assembled guests; it is probable, as Bourke suggests,[2] that the water thus used represents a survival of a former practice in which the aspersion was with the urine of the bride. The old English custom of the bride selling alcoholic liquor—the so-called Bride-Ale—on the wedding-day[3] is also likely to be ultimately derived from the same primitive source. The Jews still retain the following allied custom at their weddings: A goblet of wine is handed to the bridegroom by the best man, and after the bridegroom has sipped from it he passes it to the principal bridesmaid; she hands it to the bride, who also drinks from it. The following custom, related by Dulaure,[4] seems to be a question both of hospitality and a test of friendship· 'The Tschuktschis offer their women to travellers; but the latter, to become worthy of the offer, have to submit to a disgusting test. The daughter or wife who has to pass the night with her new guest presents him with a cupful of her urine; with this he has to rinse out his mouth. If he is brave enough to do so, he is regarded as a sincere friend; if not, he is treated as an enemy of the family.' It may be doubted whether the construction Dulaure places on this is objectively arrived at; at all events it is not likely to be the original explanation.

The magical powers of salt are fully equalled by those of urine. In connection with evil spirits and witches it played a triple part. In the first place it was used actually

---

[1] Mungo Park: Travels into the Interior of Africa, 1813, pp. 109, 135.
[2] Bourke: op. cit., p. 232.
[3] Brand: op. cit., Vol. II, p. 143 et seq.
[4] Dulaure: Les Divinités Génératrices, 1825, p. 400.

to bewitch people for evil purposes.[1] It is interesting to note that this might occur even unintentionally. In Africa, for instance, it is believed that 'to add one's urine, even unintentionally, to the food of another bewitches that other, and does him grievous harm',[2] this may be compared with the belief, mentioned above, that to give salt to someone puts him in one's power. Secondly, like salt, it was used for the detection of witchcraft and of witches.[3] Thirdly it was one of the most potent charms against evil spirits and witches, and was used as such throughout the middle ages.[4] In Ireland[5] urine, especially when combined with dung, was invaluable in frustrating the mischief of fairies. It is still used against witches by the Eskimos in disorders of childbirth.[6] The Shamans of Alaska do the same to keep off evil spirits.[7] Osthanes, the magician, prescribed the dipping of our feet, in the morning, in human urine, as a preventative against evil charms.[8] It is still a practice in France to wash in urine so as to guard against the devil and other maleficent influences.[9]

In regard to disease there was still more extensive application made of urine than of salt, both for diagnostic and for therapeutic purposes. As is well-known, urinoscopy was in the middle ages one of the principal means of

[1] Frommann: Tractatus de Fascinatione, 1674, p. 683.

[2] Bourke: op. cit., p. 376.

[3] Bourke: op. cit., p. 397. Several references.

[4] Frommann: op. cit., pp. 961, 962, Brand: op. cit., Vol. III, p. 13.

[5] Mooney: 'The Medical Mythology of Ireland', *Trans. of the American Philosophical Society*, 1887.

[6] Bourke: op. cit., p. 378.

[7] Boas: *Journal of American Folk-Lore*, Vol. I, p. 218.

[8] Quoted from Brand: op. cit., p. 286.

[9] Luzel: 'Le Nirang des Parsis en Basse Bretagne', *Mélusine*, Mai 1888; Réclus: Les Primitifs, 1885, p. 98.

recognising different diseases, and it was used for this purpose
not only in Europe but in Arabia, Tibet, and other parts
of the world;[1] for instance, in the index to the works of
Avicenna there are no fewer than two hundred and seventy-
five references to the appearance and other physical
properties of urine in disease. As in the case of salt, this
divination was connected with ideas of urine, rain, and
weather prophesying in general. The use of urine in the
treatment of disease has been so remarkably comprehensive
that it is impossible even to touch on the subject here;
Bourke[2] has collected a vast amount of information dealing
with it. It may be added that sometimes we find salt
combined with urine for medical purposes, e. g. to get rid
of a fever.[3]

The importance of salt for fecundity is if anything
exceeded by that of urine. It formed the essential constituent
of many love-philtres and magical procedures having as
their object the winning of affection.[4] Pliny describes the
aphrodisiac properties of the urine voided by a bull
immediately after copulation; it may either be drunk or
used to moisten earth which is then rubbed into the groin.
Characteristically enough, urine can also be used as an
anti-aphrodisiac or as a charm against love-philtres.[5] At
Hottentot weddings the priest urinates over the bride and
bridegroom, and the latter, receiving the stream with
eagerness, makes furrows with his nails so that the urine
may penetrate the farther.[6]

---

[1] Bourke: op. cit, pp. 272-4, 385, 386
[2] Bourke: op. cit., pp. 277-369, 375, 384.
[3] Wuttke: op. cit., p. 354.
[4] Bourke: op. cit., pp. 216, 217, 223
[5] Bourke: op. cit., pp. 224-7.
[6] Cook: in 'Hawkesworth's Voyages', 1773, Vol. III, p. 387; Kolbein:
in Knox's 'Voyages', 1777, Vol. II, pp. 399, 400; Thurnberg: in Pinkerton's 'Voyages', 1814, Vol. XVI, pp. 89, 141.

The practice described by Pliny, referred to above, has also been recommended as a remedy for the cure of impotence. The sovereign cure for this, however, consisted in urinating through the wedding-ring, i. e. into an exquisite female symbol. This practice is mentioned by most of the older writers,[1] and has persisted among the German peasantry until the present generation.[2] Pliny[3] states that the urine of eunuchs was considered to be highly beneficial as a promoter of fruitfulness in women. In Algiers a woman seeks to cure barrenness by drinking sheep's urine.[4] Schurig[5] describes as a method of inducing conception the use of a bath of urine poured over old iron, with which may be compared the magical properties mentioned above as being ascribed to the combination of salt and iron. Finally two Asiatic legends narrated by Bab[6] may be referred to, in which the symbolical equivalence of urine and semen appears in the most unmistakable manner. In the first one, from Siam, a man urinated daily on to a certain apple-tree, with the result that it bore especially large fruit. A princess ate one of the apples and thereupon became pregnant. In the other, from Cambodia, a hermit had the habit of urinating on to a hollowed-out stone. A girl who had got lost in the woods (her mother had evidently omitted to strew salt as she left the house) drank the liquid out of the stone, and likewise became pregnant.

[1] Reginald Scot: op. cit., p. 64; Frommann: op. cit., p. 997; Brand: op. cit., Vol. III, p. 305.

[2] Birlinger and Buck: Sagen, Märchen und Volksaberglauben aus Schwaben, 1861, S. 486.

[3] xxviii. 18.

[4] Ploss: Das Weib in der Natur- und Völkerkunde, 1891, Bd. I, S. 443.

[5] Schurig: Chylologia, 1725, Vol. II, p. 712.

[6] Bab: *Zeitschrift für Ethnologie*, 1906, Band XXXVIII, S. 281.

The use of salt at initiation ceremonies can also be paralleled with that of urine. A young Parsee undergoes a kind of confirmation during which he is made to drink a small quantity of the urine of a bull.[1] At the Hottentot initiation ceremony one of the medicine-men urinates over the youth, who proudly rubs the fluid into his skin.[2] Corresponding with the Christian and Jewish displacement of their initiation ceremonies (baptism, circumcision) from the time of puberty to that of infancy we find a similar displacement in respect of urine ceremonies. The Californian Indians give their children a draught of urine as soon as they are born,[3] and this custom is also in vogue amongst Americans in the country districts;[4] these are of course not pure examples of initiation. The Inuit child selected to be trained as an Angekok was bathed in urine soon after birth as a religious ceremony.[5] When Parsee children are invested with the Sudra and Koshti--the badges of the Zoroastrian faith— they are sprinkled with the urine of a sacred cow and they also have to drink some of it.[6]

The interest aroused by the taste of salt may be compared with that taken in the peculiar taste of urine, a matter that played a considerable part in medical urinoscopy. All bodily fluids, including tears, semen, sweat, blood, etc., owe of course most of their taste to the presence of salt in them. The natives of Northern Siberia habitually drink each other's urine.[7] The African Shillooks regularly wash out their milk vessels with urine 'probably', so Schweinfurth[8]

---

[1] Monier Williams. Modern India, 1878, p 178.

[2] Kolbein: op. cit., pp. 202-4; Thurnberg loc. cit.

[3] Bancroft op. cit., p. 413.

[4] Trumbull: Quoted by Bourke. op. cit., p. 240.

[5] Réclus: op. cit., p. 84.

[6] Max Müller: Chips from a German Workshop, 1869, p. 164.

[7] Melville: Quoted by Bourke: op. cit., p. 38.

[8] Schweinfurth: The Heart of Africa, 1872, Vol. I, p. 16.

thinks, 'to compensate for a lack of salt'; this is also done by the natives of Eastern Siberia.[1] The Obbe[2] and other[3] natives of Central Africa never drink milk unless it is mixed with urine, the reason given being that otherwise the cow would lose her milk; we have here a counterpart of the custom of mixing salt with the milk so as to ensure a plentiful supply. 'Chinook olives' are acorns that have been steeped for five months in human urine.[4] Of interest is the relation of urine to the manufacture of intoxicating drinks, it being thus an equivalent to alcohol, as we have noted above. When the supply of alcohol runs short in Siberia the natives eke it out by making a mixture of equal parts of urine and alcohol.[5] In Queensland there is an edible nut of a particular species of pine, which is prepared for consumption in the following way: clay pans are formed in the soil, into which the men urinate; the nuts are then steeped in this, when a fermentation takes place. The eating of the nuts causes a temporary madness, and even delirium tremens.[6]

We have next to note the analogies between the significance of salt and that of urine in regard to religious performances. In both cases the substance might be either swallowed or applied to the surface of the body, and concerning the latter practice it is expedient to make a few preliminary remarks. The religious practice of sprinkling or baptising with a holy fluid (salt and water in the Roman Catholic Church, plain water in the Protestant Church) has evidently two principal meanings. In the first

---

[1] Melville: Quoted by Bourke: op. cit., p. 200.
[2] Baker, The Albert Nyanza, 1869, p. 240.
[3] Long: Central Africa, 1877, p. 70.
[4] Kane: An Artist's Wanderings in North America, 1859, p. 187.
[5] Melville: Quoted by Bourke: op. cit., p. 39.
[6] Mann: Quoted by Bourke; op. cit., p. 38.

place it symbolises purification, particularly from sin. Probably the simplest and most accurate expression for the psychological meaning of baptism, as perhaps for that of any religious rite, is 'purification through re-birth'. The earthly incestuous libido, which is now known to be the deepest source of the sense of sin in general,[1] is overcome and purified in a homeopathic manner by passing through a symbolic act of heavenly incest. Purification by fire is a distorted form of the more original purification by water. It will be noticed that in baptism the liquid symbolises both the father's urine (or semen) and the mother's uterine waters, satisfying thus both the male and the female components of the libido. The oldest association between the ideas of liquid and purification is of course the child's experience of urine washing away faeces, thus cleansing dirt (the deepest source for the objectionableness of sexuality).[2]

In the second place baptism imbues the participant with the mystic properties conveyed by, or belonging to, the holy fluid. This meaning, which was probably the original one of the two, is well illustrated in the Hottentot rite described above, where the participant scratches his skin so as to absorb as much as possible of the precious fluid. At all events we find that the acts of ablution[3] and of swallowing are throughout treated as though they were identical. Where one is performed in one country the other is in another country in exactly corresponding circumstances, and in numberless instances the two are regarded

---

[1] Freud: Totem und Tabu, 1913, S. 144, 145.

[2] Freud: *Jahrbuch der Psychoanalyse,* Band IV, S. 49, 50.

[3] It should not be forgotten that the original form of Christian baptism was complete immersion; the relatively modern custom of christening, or sprinkling, is a later replacement of this, and is still repudiated by, for instance, the Baptist sect.

as equivalent. For example, the practice of imbibing water, particularly holy water, for the cure of barrenness, as described above, is throughout paralleled by the equally common one of bathing in water for the same purpose, and often at the same place; Hartland[1] has collected an enormous number of instances of this from every part of the world and shews that it is to-day as frequent as ever.

All the evidence, from comparative religions, from history, anthropology and folk-lore, converges to the *conclusion, not only that Christian and other rites of baptism symbolise the bestowment of a vital fluid (semen or urine) on the initiate, but that the holy water there used is a lineal descendant of urine, the use of which it gradually displaced.* Strange as this conclusion may seem it is definitely supported by the following facts selected from a vast number of similar ones.

To begin with, it is known that salt and water has historically replaced urine in various non-religious or semi-religious usages. Bourke[2] writes: 'We shall have occasion to show that salt and water, holy water, and other liquids superseded human urine in several localities, Scotland included'. The following is an example of this. One of the superstitious uses of urine was to wash the breasts of a woman after delivery, no doubt with the aim of securing a good supply of milk. Jouan[3] reports from personal experience that this was still customary in France so late as in 1847. In Scotland the custom widely prevailed of washing the breasts with salt and water in the same circumstances and for the same object.[4] Again, whenever the supply of salt falls short in a given country, particularly in an uncivilised one, the

---

[1] Hartland· Paternity, op. cit., pp. 77-89.
[2] Bourke: op. cit., p. 211.
[3] Jouan: Quoted by Bourke; loc. cit.
[4] Black: Folk-Medicine, 1883, p. 23; Napier: op. cit., pp. 36, 37.

natives are apt to resort to urine as a substitute. Gomara[1] states that human urine served as salt to the Indians of Bogota. The Latookas of the White Nile make salt from the ashes of goat's dung,[2] which again illustrates the conception of salt as the essence of excrement, particularly urine. Pallas[3] says that the Buriats of Siberia, in collecting salts from the shores of certain lakes, are careful as to the taste of the same: 'they employ only those which have a taste of urine and of alkali'; Bourke,[4] referring to this, adds 'this shows that they must once have used urine for salt, as so many other tribes have done'. The Siberians gave human urine to their reindeer in place of salt,[5] presumably to improve their yield of milk. They also used urine to obtain water from snow by melting it, just as we use salt to prevent the formation of ice on our doorsteps. The Dinkas of Central Africa use the urine of cows for washing and as a substitute for salt, but here other motives also enter in, for with them cattle are sacred animals.[6] Urine has been used for a very great number of industrial purposes, in many of which it has since been superseded by salt;[7] it is not necessary to enumerate them here.

One of the earliest uses of salt was for cleansing purposes. In Ancient Rome salt and water was used instead of toilet paper, every latrine containing a bucket of it.[8] The use of urine as a fluid for washing the body has been

[1] Gomara: Historia de las Indias, p. 202.

[2] Baker: op. cit., p 224.

[3] Pallas: Voyages, 1793, Vol. IV, p. 246.

[4] Bourke: op. cit., p. 193.

[5] Cochrane: Pedestrian Journey through Siberian Tartary, 1824, p 235.

[6] Schweinfurth· op. cit., p. 58.

[7] Bourke: op. cit, pp. 177-200.

[8] Bourke: op. cit., p. 135.

reported from the most diverse parts of the world: thus, in Alaska,[1] in Iceland,[2] in Ounalashka (in Russia),[3] amongst the Californian Pericuis,[4] the Siberian Tchuktchees,[5] and the Vancouver Indians.[6] The custom persisted in Spain until quite recent times, and even in the present generation it was to be traced among the Spanish settlers in Florida.[7] Petroff[8] states that the peasants of Portugal still wash their clothes in urine, and German, Irish and Scandinavian immigrants in the United States persist in adding human urine to the water to be used in cleansing blankets.[9] The use of urine as a mouth-wash is also very prevalent. Baker[10] writes: 'The Obbo natives wash out their mouths with their own urine. This habit may have originated in the total absence of salt in their country'. The Basques and some Hindoos do the same, and the custom used to obtain in England and Germany; in Spain and Portugal it persisted until the end of the eighteenth century.[11]

We may now return to the religious aspects of the subject. The Romans held a feast to the mother of all the Gods, Berecinthia, at which the matrons took their idol and sprinkled it with their urine.[12] Berecinthia was one

[1] Coxe: Russian Discoveries, 1803, p. 225, quoting Krenitzin.

[2] Hakluyt: Voyages, 1599, Vol. I, p. 664.

[3] Solovoof: Voyages, 1764, p. 226.

[4] Clavigero: Historia de Baja California, 1852, p. 28, Bancroft, op. cit., p. 559.

[5] Lisiansky: Voyage round the World, 1811, p. 214, Melville: In the Lena Delta, loc. cit.; Gilder, quoted by Bourke: op. cit., pp. 202, 203.

[6] Swan: 'The Indians of Cape Flattery', Smithsonian Contributions to Knowledge, No. 220, p. 19.

[7] Bourke: op. cit., pp. 203, 205. Many references.

[8] Petroff: Trans. of the American Anthropological Society, 1882, Vol. I.

[9] McGillicuddy: Quoted by Bourke: op. cit., p. 205.

[10] Baker: op. cit., p. 240.

[11] Bourke: op. cit., pp. 203-5.

[12] Torquemada: Quoted by Bourke: op. cit., p. 394.

of the names under which Cybele or Rhea, the primal earth Goddess, was worshipped by the Romans and by many nations of the East. Juvenal (Sixth Satire) describes how in the rites of the Bona Dea her image used to be sprinkled with copious irrigations of urine. In the early days of Christianity the Manichaean sect used to bathe in urine.[1] It is related of an Irish king, Aedh, that he obtained some urine of the chief priest, bathed his face in it, drank some with gusto, and said that he prized it more highly than the Eucharist itself.[2]

In modern religions of civilised peoples, however, human urine is never used, having been replaced by water, salt and water, or cow's urine. The sacred drink *hum* of the Parsees has the 'urine of a young, pure cow' as one of the ingredients.[3] In the Bareshnun ceremony the Parsee priest has to undergo certain ablutions wherein he applies to his body cow's urine,[4] and to rub the *nirang* (cow's urine) over his face and hands is the second thing every Parsee does after rising in the morning.[5] The latter ceremony is by no means a simple one; for instance, he is not allowed to touch anything directly with his hands until the sacred *nirang* has first been washed off with water. In India the urine of a cow is a holy water of the very highest religious significance. It is used in ceremonies of purification, during which it is drunk.[6] Dubois[7] says that a Hindoo penitent 'must drink the *panchakaryam*,—a word which literally signifies the five things, namely, milk, butter,

---

[1] Picart: Coûtumes et Cérémonies Religieuses, 1729, p. 18.

[2] *Mélusine,* Mai 5, 1888.

[3] Max Müller: Biographies of Words, 1888, p. 237.

[4] Kingsley: Quoted by Bourke: op. cit., p. 211.

[5] Max Müller: Chips, etc., op. cit., p. 163.

[6] De Gubernatis: Zoological Mythology, Engl. Transl., 1872, Vol. I, p. 95.

[7] Abbé Dubois: The People of India, 1817, p. 29

curd, dung, and urine, all mixed together', and he adds:
'The urine of a cow is held to be the most efficacious of
any for purifying all imaginable uncleanness. I have often
seen the superstitious Hindu accompanying these animals
when in the pasture, and watching the moment for receiving
the urine as it fell, in vessels which he had brought for
the purpose, to carry it home in a fresh state; or, catch-
ing it in the hollow of his hand, to bedew his face and
all his body. When so used it removes all external impurity,
and when taken internally, which is very common, it cleanses
all within.' Moor[1] similarly writes: 'The greatest . . . of all
purifiers is the urine of a cow. Images are sprinkled with
it. No man of any pretensions to piety or cleanliness would
pass a cow in the act of staling without receiving the holy
stream in his hand and sipping a few drops.' Hindoo
merchants at Bokhara mix with their food, that it may do
them good, the urine of a sacred cow kept in that place.[2]
At the Poojah sacrifice the Brahmans prepare the room
by sprinkling the floor with cow's urine.[3] In one of the
Hindoo fasts the devotee adopts as his food the excreta
of cows, the urine being allowed as a beverage for the
fourth day.[4] The antiquity of urine rites in India is shewn
by the fact that they are frequently referred to in the
oldest of their canonical books. The Brahminical authors
of the Maha-Bharata describe how, at the coronation of
a Maharajah, Krishna brings the urine of the sacred cow
and pours it over the King's head.[5] In the Shapast la
Shayast much stress is laid on bull's urine as a purifier.[6]

---

[1] Moor: The Hindu Pantheon, 1810, p. 143.
[2] Erman: Siberia, 1848, Vol. I, p. 384.
[3] Maurice: Indian Antiquities, 1800, Vol. I, p. 77.
[4] Maurice: op. cit., Vol. V, p. 222.
[5] Wheeler. History of India, 1867, Vol. I, p. 371.
[6] Sacred Books of the East, Vol. V, Part I.

These rites exist not only in India proper, but also on the slopes of the Himalayas,[1] and from India they were introduced into Persia; the Kharda Avesta has preserved the formula to be recited by a devotee while he holds in his hand the urine of a cow, preparatory to washing his face with it.[2]

We need not discuss the various cloud, moon, and other supposed symbolisms of the rites in question, for it is no longer tenable that these are anything more than secondary developments of more primitive interests. After dealing with the subject of animal sacrifice, and shewing that this is a later development of the original human sacrifice, a conclusion amply confirmed by the work done since his time, Bourke[3] pertinently asks: 'If the cow have displaced a human victim, may it not be within the limits of probability that the ordure and urine of the sacred bovine are substitutes, not only for the complete carcass, but that they symbolize a former use of human excreta?' This question we can to-day with a high degree of probability answer in the affirmative, for both anthropological and psycho-analytical research agree in the conclusion that excessive, e. g. religious, interest in any animal is only a substitute for a corresponding interest in some human being. There can be no doubt that the cow, for instance, is a typical mother-symbol, just as the Lamb of God in Christian mythology is a symbol of Christ, i. e. of the son.

From this point of view the devil's custom of using his urine to baptise, and bless, his worshippers at the witches' Sabbath[4] must be regarded, not—as the mediaeval

---

[1] Short. 'Notes on the Hill Tribes of the Neilgherries', *Trans. of the Ethnological Society*, 1868, p 268.

[2] De Gubernatis: op. cit., pp. 99-100.

[3] Bourke: op. cit., p. 125.

[4] Thiers: Traité des Superstitions, 1741, Vol. II, p. 367; Picart: op. cit., Vol. VIII, p. 69.

theologians indignantly thought—as constituting a wanton caricature of the Christian rites, but as a reversion to the most primitive form of these. Caricature, like wit, is often really a reversion to the unconscious source of the caricatured idea. An example of it may be quoted from another field, one which also depends on the symbolic equivalent of urine and holy water: In a caricature by Isaac Cruikshank, dated March 17, 1797, of Napoleon giving audience to the Pope, a French grenadier is represented urinating into a chamber-pot which is labelled Holy Water.[1]

The almost universal custom of rubbing a new-born child with salt, or bathing it in salt and water, has been noted above. In some parts of the world the original fluid, urine, which has been so widely displaced for this purpose by salt, is still in use, or was in historical times.[2] Soranus discusses at length the Roman custom of bathing infants with the urine of a boy who has not reached puberty (thus a peculiarly innocent and pure fluid). The Hottentots use fresh cow's urine for this purpose, while the Indians in Alaska employ horse urine.

The association between urine rites and religious dancing is especially close in many parts of the world. Bourke[3] gives a detailed account of the 'urine dance' of the Zunis in New Mexico, and draws an instructive analogy between it and the famous Feast of Fools in mediaeval Europe.[4] In a painstaking analysis of the circumstances in which dancers in Alaska bathe in urine he has further established the religious significance of this custom there

---

[1] Broadley: Napoleon in Caricature, 1911, p. 94.
[2] Numerous instances are related by Ploss: Das Kind in Brauch und Sitte der Völker, Zweite Aufl., 1911.
[3] Bourke. op. cit., pp. 4-10.
[4] Bourke: op. cit., pp. 11-23.

also.[1] The same association exists as well in various other
parts of the world, in Africa, Siberia, North America, etc.[2]
The ideas that are connected together in these ceremonies
are: alcoholic or other intoxication, religious ecstasies, urine
rites (drinking and bathing), and sexual excitement. In this
connection I venture to throw out the suggestion that
perhaps philological research might establish an etymological
relationship between the Latin word sal and the verbs
saltare and salire (= to leap or dance).[3] From saltus
(= leap) comes the English saltier (St. Andrew's cross),
the substantive salt (meaning sexual desire, especially of
animals), and the adjective salt (= lecherous),[4] further
words from the same source are assault (adsaltare), assail
(adsalire), sally, exult, and salient, all of which stand in a
psychological relationship to the present subject. The idea
of dancing is of course, now as formerly,[5] closely connected with eroticism, and often also with religion.[6]

*   *   *

Something will now be said about the symbolic significance attaching to the mingling of two liquids, which is
ultimately derived from the infantile idea, mentioned above,
that the sexual act consists in the combining of the urine
of two people. In various customs and beliefs urine has,
quite comprehensibly, been replaced by other bodily fluids,

[1] Bourke· op. cit., pp. 206-8.

[2] Bourke. op. cit., pp. 208-10.

[3] Since writing the above I find that Schleiden (op. cit., S. 17)
expresses a similar thought, suggesting that sal and salire are both
derived from the Sanscrit 'sar', a root which will be considered later
in this essay.

[4] cp. Shakespeare's 'salt as wolves in pride' (Othello: Act. III, Sc. 3)

[5] Brill: 'The Psychopathology of the New Dances', *New York
Medical Journal,* April 25, 1914.

[6] Bourke. op. cit., p. 24.

particularly the vital ones such as blood. Salt and water has also played an important part in this way.

The interchange of blood as a means of binding two people together with lasting ties is a very general rite. Hartland[1] says of it: 'The Blood-Covenant, as it is called, is a simple ceremony. It is sufficient that an incision be made in the neophyte's arm and the flowing blood sucked from it by one of the clansmen, upon whom the operation is repeated in turn by the neophyte. . . . Sometimes the blood is dropped into a cup and diluted with water or wine. Sometimes food eaten together is impregnated with the blood.[2] Sometimes it is enough to rub the bleeding wounds together, so that the blood of both parties is mixed and smeared upon them both. Among the Kayans of Borneo the drops are allowed to fall upon a cigarette, which is then lighted and smoked alternately by both parties. But, whatever may be the exact form adopted, the essence of the rite is the same, and its range is world-wide. It is mentioned by classical writers as practised by the Arabs, the Lydians, and Iberians of Asia Minor, and apparently the Medes. Many passages of the Bible, many of the Egyptian *Book of the Dead,* are inexplicable apart from it. Ancient Arab historians are full of allusions to it. Odin and Loki entered into the bond, which means for us that it was customary among the Norsemen—as we know, in fact, from other sources. It is recorded by Giraldus of the Irish of his day. It is described in the *Gesta Romanorum.* It is related of the Huns or Magyars, and of the mediaeval Roumanians. Joinville ascribes it to one of the tribes of the Caucasus; and the Rabbi Petachia of

---

[1] Hartland: Perseus, op. cit., pp. 237, 238. See in general pp. 236-58, also Strack. Das Blut im Glauben und Aberglauben der Menschheit, 1900.

[2] The resemblance of these two last-mentioned customs to the Eucharist of the Christian Churches is unmistakable.

Ratisbon, who travelled in Ukrainia in the twelfth century, found it there. In modern times every African traveller mentions it; and most of them have had to undergo the ceremony. In the neighbouring island of Madagascar it is well known. All over the Eastern Archipelago, in Australia, in the Malay peninsula, among the Karens, the Siamese, the Dards on the northern border of our Indian empire, and many of the aboriginal tribes of Bengal, the wild tribes of China, the Syrians of Lebanon and the Bedouins, and among the autochthonous peoples of North and South America, the rite is, or has been quite recently, in use. Nor has it ceased to be practised in Europe by the Gipsies, the Southern Slavs and the Italians of the Abruzzi. The band of the Mala Vita in Southern Italy, only broken up a year or two ago, was a blood-brotherhood formed in this way. Most savage peoples require their youths at the age of puberty to submit to a ceremony which admits them into the brotherhood of the grown men, and into all the rights and privileges of the tribe. Of this ceremony the blood-covenant is usually an essential part, as it is also, either actually or by symbol, in the initiation-rite not only of the Mala Vita, but of almost all secret societies, both civilised and uncivilised.'

The giving of blood, therefore, exactly like that of salt, symbolises friendship, loyalty, compact, and initiation into manhood. More than this, in many countries it is closely connected with marriage, and may actually constitute the marriage ceremony. The marriage rite of the Dusuns, in Banguey, consists in transferring a drop of blood from a small incision made in the calf of a man's leg to a similar cut in the woman's leg.[1] The marriage of the Wukas, a tribe of New Guinea, is performed by mutual cuts made

[1] Hartland: op. cit., p. 339. The original references may be found there.

by the husband and wife in each other's forehead.[1] Among
the Birhors of India the wedding ceremony consists entirely
in drawing blood from the little fingers of the bride and
bridegroom, and smearing it on each other;[2] a similar,
though more complicated, ceremony is performed by the
Káyasth, or writer caste of Behar.

Among several races of India, in the wedding ceremony
known as *sindúr dán*, the substance used is red lead,
which the bridegroom smears on the bride's forehead with
his little finger or a knife; Hartland[3] has shewn that this
is a later development of the more primitive custom, the
red lead simply replacing the blood. In some instances the
two are combined: in the Kewat caste the *sindúr dán*
rite is first carried out, and then blood is drawn from
the little finger of the bridegroom's right hand and of the
bride's left; the blood is mingled in a dish of boiled rice
and milk, and each person eats the food containing the
other's blood.[4] Similarly in the Rajput ritual the family
priest fills the bridegroom's hand with *sindúr* and marks
the bride's forehead with it; on the next day each of
them is made to chew betel with which a drop of blood
from the other's little finger has been mixed.[5] Among the
Kharwár, and also the Kurmi, the bridegroom smears the
bride with a mixture of his own blood and of paint.[6] Blood
rites of the same kind were also performed at Finnish and
Norwegian marriages.[7]

More or less elaborate symbolisms of the primitive rite
are frequent enough. An Australian bridegroom spits on

[1] Hartland: loc. cit.
[2] Hartland: op. cit., p. 336.
[3] Hartland: op. cit., pp. 334-6.
[4] Hartland: op. cit., p. 337.
[5] Hartland: loc. cit.
[6] Hartland: loc. cit.
[7] Hartland: op. cit., p. 341.

his bride, and then streaks her with red powder down to the navel.[1] A Carib will sometimes betroth himself to an unborn babe, conditionally on its being a girl, by making a red mark over the mother's womb.[2] In the East Indies, in Borneo, and in parts of Southern India, fowl's blood is used instead of human blood.[3] Blood, like urine, has also been extensively used in Europe as a love charm or philtre,[4] of which custom one example will suffice: lovers who wished to heighten the affections of their mistresses used to transfuse their own blood into the loved one's veins.[5] An example of condensed symbolism is afforded by a Mexican saga, according to which a dead man's bone (i. e. the phallus of an ancestor, or father) when sprinkled with blood produced the father and mother of the present race of mankind.[6]

We see from the facts just quoted that blood, like urine, has all over the world been treated as an equivalent of salt, as a vital or holy material. The thesis that external application is symbolically the same as drinking is confirmed in this case as well. Customs and beliefs very similar to those just mentioned could be collected in respect of various other bodily fluids, of which only one or two instances will be given. The sweat of the Finnish deity Wainemoinen was a balm for all diseases, and the same was true of the Egyptian God Ra.[7] The Scandinavian Frost-Giants were born of the sweat of the Giant Ymir.[8] It is probable that

[1] Hartland. op. cit., p. 342.

[2] Hartland: loc. cit.

[3] Hartland. op. cit., p. 343.

[4] Numerous examples are given by Hartland: op. cit., pp. 124, 125.

[5] Flemming: De Remediis ex Corpore Humano desuntis, 1738, p. 15.

[6] Southey's Commonplace Book: Edited by Warter, 1850, Vol. IV, p. 142.

[7] Lenormant: Chaldean Magic: Its Origin and Development, Engl. Transl., 1877, p. 247.

[8] Hartland: Paternity: op. cit., p. 2.

the salt taste of sweat has always struck the observation of mankind. This is certainly so with tears, where literary allusions to their saltness abound: thus in King John (Act V, Sc. 7):

Prince Henry. O, that there were some virtue in my tears,
That might relieve you!

King John·   The salt in them is hot.

*   *   *

The interest in the combination of salt and water has naturally been extended to the sea, which has always played an important part in the birth fancies of mankind. The association is evident in the use of the Greek word ἅλς (Latin *sale*) to express both 'salt' and 'sea'. The contrast between fire and water has often been seized upon to represent the contrast between male and female elements respectively. The relation between salt and fire is much more extensive than we have here described; most of the customs and beliefs mentioned above could be paralleled by similar ones in which it is necessary to throw salt into the fire in order to produce the desired effect.[1] In mythology the combination of fire and water (male and female elements) is symbolised with especial frequency by alcohol, which presumably was the essential constituent of the various sacred drinks or which we read; with singular appropriateness the North American Indians refer to alcoholic beverages as 'fire-water'.

The association between the ideas fire—salt—sea are well shewn in the following myths. From the mythical lore of Finland we learn that Ukko, the mighty God of the sky,

[1] The etymological aspects of this relationship will be discussed later.

struck fire in the heavens, a spark descended from this was received by the waves and became salt.[1] This example is especially instructive for more than one reason. In the first place we here have salt directly derived from fire, thus confirming our previous surmise of the symbolic equivalency of the two. In the next place, as Abraham[2] has clearly demonstrated, heavenly fire descending upon earth, e. g. lightning, is mythologically only another variant of the various divine drinks (soma, ambrosia, nectar) that symbolise the male fertilising fluid; this is in obvious accord with the view here maintained of the seminal symbolism of salt.

In another myth we have the Prometheus-like bringer of salt regarded as a Messiah. Lawrence[3] writes 'The Chinese worship an idol called Phelo, in honor of a mythological personage of that name, whom they believe to have been the discoverer of salt and the originator of its use. His ungrateful countrymen, however, were tardy in their recognition of Phelo's merits, and that worthy thereupon left his native land and did not return. Then the Chinese declared him to be a deity, and in the month of June each year they hold a festival in his honor, during which he is everywhere sought, but in vain; he will not appear until he comes to announce the end of the world.' The Prometheus theme of a God bringing an all-precious substance as a gift to mankind[4] is here worked into a form that closely resembles the Jewish conception of a Messiah that has to be sought and the Christian one of a prophet who was not received when he delivered his message, but who will return to announce the end of the world.

[1] Quoted from Lawrence: op. cit, p. 154.
[2] Abraham op. cit., S. 49, 62, etc.
[3] Lawrence: op. cit., pp. 154, 155.
[4] See Abraham · op. cit., for a full analysis of the Prometheus myth.

Tacitus[1] refers to the belief that salt is the product of the strife between fire and water, a belief evidently mirroring the infantile sadistic conception of coitus, but one that happens to have an objective basis in regard to the evaporating action of the sun's heat. On a lowlier plane we may refer to the connection between fire and water as shewn by some practices carried out for the purpose of obtaining children. A Transylvanian Gipsy woman is said to drink water into which her husband has cast hot coals, or, better still, has spit, saying as she does so: 'Where I am flame, be thou the coals! Where I am rain be thou the water!'[2] A South Slavonic woman holds a wooden bowl of water near the fire on the hearth. Her husband then strikes two firebrands together until the sparks fly. Some of them fall into the bowl, and she then drinks the water.[3] Of the many instances of association between the ideas of fire and urine one only need be mentioned: At the yearly ceremony held by the Eskimos for the purpose of driving out an evil spirit called Tuna, one of the performers brings a vessel of urine and flings it on the fire.[4] The ideas, therefore, of fire-salt, fire-water, and fire-urine are thus seen to be closely related in the primitive mind, a fact which stands in full harmony with the clinical psycho-analytic finding that the ideas of fire, water, urine, and semen are interchangeable equivalents in the unconscious, fire being a typical symbol for urine.

Leaving now the subject of fire we have to note a few more beliefs concerning salt and water, particularly in

[1] Cited by Schleiden. op. cit., S. 11.
[2] Ploss: Das Weib, loc. cit.
[3] Krauss: Sitte und Brauch der Südslaven, 1885, S. 531.
[4] *Report of the International Polar Expedition to Point Barrow*, Washington, 1885, p. 42

a female sense (receptive urine). In the cosmogenical myths
of the islanders of Kadiack it is related that the first
woman 'by making water, produced the seas.'[1] In South
Africa it is also believed that the sea was created by a
woman,[2] doubtless in the same way. In the creation myth
of the Australians, on the other hand, it is a God, Bundjil,
who creates the sea by urinating over the earth for many
days.[3] Among the Mexican Nahuas, again, the sea is of
female origin. there the women and girls employed in the
preparation of salt dance at a yearly festival held in honour
of the Goddess of Salt, Huixocihuatl, whose brothers the
rain-gods, as the result of a quarrel, drove her into the
sea, where she invented the art of making the precious
substance.[4] In European mythology the sea is conceived
of as either male or female, though much more often as
the latter. It stands in especially close association with the
various love Goddesses, Aphrodite, Astarte, and the rest.
Jennings writes:[5] 'Blue is the colour of the "Virgin Maria".
Maria, Mary, *mare, mar, mara,* means the "bitterness",
or the "saltness" of the sea. Blue is expressive of the
Hellenic, Isidian, Ionian, Yonian (Yoni—Indian), Watery,
Female, and Moonlike Principle in the universal theogony.
It runs through all the mythologies.' As is well known,
Friday is holy to this Goddess in most religions, and is
named after her in all European languages. On Friday,
the day of the Virgin Mary, salted meat must not be eaten
by strict Catholics (compare this with the ascetic abstinence from salt noted above), and, further, the staple food
is, appropriately enough, fish. There exists in the South

---

[1] Lisiansky: op. cit., p. 197.
[2] Lang: Myth, Ritual, and Religion, 1887, Vol. I, p. 91.
[3] Smyth: The Aborigines of Australia, 1878, Vol. I, p. 429.
[4] Bancroft: op. cit., Vol. II, p. 353.
[5] Hargrave Jennings: The Rosicrucians, 1887, Vol. I, p. 57.

of England a spell for turning the heart of a recalcitrant lover, which consists in throwing a little salt into the fire on three successive Friday nights; on the third one the lover is expected to return.[1] That the spell has to be carried out just on Friday illustrates very well how detailed is the determination of superstitions, and how careful one should be before concluding that any minor feature of one is devoid of meaning.

As might have been expected, bathing in the sea has been recommended for most of the purposes for which the combination of salt and water has been used. The following instances are characteristic. In Sardinia to drink from, or especially to bathe in, the sea is held to be a cure for childlessness.[2] Among the negroes in Guinea when a woman is pregnant for the first time she has to go through an elaborate ceremony of being purified in the sea.[3] Probably the original sense was to ensure an easy and successful labour.

The whole subject of the relation between salt and water may be concluded by referring to two practices that have nothing to do with the sea. A method of curing disease in Germany is to throw a handful of salt into water while these words are being repeated: 'I strew this seed (!) in the name of God; when this seed grows I shall see my fever again'.[4] A superstition in Bohemia says that when milk is being carried over water one should throw some salt into the water, otherwise the cow will be harmed.[5] It was remarked above that milk has the same symbolic significance as salt and here we see the two

---

[1] Henderson loc. cit.
[2] *Rivista delle Tradizioni Populari Italiane,* 1894, Vol. II, p. 423.
[3] Bosman: In Pinkerton: op. cit, Vol. XVI, p. 423.
[4] Wuttke op. cit., S. 335.
[5] Wuttke op. cit., S. 447.

substances treated interchangeably. In this connection it is
of interest that Browning, in his ' Pietro of Abano ', changes
the usual belief that sorcerers cannot tolerate salt by
describing how a magician dare not drink milk; the poet's
insight reveals the meaning of this

All's but daily dry bread· what makes moist the ration?
Love, the milk that sweetens man his meal --alas, you lack·

In several of the varieties of the Cinderella theme (e. g.
in No. 179 of Grimm's fairy tales) salt is equally plainly
taken to be equivalent of love: the third daughter, on
being asked by her father to describe her love for him,
likens it to salt.

*   *   *

We have next to consider the female, recipient
substance conceived of as a solid· namely, beliefs developed from the liquid-solid and solid-solid hypotheses of
childhood that were mentioned above. The substance most
frequently used in this respect is *bread*, which, from its
consistence and food-value, readily lends itself to symbolic
purposes. Many of the superstitious beliefs in which it is
concerned have already been referred to. Its fertilising
powers may be illustrated by the Indian practice, performed
for the cure of barrenness, of ' eating a loaf of bread
cooked on the still burning pyre of a man who was never
married, and who was the only or eldest son in his family,
and so received the fullest possible measure of vitality '.[1]
The association between bread and excrement is even
more plainly shewn in the following Slavonic beliefs. The
spirits of fruitfulness were supposed to dwell in the dung-

[1] Census of India, 1901, XVII, p. 164.

heaps, and offerings used to be made to them there. In later times witches were believed to hold their revels there, and it was not safe for a peasant to relieve himself on the spot without having in his mouth a piece of bread as a charm.[1] In England the people used to throw wheat on the bride's head as she returned from the church,[2] evidently a precursor of the more modern fertility (seminal) symbol of rice.

The wide-spread use of the combination of salt and bread for all the purposes for which salt alone is used (confirming oaths, warding off evil, etc.) has been previously described. The sexual significance of the combination comes to open expression in the following instances. In Waldenburg the bride secretly places salt and bread in her shoe so that she may be blessed with children;[3] the fecundity significance of the shoe, which is a typical yoni symbol (hence the throwing of it at weddings), has been fully described by Aigremont.[4] In the Potsdam Kreis betrothed couples place salt and bread in their shoes,[5] with of course the same meaning. In Russia salt and bread are the first articles to be carried into the dwelling of a newly married pair.[6] Among the Southern Slavs the combination in question is used as a love charm,[7] while in the more pious canton of Berne it has the function of fortifying against temptation the person who carries it.[8] Going back to Ancient Rome we find that Ceres, the grain Goddess, and Neptune, the

[1] Krauss Slavische Volksforschungen, 1908, S. 71.

[2] Moffet: Health's Improvement, 1655, p. 218.

[3] Aigremont: Fuss- und Schuh-Symbolik und Erotik, 1909, S. 55; Wuttke op cit., S. 370.

[4] Aigremont: op. cit., S. 42-64.

[5] Seligmann: op cit, S 38.

[6] Lawrence: op. cit., p 185.

[7] Krauss op. cit., S 169.

[8] Lawrence: op. cit., p. 182.

sea God, were worshipped together in the same temple;[1] the wife of Neptune, however, was called Salacia[2] (compare our word 'salacious' = libidinous).

Other substances than salt were used together with bread at times, with a similar significance. Perhaps the commonest of these was *cheese*. The combination is very potent against the evil eye, especially when carried round the neck;[3] it was also used to protect children from witches and malignant spirits.[4] In an old Welsh legend bread and cheese is used as a love charm to seduce the Lady of the Lake.[5] In this combination cheese is evidently the active element, while in others it is treated as the passive, recipient one. This is so in the various customs relating to what is called, from its association with child-birth, the 'Groaning Cheese' or 'Groaning Cake'; pieces of this, tossed in the midwife's smock, or placed under the pillow at night, cause young women to dream of their lovers.[6] The same is true of the custom, which still occasionally obtains in Europe, of using *urine* in the manufacture of cheese.[7] Urine is also used in some countries in bread-making, and there is reason to think that this was so even in Europe prior to the introduction of barm and yeast;[8] in 1886 a baker in Paris 'regressed' so far as to be detected in using water-closet refuse in the preparation of bread, which was said to deteriorate in quality as soon as the practice was put an end to.[9] The

[1] Frazer: op. cit., Second Edition, 1907, Part IV, 'Adonis, Attis, Osiris', p. 412.

[2] Plutarch: op. cit.

[3] Seligmann: op. cit., S. 38, 94.

[4] Brand: op. cit., Vol. II, p. 79.

[5] Rhys: Celtic Folklore, 1901, Vol. I, Ch. I, 'Undine's Cymric Sisters', pp. 3, 17, 18.

[6] Brand: op. cit., p. 71.

[7] Bourke: op. cit., pp. 181-2.

[8] Bourke: op. cit., p. 39.

[9] Bourke: op. cit., p. 32.

theme of moisture and dryness of bread plays a central part in an interesting Welsh legend:[1] A young man who had fallen desperately in love with a Lake Maiden sought, on his mother's advice, to woo her with the offer of some bread—a naive proposal which would be simply foolish if taken literally, but which when read symbolically is seen to be full of meaning. The maiden rejected the offer on the ground that the bread was too hard-baked. He returned, again on his mother's advice, with some unbaked dough, but was once more unsuccessful for the opposite reason to the previous one. On the third attempt, having achieved the proper consistence, he was successful. In another version of the same group of legends the suitor was enabled to capture the maiden through the magic power he had attained to by eating a piece of moist bread that she had allowed to float ashore.[2] In the Bible (Ezekiel iv. 15) it is stated that the Lord commanded the Jews to prepare their bread with cow's dung instead of with human ordure.

Finally in this connection may be mentioned the combination of *sweat* and bread. This was believed to have powerful aphrodisiac properties, doubtless an extension of the exciting effect that the odour of sweat has on many people, and at the time of the witches women were accused of rubbing dough on their bodies and giving it to men to eat in whom they wished to arouse satanic love.[3] We probably have here, as Aubrey suggested,[4] the explanation of the ancient game of cockle-bread,[5] in which the players, young women, go through the pretence of moulding bread

[1] Rhys: op. cit., pp. 4-6, 27, 28.

[2] Rhys. op. cit., p. 17.

[3] Paton: *Folk-Lore*, Vol. V, p. 277.

[4] Aubrey: Remaines of Gentilisme and Judaisme (1686), 1881 Edition, p. 43.

[5] See Brand· op. cit., p. 413.

with their back. It is a Negro, as well as a Belgian, superstition
that if you give a dog some bread soaked in your sweat he will
follow you to the ends of the earth: he is yours.[1] We have here
a repetition of the loyalty idea so characteristic of salt, the
bond, however, being cemented here by the combination of
the male and female elements in place of the male alone.

Nor is bread the only recipient substance in such
customs. Of the many other combinations may be mentioned ·
milk and resin,[2] curds and beans,[3]—both of these combinations are cures for sterility—salt and meal,[4]—a charm
to enable girls to see their future lover in a dream—
sweat and ` cake,[5]—used throughout Northern and Centra
Europe as a love charm—blood and cake,[6]—used in
Transylvania for the same purpose—and blood mixed with
the excrement of a dead person[7]—a cure for impotence.
The reverse of the same idea is presented in the superstition
that if one eats an egg without salt one will get a fever,[8]
significance being evidently attached to the combination.
The erotic meaning of this is indicated by association in the
saying that 'to kiss a man without a moustache is like
eating an egg without salt.' There is of course an extensive
nativity symbolism attaching to eggs, especially in religion.
In Bavaria and elsewhere an egg will guard against the
evil eye.[9] A Devonshire cure for ague was to bury an egg
in earth at the dead of night.[10]

---

[1] Hartland · Perseus, op. cit., p. 124.
[2] *North Indian Notes and Queries*. Vol. III, p. 96.
[3] Sacred Books of the East XXIX, p 180
[4] Wuttke · op cit, S. 244
[5] Hartland. op cit, p 123
[6] Hartland: op. cit., p. 124.
[7] Von Wlislocki: op. cit, S 140.
[8] Wuttke: op. cit., S. 311.
[9] Seligmann: op. cit., S. 330.
[10] Brand op cit, Vol III, p. 298.

The act of partaking of the same food has constantly been used to symbolise a more intimate union, representing the solid-solid infantile hypothesis described above. It is a Scandinavian saying that if a boy and girl eat of one morsel they grow fond of each other.[1] In many parts of the East Indies the betel-nut is employed as a love charm, is given as a love pledge, and the chewing of one quid by both parties is the essential part of the wedding ceremony.[2] Among the Manchus a dumpling is brought into the bed-chamber, when the bride and bridegroom each partake of a piece so as to ensure numerous offspring.[3] In Ancient Greece the bride and bridegroom used to eat of a quince together.[4] With many Hindoo tribes a woman never eats together with a man throughout her whole life, with the sole exception of the wedding-day, when after the sindúr dán ceremony described above she sits at table together with her husband. Hartland[5] records a very large number of instances, from all parts of the world, in which eating together, particularly from the same dish, constitutes an important or even essential part of the wedding ceremony, and there is no need for us to enumerate any more of these. The best known is the *confarreatio* ceremony of the Romans in which the man and woman ate together of the sacrificial cake, the *panis farreus*. Our own wedding-cake is a survival of these customs.[6]

The religious significance of the act, as illustrated by wedding ceremonies, is of considerable interest. In Christianity there has been a close association between it and

[1] Thorpe: Northern Mythology, 1851, Vol. II, p. 108.

[2] *L'Anthropologie*, Vol. III, p. 194.

[3] *Folk-Lore* Vol. I, p. 488.

[4] Plutarch: Solon, xx.

[5] Hartland: op. cit., pp. 343-53; See also Rhys: op. cit., Vol. II, pp. 649, 650.

[6] Brand. op cit., Vol. II, pp. 101, 102; Hartland: op. cit., pp. 351, 352.

the rite of the Holy Eucharist. In the old Parisian marriage ceremony the priest, after saying mass, blessed a loaf and wine; the loaf was bitten and a little of the wine drunk by each of the spouses, one after the other, and the officiating priest than taking them by the hands led them home. In a Yezidi wedding a loaf of consecrated bread is handed to the husband, and he and his wife eat it between them. The Nestorians require the pair to take the communion. Indeed, until the last revision of the Book of Common Prayer the Church of England commanded that 'the newly married persons the same day of their marriage must receive the Holy Communion', a practice that continues to be recommended.[1]

The material of the Eucharist, like all other consecrated substances, has been endowed with various non-religious powers, such as ability to ward off the evil eye, to cure sterility,[2] and so on. A curious example, full of symbolism, is the Welsh tradition that 'flying snakes'[3] originated in ordinary snakes that had become transformed by drinking the milk of a woman and eating the bread of the Holy Communion.[4] We have traced above the underlying significance of the Catholic salt and water baptism, and also that of the various customs and beliefs relating to bread. It is interesting that in Italy the combination of salt and bread is known as 'lumen Christi', and is of course endowed with magical properties.[5]

Consideration of the symbolism dealt with above, particularly the equivalency of salt and wine and the alimentary connotations of bread, makes it plain that the

[1] The preceding instances are quoted from Hartland. op. cit., p. 347.
[2] Hartland: Paternity, op. cit., p. 7.
[3] The armorial emblem of Wales is a dragon.
[4] Owen: Welsh Folk-Lore, 1887, p. 349.
[5] Seligmann. op. cit., S. 38.

deeper significance of the Eucharist and Holy Communion is throughout a sexual one. This sexual meaning forced itself into open expression with some of the Christian sects. Thus, according to St. Augustine, the Manichaeans prepared the sacred host by incorporating the Eucharistic bread with human semen, and their descendants, the Albigenses and Catharistes, preserved this custom.[1] Here, as elsewhere, heresy, by unveiling the symbolism of a given aspect of religious dogma or ritual, has uncomfortably compromised the religion it caricatures, just as the perversions of a brother often disclose the meaning of his neurotic sister's symptoms which are merely disguised manifestations of the same tendencies.

It need hardly be said that demonstration of the sexual origin and meaning of the materials used in a given religious ritual is far from explaining even the unconscious basis of that ritual. To do so with the Eucharist, for example, it would be necessary to discuss a number of other matters not directly connected with the present inquiry, particularly the incestuous basis of the union implied in the ceremony, its relation to theophagy and anthropophagy, and so on.

*   *   *

I wish here to say something about an interesting feature of superstition in general, and of salt symbolism in particular—namely, its *ambivalency*. It has often puzzled observers of superstitions to note that the very same custom or happening is supposed in one place to bring luck, in another ill luck, in the one place to lead to fertility, in another sterility, and so on. The explanation is to be found in the ambivalent attitude of consciousness to the content of the unconscious, the source of all

[1] See Bourke op. cit, p 220, where full references are given.

superstitions. If the affect, which is always positive, that accompanies the unconscious idea finds a passage-way into consciousness, as happens, for instance, in the process known as sublimation, then the attitude towards the conscious representative of this idea (i. e. towards the symbol) will be correspondingly positive, and the symbolic idea will be considered the source of all good. If, on the contrary, it is the affect belonging to the 'repressing' tendencies that gets attached to the symbolic idea, then the latter will come to be the sign of all that is unlucky or dangerous. The same ambivalency is seen in regard to all products of the unconscious, for instance in totemism – whether of the race or of the individual, the same animal can be loved in infancy and unreasonably feared in later childhood. So, as was remarked earlier in this essay, it is really irrelevant whether a given superstition is met with in a positive or a negative sense, the essential point being the evidence given by both of an excessive significance derived from the unconscious.

This ambivalency can be well demonstrated in salt superstitions. One finds that practically every attribute described above as being attached to the idea of salt may in other places be replaced by its exact opposite. We may illustrate this feature by selecting a few examples of contrasting pairs.

1. *Fruitfulness—Unfruitfulness.*

The remarkably close association between the ideas of salt and fecundity was dwelt on in detail in the earlier part of this essay (pp. 122, 123, 136, 137), and a few examples were also quoted in which the former idea was related to that of barrenness. This latter seems to have been more especially common in Eastern countries, and is repeatedly referred to in the Bible (e. g. 5 Moses xxix. 23; Job xxxix. 6;

Jeremiah xvii. 6; Psalms cvii. 33, 34, etc.); it is also remarked on by Pliny, Virgil, and other classical writers.[1] A real ground for it was no doubt the frequent sight of salty deserts and waste places where an excess of salt had prevented all growth. This real justification for the association between salt and barrenness makes still more striking the far commoner one between it and fertility, and again shews how the latter belief must have been caused by a false association of ideas, as has been maintained above.

The analogy is again evident here between the ideas of salt, of which either the absence or the excess prevents fruitfulness, and sexuality, concerning which the same is widely believed. It is thus appropriate that Lot's wife, as a punishment for regretting the (homosexual) sins of Sodom, should have been turned into a pillar (phallus) of salt.

2. Creation—Destruction.

This antithesis is of course closely allied to the last one and might also be expressed as the contrast between immortality and death. It has at all ages been a common custom to add strength to a curse by strewing salt as a symbol of destruction; historical examples are· after the destruction of Sichem by Abimelech, of Carthage by the Romans, of Padua by Attila, and ,of Milan by Friedrich Barbarossa. The custom seems to have had especial reference to the overpowering of a town (a mother symbol), another hint of the unconscious association between creation and destruction (compare the beliefs in the fructifying and the destroying sun).

3. In the same connection may be mentioned the antithesis between *the use of salt and the abstention from salt*. This has been discussed above in relation to religious observances and the question of sexual abstinence (pp. 139, 140, 141).

---

[1] Schleiden: op. cit., S. 94.

4. *Value—Worthlessness.*

The extraordinarily high sense of value often attached to the idea of salt, and also the close relation between it and that of money or wealth, has been described above (pp. 118, 119, 153), and we have now to note the opposite of this. Schleiden,[1] after quoting passages from Homer and Theocritus to the same effect, says: 'A grain or two of salt thus became an expression for the most worthless thing that one could name. We still say, when we want to denote anything trifling: "With that one couldn't even earn the salt for one's bread".' The same attitude of depreciation is shewn in the joke of the traveller who after partaking of an extremely poor meal at an inn called the landlord to him and said: 'There was one thing in this meal that I have not seen surpassed in all my travels.' On the expectant landlord inquiring what it was, the traveller crushingly answered. 'The salt'.

5. *Health—Unhealthiness.*

We have noted above (pp. 122, 141, 142) the discussion whether the partaking of salt is especially a health-bringing procedure or the exact opposite.

6. *Purity—Impurity.*

Salt has always served as an emblem of immaculateness and purity. Pythagoras says in this connection: 'it was begotten of the purest parents, of the sun and the sea' (another example, by the way, of the signification of fire and water that was pointed out above). The important part salt has played, e. g. in religion, in regard to purification need not again be insisted on. The extraordinarily close association between the ideas of salt and of the excretions, i. e. dirty processes, on the other hand, has been pointed out in detail above, and we shall presently

---

[1] Schleiden. op. cit., S. 101.

have to note the same thing in connection with the etymological history of the word. There is thus here the sharpest contrast between two opposite conceptions.

7. *Friendliness—Unfriendliness.*

Whereas the offering of salt is generally a sign of friendly intentions, we have also noted examples of the exact opposite (pp. 114, 115, 146).

We have already discussed the significance of this striking ambivalency. It is a characteristic of all ideas that have deep unconscious roots, and may roughly be said to correspond with the antithesis of 'the repressing' and 'the repressed'. The obverse of this statement is also true, that an idea which shews pronounced ambivalency in its affective values must have important associations in the unconscious. From the fact alone, therefore, that the idea of salt shews such marked ambivalency it could have been surmised that it has been invested with extrinsic significance of unconscious origin. One also gets here a further clue as to the meaning of ambivalency· it is evidently related to the contrast between on the one hand the over-valuing of sexuality in general, and the excremental aspects of sexuality in particular, in the unconscious and in infantile life, and on the other hand the under-valuing of these in consciousness and in adult life. An individual analysis, however, of the infantile origin of all the separate attributes belonging to the salt idea, e. g. the relation of purification to fertilisation, though of considerable importance, cannot be undertaken here, for it would lead us too far from the main theme of the work.

*   *   *

We may now pass to another aspect of the subject, the *etymological* one. It is becoming more and more realised by psycho-analysts that symbolisms gradually formed through 'repression' during the progress of civilisation leave traces of their original meaning as word-deposits. It is even probable that the correctness of the interpretation of a given symbol, such as the one attempted in this essay, could be accurately tested by being submitted to a sufficiently exhaustive comparison with the etymological and semantic history of the words denoting the ideas in question. From this point of view it becomes desirable, therefore, to say a little about the history of the word 'salt', though a lack of expert knowledge will necessarily render the present consideration of it very incomplete.

It seems to be definitely established that the names for salt in nearly all European languages find their earliest expression in an old Celtic word which meant 'water' or 'bog'. Schleiden[1] writes as follows: 'The Celts brought with them from their original Indo-Germanic sources some form of the root "sar", which in Sanscrit meant in the first place "to walk", "to go", "to flow", etc., and then in a derived form as "sara" also "river", "water", "sea", "pond". No such word meaning salt is to be found in the Vedas, in the Avesta, nor in any of the cuneiform writings, but in Armenian it occurs as "agh" (*gh* is a common substitute for *l*), thus constituting a bond between "sara" (= water) and the Greek ἄλς[2] (= sea-water and salt). . . . Many words that are either truly Celtic or else have passed through the Celtic language still recall the original meaning of this root word as "sea", "lake", "pond", "pool", "puddle". In Old Irish "sál" means moor or swamp, "salach" is Old Irish, "halou" Old Welsh for dirty;[3] the Old High German, Middle High German, and Anglo-Saxon "sol" means

---

[1] Schleiden: op. cit., S. 15, 16.

[2] The initial *s* has been replaced by *h* only in Greek and Welsh.

[3] So the Old Welsh 'halog' (= contaminated, impure) and 'halou' (=faeces).

a puddle or pool, the sporting words in German "suhl" (= slough) and "suhlen" (= to wallow), which are used in regard to wild swine; the Low German "sólig", meaning dirty, the French "sale" (= unclean, impure). . . . The word has always retained a specially close association with the idea of water.[1] In Greek the word "hals" with an altered gender, feminine, practically means the sea, just as "sal" did with the Latin poets. Also the rivers which contained salt water or which passed by sources of salt are called by names that in all probability are all related to "salt".' (Schleiden then gives a long list of such rivers and places).

Hehn[2] suggests that σάλος (= salum), meaning 'bog', 'lagoon', 'brackish water', belongs to the same series. It originally signified the sea outside the harbour, and thus also the swell of the sea within the harbour; we get here perhaps another hint of the relation between 'sal' and 'salire' mentioned above.

It has been suggested[3] that this root word 'sar' was applied to salt to indicate the crackling or spurting of salt when thrown into fire or water, and in support of this it may be added that in the only European languages where the word for salt does not proceed from this root (Lithuanian 'druska', Albanian 'kripe')[4] a word signifying 'to strew' is used to denote it. This suggestion is not, however, accepted by any philologist, and it seems certain that the main reason for the use of 'sar' was the connotation of the latter as 'flowing', 'bog', etc., and the resemblance of this to salt-water.

It is thus plain that the original signification of the word was 'a dirty fluid'. The facts just adduced are

[1] In New Persian also 'neme' (= salt) originally meant 'moist'
[2] Hehn op. cit., S. 25.
[3] Schleiden: op. cit., S. 17.
[4] Hehn: op. cit., S. 29.

certainly striking, and, especially in view of the derivative words that bear the closest relation to the idea of excrement, they may be regarded as an extrinsic confirmation of our conclusion—one which would hardly have been suspected without a detailed investigation—that the idea of salt and water is inherently allied to that of excretion, particularly urine. What was once a conscious association has in the course of centuries become more and more concealed, but though it has disappeared from sight it has in so doing by no means disappeared from existence.

IV

After this somewhat prolonged excursion we may now return to our original starting-point, namely, the superstitious belief that to spill salt at table is unlucky. The belief is practically universal and was as prevalent in Ancient Greece and Rome as in Modern Europe.[1] It has been applied to other precious substances besides salt: for instance, in China it is unlucky to spill the contents of an oil-jar.[2] In Germany even to play with salt is unlucky,[3] and for every grain spilt one will have to wait a day (or a week) before heaven's gate.[4]

It has been thought that the superstition in question arose from the over-spilling of the salt by Judas at the Last Supper,[5] a rationalistic explanation on a level with that which traces the superstitions concerning the number thirteen to the presence of thirteen at the same meal. Folk-beliefs of this order have a far wider and older range than purely Christian ones. The evidence adduced above points unequivocally to a quite different explanation, one

---

[1] Lawrence: op. cit., pp 167, 168.
[2] M. Cox: An Introduction to Folk-Lore, 1904, p. 10
[3] Wuttke: op. cit., S. 311.
[4] Wuttke: loc. cit.
[5] Lawrence. op. cit., p. 166.

which may be indicated by comparing the unlucky act in
question with that of Onan described in Genesis (xxxviii. 9).
In the light of it attention may be directed to the following
features of the superstition. Although the spilling of salt is
supposed to bring ill-luck in general,[1] its specific effect is
to destroy friendship[2] and to lead to quarrelling;[3] moreover
it brings ill-luck to the person towards whom the salt
falls[4] as much as to the one who has spilt it. It acts, in
other words, by disturbing the harmony of two people
previously engaged in amicable intercourse. From what has
been said above about the unconscious symbolism of eating
in company it will be intelligible why the spilling of a vital
substance at such a moment should be felt to be, some-
how or other, a peculiarly unfortunate event. To the unconscious, from which the affective significance arises, it is
equivalent on one plane to ejaculatio praecox, and on a
more primitive plane to that form of infantile 'accident'
which psycho-analysis has shewn[5] to be genetically related
to this unfortunate disorder. The original meaning of the
superstition is hinted at in the Prussian belief[6] that to spill
salt at a wedding betokens an unhappy marriage, and in
the opinion of the 'antiques',[7] who

> 'thought love decay'd
> When the negligent maid
> Let the salt-cellar tumble before them'.

It is probable that the ill-luck was formerly conceived
of as rendering the salt-spiller susceptible to the malevolent

[1] Brand: op. cit., Vol. III, pp. 160, 162.

[2] Lawrence: op. cit., pp. 169-71.

[3] Brand: loc. cit.; Lawrence: op. cit., pp. 166, 167.

[4] Lawrence: op. cit., p. 166; Brand: op. cit., pp. 161, 162.

[5] Abraham. 'Uber Ejaculatio praecox', *Internationale Zeitschrift
für Psychoanalyse*, 1916, Bd. IV, S. 171.

[6] Wuttke. op. cit., S. 210.

[7] Brand: op. cit., p. 163.

influences of evil spirits,[1] and the throwing of salt over the left shoulder, with the idea of averting the ill-luck,[2] has been thought to have the object of hitting the invisible demon in the eye and so disabling him.[3] This apparently wild suggestion has its proper meaning, which we need not go into here, but it is more likely that the true object of the proceeding was to make a propitiatory offering to the demon;[4] it has a suspicious resemblance to the Burmese custom of throwing food over the left shoulder in order to conciliate the chief spirit of evil.[5] The maleficium of evil beings is predominantly concerned with interference with sexual relations and disturbances of the sexual functions; I have elsewhere pointed out in detail that the dread of it comes from the fear of impotence.[6] Counter-charms against maleficium largely consist of symbolic acts which either assert the person's potency or serve to re-establish it; instances of both kinds may be found in connection with the averting of evil due to the spilling of salt. In the latter class may be counted the procedure of throwing some of the spilt salt, over the left shoulder, into the fire,[7] the symbol of virility; this custom is still practised in America.[8] To the former class belong the counter-charms of throwing some of the salt out of the window,[9] and of crawling under the table and coming out on the opposite side.[10] to throw something through an aperture, or to crawl

---

[1] Lawrence. loc. cit.

[2] Dalyell. op. cit., p. 101.

[3] Lawrence: op. cit, p 167.

[4] Dalyell· loc. cit.; Lawrence: loc. cit.

[5] Lawrence: loc. cit.

[6] Der Alptraum, loc. cit.

[7] Brand: op. cit., p. 161.

[8] Johnson What they say in New England, 1896, p. 92

[9] Wuttke: op. cit., S. 312.

[10] Lawrence: op. cit, p. 170.

through one, symbolises in folk-lore, dreams, and mythology, the effecting of the sexual act, a symbolism which has given rise to a large group of beliefs and customs.[1] The explanation of why the salt has to be thrown *backwards*, and why precisely over the *left* shoulder, would open up themes too extensive for us to enter on here; it is one of the many respects in which the analysis offered in this essay remains incomplete.

V

Two alternative hypotheses were set forth above concerning the origin of the excessive significance that has so widely been attached to the idea of salt, and it is maintained that the evidence detailed establishes an enormous balance of probability in favour of the second one. According to this a great part of the significance is derived, not from ideas relating to salt itself, but from ideas with which these have been unconsciously associated. Significance has been unconsciously transferred to the subject of salt from emotional sources of the greatest importance to the personality. The natural properties of salt, which in themselves can account for only a part of the feeling with which the salt-idea has been invested, are of such a kind as to render the association of it with another substance, of universal import, an easily-made, if not an inevitable one. The significance naturally appertaining to such an important and remarkable article of diet as salt has thus been strengthened by an accession of psychical significance derived from deeper sources. Freud's view that superstitions always have a hidden logical meaning, that they constitute a betrayal of unconscious mental processes, is thereby fully confirmed in this particular example, as it has been with all the other

---

[1] Róheim: 'The Significance of Stepping over', *International Journal of Psycho-Analysis*, 1922, Vol. III.

superstitions I have investigated. This hidden meaning has the characteristic attributes of the unconscious, notably in its ambivalency, its typically sexual nature, and its close relation to infantile mental processes.

The conclusion reached, therefore, is that *salt is a typical symbol for semen*. But semen itself is ontogenetically not a primary concept, being a replacement of an earlier one concerning urine, and we have correspondingly been able to trace the roots of salt symbolism to an older source than the seminal one. There is every reason to think that the primitive mind equates the idea of salt, not only with that of semen, but also with *the essential constituent of urine*. The idea of salt in folk-lore and superstition characteristically represents the male, active, fertilising principle.

An intuitive appreciation of the truth of this last sentence is afforded by the following panegyric paragraphs taken from the daily press, where they were headed: Man as 'Salt of the Earth', Science versus Suffragists.

'Whilst the suffragists are loudly claiming equality with man—if not superiority—it has been left to scientists to establish that man is literally the "salt of the earth". Two famous French savants have just announced the result of a long series of investigations, which convinces them beyond all question of doubt that woman is unalterably man's inferior, because of the smaller percentage of chloride of sodium in her blood.

'In other words, the blood of the male is more salt than that of the female, and observations of animal life show that the more salt there is in the blood the higher the intelligence and general development. The indictment does not end there, for these savants declare that their combined physiological and psychological investigations have proved that woman is inferior to man in everything— intelligence, reason, and physical force. The facial angle of the female, they add, more closely resembles that of the higher animals than the male, while woman's senses are less keen than those of man and she feels pain less.

'The scientific explanation is that the blood of the female is poorer in red blood corpuscles, and therefore relatively poorer in brine, which has been found to be the important factor in the development of the individual.'

*   *   *

The fact that the customs and beliefs relating to salt are exactly parallel to those relating to sexual secretions and excretions, the complex and far-reaching way in which the salt-idea is interwoven with matters of sex, particularly with potency and fertilisation, the universality of the beliefs in question, the faultless illumination that every detail of the customs and beliefs relating to salt receives as soon as their symbolic signification is recognised, and the impossibility of adequately explaining them on any other basis, are considerations that render it exceedingly difficult to contest the hypothesis here sustained; in fact this can hardly be done except by ignoring the facts adduced above. The validity of the hypothesis rests on the grounds that it completely fulfils both canons of scientific reasoning: it enables one to resume disparate phenomena in a simple formula that renders them more comprehensible, and to predict the occurrence of other, previously unknown phenomena in a way that is susceptible of verification.

The only opposing position that can seriously be maintained is that, however important the association in question may have been in the past, it is no longer operative—except possibly among primitive peoples, so that the only agent responsible for the persistence of the superstition in modern times is the force of meaningless tradition. This raises an extremely important general problem—namely, how far ancient symbolisms are still operative in the minds of civilised people. The tendency of the average layman would be to regard such symbolisms as merely relics from a distant past, and to look upon knowledge concerning them as having no direct bearing on matters of present-day life.

The importance they have, however, is far from being a simply antiquarian one.[1] Psycho-analytic investigation has shewn not only that symbolism plays a much more extensive part in mental functioning than was previously imagined, but also that there is a pronounced tendency for the same symbolisms to recur quite independently of the influence of other people. This is in entire accord with modern mythological and anthropological research,[2] for it is known that identical symbolisms occur in different parts of the world, and in different ages, in circumstances that preclude the possibility of their having been merely transmitted from one place to another. There appears to be a general tendency of the human mind to symbolise objects and interests of paramount and universal significance in forms that are psychologically the most suitable and available. That these stereotyped forms of symbolism are produced

[1] Roughly speaking it may be said that owing to the action of 'repression' the sexual meaning of such symbolisms retreats from view during the development of civilisation in much the same way as it does during the development of the individual. In both cases, however, the retreating from view means only a disappearance from consciousness, not from existence.

[2] It will be gathered from the whole tone of the present essay that the author attaches especial importance to the inter-relation of psycho-analytic and anthropological research. The anthropologist's material is rendered much more intelligible by psycho-analysis, and his views can there be submitted to verifiable tests with actual individual minds, while on the other hand through this material the psycho-analytical conclusions receive extensive confirmation, correction, and amplification. The comparative study of both fields is mutually instructive, and much is to be expected in the future from the work of men such as Róheim who are equally trained in both fields.

quite spontaneously is a matter capable of direct demonstration. One finds, for instance, a country farmer unconsciously exhibiting in his dreams, in his mental reactions,
and in his psychoneurotic symptoms the identical symbolisms
that played a part in the religions of Ancient India or
Greece, and in a way so foreign to the conscious life of
his environment as to exclude with certainty any source
in either suggestion or tradition. In my observations of the
seminal symbolism of salt, for instance, with actual patients
I have come across reactions indicating unconscious attitudes
of mind exactly comparable to that implied in many of
the antiquated practices detailed earlier in this essay.

The most that these external influences can accomplish
is to direct the unconscious process into a given form,
but it cannot maintain this direction of interest unless the
form of symbolism assumed becomes linked with a
spontaneous interest of the individual. Thus, a person
brought up in a society that took no interest in a given
superstition would be less likely to develop the superstition
himself than if brought up in a different society—though
he might easily do so, nevertheless, especially if he were
of the obsessional type of mind; but—and this is the
important point—a person brought up in however superstitious a society would not develop a given superstition
unless it was of such a kind as to be capable of being
associated to his personal mental complexes. This
association is a purely individual one, and without it the
superstitious belief fails to appeal; it need hardly be said
that the process, particularly in civilised communities, is
most often entirely unconscious. To put the matter more
concretely: what is meant is that with every person who
has made his own a superstitious practice regarding salt,
who follows it from an inner motive, from a 'superstitious
feeling'—even though he might consciously maintain that

he did not believe in it—analysis would shew that the idea of salt was symbolising the idea of semen (or urine) in his unconscious mind, that this association was a personal one of his own.

The reason why certain superstitions are so widely prevalent is because the ideas are such as to render easily possible the forging of associations between them and personal ideas of general interest and significance. The conditions, however, have their definite limitations: the forging of the associations must not be either too easy or too difficult. From this point of view one may venture to suggest that the general decline of superstition among educated classes is not entirely due—as is commonly thought—to the more enlightened intelligence of such classes, but is also in part due to their greater cultural inhibition of symbolical thinking in general, and of sexual symbolism in particular.

A superstition such as that of salt-spilling is usually dismissed either as being too trivial to warrant the dignity of an explanation, or else with one that is obviously superficial and inadequate. Even in the opinions on the subject enunciated in psychological text-books the writer often gives the impression of having dispensed with an investigation sufficiently detailed to establish their validity. On the other hand, attentive consideration of any given superstition reveals how much we have to learn about the subject, and demonstrates that it is often, as in the present instance, connected with aspects of the human mind that are of fundamental importance. A psychology of religion, for example, is impossible without an understanding of superstition. Here, as elsewhere, Freud has shewn that a by-way in psychology may lead to country that yields an unexpectedly rich harvest.

CHAPTER V

THE GOD COMPLEX [1]

THE BELIEF THAT ONE IS GOD, AND THE RESULTING CHARACTER TRAITS

EVERY psycho-analyst must have come across patients amongst whose unconscious phantasies is contained the curious one in which the patient identifies himself with God. Such a megalomaniac phantasy would be barely comprehensible did we not know how closely the ideas of God and Father are associated, so much so that, from a purely psychological point of view, the former idea may be regarded as a magnified, idealised, and projected form of the latter. Identification of the self with the loved object occurs to some extent in every affection, and is a regular constituent of a boy's attitude towards his father; every boy imitates his father, pretends to himself that he is the father, and to a varying extent models himself on him. It is therefore only natural that a similar attitude may develop in regard to the more perfect Heavenly Father, and indeed this is in a certain sense directly inculcated in the religious teaching that one should strive to become as like the divine model as is possible (i. e. to imitate it), and in the belief that every man is a copy of God and contains the divine spirit within him. The transition from obedient imitation to identification is often

[1] Published in the *Internationale Zeitschrift für Psychoanalyse*, 1913, Bd. I, S. 313.

a rapid one, and in the unconscious the two terms are practically synonymous. The function of representing his king or state that is entrusted to an ambassador in a foreign country or to a governor in a foreign province has many a time been transgressed in history by opportunity allowing it to be exchanged for one of greater power; the Roman Empire, for instance, was perpetually exposed to this menace. In religion we see indications of the same process, though of course they are less evident. To the common people the figures of Buddha, Mahomet, Peter, and Moses mean something more than mere representatives of God, and we find even minor prophets and preachers speaking in the name of God with an authority so astounding as to preclude the idea of its arising solely in learning; in other words one feels sure that their conscious attitude is generally the product of an unconscious phantasy in which they identify their personality with that of God.

This phantasy is not at all rare, and possibly occurs here and there in all men, it is naturally far commoner with men than with women, where the corresponding one seems to be the idea of being the Mother of God. There is, however, a class of men with whom it is much stronger than is usual, so that it forms a constant and integral part of their unconscious. When such men become insane they are apt to express openly the delusion that they actually are God, and instances of the kind are to be met with in every asylum. In a state of sanity, that is to say when the feeling for reality and the normal inhibitions of consciousness are operative, the phantasy can express itself only after passage through this censorship, and therefore only in a modified, weakened, and indirect form. It is with these external manifestations that we are here concerned, and it will be the object of the present paper to indicate how from them the presence of what may be called a

'God-complex' in the unconscious may be inferred. This unconscious complex, like any other important one, leaves permanent traces of its influence on conscious attitudes and reactions, and analysis of a number of individuals with whom it is strongly pronounced shows that the character traits [1] thus produced constitute a fairly typical picture, one clear enough to be applicable for diagnostic purposes. It is intelligible that they necessarily resemble those characteristic of the father-complex in general, being indeed simply a magnification of these, they form in fact a part of this broader group, but one sufficiently peculiar in itself to deserve to be singled out and distinguished from the rest of the group.

The inductive generalisations arrived at on the basis of my observations do not altogether coincide with those that might have been expected from deductive consideration of the attributes popularly ascribed to God. A main distinction between them, for instance, is this· Whereas the aspect of God as the Creator is perhaps the most impressive in the ordinary mind, as illustrated by the conclusiveness with which the existence of God is commonly held to be settled by the question 'who else could have created the world?' or by more abstract ratiocinations about the necessity for a 'first cause', this aspect is far from being either the most prominent or the most typical to be represented amongst the phantasies belonging to a God-complex. The most striking and characteristic of these

---

[1] When George Meredith, in 'The Egoist', endowed the chief figure of the book with certain peculiarly human attributes, his friends individually reproached him for having laid bare to the world their hidden weaknesses, each seeing in the novelist's description a mirror of his own heart. The character-traits pointed out in the present paper are so widely spread that I run the risk of laying myself open to a similar charge, as indeed does everyone who attempts to contribute something to our stock of psycho-analytical knowledge.

would seem to be the ones relating to effective power in the broadest sense (omnipotence), and most of the external manifestations of the complex can best be stated in terms of this. In my experience the main foundation of the complex is to be discovered in a colossal *narcissism*, and this I regard as the most typical feature of the personalities in question. All the character-traits presently to be described can either be directly derived from narcissism, or else stand in the closest connection with it.

Excessive narcissism leads inevitably to an excessive admiration for and confidence in one's own powers, knowledge, and qualities, both physical and mental. Two psycho-sexual tendencies are especially closely correlated with it, the auto-erotic and exhibitionistic,[1] two of the most primitive in the life of the individual, and we shall see that they play a highly important part in the genesis of the character-traits. With the second of these, the exhibitionistic, there is always associated its counterpart, the instinct of curiosity and knowledge, and this also produces some of the end-results. From the intimate inter-association, therefore, of these impulses, the narcissistic, auto-erotic, exhibitionistic, and curiosity ones, it is comprehensible why any sharp separation of the character-traits from one another according to their origin is quite impossible, for many of them could be equally well described under any one of the four, being related to all. It will thus be convenient to describe them as a whole, and not separately.

One other general remark may be made before we proceed to the details, and that is to call attention to the characteristically negative way in which these instincts are manifested in the syndrome in question; for instance,

[1] See Stekel: 'Zur Psychologie des Exhibitionismus', *Zentralblatt für Psychoanalyse,* Jahrg. I., S. 494.

excessive modesty is more often met with than pronounced
vanity. The reason for this is that' the unusual strength of
the primitive tendencies has called forth an unusually
strong series of reaction-formations, and it is these that,
being more superficial in the mind and more in harmony
with social feelings, manifest themselves most directly. In
fact one can often infer the strength of the underlying
impulses only through noting how intense are the reactions
they have evoked.

We may begin the series by mentioning some manifestations of narcissistic exhibitionism, i. e. the wish to
display the own person or a certain part of it, combined
with the belief in the irresistible power of this. This power,
which is the same as that ascribed to the tabu king[1] or
to the sun and lion symbols of mythology, is for either
good or evil, creation or destruction, being thus typically
ambivalent. In the instances under consideration the harmful
element predominates, another interesting difference between
this phantasy and the (modern) conception of God.

These first manifestations, like those throughout the
whole complex, are most typically reaction-products. Thus
obvious self-conceit or vanity is not so frequent or so
characteristic as an excessive self-modesty, which at times
is so pronounced as to be truly a *self-effacement*. The man
advances his strongest convictions in the most tentative
manner possible, avoids the word 'I' in both conversation
and writing, and refuses to take any prominent or active part
in the affairs of life. Already the exaggeratedness of this
betrays it as being an affectation, not a primary character-
tendency but a reaction to one, and this becomes still
more evident when we observe the more extreme forms
of the trait. These constitute what I consider to be the
most characteristic manifestations of all—namely, a tendency

[1] See Freud· *Imago*, 1912, Bd. I, S. 306-15.

to *aloofness*. The man is not the same as other mortals, he is something apart, and a certain distance must be preserved between him and them. He makes himself as *inaccessible* as possible, and surrounds his personality with a *cloud of mystery*. To begin with, he will not live near other people if he can avoid it. One such man told me with pride he lived in the last house of his town (a Metropolis) and that he found this already too near to the throng, so he intended to move farther away. Such men naturally prefer to live in the country, and if their work prevents this they try to have a home outside the town to which they can retire, either every evening or every week-end. They may come in daily to their work and never mention their home address to their friends, using when necessary clubs and restaurants for whatever social purposes they need. They rarely invite friends to their home, where they reign in solitary grandeur. They lay the greatest stress on privacy in general, this being of course both a direct expression of auto-erotism (masturbation) and a reaction against repressed exhibitionism. There are thus two elements in the tendency in question, the wish not to be seen, and the wish to be distant or inaccessible; sometimes the accent is on the one, sometimes on the other. Both are well illustrated in the following phantasy that a patient once confessed to me: his darling wish was to own a castle in a distant mountain at the very extremity of the country (near the sea); as he drove up to it he was to sound a terrific horn in his automobile so that the blast would reverberate along the hills (thunders of Jehovah and Zeus, paternal flatus), and on hearing it the servants and retainers were to disappear to their underground chambers, leaving everything prepared for him in the castle; under no circumstances were they ever to see him. Such men in actual life interpose all manner of difficulties in the way of being

14

seen, even on business; appointments have to be made
long beforehand or secretaries have to be interviewed, and
when the time arrives they are either late or are 'too
busy' to come at all. How prominent this feature of
inaccessibility is with the nobility, kings, popes (!) and
even important business men[1] is well known. A by-product
of the desire for distance, one which has also other roots,
is a keen interest in the matter of communication and in
improved means for enabling them to annihilate distance;
they invariably travel first-class or else by automobile, thus
keeping apart from the mob, insist on having the best
system of telephones (which presents the advantage of
allowing them to communicate without being seen), and so
on. This trait is in striking contrast with the fact that such
people do not willingly travel long distances, especially out
of their own country. They always feel best at home,
dislike going to the world and insist on making it come
to them.

The sense of this desire for inaccessibility is at once
seen when we consider its extreme exaggerations, as met
with in insanity. The late paranoiac King Lewis of Bavaria
would seem to have shewn a typical case of this. It is
said that he began by imitating Louis XIV ('obligation of
the name'—Stekel), and proceeded to identify himself
formally with Le Roi Soleil. It is further related that at
this stage he refused to interview people unless there was
a screen between him and them, and that when he went
out his guards had to warn people of his approach, to
get them to hide in time and shelter themselves from his

---

[1] H. G. Wells, in his novel 'Tono-Bungay', gives an amusing
description of the difficulties in obtaining an audience with a successful
financier. The applicants are sorted out in room after room by one
secretary after the other, and only a very few are fortunate enough to
penetrate to the Holy of Holies and come face to face with the great
man himself.

magnificent presence. Such behaviour can only indicate the belief that the rays emanating from this presence were charged with power of destruction, and the king's solicitude possibly covered repressed death-wishes. We have here a recrudescence of the old Egyptian, Persian and Grecian projection of the father as a sun-god, one that played an important part also in early Christianity. The significance of it in paranoia, as well as of the interesting and not rare 'aiglon' phantasy, was pointed out by Freud in his Schreber analysis.[1] In insanity the patient may identify both his father and himself with the sun, as in the instance just mentioned, or else only the former, as with a paraphrenic patient of mine who spent the greater part of ten years defiantly staring at the sun. In more normal people such phantasies remain in the unconscious, and only a refined form of them can penetrate through to consciousness, such as the desire for aloofness. This desire, therefore, seems mainly to express, in an indirect way, a colossal narcissistic-exhibitionistic tendency, being based on the person's belief that his proximity is fraught with tremendous power on other people, and that the glory of his presence may dazzle or even blind them; as a precaution against such terrible consequences he withdraws to a distance whenever possible. A repressed tendency that also plays a part in determining this attitude is revealed by consideration of the fear of blinding others. This of course symbolises the fear, i. e. the repressed wish, that he may castrate them, and we shall see later that both this wish and the accompanying fear of being castrated are prominent characteristics of the group of complexes under consideration.

The other trait of *mystery*, mentioned above in conjunction with that of inaccessibility, may be regarded as the mental correlate of this; thus the broad tendency

---

[1] Freud: 'Nachtrag', *Jahrbuch der Psychoanalyse*, Bd. III, S. 588.

14*

of aloofness displays itself by the desires, on the physical side of being inaccessible, on the mental side of being mysterious. The person aims at wrapping himself in an impenetrable cloud of mystery and privacy. Even the most trivial pieces of information about himself, those which an ordinary man sees no object in keeping to himself, are invested with a sense of high importance, and are parted with only under some pressure. Such a man is very loth to let his age be known, or to divulge his name or his profession to strangers, let alone to talk about his private affairs. I know of a man who has lived for eight years in a town in Western America without any of his friends there being able to find out whether he is married or not; anyone who knows something of the publicity of American private life will realise what a feat this is. Some little characteristics about writing are derivatives of the same tendency. A man of this kind writes unwillingly, particularly letters.[1] He dislikes to part with such expressions of his personality, and also finds the not-answering of letters of other people to be a convenient way of indicating his opinion of their importance.[2] In spite of a great interest in accurate language, of which we will speak later, he rarely expresses his thought clearly and directly. Very characteristic is a lengthy, involved and circuitous form of diction that at times becomes so turgid and obscure as to render it really impossible for the reader to discover what is meant. The more important is the topic (to the writer) the more difficulty does he have in parting with his valuable

---

[1] It need hardly be said that there are many other causes for this inhibition besides the ones here mentioned.

[2] Napoleon expounded this contemptuous attitude very wittily. He is said to have formed the rule, particularly during busy times, of never answering a letter until it was three months old. On being once criticised for this, he remarked taht it saved much trouble for he found that most letters answered themselves in this time.

secret. The most important part is often not written at all, but instead is constantly hinted at with repeated promises that it will be disclosed on a further occasion. In striking contrast with this is the fact that the actual hand-writing is typically clear and distinct. With some such men it is the opposite, quite illegible, but with both kinds the person is inordinately proud of it, whether of the distinctness or of the obscurity. In any event he insists that it is peculiar to himself, apart, and unique. (In general nothing offends such a man as the suggestion that he resembles someone else, whether it be in handwriting, in personal appearance, in capacity, or in conduct.) The veil of mystery and obscurity that he casts over himself is naturally extended so as to cover all those pertaining to him. Thus he never spontaneously refers to his family, speaking of them reluctantly when any inquiries are made about them, and the same applies to any affairs in which he may have become concerned. That all this privacy refers not only to narcissistic self-importance, but also to auto-erotism[1] in general, and particularly to masturbation, is too well-known to need special emphasis here. The primary narcissistic tendency leaks through in the curious trait that when the reticence is abrogated, as during psycho-analysis or during a confidential chat with an intimate friend, the person takes the greatest pleasure in talking about himself in the fullest minuteness and is never weary of discussing and dissecting his own mental attributes. He is apt to be a successful lecturer and after-dinner speaker, showing a fondness for this that contrasts with his other reactions to exhibitionism.

[1] The prominence of this in the present group of complexes explains the frequency with which the type under consideration presents the two character-traits of an interest in philosophic discussions on the nature of truth (pragmatism, etc.), with a low personal standard of honour in the matter of probity and truthfulness.

The tendency to aloofness also manifests itself on the purely mental side quite directly. Such men are both unsociable and unsocial, in the wider sense. They adapt themselves with difficulty to any activity in common with others, whether it be of a political, scientific or business kind. They make bad citizens as judged by the usual standards;[1] however interested they may be in public affairs they take no part in them, and never even vote, such a plebeian function being beneath their dignity. Any influence they exert is done so quite indirectly, by means of stimulating more active admirers. Their ideal is to be 'the man behind the throne,' directing affairs from above while being invisible to the crowd. To follow, to participate, or even to lead, in a general movement, whether social or scientific, is repugnant to them, and they use every effort to maintain a policy of magnificent isolation. In this they may achieve, as Nietzsche did, true grandeur, but more often they present merely a churlish egotism.

As is to be expected, such a strong exhibitionistic tendency as that indicated by the traits just mentioned must have a counterpart in a strongly developed complementary instinct—namely, the pleasure in visual curiosity ('scoptolagnia'), though there are fewer characteristic manifestations of these in the syndrome. They differ from the previous ones in being more often of direct origin, and not reaction-formations. There is usually present a quite womanish curiosity about trivial personalities, gossip and the like, though generally this is concealed and is betrayed only on occasion. More often a higher form of sublimation occurs, and this typically takes the form of *interest in psychology*. If the person in question is endowed

---

[1] Very characteristic is the combination of bad citzenship in a practical sense with a keen theoretical interest in social reform, which will be spoken of later.

with a natural intuition for divining the minds of others,
is a judge of human nature, he will make use of this
in his profession whatever it may be; if he is not so
endowed he tends to become a professional psychologist
or psychiatrist, or at least to take a considerable abstract
interest in the subject. This desire to compensate a natural
defect furnishes no doubt one of the explanations for the
notorious circumstance that professional psychologists so
often display a striking ignorance of the human mind. It
also accounts for their constant endeavour to remedy their
defiency by the invention of 'objective' methods of studying
the mind that are to make them independent of intuition,
and their antagonism to methods, such as psycho-
analysis, which deliberately cultivate this; the flood of
curves and statistics that threatens to suffocate the science
of psychology bears witness to the needs of such men.
To revert to our typical man: he takes a particular
interest in any methods that promise a ' short-cut' to the
knowledge of other people's minds, and is apt to apply
such methods as the Binet-Simon scale, the psycho-
galvanic phenomenon, word-association reactions, or gra-
phology in a mechanical and literal manner, always hoping
to find one that will give automatic results. The more
unusual the method the more it attracts him, giving him
the feeling of possessing a key that is accessible only to
the elect. For this reason he is apt to display great
interest in the various forms of thought-reading, cheiro-
mancy, divination, and even astrology, as well as in occult-
ism and mysticism in all their branches. This topic connects
itself with that of religion on the one hand, and the
various manifestations of omniscience on the other, both
of which will presently be discussed.

Certain less direct products of narcissistic exhibitionism
may be grouped under the heading of *omnipotence phantasies.*

These may extend over every field where power can be exhibited, so that it becomes impossible to discuss them in detail; they are particularly apt to apply to unusual ones, therefore claiming powers possessed by the few. Perhaps the commonest is that relating to money, a matter closely connected, in fact and fancy, with the idea of power. The person imagines himself a multi-millionaire, and revels in the thought of what he would do with all the power then at his disposal. This phantasy is usually associated with a pretended contempt for money in real life, and sometimes with an actual generosity and freedom in the use of it; the amount actually possessed is so infinitesimal in comparison with what he possesses in his imagination that it is too small to treasure.

The most characteristic sub-group in the present connection, however, are those relating to *omniscience*. This may be regarded as simply a form of omnipotence, for whoever can do everything can also know everything. The passage from the one to the other is clearly seen in the case of foretelling; to know beforehand when something is going to happen is in itself a kind of control, merely a weakened form of actually bringing the thing about, and the transition between a deity and a prophet is historically often a very gradual one (!).

One of the most distressing character-traits of the type under consideration is the *attitude of disinclination towards the acceptance of new knowledge*. This follows quite logically from the idea of omniscience, for anyone who already knows everything naturally cannot be taught anything new; still less can he admit that he has ever made a mistake in his knowledge. We touch here on a general human tendency, one of which the psycho-analytical movement has already had much practical experience, but it is so pronounced in the present character that it cannot be passed over without a few words being devoted to it. In the first place, men with this type of character talk even more than other men about their capacity to assimilate new ideas, and are sometimes lavish in their abstract admiration for the new. But when put to the test of being confronted with a new idea that doesn't proceed from themselves, they offer an uncompromising resistance to it. This follows on the usual well-known lines, being merely exaggerated in intensity. The most interesting manifestations are the modes of acceptance, when this does occur. There are two typical forms of these. The first is to modify the new idea, re-phrase it in their own terms, and then give it out as entirely their own; the differences between their description and that given by the discoverer of the new idea they naturally maintain to be of vital importance. When the modifications made are considerable they are always of the nature of a weakening of the original idea, and in this case the author of them usually adheres to the new conclusion. Sometimes the resistance to the new idea is indicated by the modifications being simply changes in nomenclature, or even in spelling (!), and then later reactions of the person show that he has never seriously accepted the new idea, so that his old repugnance to it will sooner or later be again evident. The second mode, closely allied to the first and often combined with it, is to devalue the new idea by describing it in such a way as to lay all the stress on the links between it and older ones, thus putting into the background whatever is essentially new in it, and then claiming that they had always been familiar with it.[1]

[1] A beautiful instance of this performance occurred recently. I had written a paper on Freud's theory of the neuroses, dealing principally, of course, with the importance of infantile conflicts, repressed sexual perversions, etc. A very distorted abstract of it appeared in a French journal, finishing with the assurance that 'since Janet's works all these ideas had long been current in France.'

Of especial importance is the subject's *attitude towards time*. The idea of time and its passage is so intimately bound up with such fundamental matters as old age and death, potency, ambitions, hopes, in short with the essence of life itself, that it is necessarily of the greatest importance to anyone who claims omnipotence and omniscience. Like all lesser things it must therefore be under his control, and this belief is revealed in a number of little traits and reactions. His own time is naturally the correct one, therefore his watch is always right and any suggestion to the contrary is not merely repudiated, but resented; this confidence is sometimes maintained in the face of the strongest evidence against it. *His* time is also exceedingly valuable in comparison with that of others, so that, quite consistently, he is usually unpunctual at an appointment, but is most impatient when others keep him waiting; time in general belonging to his domain, it is for him to dispose of, not for others. An exception is provided by those members of the group that adopt the definition of punctuality as 'la politesse des rois,' and who find pleasure in demonstrating their perfect control over time by being absolutely exact (one thinks of Kant's daily four o'clock walk).

The attitude towards *past time* chiefly concerns their personal memory. This they regard, like their watch, as infallible, and they will stoutly defend the accuracy of it to the last lengths; in support of this they cultivate with attention an exactitude in such things as quotations, dates, etc., which can easily be checked. In some cases they are proud of their excellent memory, but more typically they regard it as something obvious and are annoyed when any of their success is attributed to it.

The capacity to foretell demonstrates the power over *future time*, and this occupies a great deal of their interest. To speculate about the future of an acquaintance, an enterprise, a nation, or even the whole human race, is a matter of quite personal concern, and they freely give vent to all manner of predictions, most often of a sinister kind. One of the most characteristic of all the present series of character-traits is the person's firm belief in his ability to *foretell the weather,* and particularly rain or thunder. The vagaries of weather have always played a prominent part in the phantasy of mankind, not only on account of their obvious importance for his welfare, but because the utter variability of them seemed to point directly to the activity of supernatural beings, whether good or evil. Christian congregations that would consider it unreasonable to expect the Deity to improve the landscape at their request, or even to change the temperature, still pray earnestly for modifications of the weather, and almost the last belief about witches to die out was that they were responsible for the production of inclement weather. The weather is the part of nature that most flagrantly defies both the prescience and the control of modern science, rivalling in this respect the human mind itself; one may say that the chief evidences of spontaneity and free will to be found in the universe occur in these two spheres, so that it is little wonder that they are equally regarded as conspicuous exceptions to the natural laws of determinism and order and as manifestations of an external agency. In addition to all this, it is easy to show that the various elements have always possessed considerable symbolic significance, rain, wind, and thunder in particular being taken to represent grand sexual-excremental performances; a thunder-storm is in this connection of especial importance, because it comprises all of the three. In view of these considerations it is not surprising that the present type should take the greatest interest in the subject of the weather, and should arrogate to himself special powers of prediction in regard to it. It is practically pathognomonic of the God-complex when a man maintains that he can invariably foretell a thunderstorm, relying on signs and methods that cannot be explained to anyone else, and regards as 'false prophets' all those who use other ones.

Such men also take a great interest in the subject of *language*, one which bears a symbolic relation to the last-mentioned. They pose as authorities on literary style, and often are so, claiming a 'mastery' of their mother-tongue. The style they affect is usually good, exact but not pedantic, but tends to be involved and even obscure; lucidity is not its virtue, and they find it difficult to express clearly what they have to say. With the thorough knowledge of their own tongue goes an aversion to foreign ones, which they often refuse to learn; their own is *the* tongue, the only one worthy to be noticed. They are fond of talking, especially in monologue, and usually excel in lecturing, speech-making, and conversation.

Two character-traits that bear an even more direct relation to narcissism are those concerning the attitude towards advice and judgement. They are very unwilling to give *advice*, the responsibility being too great. Any advice that they gave would be so precious and important that not to follow it would surely be disastrous. Rather than expose their friends to this risk they prefer to withhold their advice, another instance of apparent altruism. It goes without saying that any advice tendered to them by others is contemptuously rejected as worthless.

The attitude towards *judging* is also characteristic. It is a double one, consisting of an alternation of extreme tolerance and extreme intolerance. The question of which of the two is shown seems to depend on whether the infringement to be judged is of their own will or merely of that of other people. In the former case no punishment is too harsh for the offender; I have heard such men describe, just like a child, how they would execute various people who disobeyed them, tradesmen who were behind time, and the like. In the second case, on the other hand, they are always in favour of the greatest leniency and broad-minded tolerance. They thus advocate the abolition of capital punishment, the more humane and understanding treating of criminals, and so on.

The subject of *religion* is usually one of the greatest interest to such men, both from the theological and historical side and from the psychological; this sometimes degenerates into an interest in mysticism. As a rule they are atheists, and naturally so because they cannot suffer the existence of any other God.

We may now briefly mention a few character traits that, though pronounced, are less distinctive, inasmuch as they are of such general occurrence; they only belong here because they are almost always prominent features of the present type. One of these is an exaggerated *desire to be loved*. This is rarely shewn directly, or at most by a desire for praise and admiration rather than for love. It is commonly replaced by its opposite, an apparent indifference to and independence of the opinion of others, and the repressed need often betrays itself in such ways as a theoretical interest in the action of crowd suggestion, intense belief in the importance of public opinion, pliant yielding to convention in deeds in spite of a rejection of this in words.

Like all other human beings, they are convinced in their unconscious of their own *immortality*, whether this be ensured through direct continuity or through an eternal series of rebirths; they have thus neither beginning nor end. The belief in their *creative power*, as was mentioned above, is more subordinate, at all events in comparison with other ones, than might have been expected, yet it is often pronounced enough. The belief in self-creation, and rebirth phantasies, are practically constant features. It is further revealed in such phantasies as visions of a vastly improved or altogether ideal world, naturally created by the person in question, or even of the birth of a new planet where everything is 'remoulded nearer to the heart's desire';[1] far-reaching schemes of social reform also belong here. In general there is in such men a vein of romantic idealism, often covered by a show of either materialism or realism.

The idea of *castration* always plays with our type a part of quite special importance, both in the form of castration-wishes against the father (authorities) and of fear of castration (talion) on the part of the younger generation. The latter is as a rule the more pronounced of the two, and naturally leads to a fear and jealousy of younger rivals, this being in some cases remarkably intense. Beyond the constancy with which a strong castration-complex is present there is nothing characteristic about its numerous manifestations in this type, so that I will refrain from mentioning these, particularly as they are fairly well known. The resentment with which these men observe the growing prominence of younger rivals forms a curious contrast to another character-trait, namely their *desire to protect*. They are fond of helping, of acting as patron or guardian, and so on. All this, however, happens only under the strict condition that the person to be protected acknowledges his helpless position and appeals to them as the weak to the strong; such an appeal they often find irresistible.

[1] English readers will at once think here of the numerous works of H. G. Wells that excellently illustrate this phantasy; he does not appear, however, to present any other characteristics of our type, at least not in a striking degree.

The reader will probably have realised the difficulty I have experienced in grouping such multiple traits and will therefore allow me to repeat them now in a more concise fashion. Thus, the type in question is characterised by a desire for aloofness, inaccessibility, and mysteriousness, often also by a modesty and self-effacement. They are happiest in their own home, in privacy and seclusion, and like to withdraw to a distance. They surround themselves and their opinions with a cloud of mystery, exert only an indirect influence on external affairs, never join in any common action, and are generally unsocial. They take great interest in psychology, particularly in the so-called objective methods of mind-study that are eclectic and which dispense with the necessity for intuition. Phantasies of power are common, especially the idea of possessing great wealth. They believe themselves to be omniscient, and tend to reject all new knowledge. The attitude towards time and towards the foretelling of weather, particularly thunderstorms, is highly characteristic. The subjects of language and religion greatly interest them, and they have an ambivalent attitude towards those of giving advice and of judging (e. g. punishment). Constant, but less characteristic, attributes are the desire for appreciation, the wish to protect the weak, the belief in their own immortality, the fondness for creative schemes, e. g. for social reform, and above all, a pronounced castration-complex.

An obvious consideration, and one important not to forget, is the fact that all Gods have not the same attributes—although there is much that is common to them all—so that the God-type will vary according to the particular God with whom the person identifies himself. By far the most important of these variations is that depending on the idea of the Son of God, therefore in Europe of Christ. This gives a special stamp to the type in question,

which must shortly be indicated. The three chief characteristics are: revolution against the father, saving phantasies, and masochism, or in other words, an Oedipus situation in which the hero-son is a suffering saviour. With
this type the mother plays a part of quite special importance, and her influence is often shown in the particular
attributes described by Freud in his harlot-saving type.[1]
Saving phantasies, where what is to be saved from the
'wicked father' varies from a given person (e. g. Shelley's
first wife) to the whole of mankind (democratic reform,
etc.), are thus extremely common here. The salvation is
often to be effected at the expense of a terrific self-sacrifice,
where the masochistic tendencies come to full satisfaction.
These also reveal themselves in the trait of extreme humility and altruism, especially striking in men who originally
were unusually virile and aggressive, e. g. St. Francis of
Assisi. Second only to the importance of the mother who
has to be rescued is that of the oppressive father. There
is thus constantly present an intolerance of authority of
any kind, and any person invested with this, or even only
with seniority or pre-eminence, may be viewed in the
light of this complex so that his figure is artificially distorted into the *imago* of the wicked father. With this
Christ type there invariably goes also an anti-semitic tendency, the two religions being contrasted and the old
Hebraic Jehovah being replaced by the young Christ. The
castration-complex is if possible even more pronounced in
this variety than in the main type described above.

It is interesting to see that the character evolved
through the influence of the God-complex in general tends
to belong to one or the other of two extreme kinds. On
the one hand, if the complex is guided and controlled by

[1] Freud: 'Beitrage zur Psychologie des Liebeslebens', I, *Jahrbuch der Psychoanalyse*, Bd. II, S. 389.

valuable higher factors, it may give us a man who is truly God-like in his grandeur and sublimity; Nietzsche and Shelley are perhaps good instances of this. On the other hand—what unfortunately we see more commonly, particularly in patients during analysis—we find characters that are highly unsatisfactory, with exaggerated self-conceit, difficulty in adapting themselves to life in common with ordinary men, and therefore of no great use for social purposes. Probably this can be correlated with the unconscious basis of the complex, the enormous narcissism and exhibitionism. The last named instinct is of all the sexual components the one most closely related to the social instincts, being in a sense a definition of the individual's attitude towards his fellow man, and one can see a similar ambivalence in the value of its products; on the one side, by giving a greater self-confidence and self-estimation, and a powerful motive to achieve a good standing in the estimation of others, it supplies a driving force that greatly contributes towards successfully coming forward in life, while on the other side when either exaggerated or not properly directed it gives rise to difficulties in social adjustment through a false sense of values.

In conclusion we may refer to a few considerations, which though evident have to be mentioned so as to avoid the possibility of misunderstanding. In the first place, the picture sketched above is a composite one, just like any other clinical picture. The individual details are from separate studies and artificially fused, just as a text-book description of typhoid fever is. I have never seen anyone who presented all the attributes mentioned above, and it is very possible that such people do not exist; at all events in every case some of the attributes are more prominent than others. Then I would further emphasise the fact that the present description is quite tentative, necessarily so

15

because it is based on only one person's experience of about a dozen analyses bearing on the problem,[1] in other words on evidence that is certainly insufficient to establish a sharply drawn syndrome. I am convinced that there is such a thing as a God-complex, and that some of the attributes above mentioned belong to it, but am equally convinced that the present account of it needs modification, and probably both expansion in some directions and limiting in others. The present paper is thus published mainly as an incentive to the further investigation of an interesting series of character-traits.

----

[1] Experience of many more cases during the ten years since this paper was written has only confirmed the main outlines here sketched so that no alterations have been made in it.

CHAPTER VI

THE INFLUENCE OF ANDREA DEL SARTO'S WIFE ON HIS ART[1]

IT HAS been a problem to many generations of art students to explain why Andrea del Sarto, in spite of his stupendous gifts in every branch of painting, should have failed to reach the front rank as an artist. The more carefully his work is analysed in detail the more wonder does it wring from the spectator, and especially from the connoisseur. His drawing was unrivalled in its flawlessness, and defies all criticism; he was the finest colourist of his day, and in this respect has never been excelled except by a few of the Venetian school; of chiaroscuro he was an absolute master; his composition was well-nigh perfect in its harmony; his frescoes remain to-day to show us the highest that could be reached in this domain; and his technical skill was applied with a sensitiveness of tact, a sureness of judgement, and an excellence of good taste that are beyond reproach. It is little wonder, therefore, that, even by a critical generation, he was given the title of 'il pittore senza errori'. Added to these accomplishments must be reckoned that he lived in Florence, a contemporary of Raphael and Michel Angelo, at the time when the Renaissance art reached its very acme, before there was

[1] Published in *Imago*, 1913, Bd. II, S. 468.

yet any serious sign of the decadence that was soon to set in, and when the very air was thrilling with inspiration. Yet, in spite of all this, we are confronted with the startling fact that Andrea never attained true greatness in his art, that there is something essentially lacking in his work which robs it of any claim to rank with that of the greatest masters.

A few quotations from expert judgements will describe both Andrea's excellences and his defects far better than I can pretend to do. Sir Henry Layard considers his earliest remaining work (in the Annunziata), done at the age of twenty-two, to be 'an instance of the highest level, in point of execution, attained by fresco',[1] and Leader Scott also says of it 'this might well be classed as on the highest level ever reached in fresco.'[2] Guinness writes of him: 'He interprets the secrets of nature with a force so completely victorious over every difficulty of technique that the effort appears to be to him but as child's-play, and his utterances are but a further manifestation of her intimate mysteries. . . . The works of men like Buonarotti and Leonardo betray a hundred subtleties of invention, and astonish with a sense of difficulties aimed at and overcome. But Andrea knew none of these complexities; difficulties of technique did not exist for him. . . . The supreme gift which had early gained for him the title *senza errori,* and the native simplicity of his character, left him without desire to startle; he aimed at nothing beyond the reach of his facile brush, and the longer the spectator beholds his works the deeper grows his admiration before their absorbing unity and *ensemble.* . . . It is this quality of natural simplicity and lack of exaggeration which makes del Sarto to so large a degree the artist who appeals to artists rather

[1] Layard in the 5th edition of Kugler's Handbook of Painting, 1887, Part II, p. 457.

[2] Leader Scott: Andrea del Sarto, 1881, p. 92.

than to the ordinary public, who do not understand the
noble simplicity of his work, and his stupendous powers
of technique.'[1] Of Andrea's masterpiece, the Madonna di
San Francesco, he says, 'the beauty of this picture is
beyond praise', and of the Scalzi frescoes that 'their
technique reveals the almost superhuman force of the artist,
who—within the limitations of chiaroscuro—has here
proved himself a complete master of colour. . . . They have
been equalled by no other artist in Italy.'[2] Of the famous
Last Supper picture he writes, 'No other word but brilliant
will express the jewel-like sense of colour and noble drawing
which strike the eye on entering the refectory of the Salvi
convent. It was the beauty of this marvellous creation
which saved it from destruction during the siege of Florence, when the soldiers who would have razed the convent
to the ground stopped spell-bound as they burst into the
refectory and were confronted by the noble drama which
the artist's brush had so vividly portrayed.'[3] Bottari speaks
of Andrea's 'Tabernacolo' as 'a divine picture, one of
the most beautiful works which ever issued from the hand
of man',[4] and similar panegyrics are common enough. A
sufficiently high one is contained in Michel Angelo's remark
to Raphael.

> Friend, there's a certain sorry little scrub
> Goes up and down our Florence, none cares how,
> Who, were he set to plan and execute

---

[1] Guinness: Andrea del Sarto, 1899, pp. v, 57, 58.

[2] Guinness: op. cit., pp. 21, 44, 45.

[3] Guinness: op cit., p. 42. Vasari's account of this episode (Vol.
III, p. 224) is that the picture was saved by the officer in command.
The more florid version seems to have originated with Varchi (Storie
florentine, Vol. III, p. 186).

[4] Quoted by Guinness: op. cit., p. 32.

As you are, pricked on by your popes and kings,
Would bring the sweat into that brow of yours![1]

Andrea's defects are most pithily summed up in
Reumont's phrase, 'Greatness is lacking in his works'.[2]
He seems to have had no inner vision, no inspiration, no
ideal, and his pictures fail to move the observer to anything more than a sense of admiration at their abstract
beauty and perfection; he leaves one cold at heart, and
never conveys any feeling of a something beyond that has
been mysteriously revealed. Reumont writes for instance,
'Del Sarto's Madonnas are expressive of a fresh, blooming,
often robust nature, but they do not wear the halo of the
spiritual, of the inexpressible, of the yearning towards
heaven, with which we love to see the head of the Virgin
encircled, and without which she loses her finest charm.'[3]
Guinness puts it more apologetically thus: 'But if the soul
of Andrea lay in things of sense, and he missed the vision
of ideal beauty, the secret of visible beauty was truly his,
and was rendered by him with consummate skill. . . . He
courted no rivalry, he employed no tricks, he feared no
imputations of want of originality, but went directly to his
goal, attaining, as was, alas, inevitable with his want of
poetic idealism, the fault of faultlessness. In the Birth of
St. John the skilled hand of the artist has grown almost
mechanical in its ease; the grand attitude, the noble
drapery, the perfect equipoise of composition well-nigh

---

[1] This is the rendering given by Browning in his poem on
Andrea. The original, of which it is a free translation, may be found
in Bocchi's Bellezze di Firenze. It may be of interest in this connection
to recall that Andrea once copied a picture of Raphael's (Leo X) for
Ottaviano di Medici so skilfully as completely to deceive Giulio Romano,
who had helped Raphael paint the picture.
[2] Reumont: Andrea del Sarto, 1835, S. xv.
[3] Reumont: op. cit., S. 75.

oppress by their very perfection; and this last great fresco of the Scalzo series betrays the weakness as well as the strength of Del Sarto.'[1] Vasari sums him up as follows: 'In him art and nature combined to show all that may be done in painting, when design, colouring, and invention unite in one and the same person. Had this master possessed a somewhat bolder and more elevated mind, had he been as much distinguished for higher qualifications as he was for genius and depth of judgment in the art he practised, he would beyond all doubt have been without an equal. But there was a certain timidity of mind, a sort of diffidence and want of force in his nature, which rendered it impossible that those evidences of ardour and animation, which are proper to the more exalted character, should ever appear in him; nor did he at any time display one particle of that elevation which, could it but have been added to the advantages wherewith he was endowed, would have rendered him a truly divine painter: wherefore the works of Andrea are wanting in those ornaments of grandeur, richness, and force, which appear so conspicuously in those of many other masters.'[2] Browning, in his 'Andrea del Sarto'—a poem that contains a brilliant descriptive analysis of the painter and which betrays a wealth of psychological insight[3]—makes him realise both his capacity and his deficiency:

I can do with my pencil what I know,
What I see, what at bottom of my heart
I wish for, if I ever wish so deep—
Do easily, too—when I say, perfectly,

[1] Guinness: pp. 44, 57.

[2] Vasari: Lives of the Most Eminent Painters, English Translation, 1851, Vol. III, pp. 180, 181.

[3] The reason why this is so good is because it contains a considerable piece of unconscious self-analysis on the poet's part.

I do not boast, perhaps: . . .

. . . . . .

There burns a truer light of God in them,[1]
In their vexed, beating, stuffed and stopped-up brain,
Heart, or whate'er else, than goes on to prompt
This low-pulsed, forthright craftsman's hand of mine.
Their works drop groundward, but themselves, I know,
Reach many a time a heaven that's shut to me,
Enter and take their place there sure enough,
Though they come back and cannot tell the world.
My works are nearer heaven, but I sit here.

. . . . . .

Ah, but a man's reach should exceed his grasp,
Or what's a heaven for? All is silver-grey
Placid and perfect with my art: the worse!

The prominent characteristics, therefore, of Andrea's
work are his perfection of technique, his astounding facility,[2]
his unforced sincerity and natural simpicity; with these go
a lack of inspiration, an absence of 'soul' or of deep
emotion, an incapacity to express either a great poetical
or religious idea, or an ideal thought of any kind. There
have been two explanations given of this striking antinomy,
and they are usually held, no doubt with right, to be
mutually complementary rather than contradictory. The one
invokes an inborn lack of that indefinable quality called
genius, the other the unfortunate influence of the painter's
wife. The first of these will not be entered upon here,
but it is our intention to consider the second from the
point of view of psycho-analysis, and to see whether more
light can in this way be thrown upon it.

[1] i. e. his rivals.
[2] He never painted shades one above the other, like other painters;
all was finished from the first laying on, and with an unerring accuracy
and sureness of touch.

The essential facts of Andrea's life that bear on our problem are as follows. The exact date of his birth is disputed, but was certainly in the July of either 1486 or 1488, more probably the latter. He was the third of six children, having two older brothers. He became acquainted with Lucrezia del Fede, when she was the wife of another man, about 1511 or 1512,[1] and married her, after her husband's death, in 1513. He was thoroughly infatuated with her, sacrificed both his artistic prospects and the esteem of his friends in order to marry her, and, at her bidding, deserted his parents, whom he had previously supported; this infatuation lasted, apparently without the slightest intermission or change, until the end of his life. His wife was unquestionably a beautiful and attractive woman, but the character generally given her is decidedly the reverse of favourable. She is said to have been haughty, exacting, vain, entirely selfish, extravagant, and domineering. It is thus intelligible that the whole situation brought about an estrangement between Andrea and his friends, who regarded his conduct as that of a blind fool. Vasari writes on this point: 'When the news became known in Florence the affection and respect with which his friends had always regarded Andrea changed into disapproval and contempt. . . . But he destroyed his own peace as well as estranged his friends by this act, seeing that he soon became jealous, and found that he had besides fallen into the hands of an artful woman, who made him do as she pleased in all things. He abandoned his own poor father and mother, for example, and adopted the father and sisters of his wife in their stead; insomuch that all who knew the facts mourned over him, and he soon began to be as much avoided as he had previously been sought after.

[1] His first known portrait of her is to be found in the Nativity fresco of the Annunziata, painted at some time between 1511 and 1514.

His disciples still remained with him, it is true, in the hope of learning something useful, yet there was not one of them, great or small, who was not maltreated by his wife, both by evil words and despiteful actions: none could escape her blows, but although Andrea lived in the midst of all that torment, he yet accounted it a high pleasure.'[1]

Andrea was badly paid for his work, probably because he had no rich patron; for the Annunziata frescoes, for example, he got only 70 lire each. Some five years after his marriage he was asked by King Francis to come to the French court, an invitation which he accepted with alacrity; he was absent from Florence altogether from May the 25th, 1518 to October the 17th, 1519. In Fontainebleau he was received with every mark of esteem, was highly honoured by the King and his court, and was richly paid for his work; he is said to have painted over fifty pictures while in France—though doubtless some of these were by his pupil Squazzella whom he took with him—and for one alone he received 2,100 lire. The contrast between his previous sordid existence and this life of opulence and admiration must have seemed to him nothing less than magical. Pressure on the part of his wife, however, who was probably envious of his lot and also desirous of resuming her sway over him, led him to return to Florence. According to Vasari, 'She wrote with bitter complaints to Andrea, declaring that she never ceased to weep, and was in perpetual affliction at his absence; dressing all this up with sweet words, well calculated to move the heart of the luckless man, who loved her but too well, she drove

---

[1] Vasari op. cit., p. 194. Vasari should speak with some authority on this matter, for he was one of the pupils in question. He is unfortunately an unsafe author to rely on, being given both to distortion and confabulation, but the main points of the present story are to be confirmed from other sources, e. g. from Andrea's own portraits of himself and his wife.

the poor soul half out of his wits; above all, when he
read her assurance that if he did not return speedily, he
would certainly find her dead. Moved by all this, he resolved
to resume his chain, and preferred a life of wretchedness
with her to the ease around him, and to all the glory
which his art must have secured to him.'[1] He promised
the King faithfully that he would soon return to France,
hoping to induce his wife to come back with him, but
once home he was kept prisoner by his wife, who refused
to go to France; her principal motive in this refusal is
said to have been her reluctance to leave her father, a
part which throws some light on her general hysterical
disposition. Andrea thus flung away his brilliant prospects,
resumed his old life of misery and poverty, and became
more despised than ever for his conduct; it is related
that for some time he was afraid to shew himself in
the streets of Florence on account of the sneering
remarks he overheard.[2] He made attempts a little later
to regain King Francis' favour, and sent him several
pictures, but the King never forgave him or took any
further notice of him.

Of the rest of Andrea's life there is not much to be
told. He spent it in relative obscurity and poverty, for
instance, for the two finest of the Scalzo frescoes, the
Carita and Verita, he was paid twenty lire (in 1520), and
for his Entombment picture he received merely a bunch
of candles, the price also of his Madonna of Zanobi Bracci.

[1] Vasari: op. cit., p. 206. King Francis is said to have entrusted
him with large sums of money to buy pictures for him in Florence, but
which Andrea squandered on his wife. This widely accepted story, however, seems to have been one of Vasari's inventions, for recent
investigation of the King's accounts, which were kept with scrupulous
exactitude, shows that he gave Andrea no money except for the work
he had done. (See Guinness: op. cit., pp. 28, 29.)

[2] Reumont: op. cit., S. 113.

His wife was his principal model, and so obsessed was he with her appearance that her features recur again and again in all his female types. He lived with his wife, her daughter, and her sister, thus in an altogether feminine atmosphere, and died in January 1531 (at the age of 42) of the plague, deserted by his wife who feared to expose herself to the infection. The quality of his work, with certain exceptions, steadily deteriorated during these twelve years, although they naturally betray a greater ripeness and self-confidence; according to Guinness, 'for the most part his best works were painted before he was thirty-two.'[1] (i. e. before the year he decided not to return to France). Layard says that 'his facility led later to increasing mannerisms and emptiness',[2] and it is certain that his lack of inspiration became more and more evident during these last years.

Our problem, therefore, is to ascertain, if possible, how much of his failure is to be ascribed to Lucrezia's influence, and in what precise way did it produce its effect. History has furnished us with many examples shewing that passionate and enduring devotion to a beautiful woman is not always fraught with the happiest consequences to a man's career, but at least it has been given the credit of inspiring his art if he was a painter or poet. Must we be robbed also of this illusion? Yet the judgement of the critics is that the petty annoyances caused by Lucrezia's behaviour, the way in which she drove her husband to devote himself to making money instead of to enriching his artistic capabilities, and the general squalidness of feeling resulting from her lack of appreciation and imagination, conspired to kill in Andrea whatever soul he

---

[1] Guinness: op. cit., p. 56.
[2] Layard: op. cit., p. 460.

might have had, and stifled his genius for ever. To quote
again from Browning's poem:

Had you, with these [beauties] the same, but brought
                                    a mind!
Some women do so. Had the mouth there urged
'God and the glory! Never care for gain.
'The present by the future, what is that?
'Live for fame, side by side with Angolo!
'Rafael is waiting: up to God, all three!'
I might have done it for you. So it seems.

Perhaps if we examine more closely the precise mental
relationship between the two mates, calling to our aid
psycho-analytical knowledge in so doing, we may reach a
clearer understanding of the way in which it affected
Andrea. As soon as we do this it becomes clear that love
could not have been the sole feature comprising his attitude
towards Lucrezia, and that our understanding of the
situation must be imperfect unless we also take into consideration the influence of other emotions, especially that
of hate.

There are several good reasons for coming to this
conclusion. In the first place, there is in all people a
certain amount of ambivalence of affect, so that it is hardly
possible for an intense and lasting emotion to be aroused
without its opposite being at the same time stimulated and
an increase being caused of the natural counter-tendency.
Especially is this so when, as in the present case, the
emotion is unusually strong, for then it is almost inevitably
accompanied by a counter-emotion (of variable intensity)
in the unconscious.

In the second place, no man could have suffered what
Andrea did from his wife without its provoking a natural

resentment. To be foiled in his aspirations and ambitions, to be henpecked and hampered in his daily work, to be cut off from his friends and relatives, to have his life spoilt in every respect except one (that of possessing the woman he loved): these are things that would provoke even the mildest man. Whether the one compensation counterbalances all the rest, that is, to be sure, another matter. We may grant that with Andrea it did, so that he definitely preferred his present life to existence without Lucrezia, but he would not have been human if, side by side with this constant devotion, there was not produced in him as well a counter-reaction of (repressed) hate. Further, the fact that he was able to enjoy such a life of torment indicates a pleasure in suffering, a masochism, that is always accompanied by its opposite in the unconscious, namely sadism, with the tendency to hate that is apt to go with this; we shall recur to this in a moment.[1]

Thirdly, and perhaps most important, there is a deeper ground for supposing that Andrea's love for his wife was connected with unconscious emotions of a very different kind. For there is reason to believe that the normal homosexual component of the love-impulse, particularly the feminine variety of this, was unusually developed with him. It is at all events certain that before his marriage he entered into the enjoyment of male society with the keenest zest.

When he was twenty-one years old he was persuaded by an older friend, Franciabigio, to leave his master and to set up in a studio and lodgings which the two were to share in common; for a time they even signed their work in common. After living a year or so thus, Andrea changed his lodgings so as to be in the same street as two other

[1] The account of Strindberg's marriage, given in his 'Confessions of a Fool,' is an ample illustration of this paragraph.

friends, Sansovino and Rustici. His relations with Francia
are described as having been 'of the closest possible
friendship', while of his friendship with Jacopo Sansovino
Vasari writes, 'nay, so close an intimacy and so great an
affection was subsequently contracted by Jacopo and Andrea
for each other that they were never separate night or
day'.[1] During this time Andrea is said to have been a
great favourite in his circle, to have delighted exceedingly
in lively society, and to have taken a leading part in
various jokes,[2] not always too refined,[3] that were played in
the clubs of which he was a member. It is not to be
supposed that the surrendering of these pleasures through
his marriage cost him nothing.

It is not without significance that the friends to whom
he was most especially attached were all older than himself;
Francia by five years, Sansovino by two, Rustici by
fourteen, and so on. One cannot avoid connecting this
with the fact that he had two older brothers; in many of
his pictures one sees this mirrored by the portrayal of a
playful rivalry between the infant Jesus, sheltering in his
mother's arms, and one or more older boys (St. John the
Baptist, etc.).[4] Pointing in the same direction as these facts

[1] Vasari: op cit., Vol. III, p. 184.

[2] Vasari: op. cit., Vol. V, pp. 72-6;   Scott: op. cit., pp. 86, 87.

[3] Most of these were connected with food. To those familiar with
Ferenczi's work on homosexuality it may be of interest to know that
Andrea took an especial interest in the matter of eating, he did his
own marketing every morning in order to secure the choicest tit-bits of
his favourite articles of diet, covered the walls of his house with frescoes
representing scenes of cooking, table-laying, etc. (these are still to be
seen), and was so fond of good living that, according to Vasari, it
shortened his life by lowering his resistance to the plague.

[4] Dr. Havelock Ellis has called my attention to an indication of
homosexuality shewn in Andrea's art. According to Brücke (Schönheit
und Fehler der menschlichen Gestalt, S. 39), he gave his angels boys'
arms, instead of the more customary girls' arms.

is the description of Andrea's disposition as that of 'a gentle, diffident, mild-mannered and modest man'. Finally, if Vasari's statement is true that Andrea was 'tormented by jealousy',[1] we have the plainest evidence of homosexuality, for an obsessional jealousy[2] is an almost certain indication of this.

In these circumstances Andrea's attachment to his wife may be regarded, at least in part, as denoting a flight from his repressed homosexual tendencies. She became at once his anchor of salvation, to which he must cling at all costs, as well as the barrier against the satisfying of his repressed desires. As his refuge from himself she increased his love; as the person who deprived him of the pleasure of male society she increased his hate. This hate could not be allowed to become conscious because the reason for it was repressed, and could therefore manifest itself only by evoking an exaggerated amount of love to counterbalance it.

In his attitude towards his wife there was thus a constant conflict. The matter is still further complicated by the probability that much of his homosexual masochistic desire must have found satisfaction in her peculiar temperament; in other words, he loved her as a woman loves a man,[3] a common enough occurrence in marriage. We can

---

[1] Vasari: op. cit., Vol. III, p. 194.

[2] There is every reason to believe that Lucrezia was in reality faithful to him.

[3] He sometimes actually depicted her as a man, particularly (and appropriately enough) as Michael, the Christian god of war.

Of other complex-indicators in his paintings I will mention three. (1) On the pedestal of the Madonna in his masterpiece, mentioned above, are several harpies, which are of course entirely out of place in a subject of this character; so far as I know it is the only instance of a Pagan motive occurring in any of Andrea's works, and it is so striking here as to have given the picture the name of the 'Madonna dell'Arpie'. Critics

hardly think otherwise when we contrast his own meek disposition with her domineering haughtiness; it is also significant that she was some four years older than himself. Reumont's description of him as 'a good-natured, modest, unpretentious but weak man entirely at the mercy of his own impulses as well as of his dominant wife'[1] is in full accord with this conclusion.

We now begin to understand better the enormous hold that Lucrezia possessed over Andrea. His love was maintained in a constant state of high tension because it had to serve, in addition to its own functions, that of damming back both repressed hate and homosexuality. She could demand anything of him, and treat him however she liked, for without her he was lost; he could not afford not to love her.

Returning now to our main problem, of the influence of the situation on Andrea's art, we may wonder why the current conflict did not throw him back towards older, infantile ones (regression), from which he might derive deeper sources of stimulation, or at least why he did not seek an escape from them in his work. One answer to the former question probably is that the infantile complexes

have been completely mystified by this, but, if my suggestion concerning Andrea's *unconscious* attitude towards his wife is correct, it should not be difficult of explanation (2) A favourite topic of Andrea's, which he painted no less than five times, is Abraham's sacrifice of his son Isaac Critics comment on the wonderful benignity of the father in these pictures, and the implicit trust and self-surrender displayed by the son as he sees the father's knife approach In view of our remarks above on Andrea's homosexual masochism this also becomes more comprehensible. (3) Andrea shews a special preference for painting figures seated cross-legged on the floor, in the graceful composition of which he developed a remarkable skill It is hard not to connect this with the fact that his father was a tailor and that later in life Andrea changed his surname from Agnolo to del Sarto (Sarto = tailor).

[1] Reumont: op. cit., S 214

were either not strong enough to attract the driven back
Libido or else were incapable of being sublimated in the
desired direction; this is, it is true, an unsatisfactory sketch
of an answer, but to fill it in would mean the opening up
of many topics other than those we are here concerned
with. Another answer, applicable to both questions, is that
the current conflicts were of such a kind as to allow no
escape from them, even in phantasy. How could
Andrea sink himself into his art (flight into work) when
there was Lucrezia in the body, with him at every moment?
She was practically his sole model, she ordered the workshop,
directed what her husband was to do and what not
(according to what she thought would best pay), and left
him no moment of peace in which to develop his own
individuality. With right could Browning make him say,

> So—still they[1] overcome
> Because there's still Lucrezia,—as I choose.

The last three words express the core of the situation.
The love for Lucrezia, with its superadded sources that
we have indicated above, was stronger than all else,
including the desire for artistic expression, so that in this
sense it may perhaps be said that she was responsible
for the ruin of his genius. It would be a more accurate
way of putting it to say that she forced the internal battle,
which is necessary for all artistic creation, to be fought
out in the current details of everyday life, and so allowed
him no opportunity to gather strength and inspiration that
could be applied to higher aims. Her domineering master-
fulness enabled her to choose the scene of battle, and her
egocentricity demanded that she should be the centre of it.

---

[1] i. e. Raphael and others.

But after all, the reason for the situation lay at least as much in Andrea as in Lucrezia. If she had never existed he would probably, with his special temperament, have found another Lucrezia. And here one cannot help feeling the difference between a masculine, creative temperament and a feminine, receptive one, whether they occur in the body of a man or a woman being irrelevant. Scott says very justly in this connection· 'In looking at Andrea's pictures one sighs even in the midst of admiration, thinking that if the hand which produced them had been guided by a spark of divine genius instead of the finest talent, what glorious works they would have been! The truth is that Andrea's was a receptive, rather than an original and productive mind. His art was more imitative than spontaneous, and this forms perhaps the difference between talent and genius'.[1] As regards the development of Andrea's art, therefore, Lucrezia may practically be said to have played little more than the part of a lay figure; it was his temperament that made her mean to him all that she did. The problem is thus reduced, like so many psychological ones, to one of temperamental constitution. If Andrea had not been what he was, Lucrezia could not have played the part in his life that she did; but it is probable that if *she* had not been what she was he still would have tried to make her play that part, i. e. she still would have been to him the man, and not the helpmate woman. One side of his nature was developed, but not the other. I must once more quote from Browning's poem.

I know both what I want and what might gain,
And yet how profitless to know, to sigh
'Had I been two, another and myself,
Our head would have o'erlooked the world!' No doubt.

[1] Scott: op. cit., pp. 72, 73.

.   .   .   .   .   .

In this world, who can do a thing, will not;
And who would do it, cannot, I perceive;
Yet the will's somewhat—somewhat, too, the power—
And thus we half-men struggle.

In short, if Andrea had been able to react differently
towards his everyday difficulty, he might have displayed
the genius of a creator instead of merely the talent of a
skilful craftsman. He might have been an artist, and
was—only a painter.

CHAPTER VII

THE CASE OF LOUIS BONAPARTE, KING OF HOLLAND[1]

THE LIFE-HISTORY of Louis Bonaparte, the brother of the great Napoleon and the father of Napoleon III, is of no special interest in itself, but it acquires some extrinsic importance through the part he played in contributing to his brother's downfall, an event the interest and significance of which is such as to make worth while any attempt to throw further light on the problems surrounding it. For it was Louis' attitude towards his brother's views that precipitated the incorporation of Holland in the Empire, and so added one more to the nations that presently rose and overthrew Napoleon. An attempt will here be made to increase our understanding of this attitude by adducing some psychological considerations regarding Louis' personality.

The problem can be shortly described as follows:[2] Louis was made King of Holland by Napoleon's will on June the 5th, 1806, with the very grudging consent of

[1] Read before the American Psychopathological Association, May 8, 1913; published in the *Journal of Abnormal Psychology*, Dec. 1913, Vol. VIII, p. 289.

[2] The original authorities from which the following details are taken are for the most part dealt with in Atteridge's 'Napoleon's Brothers', Rocquain's 'Napoléon et le Roi Louis', and in Masson's works, so that it is not necessary to give individual bibliographical references here.

the Dutch. He had hesitated considerably before accepting the proposal, and once having done so he proceeded to take up an independent position in opposition to his brother. Napoleon's object was, of course, to bring Holland more directly under his own control than before, to merge her interests in those of France, and to make her join in his great contest with England. It was just a few months before he issued his famous Berlin decree, after which he went on to league the whole of the Continent against England in the blockade that was intended to starve her into submission by paralysing her export trade. Holland was at that time the chief point at which this trade entered the Continent, so that she could not remain neutral, but had to take one side or the other. To join with Napoleon would involve the practical destruction of her own trade, with extreme economic distress until the end of the war, but it was essential to his project that she should make this sacrifice, for which she might be recompensed by the restoring of her colonies if England were conquered. Her narrower national interests were therefore of necessity opposed to the general Continental scheme that Napoleon was aiming at, and Louis, although he had been sent to Holland purely for the purpose of supporting and enforcing this scheme, chose to adopt the Dutch point of view and hinder his brother's plans. He would not admit that he was merely a French prince governing what was practically a part of the Empire, in the interests of the latter as a whole, but regarded himself as an independent sovereign whose duty it was to rule in the interests of his subjects, a laudable enough aim if his view of his situation had only happened to be in conformity with the real facts. This attitude, which was indicated on the day of his State entry into the Hague by his allowing hardly any French to take part in the procession, in which

Dutch cavalry formed the escort, became more and more pronounced as time went on, in spite of the most vigorous protests from Napoleon, and extended to the whole sphere of government. In a book written many years later he stated that he entertained throughout different views from his brother on every question that concerned Holland, on the problems of conscription, religion, trade, war, and so on, as well, of course, as on the all-important matter of the Continental blockade. The efforts of the French officials were vain in their endeavour to suppress the wholesale smuggling that was rendering the blockade inefficacious, and Napoleon became more and more exasperated. Finally he was driven to undertake the gradual absorption of Holland into the Greater France he was then building up. Louis, seeing clearly whither hfs brother was trending, first consented to surrender all his territory up to the banks of the Meuse, but three months later, when the French army was ordered to march into Amsterdam, he abdicated in favour of his son and fled surreptitiously into Bohemia (July 3, 1810). His where-abouts were discovered two weeks later, but he resisted all Napoleon's entreaties and commands to return to France, and proceeded to Gratz, where he lived until just before the fall of the Empire. The incorporation of the whole of Holland into France immediately followed, and this led to chronic discontent and insurrection that lasted until the final overthrow of the French yoke in 1814.

The thesis here maintained is that Louis' conduct was not altogether due to his political blindness in refusing to recognise the inexorable facts of his situation, but was in part determined by his personal attitude towards Napoleon, a matter that becomes more intelligible in the light of modern psychopathology. His lack of co-operation with his brother was not confined to the period of his short

Dutch reign, but extended over some seventeen years, until the end of the Empire. Both before these years and after them he was an enthusiastic supporter and defender of his brother, so that we see two opposite tendencies manifesting themselves in his life. More than this, the beginning of the period of hostility synchronised with a complete change in his general character and disposition; we may therefore suspect that we have to do here with something that lay near to the core of his personality.

I proceed now to give an account, as brief as possible, of Louis' life, particularly in regard to his relations with his brother. As is well known, he was Napoleon's favourite brother, was educated personally by him, and was for many years hardly separated from him. Napoleon attached him to his staff when he was barely sixteen, and he remained in this position, passing through various stages of promotion, for the greater part of the next three years, from shortly after the fall of Toulon until nearly the end of the first Italian campaign. He seemed at this time to be a very active and promising officer; at the battle of Arcola he distinguished himself by acts of especial courage and daring, and at Lodi he is said—though this has been denied—to have saved Napoleon's life. Just after this, when he was in his twentieth year, came about the striking character change, which was to reduce him for the rest of his life to being little more than a useless encumbrance to all about him. It followed on a serious illness, of which we shall say more presently, and was marked by moodiness, depression, irresolution, seclusiveness and self-withdrawal, and above all by a most pronounced valetudinarianism. His main and permanent interest now became the care of his health, he tried one after another every cure, spa, and health-resort within reach, and he used this as a pretext to refuse, or to hesitate about accepting, all the duties that were successively imposed on him. In other words, he became a confirmed hypochondriac. He protested against going to Egypt with Napoleon, and was with him there only three months before he got permission to return to France. Three years later he refused to accompany his brother in the second Italian campaign that was to end in Marengo, going instead to Aix. In 1806 he hesitated about accepting the crown of Holland on account of the dampness of the Dutch climate, and when his brother over-ruled his objections he stayed in his new kingdom only a month before leaving for Wiesbaden, leaving the government in the hands of his ministers; within a week of reaching Holland he had written to Napoleon saying that he was suffering from the change of climate and must have a holiday. In the following year, in the contest with Prussia that culminated in Jena, he hesitated to join the army, was filled with concern lest the English should descend on Holland, and behaved throughout the campaign in such a pusillanimous and timorous manner as to convince even his brother that he was totally unfitted for military command. The year after, Napoleon, seeing that he did not serve his purpose in Holland, offered him the crown of Spain, but Louis refused it, on the ground that he was pledged to Holland. Two years later came the abdication and retirement to Gratz. When the Russian campaign was embarked on he remained in Gratz, prophesying disaster to his brother. At the beginning of 1813 he wrote to Napoleon offering his services on condition that his kingdom was restored, a demand that he repeated several times throughout the year, and in November he came to France, staying at his mother's chateau at Pont-sur-Seine. Napoleon pointed out that he was being hampered in his efforts to come to terms with the Allies by his brother's absurd pretentions to the throne of Holland at such a moment, and gave orders to Cambacérès, the Arch-Chancellor of the Empire, that if Louis did not make his submission within two days he was to be arrested. Louis fled to Switzerland, but late in January of 1814 he came to Paris and made his peace with Napoleon, whom he now saw for the last time. He was asked to assist his brother Joseph in the defence of Paris, but he deserted it on the eve of the Allies' attack. On Napoleon's return from Elba he refused to join him, stayed in Italy making sinister prophesies, and was the only one of the brothers, not even excluding the recalcitrant Lucien—who returned from England after a seven years' exile—, that took no part in the Hundred Days.

During, therefore, the whole of Napoleon's period of power Louis had either refused to cooperate with him or else did so only very grudgingly and half-heartedly. Yet there were occasional moments even in this time when his old devotion to his brother reasserted itself, particularly when the latter seemed in danger, an example of this was when Napoleon was given up for lost in Egypt after the destruction of his fleet, Louis being unceasing in his insistence that the Directory should spare no efforts to send reinforcements to Egypt and relieve his brother. As was mentioned above, Louis' attitude towards his brother once more underwent a change after the downfall of the latter, and still more markedly after his death. He busied himself in his later life with making replies to Napoleon's detractors, and wrote a book, for instance, in answer to Sir Walter Scott's 'Life of Napoleon', in which he made the savagest attacks on the integrity of this author. The following passages may be quoted from this volume, as indicative of his present attitude towards his brother: 'Napoleon is the greatest man that has ever lived'; 'Since the world has existed there has never appeared a general, a conqueror, or a King, who can be compared to him'.

His own delusion of persecution he parallels, through the process of identification, by developing a similar one in regard to his brother: 'I am absolutely convinced that this gigantic undertaking (the expedition to Russia), as well as the affairs in Spain, and the taking over of Holland and the Papal States, were simply snares into which the people about him managed to seduce him, by means of his extraordinary love of fame and his equally unlimited striving to make France ever greater and mightier'; 'He would have achieved the most brilliant and decisive of all his successes had Paris only been able to hold out for a few days' (and not been surrendered through treachery).

In attempting to understand better this ambivalent attitude that has just been outlined we have first to ask ourselves whether it cannot be explained as a natural reaction to Napoleon's own rather similar attitude towards his brother. This can best be described as one of striking over-estimation of value, followed later by a gradual disappointment and increasing annoyance. To call it an alternation of love and hate, which we plainly see in the case of Louis, would be to give a very imperfect and incorrect description of it, though, and this is an important point, the external manifestations of it might be so interpreted by someone who experienced this alternation himself, just as the normal conduct of a parent is often in this way interpreted by an over-sensitive child. For Napoleon's treatment of Louis did actually resemble that of an over-fond parent on the one hand and that of an over-stern one on the other, and no doubt Louis interpreted it as such. A few illustrations will make this clearer, and it will help our understanding of the situation if we try to imagine the effect that the attitude described would have on a boy who doted on his clever and masterful brother, eight years older than himself.

Louis' first memory of his brother was that of a young officer of seventeen, on his first leave of absence to visit his Corsican home. Nearly five years later, in January 1791, Napoleon took him back with him to Auxonne, where he educated him personally and supported him at his own expense by dint of making serious sacrifices. At this time Napoleon was enchanted with his young pupil-brother, wrote home that 'he will turn out a better fellow than any of us others', and prophesied a great future for him. For a few years Louis developed promisingly and seemed to be fulfilling all the hopes his brother had built on him. It took a long time to destroy this illusion, and Napoleon clung to it for years after it had been dissipated for everyone else who knew Louis. In 1801, for instance, after Louis' disappointing behaviour in the Egyptian and second Italian campaigns, and four years after the change in his disposition noted above, we find Napoleon saying 'There is no longer any need of bothering our minds about looking for my successor. I have found one. It is Louis. He has none of the defects of my other brothers, and he has all their good qualities.' It was only gradually that he renounced this project of making Louis his successor, and then he replaced it by adopting Louis' eldest son, much against the father's will. Not until the Prussian campaign of 1806 did Napoleon realise his brother's total incapacity. From this time on his treatment of Louis became even more arbitrary than before, though he had always had a way of disposing of him that savoured of the spirit of ownership. His attitude in the later years showed still more clearly his characteristic alternation between the kindness for a favourite brother and the annoyance of a despot at one who constantly disappointed and failed him. Thus in the March of 1810, on hearing that his brother had left his Kingdom for a health resort,

he writes to De Champagny, the Minister for Foreign
Affairs, 'Prince Louis is to retire from the States of Baden
instantly, else he is to be arrested and shut up in a French
fortress to expiate all his crimes',[1] while two months later,
in a letter to Louis himself, he refers to him as 'a prince
who was almost a son to me'. Three days after this friendly
letter he writes to his brother 'Write me no more of your
customary twaddle; three years, now, it has been going
on, and every instant proves its falsehood', adding in a
postscript of his own handwriting 'This is the last letter I
shall ever write to you in my life'. In another two months
he is writing to Lebrun, his Lieutenant-General in Holland,
expressing the strongest solicitude and love for Louis. In
the November of 1813 he writes to Cambacérès, 'I am
sending you a letter from King Louis, which appears to
me that of a madman', and the day after sends him
instructions to have Louis arrested unless he gives in his
submission; but two months later he is receiving Louis in
the Tuileries with the greatest kindness.

If we now compare the attitudes of Napoleon and
Louis towards each other, we see that there are marked
differences in the two cases. Napoleon's attitude is perfectly
consistent throughout, and is in accord with his whole
character. It is that of a masterful man who becomes
disappointed at not being able to make the use he had
hoped of someone he had over-estimated to begin with,
and it is practically identical with his attitude towards
many of his followers, such as Junot, Massèna, Murat, and
others. Any change in his treatment of Louis is quite
intelligible in the light of this, and needs no further explanation. In any case it cannot be regarded as the *cause*

[1] This letter, and other similar ones, was omitted from the
Correspondence of Napoleon, published in the reign of Louis' son,
Napoleon III, and they have only recently been made public.

of Louis' change in attitude, for this had preceded it by several years and must therefore have been the prior one. Louis' attitude, which was obviously much more personal, gives, on the other hand, the impression of proceeding from some inner conflict, and this inference is greatly strengthened both by the fact that the change in it was accompanied by a severe neurotic disturbance and by a number of other considerations which will presently be mentioned.

It is already not difficult to surmise what the nature of this conflict must have been, namely his homosexual attraction to Napoleon, and having this key we can unlock most of the problems here under discussion. That the homosexual component, of the feminine variety, was unusually pronounced in Louis there is little room to doubt. To judge from the stories of his dissipations in the intervals of the Italian campaign, he was making a manful attempt to overcome this tendency and to develop the heterosexual side of his nature, when the event happened that was to change his whole life and ruin his happiness. This was an attack of venereal disease, which caused in his twentieth year a long and serious illness, and which left him a hypochondriacal invalid, permanently crippled by what in all probability was gonorrhoeal rheumatism. From this moment he became a changed man. The influence that such an event may exercise in the case of a man of a certain disposition is well-known to us from experience in daily practice, and has often been illustrated in history, notably in the case of Nietzsche. A pronounced misogyny is apt to develop, aided by the primary weakness of the heterosexual instinct, and the only avenue of escape from the homosexual tendency is thus violently closed. In Louis' case the event threw him back for a time on his old love for Napoleon, and we find Josephine in 1800 making to Roederer the strong statement, 'He loves Bonaparte as a lover does his mistress. The letters he wrote to him when he left Egypt are so tender as to make tears come to one's eyes'. This remark is made by a woman who disliked her husband's brothers, and who had a rich experience in what love letters should be like; the significance of the remark is therefore not to be underestimated.

Louis' misogyny, however, was far from being absolute, and he made several further attempts to find consolation in the arms of woman. Early in 1798 he had fallen in love with a school-friend of his sister's, a niece of Josephine, but Napoleon interfered and put an end to the affair by taking the girl from school and promptly marrying her to one of his adjutants, Lavalette. In his disappointment Louis plunged into reckless dissipation in Paris, but his soldier brother again stepped in, carried him off to Toulon on the way to Egypt, told him to stop playing the fool, and made him march reluctantly along the path of military glory. Four years later Napoleon again undertook to direct his love-instinct, this time in a more positive way by getting him to marry Josephine's daughter, Hortense. Louis at first sulked, and fled to his country estate at Baillon in order to avoid the young lady, but he ultimately gave his consent to the wedding, which took place on March the 3rd, 1802, when he was twenty-four years old. From the point of view of happiness the marriage was, as might have been expected, a complete failure. Within a few weeks his old dreamy restless mood again took possession of him, his wife became anxious and unhappy, and after two months of married life he abandoned her in Paris, so that she had to return to her mother. Seven months later a son was born, Napoleon Charles (the names of his brother and father), and the rumour became current that

Napoleon was the father. It is practically certain that the rumour was false, but it was so persistent and so widespread throughout Europe that Napoleon, after making an effort to discredit it, reconciled himself to it and concluded that, since he meant to make the boy his heir and successor, it wouldn't be altogether a bad thing if it was believed that he was his own son.

From this time Louis' old affection for his brother disappeared more completely, and was more obviously replaced by a mixture of suspicion and smothered hatred. It is not definitely known to what extent he shared the popular belief about his son, but his subsequent conduct makes it highly probable that he was unable altogether to dismiss it from his mind. He was jealous of Napoleon's intense fondness for the boy, and refused to allow him to be chosen as the successor to the Imperial throne for fear that Napoleon might adopt him and take him away; later on he refused to let his son be given the crown of Italy, and for the same reason. At the same time he gave his affection, not to his eldest son, but to the second one, about whose paternity there was never any question. His married life lasted six or seven years, and was a series of jealous quarrels with occasional reconciliations, such as during his wife's passionate grief over the death of their eldest son. She was prostrated by the occurrence and was sent to recuperate at Cauterets, in the Pyrenees; from here rumours reached Louis of her being too friendly with Decazes and Verhuell, two of his officials, and he now came definitely to believe in her infidelity. Another son, who later became Napoleon III, was born the next year, and Louis took the view, probably an incorrect one, that he was not the father, although he publicly recognised the boy as his own. He was permanently estranged from his wife after the Pyrenees visit, and in December 1809 he formally petitioned for a separation. This was the very month in which Napoleon was arranging his divorce from Josephine, a circumstance which cannot be a coincidence, for it was a most inopportune moment; it clearly shows how Louis was still identifying himself with his brother. A family council was called together, according to the French law, and to avoid scandal an informal separation was arranged, which lasted until Hortense's death twenty-eight years later. Not long after this Napoleon's son was born, Marie-Louise's child, and Louis, who was now in retirement in Gratz, reacted to the news as though the event had been purposely arranged as a personal blow against himself; he became more embittered than ever against the Emperor, who, according to him, had robbed him of his throne, taken his children from him, and had now produced a son himself who was to steal the heritage of Louis. The last relation he had with his wife was to bring a law-suit against her on the fall of the Empire to get possession of his elder surviving son, the one concerning whose paternity there was no question; he was granted this by the courts, but Hortense refused to part with the boy.

An interesting matter, and one which throws much light on Louis' conduct at the most important period of his life, is that his reactions in the sphere of international politics to a large extent duplicated those of his personal life in relation to his brother, a process known as intro-jection (Ferenczi). This is well brought out in a book he published some nineteen years after his abdication, from which I quote the following passage: 'Since a great State must necessarily exert an important influence on the others, I wanted this influence (in the case of France and Holland) to be the result of friendship, of good treatment, of mutual inclination and of benevolence on the part of the stronger

17

one in regard to the weaker, so that the interest of the latter would come into accord with its inclination.' This is evidently a parallel of his idea of what Napoleon's attitude should be towards him personally. How far he carried the identification of himself with Holland is illustrated by his cherishing the delusion that his former kingdom was mourning his absence and longing for his return, and this at the end of 1813, at a time when the Dutch were rising in insurrection against the French yoke and were massacring French officials in large numbers; Louis even went so far about this time as to write to a number of prominent men in Amsterdam assuring them that he would soon be amongst them again and that their (!) desire to have him as their permanent King would be gratified.

We may now sum up the preceding discussion. Thanks to the investigations of the past few years it is known that delusions of jealousy and delusions of persecution, the two most characteristic symptoms of the paranoid syndrome, are practically pathognomonic of repressed homosexuality, in which they take their origin, and on this ground alone, quite apart from the other evidence detailed above, we are justified in concluding that here lay the root of Louis' trouble. The delusions of persecution are the expression of disappointed love, and are brought about by means of a double inversion of the underlying content. The love is replaced by hate, a process often enough pointed out by poets and writers, and the emotion is ascribed to, or projected on to, the person towards whom it was originally directed. This explains how it is that such delusions always begin in reference to persons whom the patient had loved, though they usually extend later to others who replace these in his imagination. Finding that he cannot love them he hates them instead, and fancies that they hate him. In Louis' case this delusion remained chiefly localised to Napoleon, but we noted a tendency to extension in his conviction that Napoleon, with whom he here identifies himself, was the victim or a carefully laid plot to lure him to destruction. The psychological structure of delusions of jealousy is still simpler, there being merely a projection of the emotion, without any change in the nature of this. The patient accuses his wife of loving a man whom he himself would like to love. This also, like the previous one, may get generalised, and with Louis we see examples of both kinds. He suspects his wife of having sexual relations first with Napoleon, and then later with other men, members not of his actual family, but of his symbolic family, his court. It is instructive to see that the second of these suspicions, being a more disguised manifestation of the homosexual wish, is allowed to come to more open expression than the first one; the former was a fixed idea, while the latter was hardly more than a half-avowed suspicion.

It is not really correct to speak of delusions with Louis, at least not in the strict psychiatric sense of the word, for it is rather a question of preconscious beliefs which his reflective judgement was able to a great extent to hold in check. Louis never became a true paranoiac, though he certainly exhibited definite paranoid tendencies. All through his life we see him struggling against these, and against the homosexuality from which they sprang. As an instance of the devices he adopted to defend himself against his delusional tendencies may be quoted the following: Some years after Napoleon's death he published the statement that his brother had never been unfaithful to Josephine; Napoleon, whose amours were the talk of Europe, and who was known to have had at least thirty mistresses during his wedded life with Josephine! The object of this attempt at self-deception on Louis' part is quite plain; if Napoleon had never betrayed Josephine, it was a guarantee that he could never have betrayed Louis and that the latter's suspicion regarding his wife had been unfounded. By such desperate measures as this Louis kept his abnormal tendencies to some extent within check, and so managed to preserve his reason, but it was at a heavy cost, at the expense of becoming a nervous invalid for the whole of his life. He sacrificed his health rather than his reason, and he had no energy left to make him a useful member of society.

Of the bearing that Louis' conduct had on his brother's plans, of the difference it made to the course of history, and the not inconsiderable extent to which it contributed, directly and indirectly, to the downfall of the Empire, this is not the place to speak; the object of the present paper is merely to illustrate that knowledge gained from psychopathology, and unobtainable in any other way, may be of service in helping to elucidate even purely historical problems.[1]

---

[1] Mention may be made here of two other attempts to apply psycho-analytical knowledge to an historical problem: Abraham: 'Amenhotep IV. (Echnaton) Psychoanalytische Beiträge zum Verständnis seiner Persönlichkeit und des monotheistischen Aton-Kultes', *Imago*, 1912, Bd. I, S. 334, and Flügel: 'On the Character and Married Life of Henry VIII', *International Journal of Psycho-Analysis*, 1920, Vol. I, p. 24.

CHAPTER VIII

THE MADONNA'S CONCEPTION THROUGH THE EAR

A CONTRIBUTION TO THE RELATION BETWEEN AESTHETICS
AND RELIGION[1]

Contents

I

INTRODUCTION

The object of the present essay is to illustrate, by
the analysis of a single example, the following thesis: that
the close relation of aesthetics to religion is due to the
intimate connection between their respective roots.

[1] Published in the *Jahrbuch der Psychoanalyse,* 1914, Band VI.

The closeness of the relation, which is perhaps more striking with the higher religions, is shewn in manifold ways: sometimes by the diametrical opposition of the two, as in the iconoclastic outbursts of Savonarola or the English Puritans against art, but more frequently by the remarkable union between the two. The latter may be manifested both positively, as when art and religion are fused in worship (religious dancing, painting, music, singing, architecture; 'The works of the Lord are lovely to behold', 'God is lovely in his holiness', etc.), and negatively, as when religion condemns the same piece of conduct, now as sinful, now as ugly or disgusting.

It is widely recognised that the ultimate sources of artistic creativeness lie in that region of the mind outside consciousness, and it may be said with some accuracy that the deeper the artist reaches in his unconscious in the search for his inspiration the more profound is the resulting conception likely to be. It is also well known that among these ultimate sources the most important are psycho-sexual phantasies. Artistic creation serves for the expression of many emotions and ideas, love of power, sympathy at suffering, desire for ideal beauty, and so on, but—unless the term be extended so as to include admiration for any form whatever of perfection—it is with the last of these, beauty, that aesthetics is principally concerned; so much so that aesthetic feeling may well be defined as that which is evoked by the contemplation of beauty. Now, analysis of this aspiration reveals that the chief source of its stimuli is not so much a primary impulse as a reaction, a rebellion against the coarser and more repellent aspects of material existence, one which psychogenetically arises from the reaction of the young child against its original excremental interests. When we remember how extensively these repressed coprophilic tendencies contribute, in their sublimated forms, to every variety of artistic activity—to painting, sculpture, and architecture on the one hand, and to music and poetry on the other—it becomes evident that in the artist's striving for beauty the fundamental part played by these primitive infantile interests (including their later derivatives) is not to be ignored: the reaction against them lies behind the striving, and the sublimation of them behind the forms that the striving takes.

When on the other hand religious activities, interests and rites, are traced to their unconscious source it is found that, although—as I have pointed out in the case of baptism[1]—they make extensive use of the same psychical material as that indicated above, they differ from aesthetic interests especially in that the main motives are derived not so much from this sphere as from another group of infantile interests, that concerned with incestuous phantasies.[2] At first sight, therefore, aesthetics and religion would appear to have on the whole disparate biological origins. Freud's[3] researches have demonstrated, however—and this is not the least far-reaching of their conclusions—that infantile coprophilia belongs essentially to the as yet un-coordinated infantile sexuality, constituting as it does a prominent part of the auto-erotic stage which precedes that of incestuous object-love. From this point of view we obtain a deeper insight into the present topic, and indeed a satisfactory explanation of the problem, for, since aesthetic and religious activities are derived from merely different components of a biologically unitary instinct, components which are inextricably intertwined at their very roots, it becomes throughout intelligible that even in their most developed forms they should stand in close relationship to each other.

[1] See chapter IV, pp. 125, 162-5.
[2] See Freud: Totem und Tabu, 1913.
[3] Freud: Drei Abhandlungen zur Sexualtheorie, 4e Aufl., 1920.

II

THE LEGEND OF THE MADONNA'S CONCEPTION THROUGH THE EAR

A belief, often forgotten nowadays, but preserved in the legends and traditions of the Catholic Church, is that the conception of Jesus in the Virgin Mary was brought about by the introduction into her ear of the breath of the Holy Ghost. I do not know if this is now held as an official tenet of the Church, but in past ages it was not only depicted by numerous religious artists, but also maintained by many of the Fathers and by at least one of the Popes, namely Felix.

St. Augustine[1] writes: 'Deus per angelum loquebatur et Virgo per aurem impraegnebatur', St. Agobard[2] 'Descendit de coelis missus ab arce patris, introivit per aurem Virginis in regionem nostram indutus stola purpurea et exivit per auream portam lux et Deus universae fabricae mundi', and St. Ephrem of Syria[3] 'Per novam Mariae aurem intravit atque infusa est vita', similar passages could be quoted from various other Fathers, such as St. Proclus, St. Ruffinus of Aquileia, etc. In the Breviary of the Maronites one reads: 'Verbum patris per aurem benedictae intravit', and a hymn[4], ascribed by some to St. Thomas à Becket, by others to St. Bonaventure, contains the following verse:

Gaude, Virgo, mater Christi,
Quae per aurem concepisti,
Gabriele nuntio.

---

[1] St. Augustine: Sermo de Tempore, xxii.
[2] St. Agobard: De Correctione antiphonarii, Cap. viii.
[3] St. Ephrem: De Divers Serm. I, Opp. Syr., Vol. III, p. 607.
[4] Bodley MS., Latin Liturgy, X. Fol. 91 vo.

> Gaude, quia Deo plena
> Peperisti sine pena
>   Cum pudoris lilio.

There were many versions of this current in the middle ages; Langlois[1] quotes the following one from the seventeenth century:

> Rejouyssez-vous, Vièrge, et Mère bienheureuse,
> Qui dans vos chastes flancs conçeutes par l'ouyr,
> L'Esprit-Sainct opérant d'un très-ardent désir,
> Est l'Ange l'annonçant d'une voix amoureuse.

The event was often portrayed by religious artists in the Middle Ages. For instance, in a painting of Filippo Lippi's in the convent of San Marco in Florence, in one of Gaddi's in the Santa Maria Novella, in one of Benozzo Gozzoli's in the Campo Santa of Pisa, and in an old mosaic—no longer extant[2]—in Santa Maria Maggiore in Rome, the Holy Dove is seen almost entering the Virgin's ear. In the first named of these the Dove emanates from the right hand of the Father, in the second from his bosom; more typically, however, as in the picture of Simone Martini's here reproduced,[3] one which will presently be more fully discussed, the Dove emanates from the mouth of the Father. The Dove may either constitute a part of the Father's breath—as it were a concrete condensation of this—or it may itself repeat the emission of breath: in the Florence Bargello there are three examples of this (by Verrocchio and the Della Robbias), and it may also be seen in a picture of the Ferrarese school in the Wallace Collection, London, as well as in Martini's picture.

[1] Langlois: Essai sur la Peinture sur Verre, 1832, p. 157.
[2] Gori: Thesaurus, Tab. xxx, Vol. III.
[3] See Frontispiece.

The connection between the fertilising breath of the Dove and the child to be conceived is made plainly evident in an old panel that used to stand in the Cathedral of Saint-Leu, of which Langlois gives the following description: 'Du bec du St-Esprit jaillissait un rayon lumineux aboutissant à l'oreille de Marie, dans laquelle descendait s'introduire, dirigé par ce même rayon, un très-jeune enfant tenant une petite croix'.[1] A similar picture, by Meister des Marialebens, in which also the infant is seen descending along a ray of light may be seen in the Germanisches Museum in Nuremberg. We note that here it is a ray of light that issues from the mouth of the Dove, instead of the more appropriate breath. This equating of radiating breath and rays of light is an interesting matter to which we shall have to return later. It may have been partly determined by the greater technical facility with which rays of light can be represented by the painter, but it also has its theological aspects, for it is related to the doctrine of the monophysite Churches of Armenia and Syria (which split off from the Byzantine in the fifth century) that Jesus's body, originating in an emission of light from heaven, was made of ethereal fire and had neither bodily structure nor functions. Another example of this equation occurs in an old stained-glass window which was formerly in the sacristy of the Pistoia Cathedral,[2] also representing rays issuing from the Dove's mouth and bearing an embryo in the direction of the Virgin's head; the picture is surmounted by the lines:

> Gaude Virgo Mater Christi
> Quae per Aurem concepisti.

[1] Langlois: loc. cit.
[2] Cicognara: Storia della Scultura, 1813-1818, Vol. I, p. 324.

In a sculpture now in the Fränkisches Luitpoldmuseum at Würzburg[1] a little child carrying a crucifix is seen in the midst of the Father's radiating breath and aiming at the Virgin's right ear; the Dove here stands aside, at the right side of the head. The presence of the infant at this stage was denounced as heretical by the Catholic Church, for it contradicted the belief that He took his flesh from the Virgin Mary and so was really man.

As a counterpart to the accompanying picture or Martini's where the sacred words 'Ave Gratia plena dominus tecum' are designated passing from Gabriel's lips to the Virgin's ear—converging thus with the breath of the Dove—may be mentioned a twelfth-century altarpiece at Klosterneuburg,[2] by Nicolas Verdun, in which two rays escape from the tips of the fingers of Gabriel's right hand and are directed towards the Virgin's ear. The anomalous termination of light rays in the *ear* demonstrates the strength of the main idea, that of impregnation by means of breath—here replaced by its symbolic equivalent of rays of light—entering the ear.

Much discussion took place in subsequent centuries over the delicate questions pertaining to the mode of birth of the Holy Babe, of whether He left His mother's body by the natural route or emerged between the breasts, whether the hymen was ruptured, and if so whether its integrity was restored later, and so on.[3] It is not proposed, however, to discuss these matters here, our attention being confined to the initial stage of the process.

[1] Nr. 6 Portalstein der Hauskapelle des Hofes Rödelsee in Würzburg, 1484.

[2] Arneth: Das Niello-Antipendium zu Klosterneuburg, 1844, S. 11.

[3] See Guillaume Herzog: La Sainte Vierge dans l'Histoire, 1908, Ch. III, 'La Virginité "in partu"', pp. 38-51.

This remarkable conception of the process of impregnation, so foreign to all human experience,[1] must arouse the desire to investigate its meaning, for it evidently represents a symbolic expression of some obscure idea rather than a mere literal description of a matter-of-fact occurrence. Lecky[2] asserts that it 'of course was suggested by the title Logos', but we shall find grounds for doubting whether this rationalistic explanation does not reverse the actual order of genesis of the two ideas.

Our interest is further increased when we learn that the story is in no way peculiar to Christianity, though perhaps it is here that it reaches its most finished and elaborate form. Anticipating a little of our later discussion, we may mention at this point the legend of Chigemouni, the Mongolian Saviour, who chose the most perfect virgin on earth, Mahaenna or Maya, and impregnated her by penetrating into her right ear during sleep.[3] We shall see also that when the Mary legend is dissected into its elements each of these can be richly paralleled from extra-Christian sources, and that the main ones have proved to

[1] So foreign that Molière uses it to indicate the utmost limit of ignorance on sexual topics. In the 'Ecole des Femmes' he makes Anolphe say that Agnes has asked him

Avec une innocence à nulle autre pareille,
Si les enfants qu'on fait se faisoient par l'oreille.

[2] Lecky: History of the Rise and Influence of the Spirit of Rationalism in Europe, Cheaper Edition, Vol. I, p. 212.

[3] Norlk: Biblische Mythologie, 1843, Bd. II, S. 64 Jung (*Jahrbuch der Psychoanalyse*, Bd. IV, S. 204) makes the interesting statement, for which however he gives no authority, that the Mongolian Buddha was also born from his mother's ear; the accounts I have read, on the contrary, say that he was conceived by the ear, but born by the mouth. In a silk banner painted about 1100 A D. and recently discovered in the Cave of the Thousand Buddhas, the first appearance of the babe is depicted as being within his mother's sleeve (See Stein: Ruins of Desert Cathay, 1912, Vol. II, p. 199), a fact to which Mr. Alfred Ela of Boston kindly directed my attention.

be of almost universal interest. It is therefore certain that we are concerned, not with a purely local problem of early Christian theology, but with a theme of general human significance.

For the sake of convenience the subject will be divided up, and an attempt made to answer in order the following questions: Why is the creative material represented as emanating from the mouth, and why as breath in particular? Why is it a dove that conveys it? And why is the ear chosen to be the receptive organ?

III
BREATH AND FERTILISATION

In anthropological, mythological and individual symbolism, instances of which are too numerous in the literature to need quoting here, the *mouth* has more frequently a female significance, being naturally adapted to represent a receptive organ. Its capacity, however, to emit fluids (saliva and breath), and the circumstance of its containing the tongue, the symbolic significance of which will presently be considered, render it also suitable for portraying a male aperture; the idea of spitting, in particular, is one of the commonest symbolisms in folk-lore for the male act (hence, for instance, the expression 'the very spit of his father').

The idea of the *breath* as a life-giving agent is familiar to us from the passages in the Old Testament: 'And the Lord God formed man of the dust of the ground, and breathed into his nostrils the breath of life; and man became a living soul' (Genesis ii. 7); 'The heavens by the Word of God did their beginning take; And by the breathing of his mouth he all their hosts did make' (Psalms xxxiii. 6). Mohammedan tradition ascribes the miraculous impregnation of the Virgin Mary to Gabriel having opened

the bosom of her garment and breathed upon her womb.[1]
One of the various legends of the birth of the Aztec
divinity Quetzalcoatl relates that the Lord of Existence,
Tonacatecutli, appeared to Chimalma and breathed upon
her, with the result that she conceived the divine child.[2]

Further than this, the idea of breath has played a
remarkably extensive part in religion and philosophy, in
the lowest as well as in the highest beliefs of mankind.
In Brahmanism it becomes formally identified with the
Eternal Being,[3] and all over the world it has furnished
one of the main constituent components of the idea of
the soul (*Hauchseele*).[4]

Now when we ask what is the source of this intense
interest and importance with which the idea in question has
been invested, such an inquiry may seem almost superfluous, for it will be said that the importance attached to
the idea of breathing is inherent in the act itself. Breath,
as a symbol of life, is felt to be a natural and appropriate
choice. No manifest act is more continuously essential to
life than that of breathing, and the presence or absence
of it is the simplest and most primitive test of death; the
mysterious invisibility of breath finds a meet counterpart
in that of the soul.

Psycho-Analysis, however, has by now become familiar
with the experience of finding various matters taken for
granted as being something obvious and in no need of

[1] Sale: Koran, 1734, Note to ch. XIX, citing various Arabian
authors.

[2] Bancroft: The Native Races of the Pacific States of North
America, 1876, Vol. III, p. 271. See also Preuss: *Globus*, Bd. LXXXVI,
S. 302

[3] Deussen · The Philosophy of the Upanishads, Engl Transl. 1906,
pp. 39, 110.

[4] Wundt: Völkerpsychologie, Bd. II, 'Mythus und Religion', 1906,
Zweiter Teil, S. 42 et seq.

explanation—infantile amnesia affords one of the most
striking examples of this—and then nevertheless discovered
that behind this attitude of indifference may lie most
important problems, just where there was thought to be
no problem at all. So that, sharpened by such experiences
in the past, we should not be content to adopt a current
estimate of mental phenomena until an unbiassed examination
of the facts confirms the accuracy of it. With the matter
under consideration this is, in my opinion, not so. In spite
of the obvious reflections just mentioned, the thesis will
here be maintained that the current conclusion indicated
above furnishes only a part answer to the question asked,
and that much of the significance attached to the idea
of breath is primarily derived from a source extraneous to
it. In other words, it is maintained that we have here another
example of the familiar process of displacement, whereby
various affects that originally belonged to another idea
altogether have become secondarily associated with that
of breath.

I have two reasons for venturing to differ from the
generally accepted opinion on this matter, first because
this seems to me to be based on an erroneous estimate
of the amount of psychical interest normally attaching to
the idea of breath, and secondly because it is in open
disaccord with the principles of psychogenesis. To make
the idea in question the centre of an elaborate religion,
philosophy or *Weltanschauung*, as has been done many
times in history, seems to me to presuppose an amount
of primary interest in it which transcends that taken by
anyone not in the throes of mortal illness. And when we
explore the Unconscious, that region where so many
philosophic and religious ideas have their source, we find
that the idea of breath is much less important even than
in consciousness, occupying a rank of almost subordinate

inferiority. In the numerous cases, for instance, of neurotic symptoms centering about the act of breathing or speaking, analysis always shews that the primary importance of the act has been over-determined by extraneous factors. There is reason, it is true, to think that if we could apply the libido theory more extensively to somatic processes, along the lines opened up by Ferenczi, the act of breathing would assume an importance hard to overestimate, but there is no evidence—at all events as yet—to indicate that any serious amount of what may be termed ideational interest results from this organic importance of the act.

In the second place, it is a law of psychogenesis, founded now on extensive experience, that an idea can become psychically important in adult life only through becoming associated with, and reinforcing, an earlier chain of ideas reaching back into childhood, and that much, or even most, of its psychical (as apart from intrinsic) significance is derived from these. Thus whenever we find such an idea dating mainly from adult life we may be sure that it represents much more than itself—namely, earlier groups of important ideas with which it has become associated. These considerations are much more extensively applicable, and should therefore be regarded as correspondingly more potent, with ideas concerned with the adaptation to the world of inner, psychical reality than with those relating to the outer world, and the religious and philosophic ideas referred to—as also those concerning the act of breathing—certainly enter into the former category. Now in the present instance it must be admitted that the ideational interest attaching to the act of breathing arises for the most part relatively late, for the infant is usually unaware of the act as such, which it performs automatically, and which arouses almost as little interest as the beating of the heart; even with difficult breathing in disease it is rather the sensations of distress (precordial, etc.) that are important than the idea itself of the act of breathing. This whole argument will not perhaps be very convincing to those who have not realised through psycho-analytical experience the ontogenetic antiquity of our affective processes, but with those who have it must, in my judgement, carry considerable weight.

To trace the origin of the various affects that in later life invest the idea of breath, or of course those of any other idea, is a matter of detailed individual-psychological studies and of noting the different displacements that have occurred during the growth of the mind. If this is done, it will be found, as I pointed out some time ago,[1] that much of the interest and affect attaching to this particular idea has been derived from that of an excreted air other than breath—namely, the gas resulting from intestinal decomposition. This conclusion may seem at first sight repellent, highly improbable, and above all unnecessary, but the truth of it is supported not only by the preceding theoretical considerations and the results of actual individual analyses, but by a large amount of very definite evidence of a purely external nature. Psycho-analytic investigation has shewn that from the beginning children take a far greater interest in the act referred to than is commonly supposed, as is true of all excretory functions,[2] and that they are apt in various ways to attach great significance to it, most of which of course becomes in later years displaced on to other, associated ideas. From this point of view the extensive part played by the idea in the obscene jokes of

---

[1] *Jahrbuch der Psychoanalyse,* Bd. IV, S. 588 et seq.

[2] It should not be forgotten that the interest in question is a manifestation of the sexual instinct. The part played by breath in infantile sexuality is certainly less important than that played by the rectal excretions.

childhood, and indeed in the more allusive ones of later years,[1] becomes for the first time intelligible. It is hardly necessary to add that, owing to the repugnance of the idea, most of the infantile interest in it gets buried in the Unconscious and the phantasies concerning it forgotten.

One of these phantasies, which has a special reference to the main theme of this essay, is the identification of the material in question with the sexual secretion. In their early cogitation about what is done by the father to bring about the production of a baby many children originate the belief, to which I have elsewhere directed attention,[2] that the mysterious act performed by the parents consists in the passage of gas from the father to the mother, just as other children imagine it to consist in the mutual passage of urine. Some children, probably the smaller number, go on to connect this with the swelling of the mother's abdomen during pregnancy, and their personal experience of a swollen abdomen due to dyspepsia and intestinal decomposition may be the starting-point for reproduction phantasies of their own.[3] The possible objection that this

[1] Cp. the volumes of Krauss' Anthropophyteia, which give some notion of this. Most farcical comedians on the variety stage make almost unconcealed allusions to the act, usually in conjunction with the orchestra.

[2] *Zentralblatt für Psychoanalyse,* Jahrg. I, S. 566. In the *Jahrbuch der Psychoanalyse* (1912, Bd. IV, S. 563) a detailed report is given of one of the cases on which my conclusion was based. The explanation was subsequently, and independently, confirmed by Reitler (*Zentralblatt für Psychoanalyse,* Jahrg. II, S. 114).

[3] Larguier des Bancels (*Arch de Psychologie,* t XVII, pp 64-6), in a criticism of the present essay, holds that my conclusions 'se brisent sur un point capital' Quoting the extremely doubtful conclusions of Hartland, to the effect that many savage races are ignorant of any connection between sexual intercourse and fecundation, he asks how one can attribute to young children greater perspicacity in this respect than that possessed by savage adults. My answer is that I attribute to both a greater perspicacity than does my critic That, quite apart from

is in any way an artificial finding of psycho-analysis, or
perhaps one that refers only to present-day civilisation,
can be at once disposed of by mentioning a single counterpart from antiquity. Thus in the Satapatha-Brâhmana,[1] and
in several other passages in the Vedic literature, it is
described how the Lord of Existence, Pragapati, who had
created the original gods with the 'out (and in) breathings
of his mouth', proceeded to create the whole of mankind
with the 'downward breathings that escape from the back
part (jaghanāt)'; the identity of cosmogonic theories of
creation with infantile ones has been amply demonstrated
by Otto Rank.[2]

It will be most convenient to continue the discussion
at this stage by dissecting the natural associations existing
between the two expiratory gases, and grouping—rather
artificially, it is true—various topics under each. Air
emitted from the body, whether upwards or downwards,
has the following attributes: blowing movement, sound,
invisibility, moisture, warmth and odour.

1. Blowing Movement

The primitive notion that the down-going breath, to
use the seemly phrase of the Vedic writers, is a fertilising
principle has frequently been extended to the *wind*, as
might readily have been expected. It is significant
that the corresponding belief can be traced in every
quarter of the world, from Australia to Europe. Perhaps
the most familiar example of it is the legend of Hera,

---

actual knowledge, young children commonly imagine the begetting of
a baby to be dependent on some unknown act between the parents
may be news to him, but it is a very familiar fact to me, as to all
others who have intimate experience of the child's mind.

[1] X. Kânda, I, iii, 1 and 6; Kânda, I, ii, 2.
[2] Otto Rank: 'Völkerpsychologische Parallelen zu den infantilen
Sexualtheorien', *Zentralblatt für Psychoanalyse*, Jahrg. II, S. 372, 425.

who was fertilised by the wind and conceived Hephaistos. In the Algonkin mythology, Mudjekeewis, the West Wind and Father of the other winds, quickens the maiden Wenonah, who then bears the hero Michabo, better known to us under the name of Hiawatha.[1] In Longfellow's well-known poem of this name the courtship is described in terms that indicate the symbolic equivalence of wind, light, speech, odour and music, one which will be discussed later.

> And he wooed her with caresses,
> Wooed her with his smile of sunshine,
> With his flattering words he wooed her,
> With his sighing and his singing,
> Gentlest whispers in the branches,
> Softest music, sweetest odours,
> Till he drew her to his bosom.

The Minahassers of Celebes believe they are descended from a girl in primaeval days who was also fecundated by the West Wind.[2] The Aruntas of Central Australia still hold that a storm from the West sometimes brings evil 'ratapa', or child-germs, that seek to enter women; as the storm approaches, the women with a loud cry hasten to the shelter of their huts, for if they become impregnated in this fashion twins will result who will die shortly after their birth.[3]

Although this belief is more especially connected with the West Wind, other ones can on occasion display a similar activity. Thus in the Luang-Sermata group of islands in the Moluccas the origin of mankind is traced to a 'sky-

---

[1] Brinton: American Hero-Myths, 1882, p. 47.

[2] Schwarz: *Internationales Archiv für Ethnographie*, 1907, Jahrg. XVIII, S. 59.

[3] Strehlow: Die Aranda- und Loritja-Stämme in Zentralaustralien, 1907, S. 14.

woman' who climbed down to earth and was impregnated by the South Wind;[1] her children had access to the sky until the Lord Sun forbade it, a belief the ontogenetic significance of which is evident. Again, in the Finnish national epic, Kalevala, the virgin Ilmatar is fructified by the East Wind and gives birth to the wizard Väinamöinen; appropriately enough, the latter not only invented the harp and discovered fire, but became the instructor of mankind in poetry and music.[2] In the similar legend of Luminu-ut current in Singapore and the Indian Archipelago[3] it is not stated which wind was responsible. In classical times this belief was especially connected with the Spring Wind, Zephyrus or Flavonius, who, for instance, begot Euphrosyne with Aurora, and it is highly probable that the Floralia included a worship of this wind as well as of flowers; Ovid[4] describes how Chloris, called Flora by the Romans, was ravished by Zephyr. Widespread also are the traditions of whole regions—particularly islands—the inhabitants of which are descended from the wind, or whose women conceive only in this way. In early classical times the latter belief was entertained in regard to Cyprus, and only last century the inhabitants of Lampong, in Sumatra, believed the same of the neighbouring island of Engano.[5] Mohammedan tradition tells of a pre-Adamite race consisting entirely of women, who conceived (daughters only) by the wind, and also of an island of women thus peopled.[6] The Binhyas of

[1] Riedel: De Sluik- en Kroesharige Rassen tusschen Selebes en Papua, 1886, p. 312.

[2] Abercromby: The Pre- and Proto-historic Finns, 1898, Vol. I, pp. 316, 318, 322.

[3] Bab: Zeitschrift für Ethnologie, 1906, Jahrg. XXXVIII, S. 280.

[4] Ovid: Fasti, v, 195-202.

[5] Marsden: The History of Sumatra, 1811, p. 297.

[6] L'Abrégé des Merveilles. Translated from the Arabian by De Vaux, 1898, pp. 17, 71.

India also claim descent from the wind.[1] In an interesting poem by Eduard Mörike entitled 'Jung Volkers Lied,' the connection is clearly indicated between the belief in question and the tendency to repudiate the male sex; it is probable that all these beliefs in miraculous conception spring from the boy's desire to exclude the father from anything to do with his birth:

> Und die mich trug im Mutterleib,
> Und die mich schwang im Kissen,
> Die war ein schön frech braunes Weib,
> Wollte nichts vom Mannsvolk wissen.
>
> Sie scherzte nur und lachte laut
> Und ließ die Freier stehen:
> 'Möcht' lieber sein des Windes Braut,
> Denn in die Ehe gehen!'
>
> Da kam der Wind, da nahm der Wind
> Als Buhle sie gefangen:
> Von dem hat sie ein lustig Kind
> In ihren Schoß empfangen.[2]

[1] Saintyves: Les Vierges Mères, 1908, p. 143.

[2]
> And she who bore me as a child
> Who rocked my cradle then,
> She was a fine brawn lass so wild
> That would know nought of men.
>
> She only scoffed and laughed beside,
> And left the men alone,
> 'I'd rather be the wild wind's bride
> Than marry anyone.'
>
> The wind he came, the wind so wild,
> Bride was she, he the groom,
> By him she got a merry child,
> A boy child in her womb.

As is quite comprehensible, the same belief was by analogy also extended to animals. Freud[1] has reminded us of the ancient belief that vultures were, like the inhabitants of the islands just referred to, all female, and that they conceived by exposing their genitals to the wind; so accepted was this that Origen appealed to it in support of the credibility of Jesus Christ's virgin birth. Nor was the vulture the only bird that has been supposed to conceive in this way; in Samoa the same thing was related of snipe,[2] and both Aristotle[3] and Pliny[4] tell us that partridges can be fecundated when merely standing opposite to the male, provided that the wind is blowing from him to her.[5] St Augustine[6] gravely relates how the mares in Cappadocia are fertilised by the wind, Virgil[7] says the same of the mares of Boaetia, and Pliny[8] of those of Lusitania. In more modern times this ancient belief is found only in the form of poetic analogy, such as in the following passage from Shakespeare:[9]

When we have laugh'd to see the sails conceive,
And grow big-bellied with the wanton wind;
Which she, with pretty and with swimming gait
Following, (her womb then rich with my young squire)
Would imitate, and sail upon the land.

[1] Freud: Eine Kindheitserinnerung des Leonardo da Vinci, 1910, S. 25.

[2] Sierich: 'Samoanische Märchen', Internat. Arch. für Ethnographie, Bd. XVI, S. 90.

[3] Aristotle: Hist. Anim., v, 4.

[4] Pliny: Hist. Nat., x, 51.

[5] See also Plutarch: Moralia, Lib. VIII, Art. i, Par. 3.

[6] St Augustinus: Civ. Dei, xxi, 5.

[7] Virgil: Georgics, iii, 266-76.

[8] Pliny: op. cit., viii, 67.

[9] Shakespeare: A Midsummer Night's Dream, Act II, Sc. 2, l. 69.

Not only have the life-bringing powers been ascribed to the outer air, usually in the form of wind, but this has been extensively identified with the principle of life and creation altogether. Something will be said later of the enormous part it has played in Indian and Greek philosophy, where it has been exalted to the rank of the breath and essence of God himself, the fundamental substratum of all material and spiritual existence, the source of all life and activity, the first principle of the universe, and so on. A glance at the extraordinary mass of material collected by Frazer[1] on the subject of 'The Magical Control of the Wind' is enough to shew the astonishing significance of the idea in anthropology and folk-lore. There remain in modern times many examples of this over-estimation of the idea, particularly in poetry, of which the following may be quoted from Shelley's 'Ode to the West Wind', in which also the association between wind, birth, fire, thoughts, and words, which will presently be discussed, is well indicated:

> Be thou, Spirit fierce,
> My spirit! Be thou me, impetuous one!
> Drive my dead thoughts over the universe
> Like withered leaves to quicken a new birth!
> And, by the incantation of this verse,
> Scatter, as from an unextinguished hearth
> Ashes and sparks, my words among mankind!

The question why various beliefs in the fertilising power of the wind get attached, now to the wind from one cardinal point, now to another, cannot be completely answered without a special study. It is plain that a number of different determining factors enter into the matter. For

---

[1] Frazer: The Magic Art, 1911, Vol. I, pp. 319-31.

instance, it was believed in Thuringia[1] to be advantageous to sow barley when the West Wind was blowing, and one gets a clue to the meaning of this on learning further that the sowing should be done on a Wednesday, i. e. on Odin's day, since Odin, probably for reasons to do with the setting sun, had special connections with the west. A very general factor in the localising of the belief is its association with winds of a warm, moist, and 'relaxing' character, which commonly induce a more or less lascivious mood: a good example is the 'Föhnfieber' in Switzerland, which is certainly a form of sexual excitation. All agencies leading to sexual excitation are readily identified, especially in the Unconscious, with a fertilising principle. As winds of this character prevailingly blow from the west or south-west over the chief part of Europe, it is not surprising that in this region most of the beliefs in question are related to it. In confirmation of this supposition is the fact that the opposite type of wind, the East Wind, is popularly credited with the contrary effect. There is a saying among German sailors which runs (in Plattdeutsch) as follows:[2] 'Oste-Wind makt krus den Buedel un kort den Pint'. ('The East Wind makes the scrotum crinkled and the penis short'.)

It is nowadays generally recognised, since the belief in mankind's primary interest in physical geography has been largely discredited, that all this significance attaching to the idea of wind must have arisen mainly through a projection outward of thoughts and feelings concerning the air in immediate connection with man's body. In accord with this view is the fact that the beliefs just mentioned concerning the sexual activities of the wind can be exten-sively paralleled by similar ones relating to the breath. One

[1] Witzschel: Sagen, Sitten und Gebrauche aus Thüringen, 1878, Bd. II, S. 215.

[2] Private communication from Dr. Karl Abraham.

or two of these may be added to those already cited. The Delphi priestess in her love-embrace with Apollo was filled with his breath, which the God poured into her. In an early Mexican picture[1] a man and woman are represented as having intercourse by mingling their breath.

On the basis, therefore, of present-day views on mythology, which do not need to be expounded here,[2] we may assume that the idea of breath is primary to that of wind, and that the beliefs just related concerning the latter may be taken as some index of how important the former has been in anthropological history. That, however, the idea of another personal gas is still more primary than that of breath is a thesis that an attempt will be made to substantiate in the following pages.

2. Sound

In the description of a fertilising principle or of the Creative Being himself sound may occur either alone, when it is plainly a symbol, or as the most prominent attribute of some other phenomenon. A clear example of the former is the 'Last Trump', which is to wake the dead from their sleep and call them to eternal life. This motif also plays a part in the various miracles of raising people from the dead; it is indicated for instance in a picture by Bronzino (in the Santa Maria Novella, Florence) representing the raising of Jairus' daughter, in which an angel stands at the side blowing a trumpet. Another example of the significance of sound, where the sexual meaning comes to open expression, is afforded by a cameo, dated 1294, in

[1] Reproduced by Seler: 'Tierbilder der mexikanischen und Maya-Handschriften', *Zeitschr. f. Ethnologie*, Bd. XLII, S. 67.

[2] See Rank and Sachs: Die Bedeutung der Psychoanalyse für die Geisteswissenschaften, 1913, Kapitel II.

the Florence Bargello, in which a satyr blowing a trumpet surprises a sleeping bacchante.

In the second type, where sound is merely one of the prominent features, the phenomenon is perhaps most often conceived of in the form of *wind*. In the Old Testament the voice of God is described by Ezekiel (iii. 12) as 'a great rushing', and in the account of the advent of the Holy Ghost given in the Acts of the Apostles (ii. 2) we read: 'And suddenly there came a *sound* from heaven, as of a rushing mighty wind, and it filled all the house where they were sitting'. Similarly the South American Indians worshipped 'Hurrakan', 'the mighty wind', a name supposed to be cognate with our word 'hurricane', and the natives of New Zealand regarded the wind as a special indication of God's presence;[1] with this may be compared the Australian fear, mentioned above, of the impregnating storm, the idea of 'Father' being common to both. Even in modern times tempests have been regarded as representing God in a dangerous mood, while in all ages the creating of storms and thunder has been considered a special prerogative of the Deity (Odin, Thor, Yahweh, Zeus, etc.).

A Chinese myth[2] relates how Hoang-Ty, or Hiong, the founder of civilisation, was born of a virgin, Ching-Mou, and *thunder*. The mythology of thunder is much too extensive to be considered here, but attention should be called to the close association between the ideas of 'thunder' and 'father', one, indeed, which applies to the whole group under discussion. The Phrygian precursor of Zeus was called both Papas (= Father) and Bronton (= Thunderer).

---

[1] Taylor: Te Ika a Maui, or New Zealand and its Inhabitants, Second Edition, 1870, p. 181.

[2] De Prémare: Vestiges des principaux dogmes chrétiens, 1878, p. 433.

Frazer[1] has shewn how extensive has been the connection
between Kings and thunder, and has made it probable
that the early Roman kings imitated Jupiter's powers in
this respect; it is well known that psychologically the idea
of king is equivalent to that of father. The old Indian God
of Thunder and of Procreation, Parjanya, was represented
in the form of a bull,[2] a typical patriarchal symbol. That
the idea of thunder is exceedingly apt, in dreams and
other products of the unconscious phantasy, to symbolise
flatus, particularly paternol flatus, is well known to all
psycho-analysts; such psycho-neurotic symptoms as bronte-
phobia are almost constantly related to unconscious thoughts
concerning this, and in obscene jests the as sociation is
at least as old as Aristophanes.[3]

The association Father—God—Sound has always been
a remarkably close one, and the following description of
Zeus in this respect would hold good for the majority of
Gods: 'He gave his oracles through the voices of winds
moaning and rustling in his sacred oak grove amidst the
murmur of falling waters and the clangor of bronzen vessels
struck by wind-moved hammers.'[4] By a characteristically
human reasoning process it was assumed that supernatural
beings, including God himself, could be influenced by
sounds, of any kind, and this device has been widely
employed in connection with both the purposes for which
it was desired to attract the attention, and influence the
conduct, of the Divine Being. The beating of tom-toms in
African villages to frighten away evil spirits, and the similar
Norse procedure to prevent the sun from being swallowed
at the time of an eclipse, may be cited as examples of

[1] Frazer: op. cit., Vol. II, pp. 180-3.
[2] Rigveda (Griffith's Translation), Vol. II, p. 299.
[3] Aristophanes: Clouds, Act V, Sc. 2. Βροντή και πορδή, όμοιω.
[4] Cotterill: Ancient Greece, 1913, p. 58.

the one kind; in Greece also, loud noises were considered especially effective as apotropaic measures against the malign influences of evil demons. By the side of this Luther's statement[1] may be recalled, according to which the devil is to be driven away through the efficacy of the passage of flatus.

On the other hand, sounds, especially in the form of hymn-singing and music, have been, and still are, favourite means of intercession to obtain benefits from the Deity. A hymn called 'haha' (= breath), an invocation to the mystic wind, is pronounced by Maori priests on the initiation of young men.[2] The instrument called the 'bull-roarer', 'bummel', or 'buzzer' is said by Haddon[3] to be the most ancient, widely-spread, and sacred religious symbol in the world. It consists of a slab of wood which, when tied to a piece of string and rapidly whirled around, emits a roaring, uncanny noise. It is still used in Mexico, Ceylon, British Columbia, New Zealand, the Malay Peninsula, New Guinea, Africa, and Australia.[4] Under the name of the rhombus it figured prominently in the Dionysian mysteries in Ancient Greece, and Pettazoni[5] has recently pointed out that the 'rombo' still survives in modern Italy. It is used sometimes to invoke the presence and aid of the Deity, sometimes to drive away evil spirits. A study of the various beliefs surrounding it shews that the three main ideas with which its use is associated are: (1) thunder and wind,

---

[1] Schurig: Chylologia, 1725, p. 795; See also Les Propos de Table de Luther, Trad. franc. par Brunet, 1846, p. 22.

[2] Andrew Lang: Custom and Myth, 1884, p. 36.

[3] Haddon: The Study of Man, 1898, p. 327.

[4] Frazer gives numerous references to it in the different volumes of his Golden Bough. See also Marett, *Hibbert Journal*, Jan. 1910, and Bouvaine, *Journal of the Anthropological Institute*, Vol. II, p. 270.

[5] Pettazoni: 'Soppravvivenze del rombo in Italia', *Lares*, 1912, Vol. I, p. 63.

(2) reproduction (vegetation cults, initiation ceremonies, danger if seen by women, etc.), (3) ancestor worship (i. e. Father)—in other words, ideas that take a prominent part in the theme under discussion here. There is naturally a close connection between bull-roarers and thunder-weapons in general, which have played an important part in religious rites in most parts of the world except Egypt;[1] the hammer of Thor, the trident of Poseidon, the trisula of Siva, and the keraunos of Zeus are a few of the many variants of it the phallic significance of which is evident. In short, there are innumerable connections between the idea of thunder on the one hand and ideas of paternal power, particularly reproductive power, on the other, a conclusion reached long ago by Schwartz[2] and in full accord with the conclusions of Abraham[3] and Kuhn[4] on the sexual symbolism of lightning.

In ancient times it was believed that the young of lions were born dead and that they were awakened into life through the roaring of their sire; this is given as one of the reasons why in the Resurrection Jesus was sometimes represented as a lion, the space of three days being also common to the two beliefs. It may be paralleled by the belief mentioned by Pliny,[5] that a female partridge can be impregnated merely from hearing the *cry* of the male. The general importance of the voice in love-making is well known to biologists. With many animals, e. g. deer, most birds, etc., the love-call of the mate is one of the strongest means of attraction, and even with human beings

---

[1] See Blinkenberg: The Thunderweapon in Religion and Folklore, 1911.

[2] Schwartz: Wolken und Wind, Blitz und Donner, 1879, S. 186.

[3] Abraham: Traum und Mythus, 1909.

[4] Kuhn: Über die Herabkunft des Feuers und des Göttertranks, 1859.

[5] Pliny: op. cit., x, 51.

the *voice,* in both speaking and singing,[1] has by no means lost this primitive effect.

From the sound of the voice it is an easy transition to the idea of *Speech.* The sexual relationships of speech are made plain in every psycho-analysis of neurotic symptoms in which this function is implicated; stammering, self-consciousness concerning speech, and so on. It has been dwelt on by many writers. Sperber[2] has made out a powerful case for the view that speech originated as a development of the love-call excitation accompanying the search for symbolic sexual gratification. In mythology and folk-lore the function of speech is often treated as equivalent to loving or living, just as its opposite, dumbness, signifies impotence or death; an example of the latter symbolism is to be found in the New Testament story where, to emphasise the supernatural nature of John the Baptist's conception, the earthly father (Zacharias) is said to have been dumb (= impotent) from just before the conception until just after the birth.

[1] That infantile interest for the sound accompanying the passage of flatus may be transferred in later life to the subject of *music* was first pointed out by Ferenczi *(Zentralbl f Psychoanalyse,* Jahrg. I, S. 395, Anm. 1). The resemblance between the German words 'fisteln' (= to sing falsetto) and 'fisten' (= to pass flatus) is certainly in accord with this finding. One may in this connection recall the fact that Hermes was God, not only of music, but also of winds, speech, and money. (The anal-erotic association between money, gas, and intestinal contents is indicated by many expressions in English. Thus new words are 'coined', while new coins are 'uttered'. 'To stink of money' is to be over-wealthy. 'To raise the wind' is slang for 'to obtain money', just as 'to cough up money' is for parting unwillingly with it. 'To have a blow-out' means to have a good meal, while 'to blow' money is to spend it extravagantly; the latter expression is often, through confusion with the past tense 'blew', corrupted to 'to blue money'.)

[2] Sperber: 'Über den Einfluß sexueller Momente auf die Entstehung der Sprache', *Imago,* 1912, Bd. I, S. 405.

Speech was therefore quite naturally considered to be identical with God, i. e. the Creator, and the doctrine of the Logos has played a prominent part in most of the higher religions. One need only recall the familiar passages in St. John (i. 1 and i. 14): 'In the beginning was the Word, and the Word was with God, and the Word was God'; 'And the Word was made flesh' (embodiment of Jesus Christ). He also relates of his vision of the Being on a White Horse that 'his name is called the Word of God' (Apocalypse xix. 13). God seems to have selected with preference mere speech as the means of carrying out his wishes, for instance in the Creation itself ('And God said, Let there be light; and there was light', etc.). The association between the Holy Ghost and speech was just as intimate: the saints 'spoke by the Holy Ghost' (St. Mark xii. 36; Acts of the Apostles xiii. 2; xvi. 7), or were 'filled by the Holy Ghost and prophesied' (St. Luke i. 67), while St. Paul pointedly says that 'no man can say that Jesus is the Lord, but by the Holy Ghost' (1 Corinthians xii. 3).

The sexual equivalency of the idea of speech, or word, comes to especially clear expression in the very legend under discussion. From a number of passages in the writings of the early Fathers that bear this out I will quote two only: St. Zeno[1] writes, 'The womb of Mary swells forth with pride, not by conjugal gift, but by faith; by the Word, not by seed', and St. Eleutherius,[2] 'O blessed Virgin . . . made mother without cooperation of man. For here the ear was the wife, and the angelic word the husband'. The Virgin's conception has been constantly contrasted by ecclesiastical writers with the fall of Eve,

---

[1] St. Zeno: Lib. ii, Tractatus viii and ix, Pat. Lat., Tom. II, p. 413.

[2] St. Eleutherius Tornacensis· Serm. in Annunt. Fest., Tom. 65, p. 96.

'the second Eve' being a very usual designation for Mary. The following passage, from St. Ephrem,[1] is typical of many: 'In the beginning the serpent, getting possession of the ears of Eve, thence spread his poison throughout her whole body; to-day Mary through her ears received the champion of everlasting bliss.' It is now generally recognised[2] that the myth of the Fall in Eden represents an expurgated version of a fertilisation myth, so that such passages as the one just quoted must be simply regarded as expressing the contrast between forbidden and allowed sexual union, as typified by Eve and Mary.

It is thus plain that at least some of the significance attaching to the idea of speech has arisen in psychosexual affects, and the next question is, in which specific ones? I have elsewhere[3] indicated the probable answer to this— namely, the acts of breathing and speaking are both treated in the Unconscious as equivalents of the act of passing intestinal flatus, and a corresponding displacement of affect is brought about from the latter idea to the former ones. Indications of this association are still preserved in such expressions as 'poetic afflatus', 'clat-fart' (Staffordshire dialect for 'gossip'), 'flatulent speech', 'a windy discourse', and the contemptuous slang phrases for this, 'gas' (English) and 'hot air' (American). The word 'ventriloquism' (literally 'belly-speaking', German *Bauchreden*) is noteworthy in the same connection, and it is of interest that Ferenczi[4] has

---

[1] St. Ephrem: De Divers. Serm., I, p. 607. See also St. Fulgentius; De laude Mariae ex partu Salvatoris, St Zeno: Ad Pulcheriam Augustam, etc.

[2] See, for instance, Otto Rank: *Zentralbl. f. Psychoanalyse,* Jahrg. II, S, 389, and Ludwig Levy: 'Sexualsymbolik in der biblischen Paradiesgeschichte', *Imago,* 1917-19, Bd. V, S. 16.

[3] *Jahrbuch der Psychoanalyse,* 1912, Bd. IV, S. 588, 594.

[4] Ferenczi: Contributions to Psycho-Analysis (Engl. Transl.), 1916, p. 179.

shewn that during analysis the suppression of a remark
may be betrayed by a rumbling in the stomach.

Nor is it without significance that of the five Prânas
(the sacred breaths in the Vedas) it is the Apâna, or
down-breathing, that is the one associated with speech.[1]

3. *Invisibility and Fluidity*

These attributes favour the occurrence of the interesting association between the idea of *Thought* and the group
under consideration. Thought is usually imagined as
something flowing; one thinks of such expressions as 'he
poured out his thoughts', 'his thoughts ceased to flow', etc.,
and every psychologist is familiar with William James'
famous chapter on 'The Stream of Consciousness'. The
ideas of breath, speech and thought are symbolic equivalents,
and are all unconsciously associated with that of intestinal
gas.[2] I have elsewhere[3] brought forward reasons for thinking that the unconscious belief in the omnipotence of
thought (*Allmacht der Gedanken*), which lies at the root
of animism and magic, may be related to this association
with the idea of creative power, just as most concrete
emblems of power (sceptre, sword, cross, staff, etc.) are
well-recognised phallic symbols. The notion of thought as
a begetter also occurs, e. g. in the myth of Athene's birth
out of the brain of Zeus. There are frequent reports of
nuns in the middle ages who professed to be pregnant
because Jesus had *thought* of them.

We thus see how the Unconscious conceives of the
Mind, regarded as an objective phenomenon. In the Vedic

---

[1] Khândogya-Upanishad, iii, 13, 8.

[2] This association is also illustrated in the case already referred
to and its relation to the idea of 'auto-suggestion' expounded.

[3] *Internationale Zeitschrift für Psychoanalyse*, 1913, Bd. I., S. 429.
See also Eisler, *International Journal of Psycho-Analysis*, 1921, Vol. II.,
p. 255 et seq.

literature[1] the mind is said to be cognate with the Vyâna, or back-going breath, while in another of the Upanishads[2] we read that the Self consists of speech, mind, and breath, and that the Self should be consoled in sacrificing the desire for a wife by remembering that 'mind is the husband, speech the wife, and breath the child'.[3] Similarly for the Neo-Platonist Plotinus the world-soul is the energy of the intellect and is begotten by the intellect, the father, just as Athene, the Goddess of Wisdom, sprang from the brain of her father. In quoting the following passage from him, 'That which lies closed together in the intellect attains full development as the Logos in the world-soul, fills this with meaning and, as it were, makes it drunk with nectar', Jung[4] comments: 'Nectar, like soma, is the drink of fertility and life, i. e. sperma'. Diogenes[5] also identified the intellect with air; he maintained that air has intelligence, and that human beings are intelligent in virtue of the air that enters in from without. The latter statement is perhaps a highly sublimated expression of the infantile sexual theory described earlier in this essay.

From the ideas of thought and the mind it is but a step to that of the *Soul,* and we shall see that the same group of affects have extensively influenced this concept also. Of the primitive conceptions of the soul,[6] the lower (we do not say the primary) is that of the 'bound soul', which was imagined as the vital principle of various internal organs, and was evidently little else than a symbolisation of the vital essence, i. e. sperma. (We are not here con-

[1] Taittirîyaka-Upanishad, i, 7, 1.

[2] Brihadâranyaka-Upanishad, i, 5, 3.

[3] ibid., i, 4, 17.

[4] Jung: *Jahrbuch der Psychoanalyse,* 1912, Bd. IV, S. 179.

[5] See Brett: A History of Psychology: Ancient and Patristic, 1912, p. 46.

[6] See Wundt: op. cit., S. 1, et seq.

cerned with the motives or forces that led mankind to conceive the idea of a soul, a matter on which Freud[1] has thrown considerable light, but simply with the original content out of which this idea was constructed.) If sexual thoughts played such a prominent part in this crude conception of the soul it is reasonable to expect that they have also been operative, though perhaps in a more disguised manner, in regard to the more elaborate ones, and this we find to have been so. The most important part of the concept 'Free Soul' is that known as the 'Breath Soul' (*Hauchseele*), and it is easy to shew that the idea of this belongs to the group under consideration. The evidence for the far-reaching association between the ideas of soul and breath is so familiar that it need not be recounted here; we are constantly reminded of it by the very names for the former, from the Greek 'psyche' and the Hebrew 'nephesh' to the German 'Geist' and the English 'ghost' and 'spirit'. The fact that all these words originally meant simply 'breath' also indicates that the latter was the primary idea of the two, which is indeed evident from every point of view, and that we have here a typical example of displacement of significance.

There are at least two reasons for suspecting that the affects here concerned did not all originate in the idea of breath even, but in a still deeper one—namely, in that of intestinal gas. These are, that in the first place the affects and psychical significance which have been attached to the idea of breath, or air or wind, were disproportionate to the inherent psychical importance of the idea and so must have been derived from one of greater psychical significance (such as flatus indubitably is in infantile life and in the adult Unconscious), and that in the second place numerous

---

[1] Totem und Tabu, 1913, Kap. IV.

direct connections can be indicated between the idea of intestinal gas and the conception of the Breath-Soul.

The first argument, put in other words, is that, if a mass of feeling flowed over from the idea of breath to that of the soul greater in quantity than the amount inherently belonging to the former, then it follows that this idea must have acted, in part at least, merely as a carrier. Now it is not hard to shew that the significance attached to the ideas of wind, air, soul, and breath have been much greater than what might be explicable from the primary psychical importance of the last-named of these, omitting of course its secondary importance as an emblem of life and creation. Confining ourselves solely to Hindoo and Greek philosophy, and taking first the former, we note the following beliefs and statements in the Upanishads alone. Prâna (breath) is identified on the one hand with Brâhman, the Supreme Being, and on the other with Âtman, the primary essence of the Universe.[1] The origin of the latter is thus described: From Âtman came the Other, from this the wind, from this the fire, from this water, and from water came earth; thus the primary four of the series are expressed in terms of a gas. It is unnecessary to cite any further examples, but it may be said that by far the greater part of this whole literature is taken up with this theme, the ideas of breath, wind, and so on, being described in the most exalted language imaginable.

Similarly if we turn to Greece we find that the same group of ideas forms a central starting point for a great part, probably the greater part, of the views on philosophy, medicine, psychology, and general *Weltanschauung*. Many of the earlier monists, including Anaximenes, posited air as their ἀρχή, and the continued existence of the world was explained by a process

---

[1] Deussen: op. cit., pp. 110, 194.

of cosmic respiration,[1] the conception of which was based in detail on that of bodily respiration. Heidel, in a specially careful study,[2] has further shewn that the various atomic theories of the Greeks can principally be traced to their views about the act of breathing.[3] Diogenes, in taking air as the most important element in the world, plainly says that the necessity of breath for life is the reason why air is chosen as the primary reality; the interaction between air in the body and the air outside is the type of all vital action.[4] With the Stoics also,[5] the pneuma was of cardinal importance: it was the breath of life, the warm air closely associated with the blood, the vital principle transmitted in generation, and at the same time the soul, which is contained in the body and yet is one in nature with the surrounding World-Soul.[6] The part played by the idea of breath in moulding the Greek conception of the soul is too familiar to need insisting on. The influence of this conception extended far into Christian times. Clement of Alexandria, for instance, as well as Tertullian, maintained that the 'rational soul', which is directly imparted by God to man, is identical with that 'breath of God'[7] mentioned

[1] Heidel: 'Antecedents of the Greek Corpuscular Theories', *Harvard Studies in Classical Philology*, 1911, Vol. XXII, pp. 137-40.

[2] Heidel: op. cit, pp. 111-72.

[3] It is interesting to note that the highest achievements of modern physical science, the atomic theory and the conception of ether, both of which were anticipated in Greek philosophy, represent in both cases sublimated projections of the complex under discussion.

[4] Brett: op. cit, pp 45, 46.

[5] Brett: op. cit., pp. 166, 167.

[6] It is clear that the idea of 'cosmic consciousness', of which we hear so much in modern pseudo-philosophy, is psychologically equivalent to ideas concerning the outer air, which have been projected from more personal sources.

[7] The Hebrew 'ruach' denoted both the human soul and the breath of God.

in Genesis, in contradistinction to the 'irrational soul', which is akin to the life-principle of animals. The latter belief may profitably be compared with the Indian one mentioned above (p. 275) concerning the two breaths, upper and lower in a moral as well as in a physical sense, and the juxtaposition here of animal and divine opens up the whole topic of repression.

The pneuma concept was also one of the highest significance in Greek medicine and retained much of its importance until about a century ago, gradually fading away via the doctrine of 'humour' and 'diathesis'; its memory is perpetuated in such expressions as 'to be in a bad humour', 'in good spirits'. All causes of disease other than those relating to food and drink were summarised under the generic term 'air', a pernicious relic of which attitude we still retain in the almost universal superstition that draughts are dangerous to health (not to mention the special risks ascribed to specific forms of air such as 'night air', 'damp air', air coming through holes, etc.), and the therapeutic value ascribed to a 'change of air', or a 'change of climate' was even greater than that obtaining in our own days.[1] For centuries most physicians

---

[1] One should also think of the excessive significance which is still attached by many people to respiratory exercises. In the description of my patient referred to above there are some beautiful examples of the mystical application of these. Nor can orthodox medicine be entirely exempted from this reproach; I may cite the following examples taken at random from a medical catalogue:

1. Fletcher: The Law of the Rhythmic Breath, Teaching the Generation, Conservation and Control of Vital Force.
2. Arnulphy: La Santé par la science de la respiration. (La respiration est un des principaux procédés au moyen desquels on arrive à développer sa force magnétique, sa volonté.)
3. Durville: Pour combattre la peur, la crainte, l'anxiété, la timidité, développer la volonté, guérir ou soulager certaines maladies par la Respiration Profonde.

were attached to one or other school of philosophy, and
the most important group were those constituting the school
of Pneumatists, who subscribed to the Stoic doctrines;
physiology and philosophy thus exerted a mutual influence
on each other. The pneuma coursed through the entire
body, regulated nutrition, generated thought and semen,[1]
and, according to Aristotle, conveyed to the heart the
movements of sensation that had been transmitted to it
from without through the medium of the sense organs; on
the state of it depended the health of the individual. An
interesting example of the strength of the pneuma doctrine
was the way in which it was able totally to obscure the
significance of the discovery of the nerves,[2] it being
insisted, in spite of all the evidence to the contrary, that
these were merely ramifications of the pneuma-carrying
arteries; even later, when the relation of the nerves to the
brain and to muscular action had been established, Augustine
maintained that they were tubes of air which transmitted
to the limbs the actions commanded by the will. The
following passages from Brett[3] well illustrate the general
significance of the pneuma doctrine: 'To one who thinks
of the body as irrigated throughout by air, who attributes
the cause of pulsation to the shock of air meeting blood,
who moreover feels dimly that man is in direct connexion
with the whole universe through the continuity of this air,

[1] The view was, for instance, expressed that Hephaistos took the
form of pneuma that coursed through the arteries of Zeus to his brain
and thus led him to generate thought, i.e. to procreate Athene. (See
Creuzer: Symbolik und Mythologie, 2e Aufl., 1819-1823, Bd. II,
S. 763 et seq.)

[2] Brett (op cit., p. 284) gives a striking description of the prejudices due to the tenaciousness with which the pneuma doctrine was
held, and of the difficulty with which these were overcome before the
value of the discovery could be properly appreciated.

[3] Brett: op. cit., pp. 52, 53.

the importance of this factor must have assumed the greatest proportions.'

There is abundant evidence to shew that the idea of breath could not have been by any means the sole source of this series of doctrines, readily as this seems generally to be assumed. Proceeding first with the Greek views, we note two considerations: that the pneuma was not always brought into connection with breath as one would have expected from the current opinion, and further that their conception of respiration was a singularly broad one, many processes being included under this term besides that of breathing. Aristotle, for example, positively states that the pneuma of the body, the importance of which we have just noted, is not derived from the breath, but is a secretion resulting from processes going on within the body itself (primarily in the intestine), and Galen says, even more explicitly, that the psychic pneuma is derived in part from the vapours of digested food.[1] This association, which appears to be still active in the Unconscious, is also embodied in our daily speech: we talk of '*expressing* our thoughts', of being given 'food for thought', and so on. It would seem possible that the association has played some part in the development of certain forms of materialistic philosophy; one is struck, for instance, by the simile employed in such dicta as that of Cabanis, 'the brain secretes thought as the liver secretes bile'. We see an interesting revival of this attitude in the current materialistic trends of present-day psychiatry, which would derive the greater part of mental disorder from toxins due to intestinal disturbances—quite logically, if this organ were the source of thought, as the Greeks believed; the total absence of any evidence in support of this aetiology makes no difference to the belief in it.

[1] Brett: op. cit., pp. 118, 291.

In the second place, a little study of the accounts given by various writers makes it plain that the Greeks thought of the respiratory and alimentary systems as being throughout closely connected,[1] which is the main point we are trying here to establish. On the one hand respiration was not restricted to breathing, but included also perspiration (a perfectly scientific view), while on the other hand respiration was regarded as a variety of nutrition, which indeed it is. They not only identified the absorption of air, its subsequent changes within the body, and its final excretion,[2] with those of food, but ascribed to the influence of the former the process whereby the latter becomes sufficiently rarefied to be carried over the body; the underlying idea, with of course many modifications, seems to have been that the inspired air reached the stomach, either through the blood stream or through the oesophagus (which they believed led to the heart), and there digested the food, the internal pneuma being the product of this, and thus representing a combination of air and food. From this point of view it is clear that pneuma was not merely a symbolic equivalent of intestinal gas, but was actually and grossly identical with it. The world-wide belief that the soul escapes through the mouth[3] probably refers, therefore, to ideas concerning not only the respiratory system, but the alimentary one also; this conclusion is supported by the existence, among many tribes, of various precautions and taboos designed to prevent the escape of the soul through the mouth during eating.[4]

---

[1] See Heidel: op. cit., pp. 131-7.

[2] Hippocrates in describing the foetus says that it draws in breath through the umbilical cord, and that when it is filled with breath this 'breaks', makes a passage for itself outward through the middle of the foetus, and in this way escapes. (See Heidel: op. cit., S. 135, 136).

[3] See Frazer: Taboo and the Perils of the Soul, 1911, pp. 30-3.

[4] Frazer: op. cit., p. 116.

Study of the Vedic literature shews that the conceptions of the Indian philosophers on this matter were fundamentally similar to those of the Greeks. They devoted an extraordinary attention to the subject of the five Prânas, or breaths, but the accounts given of these in the various passages are so overlapping that it is not always easy to define the precise differences between them; in fact it is known that the definitions shifted to some extent at different periods. In spite of this, however, it is possible to determine the main outlines of the conceptions, and we may consider them in order. Prâna, the 'up-breathing', means essentially the breath proper. Where it stands alone it frequently denotes the sense of smell, consequently inspiration, but sometimes when used in conjunction with Apâna it means expiration and the latter inspiration.[1] Apâna, the 'down-breathing', though it also sometimes denotes smell and inspiration, usually means the wind of digestion residing in the bowels. It originates in the navel of the primaeval man.[2] It carries off the intestinal excrements,[3] it dwells in the bowels,[4] and presides over the organs of evacuation and generation.[5] The Vyâna, or 'back-going' breath, unites the breath proper to the wind of digestion,[6] and courses through the blood-vessels.[7] The Samâna, or all-breathing, also unites the Prâna to the Apâna,[8] and

[1] See Deussen: op. cit., pp. 276-9, where this matter is discussed in detail.

[2] Aitareya-Âranyaka, ii, 4, 1, 6. (I refer throughout to the notation in Müller's edition.)

[3] ibid: ii, 4, 3, 2. Also Maitrâyana-Upanishad, II, 6 and Garbha-Upanishad, I.

[4] Amritabindhu, 34

[5] Prasña-Upanishad, iii, 5.

[6] Maitrâyana-Upanishad, ii, 6.

[7] Prasña-Upanishad, iii, 6.

[8] Prasña-Upanishad, iv, 4.

carries the food over the body.[1] These two last-mentioned
breaths evidently make up together the Greek 'internal
pneuma'. Finally the Udâna, the 'up- or out-breathing',
sometimes called the 'wind of exit',[2] dwells in the throat,[3]
and either brings up again or swallows down that which
is eaten or drunk.[4] The Udâna, which evidently denotes
gas regurgitating from a flatulent stomach, is an interesting
counterpart to the Apâna, for while the latter is formally
identified with death itself[5] the former carries away the
soul from the body after death;[6] the connection between
them is naturally a close one, since they both represent
intestinal gas, which may escape either upwards or downwards. The ideas of death and of intestinal decomposition
are here, as so often,[7] brought near together, an additional
explanation being thus afforded for the belief that the soul
escapes from an alimentary orifice after death.

Consideration of these accounts reveals the striking
fact that four out of the five Prânas are much more closely
related to the alimentary system than to the respiratory,
being primarily concerned with the movement of food,
either within the alimentary canal itself or in the body at
large; even the fifth, the Prâna in the narrowest sense,
does not altogether dispense with this connection, for on
the one hand it is doubly united to the Apâna (flatus)
and on the other hand it has to do with the sense of
smell, which biologically is nearly related to both sexuality
and coprophilia.

---

[1] Maitrâyana-Upanishad, ii, 6. Prasña-Upanishad, iii, 5.
[2] Vedântasâra, 97.
[3] Aimritabindhu, 34.
[4] Maitrâyana-Upanishad, ii, 6.
[5] Aitareya-Âranyaka, ii, 4, 2, 4.
[6] Prasña-Upanishad, iii, 7.
[7] See chapter II, p. 101.

It seems to me, therefore, a hardy venture for anyone who has reviewed the evidence just brought forward still to maintain that no other bodily gas than breath has played a part in developing the conception of the 'Breath-Soul'.

4. Moisture

It is well known that the idea of water has played an extraordinarily extensive part in anthropological symbolism, and especially in connection with the ideas of creation and birth. The symbolic significance of water is mainly derived from its unconscious equivalency with uterine fluid, urine, and semen; it is probably the commonest symbol, both male and female, employed in birth phantasies. It is therefore quite intelligible that the ideas of water and of gas should frequently be found in proximity in these phantasies, and that they should even be treated as symbolic equivalents. A simple example is that in the myth of Prometheus, who created mankind out of water and sound. One nearer to the principal theme of this essay is that of the relation between the Holy Ghost and Baptism. In a previous essay[1] I have tried to shew that the psychological symbolism of the baptismal rite signifies 'rebirth through purification', and that purification is an idea unconsciously equivalent to fertilisation. It is thus noteworthy that the two ideas of baptismal water and the Holy Ghost (in infantile terms, urine and gas) are frequently brought together in the New Testament in relation to the idea of re-birth. Jesus, in his reply to Nicodemus, says: 'Verily, verily, I say unto thee, Except a man be born of water and of the Spirit, he cannot enter into the kingdom of God. That which is born of the flesh is flesh; and that which is born of the Spirit is spirit. Marvel not that I said unto thee, Ye must be

[1] Chapter IV, p. 163.

born again. The wind bloweth where it listeth, and thou
hearest the sound thereof, but canst not tell whence it
cometh, and whither it goeth; so is every one that is born
of the Spirit' (St. John iii. 5 et seq.), and again, 'For John
truly baptised with water; but ye shall be baptised with
the Holy Ghost' (Acts i. 5). The replacement of the desire
for earthly (i. e. incestuous) re-birth by that for spiritual
re-birth is equivalent to the wish to be purified from sin,
sin (of which incest is the great archetype) and death
being opposed to re-birth and life; St. Paul writes (Romans
viii. 2): 'For the law of the spirit of life in Christ Jesus
hath made me free from the law of sin and death'.

The tertium comparationis between water and gas is
evidently fluidity, and in the idea of *vapour* we get a fusion
of the two. For this reason vapour has always played an
important part in connection with the various topics discussed
above, and the process of evaporation, whereby water is
converted through vapour into gas, has extensively engaged
the interest and attention of mankind. In Ancient Greece
the Plutonia, Charonia, or hell-gates, where vapours issued
from the earth, were sacred, because the exhalations were
regarded as the spirits of the dead[1] (cp. the relation
mentioned above between death and Apâna and Udâna).
These spirits were looked to for increase of flocks and
herds[2] and for the fruitfulness of the soil, while women
worshipped them to obtain offspring.[3] Such beliefs are still
current in Syria:[4] for example, at the Baths of Solomon
in northern Palestine, blasts of hot air escape from the
ground, and one of them, named Abu Rabah, is a famous

---

[1] Rohde: Psyche, 6. Aufl., 1910, Bd. I, S. 213. Also Preller-
Robert: Griechische Mythologie, Bd. I, S. 283, 811.

[2] Many passages in Dieterich: Mutter Erde, 1905.

[3] Rohde: op. cit., S. 297-9.

[4] Curtiss: Primitive Semitic Religion To-Day, 1902, pp. 116 et seq.

resort of childless wives who wish to satisfy their maternal longings; they let the hot air stream up over their bodies and really believe that children born to them after such a visit are begotten by the saint of the shrine. In ancient Italy issuing vapours were personified as a goddess, Mefitis, whose chief temple was in the valley of Amsanctus. The exhalations here, supposed to be the breath of Pluto himself, are known to consist of warm, noisy blasts of sulphuretted hydrogen[1] (i. e. had the odour of flatus); the association between intestinal functions and Pluto, the god of the lower world, is brought to our consciousness by the title of the well-known purgative, Pluto water!

Heidel[2] says that 'probably no other natural phenomenon played so important a role in Greek philosophy as evaporation'. Rohde has abundantly shewn that to the Greeks the soul was essentially a vapour;[3] the later conception of the soul, however, for instance that of the Stoics, would seem to have been that of an invisible, gaseous medium which owed both its origin and its continued activities to the vapours, derived from the mixture of blood and air, that coursed through the body. The process of evaporation or distillation was evidently of cardinal importance in effecting this change from the material to the immaterial, and thus helps to explain the significance attaching to bodily heat that brought it about, of which we shall speak later. From this point of view it is also easy to grasp Diogenes' notion that thought is an activity of *dry* air, that moisture is detrimental to thinking, and that excess of moisture is the reason why the young lack

---

[1] Frazer: Adonis, Attis, Osiris, 2nd Edition, 1907, p. 170.

[2] Heidel: op. cit., p. 122. See also Gilbert: Die meteorologischen Theorien des griechischen Altertums, 1907, S. 439 et seq.

[3] It may be mentioned that our word 'breath' is cognate with the German *Brodem* (steam, odour).

intelligence.[1] The same train of thought was applied to the life of the universe, cosmic respiration being imagined in terms of moisture, the earth and sea giving forth vapour and receiving back rain.[2] It dominated further the greater part of physiology, for digestion, absorption and nutrition were essentially problems of the conversion of food into the internal pneuma and the distribution of this through the body.

The inter-relation of moisture and air in both respiratory and intestinal breath affords a physiological basis for these conceptions, the psychological origin of which, however, goes back, as was indicated above, to infantile life.

5. Warmth

In relating the variants of the idea of the Virgin Mary's conception, as portrayed in art, we noted the curious fact that rays of light were sometimes treated as the equivalent of radiating breath, issuing from the mouth, entering into the ear, and so on, and we take this as a starting point for the discussion of warmth as an attribute common to the upper and the lower breaths. The belief in question finds many parallels outside of Christianity: the legends of virgins thet have been impregnated by rays of light, usually from the sun or by fire, are exceedingly numerous and wide-spread. Bab,[3] Frazer,[4] Hartland,[5] and others have collected many dozens of such stories, with customs based on the belief, and it is not necessary to quote any specific examples here. They shew the usual

---

[1] Brett: op. cit., p. 46.

[2] Heidel: op. cit., p. 134.

[3] Bab: op. cit., S. 279 et seq.

[4] Frazer: The Golden Bough, 1900, Vol. III, pp. 204 et seq., 244, 270, 305, 314.

[5] Hartland: Primitive Paternity, 1909, Vol. I, pp. 11-13, 18, 25, 26, 89-100.

characteristics of supernatural births, the child proving to be a Messiah, a great Emperor, or what not. One rather striking feature is the frequency with which water is made to play a part in the event; the virgin is the daughter of a river-god, a star falls into water which she drinks, and so on. That the making of fire is commonly conceived of by the primitive mind as a sexual performance is well established.[1]

But beyond the symbolic equivalency just signified, an inherent connection between breath and fire (or light) is often predicated. To breathe on a fire, especially a holy one, is strictly tabooed in many countries;[2] for instance a Braham is forbidden to blow on a fire with his mouth. The relation of breath to fire in folk-lore and superstition is a very close one.[3] In Longfellow's 'Hiawatha' it is described how Gitchie Manito, the 'Creator of the Nations', blew on to the trees so that they rubbed together and burst into flame. In the Old Testament breath is constantly associated with fire, and in the Hermetic writings it is stated that souls are made from 'the breath of God and conscious fire'. In the Mithra liturgy the creative breath proceeds from the sun, and in the Stoic philosophy the cosmic Divine Fire was identical with the atmosphere. Jung[4] and Silberer[5] quote a number of interesting passages from various sources that shew the intimate association subsisting between the ideas of shining and sounding. It can therefore be said with certainty that in primitive thinking the ideas of *sound*, *heat* and *light* are as definitely

[1] Frazer: The Magic Art, 1911, Vol II, Ch. XV, 'The Fire-Drill' and p. 233.

[2] Frazer: op. cit., p. 241. Spirits of the Corn and of the Wild, 1912, Vol. II, p. 254.

[3] Frazer: The Magic Art, Vol. II, p. 239 et seq.

[4] Jung: op. cit., S. 206-8.

[5] Silberer: *Jahrbuch der Psychoanalyse*, Bd. II, S. 596-7.

interchangeable equivalents as the corresponding physical processes have been proved to be by the scientific doctrine of the transformation of energy.

We have now to inquire into the meaning of this association. Fire, or heat, is known to be one of the commonest libidinal symbols, and, as Abraham[1] has clearly shewn, it is the equivalent of soma and sperma. This, however, obviously cannot be the original source of the association, for not only is the child ignorant of the existence of sperma, but it is relatively late before it learns to appreciate even that of fire. Years ago, in his Dora analysis, Freud[2] pointed out that in symbolic language, e. g. in dreams, the idea of fire replaced that of water, particularly urine; the association is partly one of contrast, from the mutual incompatibility of the two substances. In the psycho-analyses of patients I have also found that fire can symbolise not only urine, but also flatus, as for instance in phobias concerning gas-jets,[3] and further that the primary source of fire symbolism in general is probably to be explained in the following way. The infant's first experience of heat (as distinct from the warmth of the normal body temperature) is derived from the fact that all excretions are warmer than the external temperature of the body and in addition often produce, from their irritating and acrid nature (especially marked with young children), local burning sensations. When, now, the child becomes acquainted later on with other sources of heat, particularly burning heat, he inevitably forms an association between them and the causes of his earlier experiences. This happens so regularly that, for instance, with a phobia of fire at night one can predict with certainty

---

[1] Abraham: Traum und Mythus, 1909.

[2] Freud: Sammlung kleiner Schriften zur Neurosenlehre. Zweite Folge, S. 80.

[3] This must have been so in the case described by Reitler, loc. cit.

that such a person will prove to be one who has incompletely overcome the infantile fear (and temptation) of bed-wetting. As we known that the child can express to itself the idea of sexual secretion only in terms of one or other excretion we can understand how it is that fire comes to be such a general libidinal symbol, most often of urine, though sometimes of flatus. We must thus infer, on the principles enunciated above, that the association between fire and breath is a secondary one, replacing the earlier one between fire and flatus (and urine).

There is ample confirmation of this conclusion to be found in many spheres, but we shall confine ourselves mainly to the field of Greek philosophy, so as to extend our previous considerations on this subject. In the first place, it is striking that the idea of heat, or fire, played a part of central importance in the pneuma doctrine; Aristotle, for instance, maintained that the active element in the internal pneuma was of the nature of fire, identical with the principle of fertility in semen. According to Heidel,[1] 'it is in the phenomena of fire as interpreted by the Greeks that we discover the best illustration of the processes of respiration and nutrition', and this is still the favourite method of introducing the study of chemical physiology. But the Greeks did not stay at the analogy; for them heat was the actual motive force that carried on these processes. Except among the Atomists, respiration was thought to proceed through the natural warmth of the body creating an expansion that mechanically draws in the colder air from without.[2] Similarly with nutrition. The native heat of the organism 'digested' the food, i. e. converted it into pneuma, in which form it was conveyed all through the body. It was at first believed that the

[1] Heidel: op. cit., p. 142.
[2] Heidel: op. cit., pp. 136, 141.

heat, or fire, worked no inner change in the food, merely
comminuting it and so preparing it for absorption into the
blood, but the hypothesis was carried by Aristotle to the
further stage mentioned above, his views on digestion
being accepted by Galen and most of the other later
medical authorities.[1] A great number of the Greek philosophers, however, just like the modern psycho-analyst,
refused to be satisfied with the idea of fire as a self-
sufficing primary agent, but broached the question of
its nature and origin. They concluded, or rather accepted
an age-old conclusion, that fire was sustained and fed by
water in the form of vapour, the analogy being evoked of
the sun drawing up or drinking moisture; since, however,
the very production of vapour is dependent on the heat,
it would seem as though a permanent cycle was posited,
the primordial construction of which it is impossible to
determine. It was believed that water was the primary
nutrient element *par excellence,* though this was inactive
without the influence of the fire which it itself fed. Presumably the ultimate source of the fire was the life-instinct
itself, for the greatest attention was paid to the passage
of heat from the mother to the child during pre-natal
life, but if one asks for a more explicit account of it,
particularly where it was supposed to reside, the only
conclusion at all conformable with the different accounts
seems to be that it was carried in a gaseous form, constituting thus the very essence of pneuma. In short, the
Greek theory of nutrition, just as that of respiration,
assumes the closest possible association between the ideas
of heat (or fire) and of gas (or breath in the widest
sense).

The idea of heat (or fire) played an equally prominent
part in the Greek non-physiological conceptions, e. g. the

[1] Heidel: op. cit., pp. 141-68.

philosophical and psychological ones. Some of the monists, such as Heraclitus, posited fire as their ἀρχή. The cosmic process, which, as was indicated above, was imagined in terms of respiration and nutrition, was supposed to depend on evaporation and precipitation, i. e. on an alternation of heat and cold; the continued existence of earth and sea was maintained through their emitting warm vapours and receiving back cooling showers.[1] The very word 'psyche' itself is derived from the word ψύχω,[2] which has the double meaning of 'I breathe' and 'I cool',[3] and one of the favourite images in which it was described, as it still is in poetic diction, was that of a thin ascending flame. When the Neo-Platonic Plotinus rejected the Stoic doctrine of the material origin of the pneuma, he elaborated the following ingenious view: As the association of the soul with matter implies a degradation it cannot be placed in immediate contact with the body, so it makes use of a mediating element, a form of pneuma, in which to clothe itself and be guarded from a defiling contact; this aerial garb is of the nature of fire (!), in which the soul dwells and through which it moves the body.

Another example of the association between the idea of fire and the group under consideration is that to do with *speech*. Jung[4] has brilliantly demonstrated the symbolic equivalence of speech and fire, quoting numerous beliefs

---

[1] Heidel: op. cit., pp. 134, 137-40.

[2] Prof. G. S. Brett was good enough to call my attention to Plato's sarcastic explanation of the word ψυχή = ἡ φύσιν ὀχεῖ καὶ ἔχει, 'that which conducts the nature (vitality)'. He adds: The word ὀχεῖ is not a natural one to use and is philologically connected with a number of words denoting (1) pipe, channel: (2) it is the technical word for 'ride' and in the form 'οχεύω means to perform the sexual act.

[3] Roscher: Ausführliches Lexikon der griechischen und römischen Mythologie, S. 3202.

[4] Jung: op. cit., S. 205-9.

in which the former is primary to the latter, though I cannot agree with his conclusion[1] that 'the origin of the fire-speech phenomenon seems to be the Mother-Libido'. To the many passages he cites I might add one from the Upanishads[2] in which both speech and fire are identified with the Apâna, or down-breathing. Thus fire originates in speech, and both in pneuma, particularly the intestinal one: a conclusion which is in complete harmony with the one formulated above[3] on the basis of individual analyses which shew speech to be an unconscious symbol for flatus (and sometimes urine also).

To the Assyrian Fire-God, Gibil, as to many others, was ascribed a Logos part,[4] and we have noted above the close association between speech and the Christian Trinity, particularly the Holy Ghost. It is therefore quite consistent that the Holy Ghost should be likened to fire. John the Baptist preached: 'I indeed baptize you with water unto repentance: but he that cometh after me is mightier than I, whose shoes I am not worthy to bear: he shall baptize you with the Holy Ghost, and with fire' (Matthew iii. 11). To be purified with fire (i. e. re-born) is a familiar metaphor, even in common speech, and the gaseous origin of it, indicated also in this passage, has been explained above in connection with the theme of baptism. In the Acts of the Apostles we read further (ii. 3) the following description of the descent of the Holy Ghost: 'And there appeared unto them cloven tongues, as of fire, and it sat upon each of them.'

In reference to the mention of the *tongue* in the last passage quoted it will be convenient here to say a few

---

[1] Jung: op. cit., S. 388.
[2] Khândogya-Upanishad, III, 13, 3.
[3] p. 289.
[4] Tiele: Babylonisch-assyrische Geschichte, 1886, S. 520.

words on this subject in so far as it relates to the present group of ideas. Symbolically the tongue is equivalent to the beak of the Dove, both having an evident phallic signification. Its physiological characters render it peculiarly adapted for this symbolism: thus, the facts that it is a red pointed organ, with dangerous potentialities, capable of self-movement, usually discreetly concealed but capable of protrusion (as in the defiant and forbidden exhibitionism of children), which can emit a fluid (saliva) that is a common symbol for semen.

In Bohemia a fox's tongue is worn by a timid person as an amulet to make him bold,[1] the meaning of which is patent. The term 'spit-fire', applied to anyone having a sharp tongue, is probably a relic of the belief in dragons, which emitted fire from both extremities of the body. In the Rig-Veda the fire-god Agni is called the 'beautiful-tongued one'; his tongue, like the phallic magic rods, is so powerful that it can overcome all obstacles.[2] Fire, like the tongue, is said to lick ('lingua' and allied words come from the Sanscrit lih = to lick). The dangerous-weapon idea is well shewn in a literal fashion in St. John's vision of the Being, of whom he writes (Revelations xix. 15) 'And out of his mouth goeth a sharp sword' (another favourite phallic symbol); in another passage (Revelations i. 16) he describes the Son of Man as having a sharp two-edged sword proceeding from his mouth. The Holy Ghost was not the only divine spirit to descend to earth in the guise of a tongue, for precisely the same is narrated of the Egyptian God Ptah, who, like Yahweh, created by means of the Word.

[1] Grohmann: Aberglauben und Gebräuche aus Böhmen und Mahren, 1864, S. 54.

[2] Hirzel. 'Gleichnisse und Metaphern im Rigveda', *Zeitschrift für Völkerpsychologie,* Jahrg. XIX, S. 356, 357.

Nor is the tongue bereft of connections with the alimentary group of ideas. It is, indeed, situate in the alimentary tract, and serves both for the taking in of food and for the spitting out of what may have to be expelled (bad food, phlegm, etc.); the Indians gave it the name of Atri, 'for with the tongue food is eaten, and Atri is meant for Atti, eating'.[1] It is also closely related to the gaseous ideas discussed above. In many languages, e. g. English and French, the same word is used to denote both tongue and speech, and the association between it and inspired speech or thought is indicated in the following passage from the Acts of the Apostles (ii. 4): 'And they were all filled with the Holy Ghost, and began to speak with other tongues, as the Spirit gave them utterance'. The association tongue—sexuality—speech is manifest in a number of nightmare superstitions collected by Laistner,[2] to which I will add one from Bohemia[3]—namely, that the tongue of a male snake, if cut from the animal on St. George's Eve and placed under a person's tongue, will confer the gift of eloquence; a similar explanation must hold for the well-known Irish belief of eloquence being conferred on whoever kisses the almost inaccessible Blarney stone. The tongue, therefore, is seen to be related to the ideas of fire, speech, sexuality, and divinity, a fact that will be commented on later when we discuss the idea of the combination of gas and an emitting organ.

6. Odour

This attribute differs from the preceding ones in being much more prominent with intestinal gas than with breath, and is on this account the more important for our purpose

---

[1] Brihadâranyaka-Upanishad, II, 2, 4.

[2] Laistner : Das Rätsel der Sphinx, 1889, Bd. I, S. 41, 42.

[3] Grohmann: op. cit, S. 81.

of elucidating the part played by the former. The essential relation of the sense of smell to coprophilia is well known to both ophresiologists and psycho-analysts, and it has been plainly shewn that much of the interest attaching to agreeable perfumes and aromatics is a replacement of that taken by children, and by primitive peoples, in the odour of excretions; the adult attitude towards the latter odour has become as a rule, though by no means invariably, a negative one. For both these reasons it is legitimate to infer that where the sense of smell has played a part in the formation of complex-ideas these are more nearly related to the phenomenon of intestinal gas than to that of breath.[1] Even when the odour of breath itself is prominent it is probable that it is secondary to the other; bad breath is instinctively referred to digestive disorder. In the psycho-analysis of patients who have an excessive repugnance for the odour of bad breath it is always found that this has originated in the repression of pronounced anal-erotism. The same association is often manifested in popular sayings and beliefs; 'to breathe on' was in Sparta a designation for the pederastic act,[2] and in Rome it was believed that the mouths of pederasts stank.[3]

We may begin with the part played in philosophical ideas. Heidel[4] says: 'Aromatics, which possess the power of throwing off continuous streams of effluvia without

---

[1] It may be conjectured that the antiquity of this buried association is one reason for the mysterious affective power of odours, especially in the revival of forgotten experiences (as screen-memories); as Marlitt says in her story 'Das Eulenhaus', 'Nichts in der Welt macht Vergangenes so lebendig wie der Geruch' ('Nothing on earth makes the past so living as does odour').

[2] Fehrle: Die kultische Keuschheit im Altertum, 1910, S. 86.

[3] Martial: Epigrammata, Lib. xii, 86.

[4] Heidel: op. cit., p. 125.

perceptible diminution, had great significance for Greek thought, although it generally has been overlooked.' This gives, for instance, the clue to the curious paradox that, although it is chemically pure water that is obtained by evaporation or distillation, the Greeks nevertheless held that it is through this process that various nutrient constituents pass from water to the inner fire and pneuma. They evidently seem to have regarded water not as a pure element, but as a liquid which contained in it all possible substances;[1] this belief points to an infantile origin in the idea of urine, the conception of which as an essence-containing liquid has proved fertile to many trains of thought.[2] The solution of the paradox is yielded by the observation that when a liquid evaporates the most volatile parts, not necessarily pure water vapour, are carried upwards, while the heavier, coarser parts are separated off and remain behind. The whole process, therefore, one of cardinal significance for the pneuma doctrine both of the individual and of the cosmos, was conceived as the evaporation and passing over of the volatile, quintessential elements, which were perceptible only to the sense of smell. The closest association was thus formed between this sense and the idea of essential constituent, one which is still retained in our use of the word 'essential' (cp. 'an essential oil', 'an essential idea').

The importance of odour is shewn in more direct ways than in that just indicated. One thinks at once of the extensive part played by incense in so many religions, and this in all probability replaced the earlier idea of the 'sweet savour' of burnt offerings.[3] (Taste and smell were

---

[1] See Heidel: op. cit., pp. 142, 143.
[2] See Chapter IV, p. 142, 156 et seq.
[3] See Atchley: A History of the Use of Incense, 1909, pp. 18, 76, etc.

not distinguished until relatively late in civilisation and are still popularly confounded to a remarkable extent; the Greeks, for instance, for some time denoted both by the same word ἡδονή.) The smell of the sacrifice was always considered to be specially pleasing to the god. The Fountain of Youth in Ethiopia, described by Herodotus, was aromatic and so ethereal as to be almost comparable to a vapour-bath, while the ambrosia on which the Gods fed had a marvellous fragrance. Aromatics were quite generally regarded in Greece as producing 'enthusiasm' or possession by the Godhead,[1] and inspiration altogether was connected with the same idea; the Pythia, for example, Apollo's priestess, derived her inspiration partly from the aroma of the sacred laurel and partly from the vapours issuing from her tripod.[2] It is interesting that in the Teutonic mythology also poetic inspiration was attributed to the drinking of a divine drink, Odrerir the 'poet's drink' or 'life-juice' of Odin, which is psychologically equivalent to ambrosia, nectar, soma, and semen. The sexual meaning of the drink is plainly enough indicated in the myth that Odin won possession of it by penetrating into a mountain in the form of a snake and so reaching the giant's daughter Gunnlod, whose love he of course wins; the Odrerir itself was generated by mixing honey with the blood of Kvásir, a man of wisdom who owed his existence to the mingling of two lots of saliva.[3] Customs of inducing inspiration by means of odours are very widespread; they are quoted by Frazer[4] from Bali, India, Madura, Uganda, etc. In Greece the foods partaken at the

---

[1] Rohde: op. cit., Bd. II, S. 60 et seq.

[2] Bethe: 'Die dorische Knabenliebe', *Rheinisches Museum*, Bd. LXII, S. 438-75.

[3] Mogk: Germanische Mythologie, 1906, S. 46, 47.

[4] Frazer: The Magic Art, 1911, Vol. I, pp. 379, 383, 384.

wedding feast and at the sacramental meal of the mysteries were all strongly pungent or aromatic, as were also the herbs laid beneath the dead at funerals.

On the homeopathic principle of 'like repelling like' odoriferous substances have been extensively used to counteract unpleasant or dangerous influences. In Greece, according to Heidel,[1] 'exhalations or effluvia of various kinds were the chief apotropaic and purificatory means employed in the most diverse circumstances.' Heat and cold were thought of essentially as effluvia, so that it is little wonder that fire became the purifying and apotropaic agency *par excellence,* as possessing the most evident emanations; that these were concerned in the efficacy is testified by Plato's remark, 'the demons love not the reek of torches'.[2] Almost all cathartic simples known to the materia medica of the Greeks possess a strong odour, rank or aromatic; wines were diuretic, diachoretic, or constipating according as they were aromatic or not. The efficacy of olive oil as a daily unguent and at burial was no doubt partly due to its aromatic properties; hence the use of it, or of wine, in the first bath given to the infant, and subsequently in Christian baptism. Nor should we overlook the extensive use of fumigations by Greek physicians, such as the internal fumigation of women after childbirth and as an emmenagogue.[3] But we need not go

---

[1] Heidel: op. cit., p. 126.

[2] Frazer (The Magic Art, Vol. II; The Scapegoat and Balder the Beautiful, Vol. I and II) gives many examples of the protection against evil influences, especially witches, by means of evil odours, smoke, fumigation, and so on. Luther divined the original sense of these procedures (See p. 285). In the Dark Ages evil spirits were exorcised by either purgation or by prayer and fasting; their departure coincided with the cessation of internal rumblings that goes with a state of internal emptiness (Private communication from Prof. G. S. Brett).

[3] These three sentences are taken from Heidel: op. cit., p. 127.

to the ancient Greeks for such examples. Oil at baptism
and swinging censers are still universal in the Catholic
Church; the fumigating powers of sulphur, alluded to by
Homer, are still devoutly believed in by every house-wife,
in spite of all proofs of their non-existence; no one places
any faith in medicine that has no odour; the expelling of
the demons of hysteria by evil-smelling asafoetida and
valerian has not yet come to an end; and bacteriologists
have had the greatest difficulty in dissuading surgeons
from estimating the potency of a disinfectant by the strength
of its smell.

. We thus see that the idea of odour is interwoven
with those of heat, fire, vapour, and speech (inspiration),
that odorous gas was believed to further the fruitfulness
of women,[1] herds, and land (See pp. 302-3), to be pleasing
to the gods and to drive away evil spirits and disease.
I would submit that this persistent over-estimation of the
idea, in both folk-lore and early philosophy, may in a great
measure be ascribed to the circumstance that it is a
prominent attribute of that down-going gas which is so
important in primitive thought. At all events no one would
derive it from the upper breath, the odour of which is so
much less a prominent feature.

7. Summary

We may now briefly summarise our conclusions on
the subject of breath symbolism. Starting from the consideration that the idea of breath has apparently played a part
in the history of human thought disproportionate to the

---

[1] A poetical reference to this may be found in Milton's Samson
Agonistes, who refers to Delilah as follows:

> 'Who also in her prime of love,
> Spousal embraces, vitiated with gold,
> Though offer'd only, by the scent conceived
> Her spurious first-born, treason against me.'

psychical significance inherently attaching to it, we inferred that it must have derived some of its importance by displacement from a still more primary idea. In the individual we had found by psycho-analysis that respiratory processes tend to be interpreted in the Unconscious in terms of alimentary ones, which phylogenetically they originally were and from the point of view of metabolic function still are, and which the erotogenic value of the corresponding sensations render of fundamental psychical significance in individual life. This conclusion is amply confirmed by a study of the ideas modelled on breath, the extensive material offered by Indian and Greek philosophy being specially chosen to illustrate this because of its accessibility and the prominence given there to such ideas. We found there that, just as in the child, the idea of respiration is secondary to that of alimentation; that breath receives much of its importance and interest from the conception of it as something which swallows, projects, and disseminates or expels food, besides intimately mingling with it in digestion to form vapour—the internal pneuma—which becomes the purveyor of nutrition to the system, the transmitter of both afferent and efferent nervous impulses, the generator of the fertilising principle, of thought, intelligence, and the soul itself. *It is this internal pneuma, which arises from intestinal decomposition, and in the generation of which the inspired air may or may not be supposed to take part, that is the true 'breath' largely responsible for all these secondary conceptions; and not solely, as is generally supposed, the inspired breath in the usual sense.*

In the ideas historically moulded on that of breath we recognise again what in the Unconscious are symbolic equivalents of intestinal gas: thus, wind, fire, speech, music, thought, soul, etc. The idea that is symbolised seems to possess a peculiar facility for lending itself to the most refined forms of sublimation, a quality which is psychologically to be interpreted as a measure of the intensity of the repression to which the idea is subjected.[1] Attention may be drawn to two instances of this: the part played by incense and music, especially singing, in religion; and the prevailing conception of the soul. The latter is particularly striking and the different stages of its growth can be well traced in Greek thought. Beginning with the nutrient water, the source of all things, we see the coarser constituents being precipitated and discarded, while the finer elements, the essence of essences, are distilled over into vapour (pneuma), which in its turn is purified of any grossness still remaining and is rarefied into an aerial medium, ethereal and spiritual, intangible, invisible and indefinable—the psyche; such is the power ascribed to that magic laboratory, the intestinal tract. This extraordinary capacity for sublimation is probably the reason why the conception of the soul derived from the primitive 'breath-soul' (*Hauchseele*) is definitely replacing that derived from the 'shadow-soul' (*Schattenseele*), being better adapted to express the loftiest ideas of purity and spirituality.

It is highly probable that the sublimation of the original interest proceeded historically by a series of steps, as it does in the individual, and one might venture on the following description of these. Such an attempt must necessarily be schematic, for it is not to be supposed that the evolution in question takes place in the same order in all individuals, or in all races; a given sublimated interest, therefore, may represent one of the described stages in one respect, but perhaps not in others. To begin with we have the beliefs and interests in external phenomena that in a crude way nearly resemble the original personal ones:

---

[1] See Freud on this correlation: Sammlung kleiner Schriften zur Neurosenlehre, Vierte Folge, 1918, S. 284.

thus, the belief that hot evil-smelling vapours explosively issuing from the 'bowels' of the earth lead to increased fertility and strength. The *first stage* in sublimation probably consisted in the replacement of disagreeable odours by agreeable ones, the stage of aromatics, ambrosia and incense. The *second stage* we may conceive as being brought about through the element of odour being eliminated altogether. Interest is then transferred to such ideas as those in which sound plays a prominent part, either in the form of noise (cries, savage instruments, 'bull-roarer', thunder) or in that of music; the ideas of speech and the spoken 'Word' also belong here. The *third stage* sees the removal of the attribute of sound, when we have developed the pneuma doctrine, theories of evaporation, and the idea of cosmic respiration. In the *fourth stage* moisture disappears, and interest gets concentrated on the importance of heat and fire, both as cosmic processes and as individual ones (respiration and digestion, refinements of the pneuma doctrine). With the *fifth stage* this also vanishes, and we are left with such ideas as 'the breath of God', the winds and the outer air, and so on. The *sixth and final stage* finds even this notion of blowing movement too intolerable, as recalling, however dimly, the original idea. The complex has now been 'purged of all material grossness', and is fit to render such lofty thoughts as those of 'the rational soul', universal ether, and world-consciousness. Five of the six original attributes (odour, noise, moisture, warmth, and movement) have been eliminated by progressive processes of de-odorisation, silencing, dessication, cooling and calming, and there is left only the abstract conception of a fluid that is invisible, intangible, inaudible and odourless, i.e. imperceptible and inaccessible to any of the senses. As will be noticed, however, the sublimation has only in certain cases been carried through to its uttermost extreme, and all of the attributes find various expressions at the present time as well as in the past.

It should constantly be borne in mind that much of the importance which has been attached to the present topic owes its origin in the last resort not to physiological or philosophical speculation, but to the sexual interest and sensations of infantile life. For the young child, and for the adult Unconscious, intestinal gas is before all a sexual material, the symbolic equivalent of urine and of the later semen. That it still retains some of this primary significance even in its conscious ramifications is indicated by the numerous beliefs referred to above in which the secondary ideas derived from that of breath, such as wind, speech, fire, etc., are treated as fertilising principles, and have the capacity ascribed to them of leading to conception in the literal sense.

There are two answers to the question put at the beginning of this chapter, of why it was God's breath that was chosen to represent the fertilising material in the Madonna legend, and they are of equal importance. One of them we reserve until some other features of the legend have been considered. The other is given by our analysis of the infantile source of the material in question, which has shewn that this concerns a secretion that better than any other lends itself to de-sensualisation.

IV

THE DOVE AND THE ANNUNCIATION

At first sight it would seem in the legend under discussion that the two figures of the Holy Dove and the Archangel Gabriel merely represent, in a duplicate fashion, the same idea, for both are divine agents that pour into the Virgin's ear, one breath, the other the Word; they

21

have the further common attribute of being winged beings.
There can be no doubt that they considerably overlap in
their signification, but reflection shews that this doubling,
as perhaps all symbolic reduplication, is of the nature of
mythological 'decomposition': in other words, the two
figures represent attributes, dissociated from the main
personality, which are closely akin, but not quite identical.

It is clear that the notion of a *messenger* in general
is always based on this psychological process, which
strictly speaking is a form of projection. A messenger
represents one or more aspects of the main personality;
for example, the king's thoughts on a given topic. Psychologically he may be called a part of the king, being an
agent of his wishes in the same way as the king's hand
or tongue might be. Otherwise expressed, he symbolises
the king, by representing one or other of his attributes.
The primary conception of a messenger, well illustrated
by the stories of the angels and of Satan in the Old
Testament, was thus of an agent who carried out the
king's wishes, rather than that of a mere conveyer of news.
In ages when less attention was paid to the reality-
principle this was clearly recognised, the messenger being
treated as fully responsible for the news he brought and
executed if this was bad. Even to-day we see—or did
at least until before the War—indications of this early
attribute in the special deference paid to ambassadors and
othe accredited representatives of power.

The same primitive attribute is also evident in the
present legend, for the Annunciation is exactly synchronous
with the conception; more than this, it may be said in a
certain sense actually to effect it. And it is here that we
can see the distinction between the parts played by the
angel and the Dove. For while in older mythologies, e. g.
the Greek, the Supreme Being wishing to impregnate a

mortal maiden appeared to her in the symbolic guise of an impregnating agent alone, a snake, a swan, or some other phallic symbol, in the Christian myth He is not content with this, but appears also in the guise of a man. The Archangel Gabriel thus represents the Divine Being in human form, or, more precisely, that aspect of Him which wishes to effect a human act. This wish, the cause of the act, is identical with the Annunciation, and since the wishes of God, just like those of an obsessional patient, are all-powerful, it is little wonder that we have a certain difficulty at first in distinguishing between the part played by the symbol of the wishing personality (the angel) and that played by the symbol of the means of execution (the Dove). The true significance of Gabriel is naively revealed by St. Ephrem[1] thus: 'The Archangel Gabriel was sent under the form of a venerable aged man, lest so chaste and so modest a maiden should be troubled, or seized with any fear, at a youthful appearance.'

In the Annunciation scene the Archangel Gabriel holds a *flower*, usually a lily, in his right hand. Flowers have always been emblematic of women, and particularly of their genital region, as is indicated by the use of the word 'defloration' and by various passages in the Song of Solomon. A flower in symbolic language signifies a child (an unconscious equivalent of the female genitalia); the association is formed through the origin of flowers in the mother-earth, favoured by watering and manuring,[2] and is

[1] St. Ephrem: De Divers. Serm, i, 600 In a Syriac tradition of the fourth century (The History of the Blessed Virgin Mary, Edited by Wallis Budge, 1899, p. 22) I also read that 'Gabriel appeared unto her in the form of a venerable old man, so that she might not flee from him.'

[2] The coprophilic association here hinted at is strengthened by the fact that an attractive odour is one of the most striking attributes of flowers.

represented in consciousness by the supposed innocence and sexlessness of both—as fictitious in the one case as in the other. The flower here, therefore, represents the child[1] that the divine ambassador is promising and proffering—or rather giving—to the Virgin.

The *lily* was considered a special attribute of the Madonna, representing both her motherhood and her innocence, and before the fourteenth century was always depicted in the Annunciation scene at her side; later it was placed either between her and Gabriel, as in the accompanying picture,[2] or in the hand of the latter. Both aspects of the metaphor are expressed in the following description:[3] 'Mary is the lily of chastity, but glowing with the flames of love, in order to spread around her the sweetest perfume and grace'. A delightful odour was one of the Madonna's most prominent physical characteristics, and is constantly mentioned by the Fathers: thus, Chrysostom[4] calls her 'the Paradise that is filled with the most divine perfume'.

The lily is a flower with a long history in antiquity, and has always been especially associated with the idea of innocence. The very name comes from the Greek λείριον (= simple). The Romans called it Rosa Junonis, because it was supposed to have sprung from the pure milk of the Queen of Heaven. It was associated with the Chaste Susanna, the Hebrew name for lily being 'shusham'. (In other Semitic languages it is 'susanna'; in Persia, from where the lily is said to have come, the ancient

---

[1] I have published an exact illustration of this connection (*Jahrbuch der Psychoanalyse*, 1913, Bd. V, S. 90, Fall III), the flower being there also, as it happens, a lily.

[2] See Frontispiece.

[3] Petr. Dam : De Nat. Beat. Virg., iii.

[4] Chrysostom. De Beatae Mariae Virg., vii.

capital, Susa, was named after it.[1]) It was a favourite attribute of the youthful Aphrodite. The lily has also a close connection with the soul-idea. The Greeks, particularly the Athenians, strewed lilies on the graves of their dead. The Egyptians believed that the spirit-body in heaven transformed itself into the celestial lily which the God Ra held to his nose.[2]

Turning now our attention to the other figure, the *Holy Dove*, we have two principal questions to answer: why was the Holy Ghost depicted in the form of a bird, and why particularly in that of a dove? Up to the present we have considered the idea of the Holy Ghost in its aspect as symbolising the fertilising principle, but from what has just been said it is plain that it symbolises as well the agent that transmits this in obedience to the will of the Father.[3]

---

[1] See Strauss: Die Blumen in Sage und Geschichte, 1875, S. 78-80.

[2] Wallis Budge: Osiris and the Egyptian Resurrection, 1911, Vol. I, p. 111.

[3] In this essay the idea of the Holy Ghost is treated only in its masculine aspects, as is proper in Christian mythology. As is well known, the Christian Trinity is a distortion of the original one, as obtaining in all the older religions, e. g. the Babylonian, Egyptian, Greek, etc, where it comprised Father, Mother, and Son. The sternly patriarchal Hebrew conception banned the Mother to a subordinate part and the Son to a remotely distant future, but retained their original relationship. The Christian theology changed the Mother into the male Holy Ghost (combination of phallus and fertilising principle), but in practice reinstated her importance. The attempt made by the Melchite sect in Egypt to retain the original Trinity of Father, Mary, and Messiah was crushed at the Nicene Council, though even the memory of it led Cardinal Newman to wax so ecstatic as to have his words termed 'the very poetry of blasphemy' (Hislop. The Two Babylons, p. 82). Hebrew theology and Christian worship thus form the obverse of Hebrew worship and Christian theology in their attitude towards the Mother, who could not be completely abolished from either religion. It was reserved for Protestantism to make this final step in the evolution of a

Birds have always been favourite baby-bringing symbols, and are still used for this purpose in the familiar stork legend;[1] winged phalli were among the commonest Roman amulets.[2] The ways in which this association became forged are evident as soon as we consider the most striking characteristics of birds, which we will proceed to do in order.

1. Power of Flight

Certainly the characteristic of birds which has most impressed itself on the human imagination is the extraordinary power they have of rapidly ascending into the air at will, an idea the fascination of which may be measured by the appeal made by aviation. Psycho-analysis has revealed the underlying source of this interest—namely, that the act of rising in the air is constantly, though quite unconsciously, associated with the phenomenon of erection.[3]

---

purely androgenic procreation myth, which has ended in a universal feminine protest in the countries professing this faith.

Now it is interesting to note that the idea of the Holy Spirit was intimately connected with that of a bird, and especially with that of a dove, even in its original maternal meaning. The passage in Genesis (i. 2), for instance, 'And the Spirit of God moved upon the face of the waters' should really run 'The Mother of the Gods brooded (or fluttered) over the abyss and brought forth life'. According to Wallis Budge this Ruach is feminine and has descended from an earlier mythology (probably Babylonian) as the wife of God. The act of creation in Genesis is commonly portrayed (e. g. on a stained-glass window in the cathedral of Auxerre) as being performed by a dove, and we shall see that this bird was peculiarly emblematic of most of the supreme Goddesses.

[1] An exact analysis of this has been published by Otto Rank: Die Lohengrinsage, 1911, S. 55-8.

[2] See Vorberg: Museum eroticum Neapolitanum; Ein Beitrag zum Geschlechtsleben der Römer, Privatdruck, 1910.

[3] A fact first pointed out by Federn (Cited by Freud: Die Traumdeutung, 3 Aufl., S. 204).

This characteristic of birds alone, therefore, would make them well suited to serve as phallic symbols.

Several religious similes are based, at least in part, on this association. Thus the upward flight of the bird was used to represent the aspiration of a soaring soul, and in the catacombs the idea of such souls being released from sin is depicted by birds escaping from their cages and flying upwards. In the same way the idea of a bird's flight came to represent that of resurrection, i. e. of arising again. Tertullian seems to have been the first to point out the resemblance between a flying bird with outstretched wings and the Saviour nailed to his cross, a fancy which was later much used in religious art; in most pictures, for instance, of St. Francis receiving the stigmata, the descending Saviour is portrayed, in cruciform fashion, as a bird with a human head.

2. Form of Head

The reptilian neck of birds, continued in a snake-like way into the head, the darting pointed beak, and the power of rapid protrusion, are all features that inevitably recall a snake, thus explaining why this part of the bird specially tends to be unconsciously conceived of in terms of phallic symbolism.

3. Absence of External Genital Organs

This strikes a boy's mind as strange after his experience of other animals, as well as of himself, and gives rise to a contrast association which is probably of a compensatory nature (denying the painful truth by excessive insistence); in a similar manner flowers, which are also popularly regarded as having no genital organs, are among the commonest of love-symbols. The importance of this observation, which will be discussed later, is that it leads

to fancies being formed to explain it of such a kind as
to link up with the infantile fancies of procreation we have
considered previously, and which throw much light on the
question of why a bird is chosen to depict the Holy Ghost.

4. Power of Song

This striking characteristic, almost unique in the animal
kingdom, is so obviously related to love-making that it
becomes associated with the series of symbolic equivalents
discussed in the previous chapter. Reference may also be
made here to the belief in the 'thunder-bird' current among
the North American Indians,[1] in which the sound element
is emphasised in a connection that inevitably reminds one
of the thunder beliefs and thunder-weapons mentioned
earlier.

5. Relation to the Air

It is only natural that the idea of air should play a
prominent part in phantasies concerning birds, who shew
such a supreme mastery over this element, and similarly
that birds should play a prominent part in symbolism
relating to air; indeed the absence of a bird in such
symbolism would need more explanation than its presence.
In the examples mentioned earlier of the beliefs in the
fertilisation of animals by means of wind it is noteworthy
that nearly all of them relate to birds; the idea of gaseous
fertilisation would thus seem to be readily associated with
that of birds. The connection between the two ideas has
been made use of in various cosmogonies. Thus the Poly-
nesians describe the heaven- and air-God Tangaroa as a bird
hovering over the waters,[2] and it is probable that this was

---

[1] Eels: Annual Report of the Smithsonian Institute for 1887,
p. 674; Boas: Sixth Report on the North-Western Tribes of Canada,
1890, p. 40.

[2] Waitz: Anthropologie der Naturvölker, 1872, Bd. VI, S. 241.

the original sense of the reference in Genesis to the wind of Elohim brooding over the waters[1] (See Footnote, p. 326).

After what was said in reference to the previous characteristics it is not very surprising that they should become associated with the last-mentioned one, the head, neck and beak being then regarded as a phallic organ which expels the fertilising gas. This is a more natural idea than it might at first sight appear, for, after all, whatever the nature of the fertilising substance the male organ is the typical expelling agent. I have come across this phantasy several times in the course of individual psycho-analysis, the explanation being that the person has in childhood considered the male organ to be a continuation of the rectum or its contents; the two corresponding part-instincts are always astonishingly closely connected in the Unconscious.[2] The same association probably helps somewhat to explain the fondness that so many boys have for blowing whistles and trumpets (sound of course entering into the association); as well as the use of trumpets, to which attention was called above, for the purpose of raising the dead, i. e. of infusing life into them.[3] Noise, especially in the form of trumpet blowing, often plays an important part in initiation ceremonies, a matter which will be discussed later. The same association may also be found in erotic art, of which two examples may be mentioned: In a picture by Felicien Rops, entitled 'Joujou', a nymph with satyr legs and a Phrygian cap is creating planets by blowing bubbles with the aid of a phallus which she holds to her mouth as a trumpet;[4] in one published in 'L'Art

[1] Cheyne: Encyclop. Brit., Vol. VI, p. 447.

[2] See Freud: 'Über Triebumsetzungen insbesondere der Anal-erotik', Sammlung kleiner Schriften zur Neurosenlehre, Vierte Folge, 1918.

[3] Compare the sexual significance of tongue and speech pointed out above.

[4] Das erotische Werk des Felicien Rops, 1905, Nr. 13.

de péter' a cupid is depicted blowing bubbles through a tube with the mouth and at the same time with the anus.[1] The legend of Athene, who was born out of her father's head, the product of his 'thought', has to be interpreted in the same way—to follow the hint from Plotinus mentioned above (p. 309). I would even suggest that this association[2] plays a part in determining a feature of our Madonna legend—namely, the notion that the fertilising breath of God issues from the beak of the Holy Dove. In support of this the following examples may be cited. The unicorn (a purely phallic conception) was a recognised emblem of the Christian Logos, or creative Word of God; its symbolic meaning, and its close association with breath, becomes plain from an old German picture which was very popular at the end of the fifteenth century.[3] In this the Annunication is represented in the form of a hunt. Gabriel blows the angelic greeting on a hunting horn. A unicorn flees (or is blown) to the Virgin Mary and plunges his horn into her 'lap', while God the Father blesses them from above. A second example is even less ambiguous, for in it the passage of God's breath is actually imagined as proceeding through a tube: over a portal of the Marienkapelle at Würzburg is a relief-representation of the Annunciation[4] in which the Heavenly Father is blowing along a tube that extends from his lips to the Virgin's ear, and down which the infant Jesus is descending.

[1] Reproduced in Stern's 'Illustrierte Geschichte der erotischen Literatur', 1908, Bd. I, S. 240.

[2] To this also may in part be attributed the use of such phrases as 'inflated', 'blown up', etc., as synonyms for excessive pride (narcissism).

[3] Reproduced by P. Ch. Cahier· Caracteristiques des Saints dans l'art populaire, 1867.

[4] Reproduced by Fuchs: Illustrierte Sittengeschichte; Renaissance; Ergänzungsband, 1909, S. 289.

The extent to which the idea of a bird is connected with the attributes of bodily gas enumerated in the previous chapter is indeed remarkable: thus, with sound (singing), with invisibility (difficulty with which it is caught sight of, disappearance in the air), with heat (higher bodily temperature than any other animal, nearness to the sun), with movement and wind (rapid flight, mastery over air), and so on. Two further illustrations may be given of the way in which the idea of a bird enters into this circle of 'gaseous' ideas. In the first place the soul is frequently conceived of in bird form[1] (especially in Christian art) and is then depicted, appropriately enough, as leaving the body after death by issuing from the mouth.[2] The second example, that of the phoenix, displays an extraordinary richness in the present group of associations and epitomises most of the ideas we have up to here discussed, while of interest in the present connection is the circumstance that the early Christians adopted the legend of its life-history to symbolise the resurrection of Jesus.[3] The phoenix was a golden shining bird, sometimes described as a ray emanating from the sun. It prepares for its death by surrounding itself with cinnamon, myrrh and other aromatic spices, and by addressing to the sun a song that is 'more beautiful than the sound of the nightingale, the flutes of the Muses, or the lyre of Hermes'. It dies, amidst a blaze of fragrant perfume, in a fire created by the fanning of its wings, or—as was at other times

[1] Frazer (Taboo and the Perils of the Soul, 1911, pp. 33-5) gives examples from all parts of the world.

[2] As was hinted earlier in this essay, in this belief the mouth is probably in part a replacement of the other extremity of the alimentary canal; the original form of the belief sometimes comes to open expression, an example being in the fourteenth century farce 'Le Muynier' (Dupuoy: Medicine in the Middle Ages, p. 84).

[3] Bachofen: Versuch über die Gräbersymbolik der Alten, 1859, S. 109.

believed—by the heat of the sun's rays. The first act of the young phoenix born from this fire is to carry the relics of its sire, in a casket of myrrh, to a sacred temple and pronounce over them a funeral oration.

The idea of a *rara avis*, usually a bird of fire, is common to many nations, being found in Egypt, China, and most oriental countries; the popular appeal of the idea is still witnessed by the success attending Maeterlinck's 'L'Oiseau bleu'. A Slav fairy-tale tells how a certain Prince acquired a feather from the wing of Ohnivak, the Fire-Bird, and 'so lovely and bright was it that it illumed all the galleries of the palace and they needed no other light'; he falls into a pensive decline and, summoning his three sons, says to them 'If I could but hear the bird Ohnivak sing just once, I should be cured of this disease of the heart'.[1] In Namoluk, one of the Caroline islands, it is believed that fire came to men in the following way: Olofaet, the master of flames, gave fire to the bird 'mwi' and bade him carry it to earth in his beak; so the bird flew from tree to tree and stored away the slumbering force of the fire in the wood, from which men can elicit it by friction.[2] In Shelley's 'To a Skylark' most of the preceding associations are poetically illustrated. For example: soul (Hail to thee, blithe spirit—Bird thou never wert); fire (like a cloud of fire); invisibility (Thou art unseen, but yet I hear thy shrill delight); rising flight (thou scorner of the ground); voice (All the earth and air with thy voice is loud).

With all these associations it is plain that nothing could easily be better imagined than a bird to symbolise a bringer of a wonderful message from the air. Children

---

[1] Harding: Fairy-Tales of the Slav Peasants and Herdsmen, 1896, p. 269 et seq.

[2] Girschner: 'Die Karolineninsel Namoluk und ihre Bewohner', *Baessler-Archiv*, 1912, Bd. II, S. 141.

keep a pretty reminder of them in the familiar saying 'A little bird told me', meaning 'whispered a secret to me'.

The problem of why particularly a *dove* was chosen in the present instance is most conveniently approached by first considering some of the ways in which it has played a part in other mythologies. This part has been a rather extensive one, for the dove was a sacred animal among the Assyrians, Egyptians, and Hebrews, was an attribute of Astarte and Semiramis (who was supposed to have been transformed into one after her death), and was the favourite bird of Aphrodite, whose chariot was drawn by doves. At the Syrian Hierapolis, one of the chief seats of her worship, doves were so holy that they might not even be touched; if a man inadvertently touched one, he was unclean or taboo for the rest of the day.[1] Figures of doves played a prominent part in the decoration of Aphrodite's sanctuary at Old Paphos.[2] Frazer gives reason for thinking that the Cyprian custom of sacrificing doves in honour of Adonis dated from an older form of worship in which a holy man, personifying the Goddess's lover, was sacrificed.[3]

The association of the ideas of dove and love has always been a close one, and is met with in different ages. The following is a love-charm used in Bohemia: A girl goes into the woods on St. George's Eve and catches a ring-dove, which must be a male one; early in the morning she carries it to the hearth, presses it to her bare breast, and lets it fly up the chimney (a well-known vaginal symbol), muttering an incantation the while.[4] In

---

[1] Lucian: De dea Syria, liv.

[2] A good description of this is given by Frazer: Adonis, Attis, Osiris, 1907, p. 29.

[3] Frazer: op. cit., pp. 114, 115.

[4] Grohmann: op. cit., S. 77.

1784 a mixed pseudo-freemasonry, the object of which was the pursuit of love, was formed at Versailles, the members being termed the 'Chevaliers et Chevalières de la Colombe'.[1]

The phallic symbolism of the dove is also unmistakable in the following examples. The Christian myth we are considering can be closely paralleled by the Greek one in which Zeus assumes the form of a dove in order to seduce Phtheia on one of his human expeditions, just as on other similar occasions he assumed other phallic ones, snake, bull, swan, and so on. When Catullus mentions Caesar's salaciousness he does so by using the expression 'columbulus albulus'. According to Philo, the dove was the emblem of wisdom, which in mythology, as with the snake, unicorn, etc., is always a phallic attribute,[2] and Jesus himself brought it into a contrast association with the snake: 'Be ye as wise as the serpent and as harmless as the dove' (Matthew x. 16). Von Hahn[3] relates three stories from modern Greek folk-lore in which the life of an enchanter or ogre is bound up with that of two, or three, doves; when they die, he dies also. The sense of this becomes clear when it is compared with another variant in which the life of an old man is bound up with that of a ten-headed serpent; when the serpent's heads are cut off one after another, he feels ill, and when the last one is cut off he expires.[4] But the most unequivocal indication of the symbolic signification of the dove is to be found in the extra-canonical legend which relates that a dove escaped from Joseph's genital organ and alighted

[1] Dictionnaire Larousse: Art. 'Colombe'.
[2] See Chapter IV, p. 135.
[3] Von Hahn: Griechische und albanesische Marchen, 1864, Bd. I, S. 187; Bd. II, S. 215, 260.
[4] Von Hahn: op. cit., Bd. II, S. 23.

on his head (an unconscious symbol of the erect phallus) to designate him as the future husband of the Virgin Mary;[1] the story is weakened in the writings of the later Christian Fathers, who say that the dove escaped from Joseph's rod (!).

Appropriately enough it is a dove that furnishes Zeus with ambrosia (= soma), and in the legend of St. Remy brings the bishop the oil-flask to anoint King Clovis (oil being an equivalent symbol).[2] An interesting parallel to this is the legend that Aeneas was guided by two doves to the Golden Bough,[3] for Frazer has shewn that the Golden Bough represents mistletoe growing on an oak-tree,[4] and mistletoe is as familiar a symbol of sperma (like ambrosia and oil) as the oak is of the male organ. French peasants think that mistletoe originates in birds' dung;[5] the ancients knew that it was propagated from tree to tree by seeds that have been carried and voided by birds, and Pliny[6] tells us that the birds which most often deposited the seeds were doves and thrushes.

According to Apollonius, a dove guided the Argonauts on their wanderings. The ideas of bringing, guiding and leading have much in common with that of 'messenger', and a well-known Greek legend of the dove is that in which it figures as the love-messenger carrying the *billets doux* of the poet Anacreon, who had been presented with it by Aphrodite in return for a song. Like most love-figures in mythology, including even Aphrodite herself, the dove could represent not only life, but also death;

---

[1] Protevang., St. Jacob, Cap. 9; Evang. infant. St. Mariae, Cap. 8. Cited after Maury: Essai sur les légendes pieuses du moyen-âge, 1843.

[2] De Gubernatis: Zoological Mythology, 1872, Vol. II, p. 305.

[3] Virgil: Aen., VI, 190, 293 et seq.

[4] Frazer: Balder the Beautiful, 1913, Vol. II, pp. 285, 315-20.

[5] Gaidoz: Revue de l'histoire des religions, 1880, Vol. II, p. 76.

[6] Pliny: op. cit., XVI, 247.

thus in the hymns of the Rig-Veda the dove (Kapota) is Yama's messenger of death.[1]

The dove was also associated with fire. When the Kapota touches fire, Yama, whose messenger he is, is honoured; in a Buddhistic legend Agni, the God of Fire, assumes the shape of a dove when he is being pursued by Indra in the shape of a hawk (the Sanscrit name of which, by the way, is Kapotâri, the enemy of doves.)[2] In the 'scoppio del carro' festival at Florence the holy fire is renewed every Easter Eve, and at the moment of celebrating High Mass a stuffed bird, representing a dove, (called the dove of the Pazzi), is released from a pillar of fire-works in front of the altar, flies along a wire down the nave, and ignites the fire-works on the festive car that is waiting outside the door.[3] Maury quotes as a reason why the Holy Ghost appears sometimes in the form of fire, and sometimes in that of a dove, the circumstance that in the Orient the dove was the emblem of generation and of animal heat.[4] The association with heat is retained in Christian art, where the Holy Dove is always depicted surrounded by rays of light or flames of fire.

It is comprehensible that a bird symbolising generation should also come to represent the ideas of re-birth, resurrection and salvation, which in the Unconscious are practically equivalent.[5] De Gubernatis[6] quotes a number of stories from folk-lore, in which the dove warns or saves from danger. The dove was the messenger of salvation in the Deluge myth, which is now known to represent a

---

[1] Rig-Veda, X, 165, 4

[2] De Gubernatis: op. cit , p. 297.

[3] Weston: 'The Scoppio del Carro at Florence', *Folk-Lore*, 1905, Vol. XVI, pp. 182-4.

[4] Maury. op. cit., p. 179.

[5] See my Papers on Psycho-Analysis, Second Edition, 1918, Ch. X.

[6] De Gubernatis: op. cit., pp. 297-303.

glorified birth-phantasy; the meaning is brought to clear expression in a sketch found in the catacombs of Rome, in which Noah is seen floating in a little box that flies open at the appearance of the dove with its leaf.[1] It is perhaps significant that in another Old Testament birth-myth the name of the hero, Jonah, is the same as the Hebrew word for dove. It was a dove also that appeared to the three young Hebrews in the furnace at Babylon and announced to them their deliverance from the flames. The natives at Cape Grafton say that a dove brings the babies to mothers in their dreams.[2] To the same group of ideas belongs the association between the dove and the re-birth rite of baptism,[3] both in the New Testament and in ecclesiastical decorative art. Jesus himself, the figure of salvation and resurrection, is occasionally depicted in the form of a dove;[4] for example, in a lamp in Santa Caterina in Chiusi a dove is portrayed bearing an olive branch in its mouth and having a cross on its head. The dove is in the Catholic Church also an emblem of martyrdom, i. e. of attainment of eternal life through death.

In early Christian art the soul of a dying saint was depicted as escaping from the mouth in the form of a dove,[5] this being replaced in later art by the figure of a little child. In this equating of dove—child—soul—breath we see another

[1] Reproduced in Smith and Cheetham's Dictionary of Christian Antiquities, 1875, Vol. I, p. 575.

[2] Roth, cited by Rank: Die Lohengrinsage, 1911. S. 23.

[3] It is of interest that the German words for baptism and for dove (*Taufe* and *Taube*) are derived from the same root.

[4] We have seen in order the Holy Ghost as a symbol of the creative material, the creative agent, and the child created. (In later art he is often depicted in the form of a child instead of that of a young man, just as Eros became replaced by Cupid.)

[5] Many examples are cited by Didron: Christian Iconography, Engl. Transl., 1896, Vol. I, pp. 460, 461; and Maury: Croyances et légendes du moyen-âge, 1896, Vol. II, p. 266.

example of the infantile birth theory that was discussed earlier in this essay.

An equally plain illustration of the Logos association of the dove is furnished by its connection with the idea of inspiration (spiro = I breathe). In Lybia a dove communicated the sacred oracles, and in Dodona two doves performed the same function and were supposed to cry 'Zeus was; Zeus is; Zeus will be; O Zeus, the greatest oi the Gods'. 'We noted earlier, in discussing the topics of speech and tongue, the important part played by the Holy Dove (Holy Ghost) in a similar connection. When St. Catherine of Alexandria confounded the learned doctors by her wisdom the Holy Dove kept flying over her head, and a dove, known to French art as the 'colombe inspiratrice', is frequently depicted on the shoulder of a great saint, speaking into his ear and thus inspiring him.[1] The symbolic significance of this, which should be clear from the preceding chapter, may be further illustrated by quoting the following dream related by the Welsh poet Vaughan, in a letter written in 1694: 'I was told by a very sober and knowing person (now dead) that in his time, there was a young lad father and motherless, and soe very poor that he was forced to beg; butt att last was taken up by a rich man, that kept a great stock oi sheep upon the mountains not far from the place where I now dwell, who cloathed him and sent him into the mountains to keep his sheep. There in Summer time following the sheep and looking to their lambs he fell into a deep sleep; in which he dreamt, that he saw a beautifull young man with a garland of green leafs upon his head, and an hawk upon his fist: with a quiver full oi Arrows att his back, coming towards him (whistling several measures

---

[1] Maury: op. cit., pp. 267-9; Larousse: loc. cit.

or tunes all the way) and att last lett the hawk fly att him, which (he dreamt) gott into his mouth and inward parts, and suddenly awaked in a great fear and consternation: butt possessed with such a vein, or gift of poetrie, that he left the sheep and went about the Countrey, making songs upon all occasions, and came to be the most famous Bard in all the Countrey in his time'.[1]

Etymology fully sustains our view of the sexual connotation of the dove idea, indicating its association both with phallicism and with the group of 'gaseous' ideas enumerated earlier. The word 'dove' comes from the Anglo-Saxon 'dufan' = to plunge into, and is probably allied to the Greek κολυμβίς = a diver; it is cognate with 'dip', 'dive', and 'deep', the notion of penetration evidently being the fundamental one. The more generic word 'pigeon' comes from the Greek πιπίζειν = to chirp; from the latter also comes the word 'pipe', which has the meanings of a tube (cp. the Würzburg relief mentioned above), an instrument for making smoke, to chirp or sing, and, in slang, the male organ. A whole series of words are derived from the same root (probably of onomatopoetic origin), which mean 'to blow', 'the back parts', or 'child', and Jung[2] has pointed out that the connecting link of these three apparently disparate ideas is to be found in the common infantile notion that children are born from the rectum. Thus: (1) 'pop', 'puff', 'to poop' (= to pass flatus. Compare the French 'pet' = flatus, the same word in English meaning darling, little dear, and the German 'Schatz' = darling, treasure, which also comes from a

---

[1] This letter, which has never been published, is to be found in the MS. Bodleiana, Aubrey 13, Fol. 340. I am indebted to Mr L. C. Martin for calling my attention to it and for giving me the opportunity of making use of it.

[2] Jung: op. cit., S. 230.

vulgar word for defaecation); (2) French 'poupée' and
Dutch 'pop', both meaning doll (German 'Puppe'), Latin
'pupus' = a child, 'pupula' = a girl, and English 'puppy'
and 'pupa', meaning the young of the dog and the butterfly
respectively. That words of such widely different signification
as 'pupil', 'fart', 'peep', 'fife', 'pigeon', 'puff', 'petard',
and 'partridge'[1] should all be derived from the same root
illustrates the astonishing propagating power possessed by
sexual words, to which Sperber[2] has recently directed
special attention.

The choice of the dove for the purposes above
mentioned was doubtless determined by many factors,
perhaps by extrinsic ones as well as psychological ones.
that it constituted a numerous genus and attracted much
attention in ancient times is shewn by the fact alone that
there existed in Sanscrit some twenty-five or thirty names
for pigeon.[3] It is generally said that its use in Christian
symbolism was due to its association with the ideas of
purity and immaculateness, but it is likely that cause and
effect are here reversed; even its white colour cannot be
cited in favour of this association, for most doves are not white,
while other birds, e. g. swans, most often are. A more
important feature is the tenderness they display in their
love-relations, the activity of which must, as is evident from
the extensive connotations related above, have vividly
impressed itself upon the attention. Now this tenderness
is chiefly manifested in a manner that is of particular
interest to the present theme, in what is a very prominent
characteristic of doves—namely, the soft, delightful cooing

---

[1] In view of the ancient belief that this bird could be impregnated
by either the wind or the voice it is interesting that its name should
enter into this series.

[2] Sperber: op. cit.

[3] Larousse, loc. cit.

that plays a leading part in their love-making; we still use the expression 'billing and cooing of turtle-doves' to denote a special relationship between lovers. In view of the extensive associations that subsist between the idea of birds in general, and of doves in particular, on the one hand and the group discussed in the previous chapter (sound, breath, sexuality, etc.) on the other, it seems to me probable that this striking feature of doves must have been a principal reason for the choice of them to symbolise phantasies based on the idea in question. This suggestion may be illustrated by reference to the Christian belief that 'the voice of the turtle-dove is an echo on earth of the voice of God'.[1]

This peculiar tenderness in the love-making of doves is to be correlated with a feature in the associations surrounding the idea of them on which I have only lightly touched—namely, femininity. It would lead us too far to enumerate instances of this association, but it is a curiously extensive one, so that one is forced to say that of all phallic emblems the dove is one of the most gentle and effeminate. The significance of this to our main theme will be indicated in the following section.

V

THE EAR AS THE RECEPTIVE ORGAN

The infant's psychical interests and digital manipulations relating to the lower alimentary orifice are early transferred to the nostril, which, from its nearness to a less objectional part of the alimentary canal, its relation to the sense of smell, its size, its connection with breath and with mucoid secretion, is well adapted for the purpose. A patient of mine used even to impregnate himself in his phantasy by inhaling through the nose breath that had

[1] Conway: Solomon and the Solomonic Literature, 1899, p. 123.

been exhaled from the mouth,[1] and in Genesis we read of Yahweh using a nostril for the same purpose in the creation of Adam, from which it is evident what the 'dust of the ground' out of which Adam was moulded must have originally signified.[2]

By the time of the Christian era, however, a greater refinement had taken place, one corresponding with the increasing displacement that is to be observed in the progress of individual repression, and the nostril, which can receive a palpable gas, is replaced by the ear, which can receive only impalpable sound—for instance the Word of God—a rarefied abstraction of the primitive gas idea. That in the Madonna legend[3] the ear symbolises the lower alimentary orifice, and not the vagina, is a conclusion based not only on logic, for the idea of the vagina would be a meaningless intrusion into a series of themes that have nothing in common with it (they are all of infantile origin, while the child knows nothing of the existence of the vagina), but through numerous analyses of persons in whom this orifice has acquired a symbolical significance; such habits as nose and ear-picking, for

---

[1] *Jahrbuch der Psychoanalyse*, 1912, Bd. IV, S. 598.

[2] I have elsewhere dealt with the symbolism of dirt at some length: *Jahrbuch der Psychoanalyse*, 1913, Bd. V, S. 90, Fall III.

[3] That in this legend the ear was thought of as the receptive organ in a quite concrete sense is clear from the evidence produced earlier in this essay, and is proved by consideration of such a presentation as the Würzburg relief alone. To the numerous passages already quoted from the early Fathers the following two may be added: 'And because the devil, creeping in through the ear by tempt-ation, had wounded and given death to Eve, Christ entering by the ear to Mary, dried up all the vices of the heart, and cured the woman's wound by being born of the Virgin' (St. Zeno: Epist. ad Pulcheriam Augustam); 'None other was born of Mary, than He who *glided in through her maternal ear,* and filled the Virgin's womb' (St. Gauden-tius: De diversis Capitulis, Serm. xiii).

instance, invariably prove on analysis to be derivatives of, and substitutes for, anal masturbation. The exact symbolical equivalency of the two orifices, however, can be demonstrated quite apart from psycho-analysis.

In several of the mediaeval pictures of hell the devil is portrayed in the act of swallowing sinners (through the mouth, of course) and excreting them through the ear alone, the cloaca alone, or through both indifferently and simultaneously; instances of each of these in Florence alone are to be found in the Baptisteria, in Orcagna's fresco in the Santa Maria Novella, and in Fra Angelico's picture in the Academy. We see here a complete parity of the two orifices, one which can be matched by beliefs drawn from another part of the world, India: In the Ramayana[1] a sun-hero, Hanumant, is described as entering into the mouth of a sea-monster and emerging through the 'other side' at the tail, evidently through the cloaca; in another part of the poem, however, he is made to emerge through the ear, the two orifices being again treated as equivalent. According to the Taitiriyaka-Upanishad,[2] the Apâna, or down-going breath, corresponds with the ear.

The ear figures as the receptive organ in other and earlier myths than the Christian one, which is doubtless derived from them. The Mongolian legend of Maya, who was impregnated through this orifice during sleep, has been referred to already (p. 268). Just as Eve, after having been seduced by the 'serpent', tasted of the fruit of knowledge,[3] so Cassandra became a prophetess when the

---

[1] Frobenius: Das Zeitalter des Sonnengottes, 1904, Bd. I, S. 173, 174.

[2] I, 7, 1.

[3] i. e. the knowledge of sexual matters. See Ludwig Levy: op. cit.

'serpent' licked her ear. The Sumerian word-sign for 'ear' in its earliest form was written by the pictograph of a pair of ears, with the phonetic value of 'wa' in the Sumerian and 'uznu' in the Semitic-Akkalian or Assyrian; it is defined in the bilingual cuneiform of about 2000 B. C. and later as 'the bent member'.[1] In these glosses the Semitic 'uznu' or 'ear' is also defined as a title of the Mother-Goddess Ishtar, and particularly of her form as Antu, the Creatress and Goddess of generation, a usage which is explained as arising from the idea 'bend down, bend over' in sexual intercourse.[2] This is perhaps the source of the large ears assigned to the woman in the presence of the Father-God as figured on the ancient Babylonian seals described by Pinches.[3] This word-sign for 'ear' is moreover used as a synonym for the 'cedar',[4] which through its ever-greenness was the 'Tree of Life' of the Garden of Eden in the Hebrew legend[5] and an emblem of the Mother-Goddess Ishtar. In the Persian cosmogony the first man was created by the Divine Being inserting his 'hand' into the ear of the female one; in another version, on which the preceding Babylonian myth throws light, it is his 'main branch' that is inserted. This 'main branch' is presumably the branch held in the hand of the Father-God in the archaic Babylonian seal-cylinders of the third and fourth millenium B. C.;[6] it may perfectly well be the origin of the modern expression 'olive branch' for a child, since the olive

[1] Prince: Sumerian Lexicon, 1908, pp 1, 373; Barton: Babylonian Writing, 1913, p. 179.

[2] Prince: op. cit., pp. 338, 339.

[3] Pinches: *Proceedings of the Society of Biblical Archaeology,* 1917, Vol. xxix.

[4] Barton: loc. cit.; See also Muss-Arnolt: Assyrian Dictionary, p. 103.

[5] See Cheyne: Traditions of Ancient Israel, passim.

[6] Ward: Seal Cylinders of West Asia, 1910, pp. 96, etc.

came in Greece and Rome to replace the cedar as the special tree of the Virgin Mother-Goddess, Athene. In connection with the ancient Semitic-Babylonian hymn on the 'Wailing of Ishtar' for the killing of her son-lover Tamnuz the origin of the wailing of the Jewish women of Jerusalem for Tamnuz is described by Ezekiel in a familiar passage,[1] but it would seem that the word usually translated as 'cedar' might well mean 'ear', when the stanza in question would read.

'Ah me, my child (now) far-removed!
My son-consort, the far-removed!
For the sacred *ear* where the mother bore him,
In Eanna, high and low there is weeping,
Wailing for the house of their lord, the women raise'.[2]

A faint indication of the meaning of this symbolism is furnished in the pictures[3] where the Archangel Gabriel makes his appearance through a door at the *back* of the Virgin, who is aware of his presence without seeing him. This expresses the same idea as the Kwakiutl myth of the hero who was conceived by the sun shining on the small of his mother's back.[4] We are not told whether Jesus was actually born, like Rabelais' Gargantua, through his mother's ear, as well as being conceived through it; the real passage is hinted at in St. Agobard's description (See p. 264) of how the holy fertilising principle, after entering by the ear, emerges 'through the *golden* gate'.

[1] Ezekiel viii, 14.
[2] This rendering, based on Longdon's translation in his 'Tamnuz and Ishtar', is by Dr. Jyotirmoy Roy of Calcutta, who also kindly suggested to me several of the preceding points.
[3] Many examples are referred to by Mrs. Jameson: Sacred and Legendary Art, 1890 edition, Vol. I, p. 124.
[4] Boas and Hunt: Jesup Expedition. Bureau of Ethnology, Vol. I, p. 80.

That the danger of this form of conception is regarded by Catholics as not having entirely passed is shewn by the custom with which all nuns still comply of protecting their chastity against assault by keeping their ears constantly covered, a custom which stands in a direct historical relation to the legend forming the subject of this essay.[1] This is the acme of chastity, for it protects even against the most innocent form of conception, one reserved for the most modest women. An Indian legend, which may serve as a pendant to the Persian one mentioned above, well illustrates this connection between aural conception and modesty. Kunti, the mother of the five Pandava princes, the great heroes of the Mahabarata, when still a virgin, made use of a *mantra* charm to test its alleged power of calling up the Gods. It worked, and the Sun God appeared to her. She became very confused and bade him go, but he said that as she had called him she could not refuse him a reward. On learning that the reward the God wanted was carnal knowledge she explained that she was a Virgin. To this objection the Sun God suggested sexual intercourse via the ear, and to this she consented, with the result that the hero Karna (whose name means ear) was conceived.[2] The same association with extreme innocence is also indicated in the passage quoted above from Molière (p. 268).

*   *   *

We may conclude the present topic by briefly considering an animal myth which offers interesting resemblances to the legend under discussion and which also possesses certain historical connections with it. The myth of the

[1] See Tertullian: De Virginibus Velandis.
[2] Mahabharat-Adiparva, Ch. III, 1-20. I am indebted to Dr. Roy for calling my attention to this legend.

phoenix and other fire-birds, of which the aureole-surrounded
Holy Dove is the lineal descendant, is paralleled by that
of the salamander, the fabulous lizard born, like those, of
fire. It would not be easy to imagine animals more unlike
each other than a dove and a *lizard*, or *crocodile,* and
yet the positions both have occupied in mythology and
religion shew a far-reaching similarity, one which should
throw a new light on the legend of the Virgin Mary.
The lizard has been an extensive object of worship, by the
Slavs in Europe as late as the sixteenth century,[1] by the
Egyptians in the form of the crocodile, by the Mexicans in
that of the alligator; the crocodile is the protective totem
of one of the chief Bechuanaland tribes.[2] It was specially
sacred to the sun, and was, largely on that account,
adopted by the Gnostics as a symbol of the Life-Giver;
the Sun God Sebek was figured as a crocodile-headed
man. On the other hand it was identified at Nubti with
Set, one of the fore-runners of our devil, and—like most
phallic animals, lion, dragon, serpent, etc.—it had to be
overcome by the young God-Hero; thus at Adfou it was
supposed to have been speared by the young Sun God
Horus. In the Book of Gates the monster serpent Apep
is described as being accompanied by a friend in the
shape of a crocodile which had a tail terminating in the
head of a serpent, its name being Sessi.

There seem to have been two principal associations
between the idea of a lizard, or crocodile, and that of
the Deity. One was the observation that 'it veils its eyes
with a thin transparent membrane which it draws down
from the upper lid, so as to see without being seen,
which is the attribute of the Supreme Deity' (Plutarch);
this idea is naturally connected with that of the Sun-

---

[1] Morfill: The Religious Systems of the World, p. 272.
[2] Bent: The Ruined Cities of Mashonaland, 1891, p. 15.

Father,[1] and in Egypt the crocodile was the chief symbol of Cheops, the 'Ever-Existent Eye'. A more important association, however, and one which is closely related to the group of ideas under discussion here, was that the crocodile was the symbol of silence, being 'the only land animal which lacks the use of its tongue' (Pliny); 'it is said to have been made an emblem of the Deity, as being the sole animal destitute of a tongue. For the Divine Reason stands not in need of voice, but walking along a silent path and rule guides mortal affairs according to justice' (Plutarch). Representing the silence of the wise, it became the emblem of the mind, of reason, of intelligence, and particularly of wisdom;[2] as such it figures on the breast of Minerva, the Goddess of Wisdom. The only instance of its use in this respect that I know of in Christian art is in Seville, where one dating from the Moorish occupation still stands over the portal of the entrance to the Cathedral leading from the Patio de los Naránjos, there is, of course, the well-known crocodile on St. Theodore's column in the Piazzetta in Venice, which doubtless had an apotropaeic signification.

The attributes of the crocodile that have attracted interest thus appear to be mainly negative: it is an animal which has no visible genital organs, and is said to have no tongue and to be dumb—two ideas which, as we have seen earlier, symbolise impotence.

Side by side, however, with this conception of the crocodile as an impotent animal, one having the most elementary defects, we find the precise opposite—namely, the idea that it represents a glorification of phallic power; consideration of this remarkable antithesis will prove highly instructive for the main theme of this essay. The phallic

[1] Cp. Chapter V.
 For the symbolism of this see pp. 135, 334.

significance of the crocodile may be suspected from the circumstance alone that it is closely associated with the ideas of wisdom, the sun, and the snake, but grosser facts than these can be cited. In the text of Unas, written during the Sixth Dynasty, are passages expressing the desire that a deceased person may attain in the next world to the virility of the crocodile and so become 'all-powerful with women'.[1] At the present day in the Egyptian Soudan the belief is acted on that the penis of the crocodile eaten with spices is the most potent means of increasing sexual vigour in the male.[2] Both in Ancient Egypt and in the modern Soudan the belief has prevailed that the crocodile has the habit of carrying off women for sexual purposes. Two physiological facts concerning the animal probably contribute to these ideas· the copulatory act is unusually ardent and lasts a long time; and the male organ,[3] though never visible while the animal is alive—being concealed within the cloaca—is unusually large.[4]

The ancients, in pondering over the question of how the crocodile propagated its species, indicated consideration of both these opposite attitudes. They concluded that it must take place in some way that expressed the animal's independence of the ordinary means and, following the path of associations indicated above, reached the belief

[1] Budge: op. cit., pp 127, 128.

[2] Bousfield: 'Native Methods of Treatment of Disease in Kassala', *Third Report of the Wellcome Research Laboratories,* p. 274 Stanley: Through the Dark Continent, 1878, Vol. I, p. 253. Budge: op. cit., p. 128

[3] It is perhaps of some interest in the present connection to note that this organ is situate in the rectal part of the cloaca, being separated from the anterior urinary chamber by a wide transverse fold. Of further interest in relation with the 'gaseous' group of ideas is the circumstance that during the rutting period a pungent odour is emitted from the submaxillary glands of the creature.

[4] Gadow: in the Cambridge Natural History, Vol. VIII, p. 445.

that the female *conceivea, like the Virgin Mary, through the ear*. According to this the crocodile would represent a force greater even that that of the Deity whose Word was all-powerful and all-creating,[1] for to execute its wishes it needed not even speech, being possessed of the still more potent Silence of the Wise. We have here, therefore, a beautiful example of the 'omnipotence of thought', which is evidently higher than the 'omnipotence of speech'; invisible and silent action is the highest limit of imaginable power. The ear is the orifice best designed to receive thought, even though this be inaudible to the uninitiated.

According to King,[2] it was this belief about the crocodile's natural history that later made it come to be regarded by the early Christians as 'the type of the generation of the Word, that is, the Logos or Divine Wisdom'. Plutarch (De Iside et Osiride) makes a similar statement about the cat· he refers to the belief that the cat 'conceives through its ears, and brings forth its young through its mouth, and the Word, or Logos, is also conceived through the ear and expressed through the mouth'. In the Egyptian Book of the Dead four crocodiles are said to reside in the four quarters of the world, and to attack the dead in order to seize the magic *words* on which they depend for existence in the Other World.[3]

The great characteristic on which I wish to lay emphasis in the preceding beliefs concerning the crocodile is their striking *ambivalency*. Herodotus[4] noticed that the creature was held sacred in some parts of Egypt and was slain as a noxious reptile in others, and the double attitude

---

[1] Like, for instance, that of Ptah (First Dynasty).

[2] King: The Gnostics and their Remains, Second Edition, 1887, p. 107.

[3] Budge: op. cit, Vol. II, p. 239.

[4] Herodotus: ii, 69.

here indicated may be traced throughout Egyptian religion. We have remarked above on the contrasting beliefs whereby the crocodile was endowed, now with absolute impotence, now with the maximum of procreative power.

* * *

Proceeding from this we may venture to develop a view that will afford a more complete answer to the question instituted at the beginning of the present inquiry —namely, why breath was chosen in the Virgin Mary legend to represent the fertilising material. The view is that *the idea of gaseous fertilisation constitutes a reaction to an unusually intense castration-phantasy.* It is one of the most remarkable of the various modes of dealing with the primordial Oedipus situation.

The idea of intestinal gas is inextricably associated with three others—of the father, of the male organ, and of power. We have already considered here and there each of these connections, so that only a few words need be added by way of summary.

Little need be said about the association between the idea of *father* and the various 'gaseous' ones discussed above, for in most of the examples quoted the latter have constituted attributes of the Heavenly Father himself, the Deity. The breath of a Maori chief (= father) is so powerful that he dare not blow on the fire, for a brand might be taken from the fire by a slave and so cause his death; or the sacred breath might communicate its qualities to the fire, which would pass them on to the pot on the fire, whence they would reach the meat in the pot, the future eater of which would surely die.[1] In the phoenix myth, one of the most characteristic of the whole series, the

[1] Taylor: op. cit., p. 165.

idea of piety to the father is of central importance, a sign of ambivalency. That this association applied not only to the more refined derivatives, but also to the gaseous notion itself, is indicated by the fact that oriental nations, and also Rome, worshipped a special Deity who presided over the function in question.[1] The connotations of intestinal gas are almost exclusively male and predominantly refer to the father, one reason for this being fairly obvious in the greater reticence displayed by women and the much greater openness by men in regard to the act concerned, especially during effort (e. g. coitus).

The association with the idea of the *male organ* has also been pointed out and explained above (p. 329). Something more may be added on the subject of initiation ceremonies, for it is now recognised that these are the expression of castration threats.[2] Throughout Australia women are strictly forbidden ever to see the bull-roarer (See p. 285), so essential is the relation of this to the idea of maleness; the Chepara tribe punish with death a woman who casts eyes upon it, or a man who shews it to a woman.[3] In Brazil also no woman may see the equivalent jurupari pipes on pain of death.[4] The association penis—gas (noise)—castration is well illustrated by the Kakian initiation ceremonies, the following account of which I abstract from Frazer.[5] The Kakian ceremonial house is situate under the darkest trees in the depth of the forest and is so built as to admit so little light that it is impossible to see what goes on within; the boys are conducted there blindfold. When all are assembled before the house the

[1] Bourke: Scatologic Rites of All Nations, 1891, pp. 129, 154-7.
[2] See Reik: Probleme der Religionspsychologie, 1919, Cap. 3, Die Pubertätsriten der Wilden'.
[3] Lang. op. cit, p. 34.
[4] Lang. op cit. p. 43
[5] Frazer: Balder the Beautiful, 1913, Vol. II, pp. 249, 250.

High Priest calls aloud on the devils, and immediately a hideous uproar is heard to proceed from the house. It is made by men with bamboo trumpets who have been secretly introduced into the building, but the women think it is made by the devils and are greatly terrified. Then the priests enter, followed by the boys, one at a time. As soon as each boy disappears within the precincts a dull chopping sound is heard, a fearful cry rings out, and a sword or spear, dripping with blood, is thrust through the roof of the house. This is a token that the boy's *head has been cut off*, and that the devil has carried him away to regenerate him. In some places the boys are pushed through an opening made in the shape of a crocodile's jaws or a cassowary's beak, and it is then said that the devil has swallowed them. The boys remain in the shed for five or nine days. Sitting in the dark, they hear the blast of the bamboo trumpets, and from time to time the sound of musket shots and the clash of swords. As they sit in a row cross-legged, the chief takes his trumpet and, placing the mouth of it in the hands of each lad, speaks through it in strange tones, imitating the voice of the spirits; he warns the lads, under pain of death, to observe the rules of the Kakian society.

The association with the idea of *power* has also been manifest throughout all the examples quoted above, and is an extraordinarily intimate one. To create or destroy with a word, a wind, a breath, or a vapour obviously implies a higher degree of power than to do so with an instrument of might, however wonderful and impressive this might be. With the primary idea (intestinal gas) the sense of power is in adult life usually manifested in the form of contempt; in many countries the passage of wind is regarded as the deadliest possible insult and in certain circumstances may involve such penalties as expulsion from

23

the tribe or even death.[1] In an analysis, carried out from
a different point of view, of two Old Testament myths,
Lorenz[2] has shewn how the might of God against his most
desperate foes was displayed, in the one case by means
of wind, in the other through the blowing of trumpets.
The myths in question are those of the destruction of the
tower of Babel and the walls of Jericho, and he shews,
as I think convincingly, that both of these are variants
of the Titan motive. In the first of them the destruction
is brought about by a mighty *wind* that disperses the
people by confounding their *speech*, in the second by God
getting his chosen people to give a loud *cry* and to *blow
their trumpets*.

The preceding considerations are in full accord with
the conclusions I have reached on the basis of psycho-
analytical experience with actual persons. In such study
it becomes plain that the infantile complex concerned with
gaseous fertilisation is integrally related to the castration
thoughts. The total complex is a characteristically ambivalent
one, corresponding with the child's ambivalent attitude
towards his father, and its manifestations express at once
a denial of his power and an affirmation of his supreme
might; his impotency and his omnipotence. Through the
conception of the male organ as a flatus-emitting agency
(See p. 329) these two opposite components become fused
into a perfect unity.

Further psycho-analytic study throws still more light
on the nature of this paradoxical attitude. It has elucidated
the source of the two-fold attitude towards the father. The
hostile and depreciatory one, the wish that he were
impotent, originates in the rivalry between the boy and

[1]   Bourke: op. cit, pp. 161, 162.
[2]   Lorenz: 'Das Titan-Motiv in der allgemeinen Mythologie',
Imago, 1913, Bd. II, S. 50-3.

father over the possession of the mother. The admiration, which exalts the father's greatness, has a more personal source: it is a substitute for the primary narcissism and feeling of omnipotence which the child is unable to sustain in the face of experience, a failure which is largely contributed to by the presence of the obviously powerful Father. By transferring his own congenital sense of omnipotence[1] to the Father and identifying himself with him, he is enabled to maintain the feeling of power for some time longer, until the time comes for him to discover his Father's limitations also, when he has to repeat the same psychological process by substituting a heavenly for an earthly Father. There is a further important gain in both cases—namely, the reconciliation with a potentially hostile being, and the allaying of a sense of sin that arose from disobedient or hostile thoughts concerning him.

The curious way in which the attitude towards the Father is dealt with and reconciled in the compromise we have considered above, and even the specific form of this compromise, is also a mirror of changes within the individual himself, changes which are only secondarily transferred to the idea of the Father. For, in my experience, the particular group of phantasies that have constituted the main theme of this essay arise in persons who, chiefly on account of the incest barrier, have experienced a difficulty in passing from the pregenital stage of development to that of the genital one,[2] and who have thereby reacted by reverting to the former stage. In this earlier stage, which is principally composed of a combination of sadism and anal-erotism, the element most suitable for

[1] See Ferenczi: op. cit., Ch. VIII, 'Stages in the Development in the Sense of Reality'.

[2] See Freud: Sammlung kleiner Schriften zur Neurosenlehre, Vierte Folge, Cap. III, 'Die Disposition zur Zwangsneurose'.

fusion with the genital attitude that could not be encom-
passed is that of the passing of flatus, with its close
relation to the sense of power,[1] to expulsion and projection.
As was pointed out above, the uniting of these elements
to the actual genital one, in the phantasy of a flatus-
expelling organ, fulfils all the wished-for conditions to an
extent that one could hardly otherwise conceive. That the
idea of supreme power is here recaptured under the guise
of phantasies that have numerous feminine, anal, masochistic
and homosexual implications—e. g. by means of the gentle
dove—is in entire accord with the fundamental method
of Christian salvation, so that further studies on these
lines should lead to a deeper understanding of the psychology of this idea.

VI

CONCLUSION

If we now regard the theme as a whole, we cannot
but be impressed by the ingenuity and fine feeling with
which an idea so repellent to the adult mind has been
transformed into a conception not merely tolerable, but
lofty in its grandeur. In the endeavour to represent the
purest and least sensual form of procreation that can be
imagined, the one most befitting to the Creator Himself,
the mind worked surely and on the soundest lines by
reaching for its basis to the crudest and grossest idea
obtainable; it is always through such violently extreme
contrasts, as we know from the analytic study of literature,
that the grandest psychological effects are achieved. Of
all infantile theories of procreation that persist in the
Unconscious there is perhaps not one more repellent than
that described above, and no more astounding contrast

[1] See my Papers on Psycho-Analysis, 2nd. Ed., p. 546.

could well be conceived than the original form of this and the form given to it in the legend here analysed. In the original one we have a Father incestuously impregnating his daughter (i. e. a son his mother) by expelling intestinal gas, with the help of the genital organ, into her lower alimentary orifice, one through which her child is then born. In the legend, the site of exit is completely omitted, and that of ingress is denoted by the receptive organ of music, an orifice with fewer sensual implications than any other in the whole body, than the navel, the mouth, or even the eye. What more innocent symbol exists than that gentle messenger of hope and love, the dove? And in the tender breath of the dove, reinforced by the solemn words of the Archangel, who would recognise the repulsive material thus symbolised, with its odour replaced by the fragrance of lilies, its moisture and warmth by the aureole of light and fire, and its sound by the gentle cooing—'the echo on earth of the very Word of God'.

The Christian myth is perhaps the most gigantic and revolutionary phantasy in history, and its striking characteristic is the completely veiled way in which this phantasy is carried through to success under the guise of sacrificial submission to the Father's will. It is therefore entirely appropriate that such an important episode as the birth of the hero should be portrayed by symbolisms that signify a complete denial of the Father's power, and which at the same time, under the mantle of the Father, glorify the son's might in the most supreme terms imaginable.

Turning lastly to the accompanying picture by Martini[1] (see Frontispiece), painted over six hundred years ago, we see, although its marvellous colour cannot be here

---

[1] The picture is usually attributed to both Simone Martini and Lippo Memmi, but the latter painted only the setting and the angels at the side, which are not here reproduced.

reproduced, that the whole theme which has occupied us is portrayed with a charm and fidelity hardly to be surpassed. One of our leading critics, Edward Hutton, writes of it: 'Who may describe the colour and the delicate glory of this work? The hand of man can do no more; it is the most beautiful of religious paintings'. To shew how deeply the artist has reached for his inspiration I will call the reader's attention to one little detail, a trait characteristic of Martini's Annunciation pictures, though often copied from him later by other painters.[1] It has to do with the campanulas that stand between Gabriel and the Virgin. Our artist indicated, quite unconsciously, why the lily is the flower chosen for the present purpose. Of all flowers the lily is the most noted for the delicate fragrance of its odour: better than the luscious and half-lascivious rose, the heavy jasmine, or the fleeting wild flowers, the lily can serve as no other flower can to express the acme of purity that is necessary to conceal the exactly opposite original idea. In the picture, the artist makes the words of Gabriel, which are the counterpart of the Breath of God, pass through the lilies, as if to purify the fertilisation principle of the last trace of early uncleanness, to cleanse it of any possible remaining dross.

In work done, as this must have been, under the direct inspiration of the Unconscious, we realise the difference between true and pseudo-art. It also illustrates how happy was the union between Christian religion and art, before the divorce came with the decadence of the Renaissance and the reign of 'Puritanism' in religion. The whole

[1] For instance, by Taddeo Bartoli (in the Siena Academy). A very clear hint as to the function of the holy words is given by those painters who make them issue from the Archangel's mouth in the form of a *snake*. (An example of this is offered by the altar at Klosterneuburg, reproduced by Beissel: Geschichte der Verehrung Marias in Deutschland während des Mittelalters, 1909, S. 466.)

topic of this essay shews how important was the part
played by aesthetic feeling in the elaboration of religious
beliefs—the legend we have analysed may well be compared
to an exquisite poetic conception—a fact that is throughout
intelligible when we remember how intimate is the association
between the unconscious roots of both. Religion has always
used art in one form or another, and must do so, for
the reason that incestuous desires invariably construct their
phantasies out of the material provided by the unconscious
memory of infantile coprophilic interests; this is the inner
meaning of the phrase 'Art is the handmaid of Religion'.
The increasing separation between the two, and the
diverting of art to other purposes, constitutes the first
serious stage in the transformation of religion, and
in the supersession of the pleasure-principle by the reality-
principle.

CHAPTER IX

WAR AND INDIVIDUAL PSYCHOLOGY[1]

THE aim of this essay is to raise the question whether the science of Psychology can ever shew us how to abolish War. It is a question that must have occurred to many of those who have been able to reflect on the events of the past months, and it is one of the most far-reaching questions that mankind as a whole has to face, one on which its future may to a great extent depend. We are beginning to realise as never before—for it is to be supposed that at the time of other cataclysms, such as during the destruction of the Roman Empire, mankind was less conscious of itself than now—how powerful is the check that War may impose on the advance of civilisation, and the sight, together with the accompanying horrors, has naturally stimulated the desire, always widespread even in times of peace, to devise if possible a means of surmounting this formidable obstacle.

This desire has already manifested itself in the formulation of many schemes, mainly legal and political—from systems of international policing to conventions for compulsory arbitration—and the evidently unworkable nature of these may be taken as a measure of the emotional pressure that has brought them into being. It is characteristic

[1] Published in the *Sociological Review*, 1915, Vol. VIII, p. 167.

of emotional states that they lead to attempts at immediate action instead of to thought, the preliminary investigation necessary to secure suitable action being dispensed with. The general attitude of pacifists is that, both on the moral and the material side, the evils of War are evidently greater than its benefits, even if the latter are admitted, and that consequently steps must be taken at all costs to prevent its occurrence. The sense of urgency is felt so acutely that any calm study of the factors involved is regarded as an intolerable delay, while any expression of doubt as to the desirability of the goal is repudiated with impatience. Ill-considered and, in all probability, unsuccessful action is the natural result of such an attitude. Certain cooler-headed and more thoughtful people, on the other hand, who take a longer view of the question, realise better its complexity, and see that the matter demands an intimate knowledge of human motives, desires and emotions. They therefore turn to Psychology for assistance in a problem which obviously belongs to its domain, and ask psychologists how it is to be solved. It is the purpose of the present essay to consider what kind of answer can be given to such an inquiry.

Now this answer must always be the same whenever any science is approached with a similar question, one with a purely utilitarian aim. Suppose, for example, that an engineer is asked to devise a plan for carrying out a given practical purpose, e.g., building a bridge. He can answer the questions about the possibility of the undertaking, the means that would have to be adopted, and the probable cost, in lives and money, that would be incurred. What would not be in his sphere is the question of whether or no the undertaking *should* be entered upon. All he can do is to supply the data relating to the points just mentioned, leaving to the promoters of the undertaking

the decision of whether they considered it worth while
to carry it out. Science is thus the handmaid of the
human will: it is not within her province to dictate what
ought to be done in a given situation, but only to point out
what will have to be done if a desired end is to be attained.

Psychology, however, holds a peculiar rank among the
sciences in that it is concerned also with the instrument
of valuation, the mind. When approached with a utilitarian
problem, therefore, it has two additional functions to fulfil
which do not appertain to any other science. In supplying
the data to enable a decision to be made it has first to
answer the three questions mentioned above, viz., as regards
possibility, means, and cost. But there are two further
sets of important data that Psychology has to supply.
The first of these relates to the decision that a given end
must be achieved, the second to the choice of means.
Fundamentally the two points come to the same, it being
the place of Psychology in both cases to call attention to
the mental factors that may unconsciously influence decision,
so that they may be taken into consideration in making
a judgement. This is a matter on which the greatest
emphasis has to be laid, because the importance of such
factors is commonly neglected or else grossly underestimated,
and it will therefore be discussed here at some little length.
Coming now to the question at issue, whether Psychology
can teach us how to abolish War, we see that the first
thing to do is to re-state the problem under the following
headings: Is it possible? If so, how can it be done? What
would the cost involve? And, finally, what is the full
significance of the desire to accomplish this end?

It may as well be said at once that Psychology can
as yet give no positive answer to any one of these
questions, a fact which for the impatient will forthwith
dispose of any further interest in whatever it may have

to say on the matter. With those, however, who are chary of nostrums, and brave enough to suspend their judgement until the painful process of attaining truth is achieved, the following considerations should carry weight. In the first place, Psychology is already in a position to offer a considerable body of information directly bearing on the problem, and, in the second place, it is only through a richer and deeper knowledge of Psychology that a final solution of it is possible. It is hardly likely that this conclusion will be doubted on reflection, for it should be evident that even physical factors, e. g., economic ones, owe their influence only to the effect they have on human motives and instincts: it is in the sphere of these latter that we have to seek in order to obtain a better understanding of the causes of War.

It will be expedient to open the discussion by considering further the important matter mentioned above—namely, the influence of emotional factors on decision and judgement. Within the last twenty years a method of investigation, known as psycho-analysis, has been devised and elaborated by Professor Freud of Vienna, which has permitted access to a hitherto veiled part of the mind, designated the Unconscious, and the explorations thus carried out have yielded information of very considerable value about the unsuspected significance of this more emotional region of the mind. It would appear from these investigations that man is endowed with a far more intense emotional nature than is generally imagined, and that powerful barriers exist the function of which is to restrain its manifestations. All the emotions of which we become aware, either in ourselves or in others, represent only tricklings through from the volcanic reservoir that is pent up in the unconscious region of the mind, i. e., that region of which we are unconscious. The dams that impede a freer flow of emotion are the restrictions against uncurbed action that have been painfully acquired during the civilisation of the race and the training of the individual, and the reason for their existence is the fact that the pent-up or 'repressed' emotional life is of a rude and savage character incompatible with the demands of civilised standards. In this buried mental life, which is prevented from readily translating itself into action, phantasies play a very extensive part, and these are fundamentally of a pleasurable kind. Any disagreeable piece of reality that may succeed in penetrating to this region of the mind is at once treated as material to be used for the building up of some pleasurable fancy; it is remoulded in terms of some wish, and thus robbed of all its unpleasant features. The Unconscious cannot endure any contradiction of its desires and imaginings, any more than an infant can; intelligibly so, because it mainly comprises the infantile and inherited portion of our mind. Perception and, in an even higher degree, judgement are thus grossly distorted by these powerful emotional agents.

We are, it is true, to some extent familiar with this process of distortion in conscious mental life also. The expression 'the wish is father to the thought' is proverbial, and everyone will admit, in the abstract, that prejudices can influence opinions and judgements, at least those of other people. The science of History, and in a very imperfect way that of Law, makes some attempt at estimating and allowing for errors due to this factor, and in scientific research it is generally recognised that evidence of an emotional influence (jealousy, ambition, etc.) casts suspicion on the validity of the conclusions and even on that of the observations. But what is not generally recognised is that influences of this nature are far more extensively exerted than might be imagined, and that the most potent

ones are those proceeding from sources of which we know
nothing, namely from the unconscious region of the mind.
In an emotional situation, such as is evoked by a horror
of war, any judgement arrived at will infallibly be dependent
only in part on the external evidence; in a greater part
on unconscious emotional influences. If, therefore, we desire
to form a judgement purely on the relevant evidence, i. e.,
a judgement that is in accord with reality and so is likely
to be permanent, it is essential to neutralise the influence
of those other factors, and this, of course, cannot be done
until it is known precisely what they are. As will presently
be explained, this knowledge can be adequately based
only on a study of Individual Psychology.

Similar considerations apply to the causes of War.
The causes of any given war are exceedingly numerous,
and these are usually so inter-related as to make the
unravelling of them one of the most difficult of tasks; it
is further notorious that success in this undertaking is rarely
more than approximate. The most important part of the
task is, of course, not the mere enumeration of a list of
causes, but the ordering of them according to their scale
of values. They constitute a hierarchy in this respect, and
may be divided into the exciting causes, which merely
precipitate the war, and the deeper or more underlying
ones, which bear the main responsibility for it. Whereas
popular opinion concentrates its attention almost exclusively
on the former, the philosophic historian seeks to uncover
and comprehend the latter. How difficult this is may be
judged from the circumstance alone that it takes about
a century before all the material is published on which
alone valid conclusions can be founded. In the present
war, for example, it would seem impossible as yet to
answer even the apparently elementary and simple question
of which was the more important causative factor

leading up to it—the so-called inevitable conflict between Teuton and Slav or the need for German expansion overseas; in other words, whether the War is primarily one between Germany and Russia or between Germany and England.

Supposing, however, that all the political factors bringing about a certain war have been elucidated, we are still left with the problem of the causation of war in general. That is to say, the question arises whether there is not in the human mind some deep need, or some set of recurrently acting agents, which tends to bring about wars more or less regularly, and to find or create pretexts for wars whatever the external situation may be. This would involve the conclusion that man cannot live for more than a certain period without indulging his warlike impulses, and that history comprises an alternation of wars and recuperations. Another possibility, not identical with the preceding, though allied to it, is that man tends to prefer the solution of various socio-political problems by means of War to their solution in any other way: this might be because of the instinct just referred to or else because the other solutions are more difficult and irksome, or it might be due to both reasons combined. There is undoubtedly much that could be adduced in favour of this view, unpalatable as it may seem, and we should be prepared in any unbiassed investigation for the possibility that it is true. We have, for instance, the unvarnished fact that wars do invariably recur in spite of the best intentions to the contrary, and it might very plausibly be argued that what happens historically is a periodic outburst of warlike impulses followed by a revulsion against War—usually lasting for one or two generations—which is again succeeded by a forgetting of the horrors involved and a gradually accumulating tension that once more leads to an explosion. This feature of periodicity would be well worthy of a special study,[1] but we must leave aside here historical questions of a kind which are not directly germane to the psychological considerations of the present paper.

Returning to the problem of the Psychology of War, we may at this point consider an objection that is likely to be brought against the mode of approach here adopted, namely, that of Individual Psychology. Many will take the view that, since War is obviously a social problem, it should be to either Sociology or Social Psychology that we should have recourse in order to obtain a better understanding of the nature of it. This might even more strongly be urged in the case of modern war, which is essentially the affair of whole societies, and in which the social phenomena of imitation, contagion, crowd psychology, and mass suggestion play an important part. Fully to meet this objection would necessitate a detailed discussion, impossible here, of the relation of Social to Individual Psychology in general. There are two schools of thought in the matter, the main point at issue being as follows On the one hand it is contended that it is possible to pursue the subject of Social Psychology independently of the data afforded by Individual Psychology, on the ground that there are peculiar data pertaining to the interaction of social mass units which are provided by the former subject and which are accessible only to those who make a study of it. The second school maintain the contrary of this, namely, that Social Psychology must throughout be based on Individual

---

[1] Several writers, for example, have commented on the interesting circumstance that on the four last occasions the turn of the century has roughly coincided with a general European war of the same nature, consisting, namely, in a coalition against the predominance of the most powerful nation.

Psychology, for three reasons. In the first place, the unconscious emotional influences and prejudices spoken of above affect judgement to a much greater extent in the domain of the mental than in that of the non-mental sciences, so that a student of Social Psychology is at a grave disadvantage unless he has on the basis of Individual Psychology submitted his own mind to a thorough analysis and in this way acquired a knowledge and control of the distorting influences in question. In the second place, the study of motives, emotions, instincts, etc., can for technical reasons be properly carried out only by the methods of Individual Psychology, where the material is susceptible of objective experimental control. Finally, there is good reason to believe that in what may be called the 'social situations' that are the subject of socio-psychological study no new factor is added that may not be observed apart from such situations. 'Social' mental activities are nothing more nor less than the sum of individual mental activities. The reason for this has been pointed out by Wilfred Trotter,[1] who in his essay on the most exquisite of socio-psychological forces—the herd instinct—adduced considerations to shew that man is literally never anything but a social animal, and that all the agents specially insisted on by social psychologists, mob infection, press suggestion, etc., are constantly operative under all circumstances. The reason why some social psychologists have been misled into adopting the opposite conclusion is largely that the manifestations of certain instincts acted on by 'social situations' may differ somewhat in their external form from those occurring apart from these situations, the underlying unity of the two sets being thus overlooked.

[1] *Sociological Review*, 1908. Reprinted in his Instincts of the Herd in Peace and War, 1916.

Something may profitably be said at this point on the mode of operation of these 'social situations,' for the matter has a direct bearing on the problem of the essential nature of war. It is necessary to recur to a topic mentioned earlier, that of the 'repressed' unconscious impulses that are incompatible with civilised standards of thought and behaviour. The normal fate of these impulses is not annihilation, as might be supposed from the fact of their total disappearance from view in the course of education and development. On the contrary, they remain active throughout life, and furnish probably the greater part of all our interest, energies, and strivings. They cannot manifest themselves, however, unless they first go through a process of transformation, to which the name 'sublimation' has been attached, whereby the energy investing them becomes diverted along other, associated channels that accord better with the demands of social standards. The deflection of an ungratified maternal instinct into philanthropic channels is a familiar instance of this. Mental disorder, including the various forms of 'nervousness,' results from an inability of this process to work smoothly, and the very great prevalence of this in one shape or another, from slight eccentricities and character anomalies to the gravest kinds of insanity, affords some measure of how imperfect is the sublimating mechanism. Further, there is present in the mind a constant tendency to relapse in the direction of cruder and more primitive manifestations of the repressed impulses, and advantage is taken of every excuse to do so: examples are the relaxation of standards of modesty in clothing at the seaside and on the stage, the conduct responsible for the recent agitation about 'war babies', and the temporary paralysis of ethical restraints by alcohol. Now the influence of social situations is very apt to be in just this direction of undoing the effects of sublimation, thus leading to the adoption of a lower or more primitive standard of behaviour.[1] A mild example of this may be seen in the circumstance that most committees will display types of behaviour, involving perhaps injustice, meanness, inconsiderateness, and lack of responsibility, of a kind that would be disavowed by any single member acting independently. The bloodthirsty and often indiscriminate cruelty of mobs is notorious, and in general it may be said that any large body of men can be got to commit acts that would be impossible to the component individuals. But it is important to realise that this massive social contact creates none of these impulses; it only releases them, by affording a certain sanction to them. The impulses themselves are deeply rooted in human nature, and lead to endless other manifestations besides those just indicated. These fall into three main groups: (1) social, those of social value, produced by sublimation; (2) asocial, those of no social value, neurotic and other mental disturbances, due to a partial failure of the sublimating process, i.e., to mental conflict; (3) anti-social, due to paralysis of sublimation, whether this be brought about by massive social contact or in any other of the numerous ways in which this is possible. The manifestations of social situations so largely studied by social psychologists must, therefore, in no sense be regarded as isolated phenomena.

It is from this point of view that we obtain what is perhaps the most profitable perspective of the nature of War. The essence of war surely consists in an abrogation of standards of conduct approved of by the ethical sense

[1] The reason why the influence of social situations is most often in the direction of lowering the standards of thought and behaviour can only be briefly indicated here. It is because sublimations are mainly individual creations, whereas the unconscious repressed impulses are more uniformly and generally distributed; a relapse therefore takes place in the direction of the greatest common measure of the whole, i.e. in the direction of these impulses.

of civilised communities. By this is meant that in War an attempt is made to achieve a given purpose by means which are otherwise regarded as reprehensible. The best proof of this statement is to be found in the simple fact that no nation or government dares to assume the responsibility for initiating any war. At the present time, for instance, they are one and all engaged in an eager search for sanctions to justify their action in proceeding to war, and a cynical observer might almost say that the chief conflict in the war is over the question of who began it. On every side it is agreed that to have caused the war is a disgrace, the blame for which must at all costs be imputed to the enemy. To admit responsibility for it is universally regarded as tantamount to a confession of guilty wrong-doing, the thought of which is too painful to tolerate. Every nation whole-heartedly maintains the view that it was forced to go to war, regretfully and entirely against its will, by the wicked machinations of some other nation. Now this is just the attitude which in private life we see adopted towards any anti-social act or any act of which the ethical sense of the community does not approve. The person concerned makes every endeavour to shift his guilt or responsibility on to others or on to circumstances, and seeks to defend his conduct under cover of all imaginable excuses, pretexts, and rationalisations. This need for defence is in itself a proof that the act runs counter to the prevailing ethical sense. Seen from this angle, peace may be compared with the institution of monogamy, which society accepts in theory, but never in practice.

It is plain that the actual deeds of which War consists are so counter to the conscience of mankind that they can never be deliberately performed without some preliminary vindication; otherwise it would be mere murder and destruction of the savagest kind. The general theory

24*

of War is, of course, that the deeds comprising it are in themselves wholly repellent and abhorrent, but that they are justified by the necessity or desirability of the purpose to be achieved. As was indicated above, however, an alternative and equally possible view is that the repressed impulses leading to warlike acts accumulate such force from time to time as to incline the scales in favour of a bellicose solution whenever the opportunity offers itself in the form of problems otherwise difficult of settlement. Nietzsche, in 'Thus Spake Zarathustra', contrasts the two attitudes thus: 'Ye say it is the good cause which hallow- eth even war? I say unto you: it is the good war which halloweth every cause.' The fact that the second view appears repugnant and almost unthinkable is in itself no evidence against its possible truth, for *ex hypothesi* it relates to the unconscious and repressed part of the mind, the part that is repudiated by our waking consciousness, but which none the less exerts the greatest influence on the latter. It is not without significance that every belligerent tends to impute to his enemy this motive for War; the Germans have a proverb *Der Hass sieht scharf*, which means that hate enables one to uncover the motives of an enemy to which the latter is blind.

Even if we accept the more flattering view of War, to the effect that 'the end justifies the means,' it is necessary to remember that historically the attitude of mind implied in this has frequently been allowed to serve as a cover for acts in which the means supplied the principal motive—a familiar instance being the passion for cruelty indulged in under the cloak of the Inquisition. It is an empirical rule of wide validity in psychology that the consequences of an act, so far as they could have been predicted, have to be taken into account as a prob- able motive, and usually the chief one, in performing the act, even when the author of it repudiates this conclusion. Applying this rule to the present question, we are led to ask whether the terrible events of War, the cruelties and so forth, are not connected with the underlying causes of War itself. Therefore, for more reasons than one, it remains a problem for psychological investigation whether the end or the means of War must be regarded as the ultimate cause of it. There is reason to suppose that both are operative, and also that the second set of factors is seriously underestimated, but it would be valuable to know which of the two is the more important. It will thus be necessary to institute studies into two broad groups of motives, on the one hand those alleged by the conscience and on the other the darker ones to be discovered only by a more indirect mode of approach. A few words may be added concerning each of these groups, so as to indicate some of the directions in which further research would seem to be desirable.

Most of the motives belonging to the first group can be summed up under the word Patriotism, for it is much to be doubted whether the operations of cosmopolitan financiers have ever directly dictated the outbreak of any war and they have rarely been a factor of any importance at all. Patriotism, or devotion, love and loyalty towards one's country (or smaller unit), involves the willingness to fight for its interests, this taking the various forms of defending its material interests, avenging a slight on its honour, extending its prestige and importance, or resisting encroachments. The ultimate psychological origin of this complex sentiment is to be found mainly in the individual's relation to his parents, as Bacon hinted in his remark that 'Love of his country begins in a man's own house.'[1] It has three sources—in feelings about the self, the mother,

[1] De Aug. Scient, Bk. VI, Ch. iii.

and the father respectively. The last-mentioned is probably the least important of the three, but is more prominent in some cases than in others, leading then to patriarchal conceptions in which the head of the state is felt to be the father, and the state itself the father's land. More significant is the relation towards the mother, as is indicated by the fact that a country is as a rule conceived to have the feminine gender (in the expression *la patrie* we see a fusion of both conceptions). Most important of all is the source in self-love and self-interest, where the self becomes more or less identified with one's fellow citizens and the state is a magnified self. Psycho-analysis has shewn that these three feelings are far more complex and deeply rooted than is generally supposed, and that they exert a correspondingly weighty influence in the most manifold relations of life, often in quite unsuspected ways. On the precise fate of these feelings during the stage of early mental development depends the greater part of a man's character, dispositions, including the form of his Patriotism, whether aggressive, assertive, vainglorious, or the contrary; it would be tempting to compare the type of Patriotism usual in different countries with the various types of family relationship characteristic of each, for instance in Germany, England, and America. Even the finer shades of conduct in diplomatic relations, and the decisions on intricate questions, are to a large extent determined by the precise manner in which the three feeling-complexes just mentioned have been developed and inter-connected; it should not be forgotten that the greater part of them is unconscious, an example being the concealed hostility towards the father and passion for the mother that makes up what has been called the Oedipus complex.

The second group of motives concerns a darker side of human nature. It is necessary to penetrate behind a

veil which is well adapted to obscure it. This is the veil
of restraint and discipline, the inculcation of obedience,
loyalty, and devotion to the military unit and its commander,
attitudes of mind which are akin to the first group of
motives just discussed; they can hardly be regarded as
important causes of War, for the emotions concerned are
just as easily indulged in times of peace. Behind the façade,
however, are to be discerned evidences of far less respectable motives. War is, of course, the replacement of peace-
ful methods of dealing with certain other people, through
discussion, consideration, and so on, by the method of
brute force, and that this reversion to a more primitive
level of civilisation is of its very essence is shewn by the
nature of the deeds that throughout compose it. Civilised
warfare is a contradiction in terms, for under no circumstances is it a civilised act to blow another person's head
off or to jab a bayonet into him, nor can we after recent
events be any longer subject to the illusion that it is
possible to exclude savagery from the warfare of civilised
nations. Four repressed instincts play a cardinal part in
all war: the passions for cruelty, destruction, lust, and
loot. It is popularly held that the manifestations of these
are incidental to War, and not inherent in it; that they
are regrettable, though perhaps unavoidable, complications
which should be reduced to a minimum. But it is found
in practice that where one of these passions is suppressed
another flames out the more to take its place; one army
may rape where the other loots. The most puritanical
army of which we have record, Cromwell's Ironsides,
indulged in orgies of sacrilege, pillage, and massacre—under,
of course, the usual cover of military necessity, etc. One
of these passions, the lust to kill, is so indispensable that
without it an army would be paralyzed. The full analysis
of these various passions, the sadistic blood-lust, the

impulse to pillage and destroy, and so on, is of obvious importance for a proper understanding of their significance in regard to both the causation and conduct of War.

Where, therefore, the romantic idealist sees only the pure flame of patriotism feeding noble impulses to heroism and self-sacrifice, the psychologist detects the operation also of deeper forces dating from a past that is only too imperfectly overcome. Behind the guise of altruism work impulses of a more egoistic order, and who shall say which of the two is the more important, the visible or the invisible? What can definitely be asserted is that there is no hope of attaining to a real understanding of the meaning of War unless both are taken into full account and appraised at their true value. Whoever undertakes a psycho-analysis of men deciding to enlist in war time will be astonished at the complexity and strength of the unavowed motives darkly impelling him and reinforcing his altruism, from the fascinating attraction of horrors to the homosexual desire to be in close relation with masses of men, and one can only urge scepticism and caution in accepting conclusions on these and allied matters until our knowledge of every layer of the human mind is more complete than it is at present.

It may also be not out of place to sound a warning for those who accept the view that War is a reversion to a more savage state of conduct, but who draw the inference that the way to avoid it is through a still greater repression of the more primitive instincts that we inherit from the past. Doubt is cast on the validity of this apparently plausible conclusion by the following considerations. The investigations of psycho-analysis[1] have shewn that the influence on conscious life of these impulses that

[1] Those wishing to inform themselves further on this subject may be referred to the writer's 'Papers on Psycho-Analysis', 2nd Ed., 1918.

are in a repressed state in the unconscious mind is of an altogether unsuspected importance, and, what is more, that they are indestructible. Through the process of sublimation, however, they become of the highest value in furnishing much of the energy for our social activities, so that the only hope of diminishing their anti-social effects is to further this process. Now sublimation takes place automatically when repression is carried up to a certain point, the repressed impulses finding another outlet. In this there is necessarily an element of renunciation (of the original aim of the impulse), a circumstance which imposes an inevitable limit on what is possible in this direction. There are not wanting indications suggesting that we are nearly reaching the limit of natural sublimation, and when this happens there comes about a very unsatisfactory state of affairs. For if repression is carried too far, the energies in question revert to their unconscious sources, and lead either to neurotic disorders or to an accumulated tension which may be followed by an outbreaking of the impulses in more or less their original form. A lessening of the repression in such a case will allow better sublimation to take place than before.

If the present situation of civilisation is accurately described in these terms, it follows that there are only two possible ways of dealing further with these unruly impulses, and it is likely that both will be adopted when such matters are better understood. One is to relax the repression at points where it has lost its value and become harmful; certain aspects of the sex problem (more intelligent organisation of the marriage institution) occur to one in this connection. This is like the plan which we, alone among the nations, have adopted in the governing of subject races, and still more so in our relations with the Colonies. What the opposite attitude leads to is well shewn historically by the French Revolution and the American War of Independence. This principle has also been adopted socially in many spheres, notably in that of penology, and always ultimately with beneficial results. The other plan, which is not only compatible with, but also related to the first, consists in preventing excessive repression by allowing children to be more aware of certain sides of their nature, and so substituting conscious control for blind repression. A corollary of this is the provision of suitable outlets for the impulses in question; the value of various sports in this connection is undoubtedly great. One of the appeals made by War is that it offers a permissible outlet for a variety of impulses that are insufficiently gratified in times of peace; this is often described as the spirit of adventure seeking to escape from humdrum conventionality. The credit of first clearly perceiving that War could never be abolished unless suitable outlets were provided for the impulses leading to it belongs to William James. In his famous essay on 'The Moral Equivalents of War' he suggested that such impulses should be deliberately guided into suitable paths, an example he gave being Alpine climbing to gratify the desire for danger. What was completely lacking in his day, however, was any knowledge of the springs of conduct and of the unconscious sources of warlike impulses. Thanks to Freud's penetrating researches, we are now at least in a position to undertake further investigations in this direction that hold out every promise of success.

The argument of this paper may now be recapitulated. It is the place of Psychology to point out the almost irresistible tendency of the mind to believe that a given aim is possible of achievement when there is present a burningly intense desire to achieve it. Under these circumstances the mind tends greatly to underestimate the difficulties in the way, and also the cost involved. Psychology has further to ascertain what this judgement of values depends on and ultimately signifies. When all the data involved are put before those who have to pass such judgements it is quite possible that reflection may lead to reconsideration of the criteria on which there had been a tendency to make a hurried decision.

Although these considerations are evident enough psychological knowledge has realised that it is far harder to apply them than is commonly imagined, and proffers the explanation of this· namely, that the main influences distorting judgement are unconscious ones, the persons concerned being therefore unaware of their effect. This matter has a direct bearing on judgements relating to the causation and preventibility of war. It is at present quite an open question whether it is possible for mankind to abstain from war, whether the desire to abstain at all costs does not fundamentally signify something more deleterious to human development than the contrary attitude, and whether the psychological benefits that regularly recurring warfare brings to a nation are not greater than the total amount of harm done, terrific as this may be.

Some clues were then indicated for the direction in which psychological research may profitably be further developed with a view to determining the ultimate meaning of War in general. This has to reach beyond the ostensible motives given by the belligerent, and to enquire also into the nature and origin of the various warlike impulses the presence of which is indispensable for a bellicose solution of a problem ever to be regarded as tolerable. It is even possible that the strength of these impulses, for the most part concealed from view, is greater than that of the conscious motives; in any case they are certainly o importance in rendering the latter more acceptable and plausible. Something has been said also about the source of the warlike impulses, and about the possibility of finding other than warlike outlets for their activity.

It is only when we have a fuller understanding of the motives and impulses concerned in War based on a detailed and exact knowledge of Individual Psychology that we can begin to form a just appreciation of the merits and demerits of War and of its general biological and social significance. War furnishes perhaps the most potent stimulus to human activity in all its aspects, good and bad, that has yet been discovered. It is a miniature of life in general at its sharpest pitch of intensity. It reveals all the latent potentialities of man, and carries humanity to the uttermost confines of the attainable, to the loftiest heights as well as to the lowest depths. It brings man a little closer to the realities of existence, destroying shams and remoulding values. It forces him to discover what are the things that really matter in the end, what are the things for which he is willing to risk life itself. It can make life as a whole greater, richer, fuller, stronger, and sometimes nobler. It braces a nation, as an individual, to put forth its utmost effort, to the strange experience of bringing into action the whole energy of which it is capable.

The results of this tremendous effort are what might have been expected. On the one side are feats of dauntless courage, of fearless heroism, of noble devotion and self-sacrifice, of incredible endurance, of instantaneous and penetrating apprehension, and of astounding intellectual achievement; feats which teach a man that he is greater than he knew. The other side need not be described in these days of horror. To appraise at their just value these two sides of war, to sound the depths as well as explore the heights, what is this other than to know the human mind?

CHAPTER X

WAR AND SUBLIMATION[1]

IT is proposed to discuss in this paper the relationship of the uncivilised impulses of man to the civilised ones, with special reference to the problems in this connection suggested by the spectacle of war. The term 'sublimation' in the title does not, therefore, cover the whole ground of the paper, for, although the process denoted by this is perhaps the most characteristic of those whereby the one set of impulses becomes subordinated to the other, it is by no means the only process of the kind.

In the conduct of war, and implicit in the very conception of war, sundry impulses come to expression of a kind that are apparently non-existent, or at all events latent, in the same people during peace, and with which we are hardly familiar outside the criminal classes; they may include such disapproved-of tendencies as cruelty, deceit, and ruthless egotism, with such acts as killing, looting, and savagery of various kinds. This statement, it is true, does not accord with the popular and romantic view of war, which holds that it is valid only of the enemy, and that the conduct of the soldiers on its own side differs from that in peace in merely one particular, namely, in the fact

[1] Read before the British Association for the Advancement of Science, Section of Physiology, September 10, 1915. Published in the Reports of the Association, Vol. 85, p. 699.

that they kill their opponents. That it should have to differ even in this particular is regarded as an unfortunate necessity, and in no way related to any innate desire to kill. But it does not need very much knowledge of the unvarnished facts to realise the outstanding truth that in war things are done by large numbers of men on both sides of a kind that is totally foreign to their accustomed standard of ethical conduct during peace, and the question arises what is the source of the impulses thus vented and the relationship of these impulses to the controlling forces of civilised life?

An important clue to the problem is afforded by the circumstance that similar impulses are readily to be detected in the conduct and mental attitude of most children in the first few years of life, although their significance here has for certain reasons been greatly underestimated. It should be evident that if an adult were to display the same disregard for the rights and feelings of others, the same indecency, cruelty, and egotism as that characteristic of the infant he would very definitely rank as an asocial animal, and it is partly this remarkable contrast between the two, separating them into two worlds, that accounts for the extent to which the continuity of individual life from the infant to the adult is generally overlooked. There can be no doubt that the asocial impulses we are discussing are part of the inherited characteristics of mankind, and it is throughout intelligible that both the infant and the savage stand in this respect nearer to the animals from which we are descended. In the course of individual development these impulses are replaced by tendencies of an opposite nature, such as consideration for others, honesty, altruism, and horror of cruelty. It is generally believed that they disappear owing to the implantation or development of the more civilised tendencies, but psycho-analytic investigations shew that the process is more subtle and complex than is indicated in such a statement. There is an intricate inter-relationship between the two sets of tendencies, the precise details of which should form an important subject of study. A foundation for such study is the conclusion arrived at by all psycho-analysts, and perhaps one of the most startling of their conclusions, that the primitive, asocial tendencies never really disappear at all, but continue their existence throughout life in the buried, unconscious region of the mind. This part of the mind, indeed, essentially consists of the mpulses that we are considering, that is, of all the wishes, longings, and instinctive tendencies that are incompatible in their nature with the ethical and civilised standards prevailing in consciousness, and which, consequently, have been split off from consciousness, prevented from entering it, and 'repressed' into the unconscious. From here the asocial impulses exert a far more considerable influence on conscious activity than might be imagined, and they may even be called the ultimate source of such activity. It is with the interaction between the unconscious and consciousness that the science of psycho-analysis is primarily concerned.

A description of the normal unconscious mind would astonish and assuredly shock its owner. It is absolutely non-moral in nature, or, as judged by conscious standards, immoral. Through it course all manner of unrestrained fancies and desires, characterised by a complete disregard for the ethical and aesthetic canons of social life. A wish for the death of another person, even that of a loved relative, may arise on the slightest provocation, the crudest forms of indecency are gratified in the imagination, and the most extravagant flights of self-glorification are indulged in to the heart's content. In short, the picture may bear no resemblance to the person's conscious character.

The interest that a knowledge of the unconscious has for the psychological understanding of the phenomenon of war is twofold. In the first place, as I have suggested elsewhere,[1] it is probable that the constant pressure of these savage, unconscious impulses plays a part, the extent of which is quite unknown, but which may be very great indeed, in raising the threshold of acceptability for pacific solutions of international difficulties, and thus operates, probably in periodic waves, in favouring a bellicose one. In the second place, we find in war an instructive example of the type of influence which has the power of releasing repressed impulses, and thus allowing external manifestation of them in a fairly direct form; it is with this latter question that the present paper is chiefly concerned.

In order to understand what happens in the release of a repressed impulse we have next to consider the fate of such an impulse under various circumstances. This fate is manifold, but there are two broad groups of processes that may come about, the distinction between which I wish to emphasise at the outset. The repressing forces may on the one hand profoundly affect the impulse itself, or, to be more accurate, its mode of functioning; or on the other hand it may merely hold the impulse in check. The external result is very similar in both cases, the conduct of the person falling into line with what is demanded by social convention, but the psychological difference between the two is profound, though its full social significance is only evident under the stress of influences, such as war, which inhibit the action of the repressing forces.

The repressed impulses, as of course all impulses, are of a dynamic character, and they exert a constant activity in the direction of external expression, which is

[1] See Chapter IX.

called in psycho-analysis the 'wish-fulfilment'. In this, however, they meet with the opposition of certain forces of a contrary kind, which emanate partly from without, and partly from within. The main source of them is the pressure of education in the widest sense, exerted first by the parents and later on by the whole cultural environment as well, though no doubt the child is born with a susceptibility to this influence in the form of various predispositions. A simple illustration of the effect of repression is the case where the impulse is, as it were, weakened and made milder on its path towards expression, the resulting manifestation agreeing in kind, but not in intensity, with the original impulse. In this way, for instance, a definitely sexual attraction may reveal itself consciously as merely a slight liking, manifesting itself externally in the form of polite attentions, and a murderous desire may come to expression merely as a chuckle whenever the object of the feeling meets with a slight reverse of fortune, or as a cordial opposition to whatever views he may hold. In such cases as these the repressing force presents itself in the form of an obstacle, a filter through which the affect accompanying the repressed impulse can only percolate.

It will readily be seen that the social consequences of a process such as that just indicated may be entirely satisfactory, the energy investing the repressed impulse being neither lost nor dammed up, but being applied in a quite permissible and even advantageous social direction. But only too often the process does not go on so smoothly as this. The repressed affects may, for instance, become heaped up in the form of an unconscious complex, from which they can then be discharged in an excessive manner on to an associated conscious idea, leading to a violent distortion of judgement, a common example of which is

25

a strong political bias unconsciously dictated by self-interest. More serious consequences still will be noted presently.

We have next to speak of the transformations that may be brought about in the actual impulses themselves. Perhaps the most typical of these, and the most extensively studied, is that known as 'sublimation'. This has been defined by Freud [1] as 'the capacity to exchange an originally sexual aim for another one which is no longer sexual, though it is psychically related to the first.' By it is meant not a vague displacement of normal sexual desire by another, unrelated interest, but an unconscious and automatic deflection of energy from the individual biological components of the sexual instinct on to other fields which are symbolically associated with the first. It is a process that concerns the life of the young child far more than that of the adult, and it must clearly be recognised that it refers much more to the peculiar and less differentiated form of sexuality known as infantile sexuality than to the familiar adult type.[2] It will be remembered that, for reasons that cannot be gone into here, Freud includes under the term 'sexual' many processes, especially in childhood life, to which it is not usually applied. Be that as it may, the fact that energy and interest can be in this way deflected from the sexual sphere is well recognised by psychologists and educationalists, although its importance and the extent to which the process normally goes on without being remarked are certainly as a rule underestimated.

The primary impulses that have to be modified before attaining adjustment to the standards of social life may for practical purposes be divided into two groups, according

[1] Sammlung kleiner Schriften zur Neurosenlehre, Zweite Folge, S. 181.

[2] This subject is developed in a chapter of my 'Papers on Psycho-Analysis', 1918, Ch. XXXV.

as they serve the interests of the individual or those of the species. The latter, the sexual impulses, are transformed by sublimation in the manner just indicated. The other set, which may be called the impulses belonging to the ego, are equally in need of modification for social purposes, for in their original shape they are quite egocentrically orientated and tend to function in ways that ruthlessly ignore the rights and feelings of other people. A characteristic process whereby these egoistic impulses become modified is through their becoming invested with erotic feeling, the word erotic being here used to denote all possible varieties of love. They are in this way subordinated to the mutual interests of the individual and his environment, and direct pleasure is experienced in their functioning along lines that are acceptable to civilised social standards.

In both these cases we may speak of a refinement of the primary impulses, the very nature of which is profoundly affected. A curious circumstance, however, one that cannot be illustrated by any analogy from the physical world, is that the impulses continue to exist side by side in both their original and in their altered form. A possible explanation for this may be reached from consideration of the varying depth in the unconscious to which the educative influence penetrates, for it is certain that it never affects the repressed impulses down to their ultimate source in the inherited instincts. Evidence for the truth of this statement may be obtained from the analysis of dreams, in which the repressed impulses are to be discovered in their original form, and sometimes with very little disguise. The practical external result, none the less, is that the individual's conduct is in complete accord with the ethical, aesthetic and social standards of civilised life, and that it is so without any sense of compulsion, but as a spontaneous and natural expression of the personality. One may say that adoption of these standards has become second nature, so thoroughly are they incorporated into the personality. A further important matter is that this state of affairs is a durable one, and will stand a considerable amount of strain. The individual is in no sense dependent of external approval, but will act well whatever the circumstances, even when to do so is to his manifest disadvantage; it is not in his power to do otherwise.

The refinement just described is of course the ideal more or less consciously aimed at by civilising agents, though it is not often fully achieved. In contrast to it stand other effects of repression, which, though they may equally result in 'good' behaviour, do so merely through exercising an external pressure, there being no change whatever in the nature of the impulses themselves. It is as though the individual consented to behave well, against his nature, because the consequences would otherwise be disagreeable in the form of social disapproval, dislike, or actual punishment. Like Nietzsche's 'culture-Philistines', they obey and follow an ideal that is not really their own, and it is therefore intelligible that their allegiance to it can never be absolutely depended on. They are usually under a certain strain, and are always subjected to more or less inner mental conflict, though the greater part of this may be unconscious. Superficially it may not be easy to distinguish the two types just described—and of course the line between them is in no sense an absolute one—but the difference becomes pronounced when the stress of external social pressure is removed. In these circumstances the conduct and standards of the type first described remain relatively unchanged, while those of the second type rapidly deteriorate. A trite illustration of what is meant may be seen in connection with table manners and other personal habits; with some people these remain quite the same whether they are alone or in company, but with the majority of people this is certainly not so. The same is true of much more important matters, including the cardinal laws of morality. When an individual no longer feels himself to be under the eye of the social censor he becomes more true to himself, aud the result of this will depend on whether his primitive instincts have undergone a real refinement by civilisation—in the way indicated above—or only an apparent one. There are many circumstances under which this may happen. The sensitiveness to the social censor may be paralysed by physical agents, for example alcohol or the toxins of bodily disease (e. g. syphilis of the brain), or they may be temporarily inhibited by the action of powerful emotions, such as anger. More serious socially is the situation when the change is not in the individual, but in the conscience of the social body itself. This is the secret of the so-called 'danger of mob violence', when passions are no longer restrained because the surrounding social attitude has ceased to be inimical to their functioning. To the same category belong many of the phenomena of war, indeed the most essential ones. The lust for murder, for instance, which slumbers in every man's heart, runs counter to the strongest possible disapproval and penalties on the part of the state and of society in general, but in war time society not merely averts its gaze, but deliberately incites this lust and affords it full opportunity for gratification.

Psycho-analytical experience fully accords with the evidence at present being yielded by the War in the conclusion that the refinement of our primitive instincts has proceeded to a far less extent than we flatter ourselves, and that the large majority of people belong to the second type described above, where this refinement is more apparent than real.[1] And there is still more to be said in the same direction. Society, after making the discovery that a level of conduct which is natural to the few can be compelled from the many, has been encouraged to raise her standards still higher, to an extent that an increasingly large number of people find it difficult to comply with. The forced efforts to do so result in a variety of artificial reactions, character peculiarities, over-compensations, neurotic symptoms, and so on, all of which are necessarily unstable in nature. As Freud puts it, such people may be said, in a psychological sense, to be living beyond their means. When the real test comes, i. e. when they are left to their own resources without the supporting pressure of a civilised environment, their false acquisitions fall away from them just as a *parvenu* loses his veneer of good manners in similar circumstances, and they revert to a lower level of conduct. An inexplicable change seems to have come over them, but this change is only in their external behaviour; their real nature remains what it always was. All that has been lost is a false ideal, an illusion.

In this paper I have done nothing but sketch the outlines of a problem which I believe to be of great importance for psychology, and for social psychology in particular. Further investigation is needed to determine in what precise details the two types differ, and how these differences come about, why it has proved possible for one man to incorporate a given civilised standard into his inmost nature—to identify himself with it, as would be said psycho-analytically—and not for another.

---

[1] See a recent paper to the same effect by Freud: 'Zeitgemäßes über Krieg und Tod', *Imago*, 1915, Bd. IV, S. 1.

CHAPTER XI

A LINGUISTIC FACTOR
IN ENGLISH CHARACTEROLOGY[1]

THE definition of national character traits is notoriously treacherous ground, but in all attempts to describe those most typical or general among English people one is always mentioned with such unvarying emphasis that it is hard to resist the conclusion that it must relate, however roughly, to some group of observable phenomena. I refer to the striking insistence of the English on propriety, which is commented on not only by practically all foreign observers, but also by Americans and our fellow-subjects from overseas, not to speak of the 'Keltic fringe' in our own islands. That it degenerates into prudishness here more often than in any other country, at least in the Old World, will also, I think, be widely admitted. The trait is probably to be correlated in some degree with the proneness to reserve, the absence of social gifts, the dislike of betraying emotion of any kind, and the horror of self-display, vaunting, braggadocio, gasconade, rodomontade—one sees that we have to use foreign terms to indicate attitudes so foreign to us—which also belong to the judgements passed on the English by foreigners. Psychologically the group in

[1] Read before the British Psychological Society, March 14, 1920. Published in the *International Journal of Psycho-Analysis*, 1920, Vol. I.

question might perhaps be described in McDougall's language as a deficiency in the self-regarding instinct. Psycho-analysts would call attention to the secondary nature of the phenomena as indicating the existence of what is called a reaction-formation, and indeed that something is being actively controlled or avoided is fairly evident; they would probably ascribe the traits to a reaction against more than one complex, repressed exhibitionism being perhaps the most prominent. However this may be, it has occurred to me that there is possibly a connection between this group of character traits—which, for convenience, might be referred to as the propriety trait—and a peculiar historical feature in the development of the English language, but before submitting this idea for your consideration I shall have to make a few remarks on some general psychological aspects of speech.

There are good grounds for believing that speech originally was a far more concrete activity than it now is, and it has indeed been maintained that all speech represents pretermitted action.[1] Plain indications of this are to be observed among less cultivated human beings, especially children and savages. Freud,[2] for instance, following Groos, points out that children treat words as objects in the various games they play with them, while Frazer,[3] in his section on Tabooed Words, brings forward a mass of evidence illustrating the extraordinary significance attached by primitive races to words and especially to names. He says, following Tylor: 'Unable to discriminate clearly between words and things, the savage commonly fancies that the link between a name and the person or thing

---

[1] Ferenczi: Contributions to Psycho-Analysis. 1916, p. 120.
[2] Freud: Der Witz und seine Beziehung zum Unbewußten. 1905, S. 105.
[3] Frazer: Taboo and the Perils of the Soul. 1911, Chapter VI.

denominated by it is not a mere arbitrary and ideal association, but a real and substantial bond which unites the two in such a way that magic may be wrought on a man just as easily through his name as through his hair, his nails, or any other material part of his person. In fact, primitive man regards his name as a vital portion of himself and takes care of it accordingly.' He cites[1] the example of the Sulka of New Britain who when near their enemies speak of them as 'rotten tree-trunks', 'and they imagine that by calling them that they make the limbs of their dreaded enemies ponderous and clumsy like logs. This example illustrates the extremely materialistic view which these savages take of the nature of words; they suppose that the mere utterance of an expression signifying clumsiness will homoeopathically affect with clumsiness the limbs of their distant foemen. Another illustration of this curious misconception is furnished by a Caffre superstition that the character of a young thief can be reformed by shouting his name over a boiling kettle of medicated water, then clapping a lid on the kettle and leaving the name to steep in the water for several days.' Of the innumerable examples from the field of taboo one may be quoted:[2] the Alfoors of Poso are not only not allowed to mention the names of their parents-in-law, a common enough prohibition, but if such a name happens to be the same as that of a thing—e. g. in English a Mr. Lake—then they may not mention even this thing by its own name, only by a borrowed one. Even with us the use of bad language by children is treated as a sin of no mean order, and the law of England can still condemn a man to imprisonment for making use in public of certain forbidden (obscene) words, the utterance aloud of the heinous words being in both cases regarded as equivalent to a nefarious deed.

[1] ibid., op. cit., p. 331.   [2] ibid., op. cit., p. 340.

The nature of this primitive material conception of words and speech can be described more exactly. One of the conclusions emerging from Freud's work on the psychology of wit and of dreams is that all words originally possessed distinct motor and perceptual qualities, which they gradually lose more or less completely in the course of mental development. As has been interestingly expounded by Ferenczi,[1] there is a class of words, namely, obscene words, which, probably because of their being excluded from the usual course of development, still retain these qualities in a full measure. On the perceptual side Ferenczi[2] remarks that a word of this kind 'has a peculiar power of compelling the hearer to imagine the object it denotes in substantial actuality', and adds 'one may therefore infer that these words as such possess the capacity of compelling the hearer to revive memory pictures in a regressive and hallucinatory manner'; he calls attention to the fact that delicate allusions to the same ideas, and scientific or foreign designations for them, do not have this effect, or at least not to the same extent as the words taken from the original, popular, erotic vocabulary of one's mother-tongue. On the motor side the following three illustrations may be mentioned: the aggressive tendency which Freud has shewn to underlie the uttering of obscene jokes—this being a substitute for a sexual aggression; the curious perversion of coprophemia in which the sexual act consists solely of uttering indecent words to women; and the obsessional neurosis, where the act itself of thinking is curiously sexualised in the preconscious in such a way that the impulsion to think certain thoughts comes as a substitute for forbidden acts. In all these cases the act of thought or speech is psychologically the full equivalent of an actual deed.

[1] Ferenczi: op. cit., Chap. IV.
[2] ibid., op. cit., p. 116.

As was remarked above, in the course of mental development the motor and perceptual elements become more and more eliminated from words, and in purely abstract thought they disappear altogether. It may be recalled that Galton many years ago pointed out how much less capable of abstract thought are as a rule persons of a pronouncedly visual or auditory type as contrasted with those whose thought processes contain only feeble perceptual elements. One may also in this connection refer to Freud's latest conclusion on the unconscious,[1] namely, that the essential difference between unconscious and conscious ideas is that the former consist only of ideas (which easily regress to images) of the object or process, whereas the latter contain as well the idea of the corresponding word. Thus unconscious mentation and abstract thought stand at the two opposite ends of the scale in this respect, the ideas of the former being near to perceptual imagery, those of the latter being almost completely divested of it.

It is evident that this process of gradual abstraction effects a great economy of thought; indeed, without it none of the higher forms of thought could occur. It is probable that this economical factor is of prime importance in bringing about the process in question, but it has to be remarked that this is accompanied by other important psychical changes as well, which probably also stand in a causal relation to it. I refer to the inhibition in feeling that goes with the progress from the motor-perceptual stage to the abstract one, and the valuable saving in expenditure of emotional energy that this signifies. There is thus a double economy, an intellectual and an affective one. The affective economy, to which I wish to draw special attention, may be illustrated from two sides. On

[1] Freud: Sammlung kleiner Schriften zur Neurosenlehre, Vierte Folge. 1918, S. 334.

the one hand, when there is a need to express unusually strong feeling recourse is commonly had, through regression, to the use of just those words which have retained their motor and perceptual elements, as in oaths and obscene language, a procedure much more manifest in the male sex because of their having been to a less extent the subject of repression in this sex. The desire for expression combined with a sense of incapacity for it, so common in the young, similarly results in the phenomenon of slang. On the other hand, when there is a special need to inhibit feeling recourse is had to the use of abstract, or at all events less familiar words. It is well known that an otherwise forbidden idea can be readily expressed if only it is veiled in a euphemism or translated into a foreign tongue. Most books on sexology, for instance, contain whole passages written in Latin. The reason is that the vulgar, familiar words would tend to arouse embarrassing feelings, in both speaker and hearer, which can be avoided by the use of foreign, unfamiliar, or abstract words which have been acquired only in later years.

After this long digression I now return to the theme of English characterology. Without entering on a discussion of the numerous individual, social, or racial forces making for repression and inhibition, I can only think that such a process must be favoured if one of the main instruments by means of which it is carried out is peculiarly accessible. Thus, if it is unusually easy to give vocal expression to forbidden ideas in a way that inhibits the development of feeling it seems to me to follow that in such circumstances feeling will be more readily and extensively inhibited. Now it is clear that this is just the situation in which the English race has been placed for nearly a thousand years. The Saxon and Norman languages, after living side by side for about two centuries, gradually coalesced to form

English, but to this day there is in most cases an obvious difference in the 'feel' of the words belonging to each, and still more between words of Saxon origin and Latin words more recently introduced than their Norman-French precursors. All literary men recognise the distinction clearly, and every text-book dealing with style in writing urges the student to choose the Saxon words wherever it is possible without being precious, as being more vivid, robust and virile, i. e. because of their greater capacity to arouse plastic images and feeling-tone. Our store of synonyms is unequalled by that of any other European language, and the difference in the respects I have mentioned between such pairs as house and domicile, fatherly and paternal, book and volume, is quite patent. The existence of this double stratum of words enables us to indulge in fastidiousness to a degree not open to any other nation. Most culinary terms are, for historical reasons, of Romance origin, and the difference between being invited to a dish of veal or pork and one of calves' flesh or swine flesh is very perceptible. No other nation is unable to use its native word for belly if need be, but we have to say 'abdomen', and that only with circumspection. In English a lady is gravid, pregnant, or *enceinte,* there being no single native word to describe the phenomenon. The process in question can often be followed in its stages, such as when the Saxon word 'gut' gets replaced first by the Norman-French 'bowel', and then, when this is found too coarse, by the Latin 'intestine'.

The suggestion I make, therefore, is that the development of the outstanding English character trait of propriety has been fostered by the peculiar nature of the English language, one resulting from the success of a Norman adventurer some thousand years ago.

CHAPTER XII

THE ISLAND OF IRELAND [1]

A PSYCHO-ANALYTICAL CONTRIBUTION TO POLITICAL PSYCHOLOGY

IT must often have struck dispassionate observers as a curious problem that Ireland should differ so profoundly from both Scotland and Wales in her reaction to the stimuli provided by England. On the extent of the difference it is not necessary to dwell; the evidence of it is to-day before our eyes. It is the object of this paper to suggest along psycho-analytical lines that one important factor effecting this difference, the geographical relationship of the countries, operates in a more subtle and complex manner than might be suspected. In so doing it is clear that we are deliberately isolating one factor only and have no intention of underestimating the numerous other well-recognised ones, historical, dynastic, economic, and so on.

Most people would, I think, agree that the psychological motives impelling Scotland and Wales to unite amicably with England are more evident, and call less for explanation, than those which have perpetuated strife between Ireland and England. The relations between Scotland and England, for instance, are typical of those subsisting between two strong and well-matched men, who after a period of angry fighting agree to be reconciled and to

[1] Read before the British Psycho-Analytical Society, June 21, 1922.

join in a partnership of mutual benefit. This issue was doubtless facilitated by the circumstance that the race and culture of both countries were predominantly Anglo-Saxon; indeed, with the exception of the Western Highlands, the differences between Scotland and Northern England are hardly greater than those between Northern and Southern England. The same reason cannot be evoked in the case of Wales and England, where both the racial and cultural differences are profound and yet the two nations have found it possible to live harmoniously together in the closest contact for many centuries; nor can it be said that the dynastic union in Tudor times played more than a transitory part in producing this result. One might liken the relation of the two countries to each other as resembling that between two brothers of unequal size, with good-humoured tolerance on the one side and a combination of petulance and admiration on the other.

Between England and Ireland, on the other hand, we have a continuous record of dragooning, despoiling and bullying on the one side and of dogged and contumacious resistance on the other, there being relatively little attempt at any period in the past seven centuries to agree to any form of tolerable union. The first question that arises is whether the state of affairs represents a perfectly natural reaction on the part of Ireland to an exceptional degree of tyranny from England or whether on the other hand there was not some special feature in the Irish character that provoked friction and prevented the union that one has seen in various parts of Europe between different nations and races.

Being concerned here only with the nature of the Irish reaction I intend to pass by any analysis that might be instituted into England's attitude. That the latter cannot be held responsible for the whole situation is clear from

a comparison between Wales and Ireland. The position of
Wales in respect to England has been for many centuries,
from a purely military point of view, identical with that
of Ireland, so that the greater resistance offered by Ireland
against absorption into the United Kingdom could hardly
have been due to any better possibility of success. It
seems safe, therefore, to search for some explanation in
the national differences between the two peoples. The task
here at once becomes obscure, for there is no profound
racial difference between the two. Both Irish and Welsh
consist essentially of a Mediterranean stock, with a primitive
Neolithic substratum, which in both cases completely
accepted, presumably through conquest, the Keltic culture
and language. We can hardly ascribe any far-reaching
national importance to the greater admixture of Danish
stock in some of the coastal regions of Ireland or to the
more complete Romanization of the Britons. Yet within
historical times we note three outstanding divergences in
the behaviour of the two peoples: (1) Wales early established a harmonious relationship with England, which has
always proved impossible with Ireland; (2) Ireland was
uninfluenced by the Reformation, whereas Wales passed
to the extreme of radical Protestantism; (3) The Welsh
have on the whole been a more peace-loving people than
the Irish, both nationally and individually.

Of the many factors accounting for this result the
only one with which we are here concerned is the circumstance that Ireland is an island. It has often been pointed
out that the psychology of islanders tends to differ from
that of related peoples on the mainland and we ourselves
are no exception to that rule. The insularity of the British,
with all that that word connotes, is proverbial on the
Continent. It is probable, however, that the relative size
of the island is of considerable importance in this con-

nection and that the insularity of, for instance, Australia, Japan, and Great Britain is a very different thing from that of smaller islands, even though there may be features common to them all. The numerous ways in which the geographical fact of insularity may influence the mentality of the islanders, the sense of aloofness, peculiar forms assumed by the desire for security, and so on, would make an elaborate chapter, from which it is only possible here to select one special aspect. This aspect concerns the tendency of the geographical insularity to become unconsciously associated with particular complexes, affording in this way a certain mode of expression for these.

The complexes to which the idea of an island home tends to become attached are those relating to the ideas of woman, virgin, mother and womb, all of which fuse in the central complex of the womb of a virgin mother. This means, of course, one's own birth-place. In the secret recesses of his heart every male being cherishes the thought that his mother is a virgin, this representing the repudiation of the father which psycho-analysis has shewn to be a normal constituent of the universal Oedipus-complex. That important consequences in life may follow, as will presently be indicated, from the association of one's actual home and country with the profound source of feeling just mentioned is not surprising.

The evidence for the existence of this unconscious association is of two kinds. On the one hand there is the psycho-analysis of individual phantasies about wonderful islands, which are so common as to provide a constantly recurring theme for poets and novelists. In such investigations I have repeatedly obtained unequivocal evidence of the association in question. Secondly one finds scattered throughout literature and mythology innumerable references to a special mystical appeal that islands make to the imagination, and study of the precise form taken by this affords plain indication of the same conclusion.

To begin with, that the idea of one's native land, whether an island or not, is generally associated with the idea of a female being having both virginal and maternal attributes is evident from the familiar fact that most countries are commonly represented in this allegorical form: one has only to think of Britannia, Columbia, Germania, Italia, and the rest. These personages, in spite of their matronly characteristics, never have any husband. The thesis here maintained, however, goes beyond this simple fact: it is that the association mentioned above is much more closely forged and much more strongly invested with feeling if the homeland is an island. It will, I think, be generally agreed that the conception of Britannia has much more significance to us than has that of Columbia for citizens of the United States.

Most of what is here quoted from the second group of evidence, taken from popular and literary sources, will have a direct reference to Ireland, but similar instances bearing on the theme will also be cited from other countries. In the first place it may be doubted if any other country has such a variety of feminine names. In addition to the customary one of Erin, which would content most countries, Ireland is also called by, amongst other names: Cáitlin Ni Houlihan, Morrin Ni Cullinan, Roisin Dubh (little black Rose), Shan Van Vocht (old woman), Seau Bheau Bhoct, Dark Rosaleen, and by the names of three queens of Tuatha Di Danann, Eire, Bauba, and Fodhla. References to Ireland as a woman, and especially as a mother, are innumerable in poems, speeches and writings; the following may serve as typical examples.[1]

---

[1] For these I am indebted to Miss Violet Fitzgerald.

I am Ireland.
I am older than the Old Woman of Beare.
Great my glory,
I that bore Cuchulainn the valiant.
Great my shame
My own children that sold their Mother.[1]

And Mother, though thou cast away
The child who'd die for thee,
My fondest wishes still should pray
For cuisle geal mo croidhe.[2]

Thou hast slain me, O my bride, and may'st serve thee
                              no whit,
For the soul within me loveth thee not since yesterday,
                              nor to-day.
Thou hast left me weak and broken in mien and in shape
Betray me not who love thee, my Little Dark Rose.

Had I a yoke of horses I would plough against the hills,
In middle-Mass I'd make a gospel of my little Dark Rose.
I'd give a kiss to the young girl that would give her
                              youth to me
And behind the kiss would lie embracing my Little Dark Rose.

The Erne shall rise in rude torrents and hills shall be rent,
The sea shall roll in red waves and blood be poured out,
Every mountain glen in Ireland and the bogs shall quake
Some day ere shall perish my Little Dark Rose.[3]

[1] P. Pearse: I am Ireland.

[2] Michael Doheny: A cuisle geal mo croidhe. Doheny escaped to America in 1848 after taking part in the O'Brien rising.

[3] Traditionally ascribed to Hugh O'Donnell, 1602; translated by Patrick Pearse.

Fallen her own winsome beauty
From her lovely shapely face,
Full breasted nurse of fair hosts,
No heir is left to her.

She hath no friend, no mate,
No lover in her bed,—
A woman with no strong man's protection!
No man lieth beside her
Of the true blood of her heart's affection.

She hath no hope of any husband
For the true Gaelic blood
Over the stormy white-bayed sea is gone.
For this her mind is heavy.
The gentle widow shall not find
A lover or a friendly mate
Until the true Gaels come again—
With freemen's shouts inspiring dread,

No wonder that the isle ot strengths,
Once beloved, should now repine
For the Gaelic race of noble deeds,
Who once cherished her full well.

The nurse of the fosterling though she be
Widowed ot every husband
O Mary, how pitiful her fate,
Bereft of all her ancestral beauty!

Without protection against the island's evil
Alas, the deformity of her condition
Those who possessed her thus,—
The ancient mother of the sons of Mileadh.

A harlot without respect or honour
Is this land of Partholon's stronghold.
Her reason hath withered without reward,
And her seed is subject to savages![1]

'Yet I do not give up the country. I see her in a
swoon, but she is not dead: though in her tomb she lies
helpless and motionless, still there is on her lips a spirit
of life, and on her cheek a glow of beauty.'[2] 'Nurse of
our bringing up is she, and when you have looked at her
she is not unlovely.'[3] But perhaps the most moving description of all is to be found in W. B. Yeats' play
'Cathleen ni Houlihan', where the spirit of Ireland is
depicted as a poor wandering old woman whose sorrows
impel the young men (the scene is cast in 1798) to for-
sake all else, even their brides on their wedding-day, and
follow her call. The young hero in the play does this and
the play closes with a question put by his family to a
young boy who has just entered: 'Did you see an old
woman going down the path?', to which he answers
'I did not, but I saw a young girl, and she had the walk
of a Queen'. We get here the identification of maiden,
old woman, and queen (i. e. mother) so characteristic of
the unconscious conception of the mother.

We now pass to apparently a different theme, the
connection of which with the previous one, however, will
be pointed out later. In every region of the world the
belief may be found that there exists somewhere, usually
in a Western sea, a magical island which is identified

[1] Geoffrey Keating: My Pity How Ireland Standeth. 1644 or 1650;
translated by Pearse.
[2] Anti-Union speech by Grattan, May 26, 1800.
[3] O'Grady, Catalogue of Manuscripts in the British Museum, 1894,
No. 385.

with heaven. In Europe it goes under various names:
Meropis, the continent of Kronos, Ogygia, Atlantis, the
Garden of the Hesperides, the Fortunate Isles, and so on.
The actual position of the island was depicted on many
mediaeval maps, such as the one made by Lambertus
Floridus in the twelfth century, now in the Bibliothèque
Nationale, Paris, the Hereford map of the thirteenth
century, and the twelfth century map of the world in
Corpus Christi College, Cambridge.

There are three features regularly attaching to this
concept: (1) in that land all wishes are fulfilled; (2) from
it new souls emanate; (3) it is the land to which the dead
depart. These three features will be considered in order.
With the *first* of them psycho-analysts are very familiar.
The phantasy of a life where all wishes are easily fulfilled, the
unconscious 'omnipotence of thought', represents the desire
to live over again the once-tasted experience of such an
existence. The notion that such a life is possible is not
so fantastic and pretentious as it may appear; we all
actually experienced it at one period and we simply desire to
return to this experience. I refer, of course, to the period of
complete gratification passed through during intra-uterine
life, the perfection of which gradually 'fades into the light
of common day', as Wordsworth put it, in the succeeding
stage of infancy and childhood. It is true that the joys
to be tasted in the Fortunate Isle are depicted in more
adult terms than this humble origin would suggest, a
comprehensible enough fact, but it is noteworthy that the
part played by feeding, the chief pleasure in infancy, is
remarkably prominent in most of the descriptions. Few of
these islands are without their fountain of life and eternal
youth as well as a bounteous supply of golden apples, in
which symbols it is not hard to recognise the mother's
milk and breast; fruit, particularly apples, are a constant

symbol of the breast in the unconscious. So natural, indeed, did the idea of luscious feeding seem to be in connection with the concept of a Fortunate Isle that the Mediaeval caricatures of it—Cockaigne and Schlaraffenland, for instance—deal with little else; roast geese parade the streets, adding the finishing touches to their condition by continually turning as they walk, wine flows in rivers, and so on. There can be little doubt that unconscious memories of the mother's womb and breast extensively contributed to the formation of this phantasy of a wishless Paradise. The relation of it to the memory of the mother was plainly brought out in Sir James Barrie's play 'Mary Rose'. It will be remembered that the Peter-Pan-like heroine of the play, who quarrels with her husband and is afraid of her father but is devoted to her mother and her child, i. e. has an intense maternal fixation, is charmed away by the irresistible spell of a magic island, which is depicted in the form of a woman with wooing music. Incidentally, music, i. e. the mother's soothing lullaby, is extensively associated with the ideas of children and the third of our themes, death. Throughout Northern Europe children were cautioned not to hearken to the sweet songs of the Elves (the music of which is known in Germany as Alpleich or Elfenreigen, in Sweden as ellfr-lek, in Iceland as liuflingslag, in Norway as Huldreslát) lest they be spirited away by Frau Holle, and Baring-Gould[1] has interestingly traced the same idea in many of our Dissenting hymns, e. g. 'Hark! hark, my soul! Angelic songs are swelling', 'Sweet angels are calling to me from yon shore'.

The *second* feature, that the island is where children originate, is the one that most unambiguously points to a maternal source. A place where children are born

[1] Baring-Gould: Curious Myths of the Middle Ages, p. 425.

evidently can be nothing else but a symbol for the mother's womb. Largely through Otto Rank's detailed work,[1] we have become familiar with the extraordinarily extensive part played by the idea of water in myths and beliefs relating to birth, so that it is not surprising to find a place so closely connected with water as an island functioning as a common womb symbol; in individual psychoanalyses one is familiar enough with this. The frequent unconscious process of inversion of course aids this (a place contained by water instead of a place containing water). As is well known, in folklore and mythology babies mostly come from a river, a well, a pool, or the sea, at all events from a watery place where they are stored. In Wordsworth's poem quoted above, 'Intimations of Immortality from Recollections of Early Childhood', after speaking of the boy's birth from 'that imperial palace whence he came', he goes on to say:

> Hence, in a season of calm weather
> Though inland far we be,
> Our souls have sight of that immortal sea
> Which brought us hither,
> Can in a moment travel thither,
> And see the Children sport upon the shore,
> And hear the mighty waters rolling evermore.

The meaning of the *third* feature, that the Fortunate Isle should also be the abode of the dead—they are often for this reason called the Isles of the Blessed—is less obvious and only becomes intelligible when one remembers the idea, again commonly found both in folk belief and in the individual unconscious, that in dying one simply

[1] Otto Rank: Die Lohengrinsage, 1911, S. 26-32, etc.

returns to the place whence one came: 'dust thou art
and unto dust thou shalt return'. The unconscious mind
cannot apprehend the idea of annihilation and substitutes
for it that of return to the Nirvana existence of pre-natal
life. It is probable that on this is largely founded the
belief in re-birth and reincarnation.[1] From this point of
view it is quite comprehensible that what might be called
the uterine conception of death is again closely associated
with the idea of water.[2] That souls of the dead have to
cross water before arriving at their final abode is an idea
of which thousands of examples could be quoted, from
the Greek Styx to Böcklin's Toteninsel. It is curious to
note that remains of this pagan belief are to be found in
many English hymns:

> Shall we meet beyond the river,
>   Where the surges cease to roll,
> Where in all the bright Forever
>   Sorrow ne'er shall press the soul?
>
> Shall we meet in that blest harbour,
>   When our stormy voyage is o'er?
> Shall we meet and cast the anchor
>   By the fair celestial shore?

The following lines occur in the Lyra Messianica, in
a poem on 'The Last Voyage'.

> On! on! through the storm and the billow,
>   By life's chequer'd troubles opprest,
> The rude deck my home and my pillow,
>   I sail to the land of the Blest.

---

[1] See Chs. XXXVIII and XXXIX of my Papers on Psycho-
Analysis, 1918.

[2] See Otto Rank: op. cit., and Psychoanalytische Beiträge zur
Mythenforschung, 1919.

> Ye waters of gloom and of sorrow,
>> How dread are your tumult and roar!
> But, on! for the brilliant to-morrow
>> That dawns upon yonder bright shore!
>
> Now, ended all sighing and sadness,
>> The waves of destruction all spent,
> I sing with the Children of gladness
>> The song of immortal content.

Or I may recall the familiar stanzas of Tennyson's
'Crossing the Bar'

> Sunset and evening star,
>> And one clear call for me!
> And may there be no moaning of the bar,
>> When I put out to sea.
>
> But such a tide as moving seems asleep;
>> Too full for sound and foam,
> When that which drew from out the boundless deep
>> Turns again home.

We thus see that all aspects of the idea of an island
Paradise are intimately connected with womb phantasies,
with our deepest feelings about birth, death, and mother.
Now the point I wish to make here is that this connection,
although common enough elsewhere, is extraordinarily close
in Irish thought. Without fear of contradiction it may be
said that there is no culture so impregnated throughout
with the various beliefs and legends associated with the
idea of an island Paradise.[1] The number of Erse names

---

[1] The fullest accounts are collected in Jubainville's L'Epopée
celtique en Irlande, 1892, and in the 'Essay upon the Irish vision of
Happy Otherworld and the Celtic Doctrine of Re-Birth' by Alfred Nutt, the
greatest authority on this subject, in Vol. II of Meyer's Voyage of Bran, 1897.

for it is in itself indicative evidence of this. Thus: Thierna na oge, the Country of Youth; Tir-Innambéo, the Land of the Living; Tirno-nog, the Land of Youth; Tir Tairngire, the Land of Promise; Tir N-aill, the Other Land; Mag Már, the Great Plain; Mag Mell, the Agreeable Plain. The Gaelic Flath Innis, the Noble Isle, to which the souls of the departed go, is evidently a variant of the same idea. The beliefs are made up of the elements we have considered above. We find there the fountain of life, the golden apples, children come from it and the dead return to it. Heroes set out to secure the wonderful Cauldron of Re-Birth, a typical womb symbol, just as elsewhere they did for the Holy Grail. Altogether the idea of re-birth in relation to the island of the Other-World plays a quite extraordinary part in Irish mythology.[1] The Fortunate Isles of the Irish were invariably in the West. From the Odyssey (xx, 356) onward the West has always been associated with the idea of death, and long before the War the usual expression in Munster for dying was 'to go west'.

We thus see, first that the idea of Ireland has been intimately associated with the ideas of woman, mother, nurse, and virgin[2] and, secondly, that no other country has shewn such an extensive and tenacious belief in the conception of a Western Isle possessing the uterine attributes of happiness, birth and death. It is no very far step to infer that the two themes are connected, that the Magic Isle was a glorified idealisation of the Irishman's own birthplace, Ireland; indeed the Norse, who adopted many Irish beliefs before their Leinster kingdom was destroyed

---

[1] See Alfred Nutt, op. cit.

[2] It is of interest that several writers have connected the national musical instrument of Ireland, the harp, with the sistrum of Isis, a well-known emblem of virginity.

at Clontarf in 1114, actually called it by the name of Ireland hit Mikla (Greater Ireland). It is therefore quite comprehensible that the average Irishman should react to the idea of foreign invasion in a different manner from the conscientious objectors when faced with the usual question in their trial: what would you do if a German assaulted your mother? The primordial nature of the response that most men make to such a situation is due, as psychoanalysis has amply shewn, to the deeply rooted Oedipus complex, to the sadistic conception formed by most boys of the cruel and violent nature of the father's love demonstrations towards the mother.

Granted that this may have been true of the Irish in the past, have we any evidence that such ancient beliefs should have lingered on unconsciously and affected the people in modern times? Quite apart from general expectations based on the permanence of the underlying complexes, there is a wealth of evidence indicating an affirmative answer to this question. It seems almost impossible for Irishmen to express their feelings on political subjects without using imagery similar to that described above, and they have shewn by their conduct that this imagery is pregnant with meaning to them. It is no chance that Ireland, alone of the constituent elements of the British Empire, refused in the sixteenth century to relinquish the Catholic cult of the Virgin-Mother, and that virginity is nowhere held in higher esteem. And it is perhaps more than a coincidence that some of the most implacable leaders of the Republicans, such as De Valera, Erskine Childers, etc., are Irish only on their mother's side.

Let us take as an example the first of the modern leaders, Charles Stewart Parnell, so long the adored chief of the Nationalist party. 'The Parnells were supposed either to have concealed Fenians in their house, or documents of a compromising kind, or weapons. At all events a search party arrived, insisted on going through the house, would not be denied entrance anywhere, actually would penetrate to Mrs. Parnell's bedroom and turn possible hiding places upside down there with sacrilegious hand. That at least is how the young man at Cambridge received it when all was related to him. It was rank sacrilege and violation of what should have been the sanctity of his mother's room. . . . He brooded upon it probably more than a little morbidly. It grew to seem a monstrous thing. Its memory and its infamy influenced his whole nature. It turned him into a hater, a hater of the England by whose order this thing had been done. . . . The men of the search party that had invaded his mother's bedroom do not seem to have found anything . . . unless it were a sword belonging to Charles which they took away with them. What he wanted with, or what right he had to the sword I do not know, but probably the taking of it from him was another coal laid on the fire of his wrath.'[1] Or I may quote the following passage from Killiher's 'Glamour of Dublin', 1920: ' alone amidst the gross batterings of material things, she stands patient with her old sacred civilization—a reverence for youth, a worship of womankind unique in an age of apostasy, a devotion to lost causes that are so often but virtue herself in distress—all these the stigmata of her martyred but indestructible soul.

> And we love thee, O Bauba!'[2]
> Though the spoiler be in thy hall,
> And thou art bereft of all,
> Save only that Spirit for friend
> Who shapes all things in the end:

[1] Hutchinson: Portraits of the Eighties, 1920, pp. 30, 31.
[2] One of the many feminine names for Ireland.

> Though thine eyes are a sword that has slain
> Thy lovers on many a plain,
> When glad to the conflict they pressed
> Drunk with the light of thy breast
> To die for thee, Bauba!'

I will finish with a few passages taken from speeches made in the spring of this very year. De Valera, in a speech on February 22, said: 'There were people who held Ireland was a mother country, and would never consent to making her a kind of illegitimate daughter. . . . Ireland, being a mother country, had a right to be in a position worthy of the dignity of a mother country.' In the same month Michael Collins wrote in a similar strain: 'at a conference in London with the British representatives I made it quite clear that Ireland was a Mother country, with the duties and responsibilities of a Mother country.' On April 30 De Valera said of the Free Staters: 'They wanted them to come and hold Ireland while the shackles were being put upon her.' So the oldest and the youngest records of the Irish concur in resenting with the bitterness of despair, and now at last of triumph, the rape and violence offered to their beloved mother-land.

The point of view brought forward in this essay is—I will not say too slight—but too isolated for one to draw safe practical conclusions from it. But I may perhaps be permitted to suggest that possibly history would have been different if England had had more inkling of the considerations here mentioned and had, instead of ravishing virgin Ireland as though she were a harlot, wooed her with the offer of an honourable alliance. That this was the only hopeful attitude was not seen until the chief power in England was entrusted to a citizen of another small Celtic land.

CHAPTER XIII

A PSYCHO-ANALYTIC STUDY OF THE HOLY GHOST[1]

WHATEVER time may reveal about the historical personality of the Founder of Christianity, there is no doubt in the minds of those who have instituted studies into the comparison of various religions that many of the beliefs centering about Him have been superadded to the original basis, having been derived from extraneous Pagan sources, and the name of Christian mythology may very well be applied to the study of these accretions. As Frazer[2] puts it; 'Nothing is more certain than that myths grow like weeds round the great historical figures of the past'.

Some of the more important elements of this mythology have already been investigated by means of the psycho-analytic method by Freud.[3] According to him, the central dogma itself of the Christian religion—the belief that mankind is to be saved from its sins through the sacrifice of Jesus Christ on the cross—represents an elaboration of the primitive totemistic system. The essence of this system he sees in an attempt to allay the sense of guilt arising from the Oedipus complex, i. e. the impulse, gratified in primordial times, towards parricide and incest, there

[1] Read at the Seventh International Psycho-Analytical Congress, September 27, 1922.

[2] Frazer: Adonis, Attis, Osiris, 3rd Ed., 1914, p. 160.

[3] Freud: Totem und Tabu, 1913, S. 142.

415

being good reason to think that this complex is the ultimate source of the 'original sin' described by the theologians. This was the first great sin of mankind and the one from which our moral conscience and sense of guilt was born. The early history of mankind in this respect, the tendency towards this great sin and the moral reaction against it, is repeated by every child that comes into the world, and the story of religion is a never-ending attempt to overcome the Oedipus complex and to achieve peace of mind through atonement with the Father. Freud has pointed out that the most striking characteristic of the Christian solution as compared with others, such as the Mithraic, is the way in which this atonement is achieved through surrender to the Father instead of through openly defying and overcoming him. This surrender, the prototype of which is the Crucifixion, is periodically repeated in the ceremony of the Holy Mass or Communion, which is psychologically equivalent to the totemistic banquet. In this way the Father's wrath is averted and the Son takes his place as co-equal with Him. In the banquet is lived over again both the celebration of the original deed of killing and eating the Father and the remorseful piety which desires re-union and identification with him. It will be seen that, according to this view, the Christian reconciliation with the Father is attained at the expense of over-development of the feminine component.

The present communication will, it is hoped, afford confirmation of Freud's conclusions by a study on parallel lines. Some ten years ago I published in the *Jahrbuch der Psychoanalyse* an essay on the impregnation of the Madonna and what I have to present here is largely based on a recently written expanded edition of the essay which is to appear in English.[1] The research there pursued led incidentally to consideration of the following problem.

[1] Chapter VIII of this book.

In the Christian mythology a startling fact appears. It is the only one in which the original figures are no longer present, in which the Trinity to be worshipped no longer consists of the Father, Mother and Son. The Father and Son still appear, but the Mother, the reason for the whole conflict, has been replaced by the mysterious figure of the Holy Ghost. ·

It seems impossible to come to any other conclusion than the one just enunciated. Not only must the Mother logically constitute the third member of any Trinity whose two other members are Father and Son, not only is this so in all the other numerous Trinities known to us, but there is a considerable amount of direct evidence indicating that this was originally so in the Christian myth itself. Frazer[1] has collected some of the evidence to this effect and makes the conclusion highly probable on historical grounds alone. The original Mother, who was accepted by for instance the Ophitic sect as the third member of the Trinity, would appear to have been of mixed Babylonian and Egyptian origin, although there are not wanting indications to shew that a misty Mother-figure floated in the background of Hebrew theology also. Thus the passage in Genesis (i. 2) ' And the Spirit of God moved upon the face of the waters' should properly run ' The Mother of the Gods brooded (or fluttered) over the abyss and brought forth life', a bird-like conception of the Mother which must remind us not only of the Holy Dove (i. e. the Holy Spirit that replaces the Mother), but also of the legend that Isis conceived Horus while fluttering in the shape of a hawk over the dead body of Osiris. While the sternly patriarchal Hebrew theology, however, banned the Mother to a subordinate part and the Messiah-Son to a remotely distant future, it nevertheless retained the normal relationship

[1] Frazer: The Dying God, 1911, p. 5.

of the three. It is probable, therefore, that any elucidation
of the change from Mother to Holy Ghost would throw
light on the inner nature of the psychological revolution
betokened by the development of Judaism into Christianity.

The mode of approach here adopted will be by considering the circumstances of the conception of the Messiah.
This approach is justified on two grounds. In the first
place, as is well known, the figure of the Holy Ghost
appears in the myth only as the procreative agent in the
conception of the Son, and as an ambrosial benediction
poured out on to the Son when the latter undergoes the
initiatory rite of baptism (later on also in connection with
the followers of the Son). In the second place, Otto
Rank[1] has long ago shewn that the tendencies of a myth
are revealed already in its earliest stages, in what he has
termed the Myth of the Birth of the Hero. Consideration
of the Christian myth makes it probable that this law
holds good here also, so that a study of the conception
of Jesus may throw light on the main tendencies and
purposes of the whole myth.

To begin with, the very idea of a conception being
induced by a supernatural and abnormal means yields a
clue to the mythical tendency. It tells us at once that
there is some conflict present in the attitude towards the
Father, for the unusual route of impregnation implies, as
we know from other studies, a wish to repudiate the idea
of the Father having played any part in it. There may
or may not be present as well the opposite tendency to
this—the desire to magnify admiringly the special power
of the Father. This ambivalency is clearly seen in the
primitive belief that children are begotten not of their Father,
but through impregnation of the Mother by the particular
clan totem, for the totem is simply an ancestral substitute

[1] Otto Rank: Der Mythus von der Geburt des Helden, 1909.

for the Father, a super-Father. It is thus not surprising to learn that the Christian myth must, like most other religious myths, be concerned with the age-old struggle between Father and Son.

It will be remembered that the conception of Jesus took place in a most unusual manner. As a rule, whenever a god wishes to impregnate a mortal woman, he appears on earth—either in human form or disguised as an animal with specially phallic attributes (a bull, a snake or what not)—and impregnates her by performing the usual act of sexual union. In the Madonna myth, on the other hand, God the Father does not appear at all, unless we regard the Archangel Gabriel as a personification of Him; the impregnation itself is effected by the angel's word of greeting and the breath of a dove simultaneously entering the Madonna's ear. The Dove itself, which is understood to represent the Holy Ghost, emanates from the Father's mouth. The Holy Ghost, therefore, and His breath play here the part of a sexual agent, and appear where we would logically expect to find a phallus and semen respectively. To quote St. Zeno: 'The womb of Mary swells forth by the Word, not by seed', or, again, St. Eleutherius: 'O blessed Virgin . . . made mother without cooperation of man. For here the ear was the wife, and the angelic word the husband'.

It will be seen that our problem is immediately complicated. To find that the mysterious figure replacing the Mother is a male being, who symbolises the creative elements of the Father, only adds a second enigma to the first. Before taking this up, however, it is necessary to consider more closely the details of the impregnation itself.

A comparative analysis of these leads to an unexpected conclusion. When we seek to discover how the idea of breath could have become invested in the primitive, i. e. unconscious, mind with the seminal connotation just indicated, we find that it does so in a very circuitous way. As I have shewn in detail in the work referred to above, the idea of breath does not have in the primitive mind the narrow and definite signification we now give to it. A study of Greek and Hindoo physiological philosophy in particular shews that breath used to have a much broader connotation, that of the so-called pneuma concept, and that an important constituent of this concept—probably the greater part of at least its sexual aspects—were derived from another gaseous excretion, namely that proceeding from the lower end of the alimentary canal. It is this down-going breath, as it is termed in the Vedic literature, which is the fertilising element in the various beliefs of creation through speech or breath. Similarly, analysis of the idea of the ear as a female receptive organ leads to the conclusion that this is a symbolic replacement, a 'displacement from below upwards', of corresponding thoughts relating to the lower orifice of the alimentary canal. Putting these two conclusions together, we can hardly avoid the inference that the mythical legend in question represents a highly refined and disguised elaboration of the 'infantile sexual theory', to which I have elsewhere drawn attention,[1] according to which fecundation is supposed to be effected through the passage of intestinal gas from the Father to the Mother. I have also pointed out why this most repellent of sexual phantasies should lend itself better than any other to the conveyance of the most exalted and spiritual ideas of which the mind is capable.

Now there are certain characteristic features accompanying this infantile theory which we can discover by means of individual psycho-analyses of persons holding

[1] *Jahrbuch der Psychoanalyse*, 1912, Band IV, S. 588 et seq.

it, as well as from a study of the comparative material in association with it. Superficially considered it would appear to imply a denial of the Father's potency and to represent a form of castration wish, and no doubt this is in part true. Yet, on the other hand, one is astonished to find that throughout all the numerous associations to the idea of creation in connection with wind there is nearly always implied the very opposite idea of a powerful concrete phallus which expels the wind. Thus in most of the beliefs attaching in all parts of the world to the idea of divine creative thunder there is also present some sort of thunder-weapon, the best-known and most widely spread of which is the bull-roarer. Further than this, the idea of impregnation by means of wind itself would seem to be regularly regarded by the primitive mind as a sign of peculiarly great potency, as if the power to create by a mere sound, a word or even a thought, were a final demonstration of tremendous virility. This reaches its acme in the notion of conception without even sound, by a silent thought alone, such as in the belief cherished by various nuns in the Middle Ages that they had conceived because Jesus had 'thought on them'.

An excellent example of this complex of ideas, interesting from several points of view, is afforded by certain Egyptian beliefs about the crocodile. They also bear directly on the present theme, for the crocodile was taken by early Christians to be a symbol for the Logos or Holy Ghost; moreover, the creature was believed to impregnate his mate, just like the Virgin Mary, through the ear. Now on the one hand the crocodile was notable to the ancients for having no external genital organs, no tongue and no voice (symbolic indications of impotency), and yet on the other hand—in spite of these purely negative qualities (or perhaps just because of them)—he was regarded as the highest type of sexual virility, and a number of aphrodisiac customs were based on this belief. The crocodile was an emblem of wisdom, like the serpent and other phallic objects, and as such figures on the breast of Minerva, so that the ancients seem to have reached the conclusion that the most potent agent in all creation was the Silence of Man, the omnipotence of thought being even more impressive than the omnipotence of speech.

We know that this over-emphasis on paternal potency is not a primary phenomenon, but is a transference from personal narcissism in response to the fear of castration as a punishment for castration wishes. We thus come to the conclusion, which is amply borne out by individual psycho-analyses, that a belief in a gaseous impregnation represents a reaction to an unusually intense castration phantasy, and that it occurs only when the attitude towards the Father is particularly ambivalent, hostile denial of potency alternating with affirmation of and subjection to supreme might.

Both of these attitudes are indicated in the Christian myth. The occurrence of impregnation by *action à distance,* merely through messengers, and the choice of a gaseous route, reveal an idea of tremendous potency, one to which the Son is throughout subjected. On the other hand, the instrument employed to effect the impregnation is far from being a specially virile one. Though the Dove is evidently a phallic symbol—it was in the guise of a dove that Zeus seduced Phtheia, and doves were the amor-like emblems of all the great love-goddesses, Astarte, Semiramis, Aphrodite and the rest—still it plainly owes its association with love principally to the gentle and caressing nature of its wooing. We may thus say that it is one of the most effeminate of all the phallic emblems.

It is thus clear that the Father's might is manifested only at the expense of being associated with considerable effeminacy. The same theme is even more evident in the case of the Son. He attains greatness, including final possession of the Mother and reconciliation with the Father, only after undergoing the extremity of humiliation together with a symbolic castration and death. A similar path is laid down for every follower of Jesus, salvation being purchased at the price of gentleness, humility, and submission to the Father's will. This path has logically led in extreme cases to actual self-castration and always leads in that direction, though of course it is in practice replaced by various acts symbolising this. There is a double gain in this. Object-love for the Mother is replaced by a regression to the original identification with her, so that incest is avoided and the Father pacified; further the opportunity is given of winning the Father's love by the adoption of a feminine attitude towards him. Peace of mind is purchased by means of a change in heart in the direction of a change in sex.

We return at this point to the problem raised above of the psychological signification of the Holy Ghost. We have seen that He is composed of a combination of the original Mother-Goddess with the creative essence (genital organs) of the Father. From this point of view one approaches an understanding of the peculiar awfulness of blasphemy against the Holy Ghost, the so-called 'unpardonable sin', for such an offence would symbolically be equivalent to a defilement of the Holy Mother and an attempted castration of the Father. It would be a repetition of the primordial sin, the beginning of all sin, gratification of the Oedipus impulse. This is in complete harmony with our clinical experience that neurotics nearly always identify this sin with the act of masturbation, the psychological significance of which we now know to be due to its unconscious association with incestuous wishes.

So far the figure of the Holy Ghost may be held to correspond with the terrible image of the phantastic 'woman with the penis', the primal Mother. But the matter is more complicated. On union of the Mother with the Father's creative agent all femininity vanishes, and the figure becomes indisputably male. This reversal of sex is the real problem.

For the reasons given above this change in sex must have something to do with the act of begetting, and here we are reminded of another curious change in sex connected with the same act. In his brilliant researches into the initiation rites and couvade ceremonies of savages Reik[1] has shewn that the most important tendency permeating these is the endeavour to counter the Oedipus-complex—i. e. the wish for Father-murder and Mother-incest—by a very peculiar and yet logical enough device. Acting on the deeply-seated conviction that the foundation of the fatal attraction towards the Mother is the physical fact of one's having been born by her, a conviction which has some real basis, savages enter upon various complicated procedures the essential aim of which is so far as possible to annul this physical fact and to establish the fiction that the boy has been at all events re-born by the Father. In this way the Father hopes to abrogate the incestuous wishes on the one hand and to bind the youth more closely to him on the other, both these aims diminishing the risk of parricide. Put in terms of the instincts this means that an incestuous heterosexual fixation is replaced by a sublimated homosexuality.

When we reflect how widely spread is this tendency —the rites themselves, as Reik remarks, are found in every part of the world—it would not seem too bold to

---

[1] Reik: Probleme der Religionspsychologie, 1919, Ch. II and III.

ascribe to it also the substitution of the male for the female sex in the case under discussion. I would therefore suggest that *the replacement of the Mother-Goddess by the Holy Ghost is a manifestation of the desirability of renouncing incestuous and parricidal wishes and replacing them by a stronger attachment to the Father*, a phenomenon having the same signification as the initiatory rites of savages. Hence the greater prominence in Christianity, as compared with Judaism, of personal love for God the Father. In support of the conclusion may further be quoted the extensive part played by sublimated homosexuality throughout the Christian religion. The exceptional precept of universal brother-love, that one should not only love one's neighbour as oneself but also one's enemies, makes a demand on social feeling that can be met, as Freud has pointed out, only from homosexual sources of feeling. Then the effeminate costume of the priests, their compulsory celibacy, shaven head, and so on, plainly signify deprivation of masculine attributes, being thus equivalent to symbolic self-castration.

The figure thus created represents an androgynic compromise. In surrendering some elements of virility it gains the special female prerogative of child-bearing, and thus combines the advantages of both sexes. The hermaphroditic ideal offered to the world by Christianity has proved of tremendous importance to humanity. We have in it a great reason for the enormous civilising influence of Christianity, since the civilising of primitive man essentially means the mastery of the Oedipus complex and the transformation of much of it into sublimated homosexuality (i. e. herd instinct), without which no social community can exist. We realise also why a real conversion to Christianity is typically described as being 're-born of the Holy Ghost', and why immersion in water (a birth symbolism) is the official sign

of it; we have here, further, the explanation of the curious
finding, which I have pointed out previously,[1] that the
baptismal fluid is lineally derived from a bodily fluid
(semen, urine) of the *Father*. It should, incidentally, be no
longer strange that the most vivid forms of religious conversion are seen either at puberty, i. e. the homosexual
phase of adolescence, or, in adult life, with drunkards; it
will be remembered that drunkenness is a specific sign of
mental conflict over the subject of repressed homosexuality.

The conclusions thus reached accord well with those
reached by Freud along other lines regarding the connection
between Christianity and totemism. Christianity constitutes
in large part both a veiled regression to the primitive
totemistic system and at the same time a refinement of
this. It resembles it in the sharpness of the ambivalency
towards the Father, though in it the hostile component
has undergone a still further stage in repression. It also
agrees with the tendency of the primitive initiation ceremonies
as disclosed by Reik, but it indicates a progress beyond
these inasmuch as the shifting of procreative importance from
the female to the male sex is put backward from the
time of puberty to that of birth, just as, incidentally, the
initiatory rite of baptism subsequently was. Instead of the
maternal birth being nullified by a symbolic paternal re-
birth at the time of puberty, the birth itself is mythologically treated on these lines.

In discussing the fate of the original Mother-Goddess
and her transformation into the Holy Ghost we have passed
by a very obvious consideration. Although in the Christian
Trinity itself the Holy Ghost is the only figure that replaces
the primal Mother, nevertheless there is in Christian
theology a female figure, the Virgin Mary, who also plays

[1] Chapter IV, p. 164, etc.

an important part. It would thus be truer to say that the original Goddess has been 'decomposed'—to use a mythological term—into two, one of which goes to make the Holy Ghost and the other of which becomes the Madonna. To complete our analysis a little should be said about the latter figure.

By a divine Father or Mother, i. e. God or Goddess, we mean, from a purely psychological point of view, an infantile conception of a Father or Mother, a figure invested with all the attributes of power and perfection and regarded with respect or awe. The decomposition in question, therefore, signifies that the divine, i. e. infantile, attributes of the original Mother image have been transferred to the idea of the Holy Ghost, while the purely human, i. e. adult, attributes have been retained in the form of a simple woman. Apart from the change in sex that occurs in the former case, which has been considered above, the process is akin to the divorce that normally obtains during the years of adolescence, when the youth, following the dichotomy of his own feelings, divides women into two classes—human accessible ones and unapproachable forbidden figures of respect, the extreme types being the harlot and 'lady' respectively. We know from countless individual psycho-analyses that this splitting is simply a projection of the dissociation that occurs in the feelings originally entertained by the boy for the Mother; those that have been deflected from a sexual goal become attached to various figures of respect, while the crudely erotic ones are allowed to appear only in regard to a certain class of woman, harlot, servant, and so on. Both the 'lady' and the harlot are thus derivatives of the Mother figure. So we infer that the division of the original Goddess into two figures in Christianity is a manifestation of the same repression of incestuous impulses.

Light is thrown on the part played by the Virgin
Mary both by these considerations and by comparison of
the woman in Christian mythology with the woman of
other Trinities. For this purpose we may select the three
that have been so fully studied by Frazer, three which
seriously competed with Christianity in its early days and
which were the sources of some of its most prominent
elements. I refer to the three Saviour-Gods Adonis, Attis
and Osiris. With all these we have a Son-Lover who dies,
usually being castrated as well, who is periodically mourned,
chiefly by women, and whose resurrection betokens the
welfare or salvation of humanity. Two of these contrast with
the third in the following interesting respect. With Adonis and
Attis the Mother-Goddess, Astarte or Cybele respectively,
towers in importance over the young Saviour; Osiris on
the other hand is at least as distinguished and powerful as
an Isis. Frazer writes:[1] 'Whereas legend generally represented Adonis and Attis as simple swains, mere herdsmen
or hunters whom the fatal love of a goddess had elevated
above their homely sphere into a brief and melancholy
preeminence, Osiris uniformly appears in tradition as a
great and beneficent king'. Later on,[2] however, he suggests
that 'This . . . . . . seems to indicate that in
the beginning Isis was, what Astarte and Cybele continued
to be, the stronger divinity of the pair'. Thus, in the
series: Astarte, Isis, Mary we have a gradation in the
diminishing greatness of the primal Mother. Although Mary
retains the attributes of perfection, she has lost those of
divine and unapproachable grandeur and becomes simply a
good woman. This subordination of the primal Mother, and
her deprivation of the infantile conception of divinity,
would seem to accord well with the view expressed above of

[1] Frazer: Adonis, Attis, Osiris, 1914, pp. 158, 159.
[2] ibid. p. 202.

the tendency in the Christian myth to exalt the Father at the expense of the Mother. The significance of this is, as has been indicated, to counter the incest wish by instituting a closer bond with the Father.

Reflection on the history of Christianity shews that its object has been gained only in part, that the solution provided of the Oedipus complex was not one of universal applicability, and that the age-old conflict between Father and Son has continued to lead to further efforts to solve it. The transition from the Mother to the Holy Ghost was not accomplished without a struggle even at the beginning, as might have been expected in a community always accustomed to Goddess worship. Several sects tried to maintain the divinity of Mary, the obvious successor of Isis, Hera, Astarte, Aphrodite and the rest, and the Melchite attempt to retain the original Trinity of Father, Mary, and Messiah was crushed only at the Council of Nice. For a thousand years matters proceeded quietly, perhaps because of the astounding syncretizing activity of those years in assimilating Pagan mythology of all kinds, including most of that pertaining to the earlier Mother-Goddesses. After this time, however, voices were increasingly raised in favour of according the Virgin Mary a loftier part in the hierarchy. This tendency won the day in the Catholic Church and may be said to be still proceeding, for it is hardly more than half a century since the last step was taken of pronouncing that she herself was also conceived immaculately. The human need for a Mother to worship was too strong, so that She had to be reinstated. Christianity here, therefore, as in so many other respects, effected a compromise between the Hebraic tendency towards an androgenic conception and the Classical tendency towards acknowledgement of the Mother-Goddess as a central figure.

The peculiarly Christian solution, which was later adulterated by Catholicism, was thus a lineal descendant of the Hebraic tendency. The Protestant Reformation was clearly an attempt to reinforce the original solution and to carry it to its logical conclusion by abolishing all traces of Mariolatry from religion; only those who have witnessed the horror with which the 'Red Woman' is mentioned among the extreme Protestant sections of the community can fully appreciate the strength of this impulse. It is interesting, further, to note that the more completely is this process carried out the less necessity is there to adopt a homosexual attitude in religion; the extreme Protestant ministers not only marry, but discard all special costume and other indications of a feminine rôle, whereas all the self-castrating tendencies are more evident where Mariolatry is highly developed. One might perhaps say that the Protestant solution of the Oedipus complex is the replacement of the Mother by the Woman, while the Catholic one consists in the change of the masculine to the feminine attitude.

INDEX

When the number of the page on which a quotation occurs is given in Roman figures, the full title of the work from which the quotation is taken will be found on the last page before this the numbering of which is given in italic figures

431